Ethnos of the Earth

By constructing the first transnational and interlingual conceptual history of ethnicity, *Ethnos of the Earth* reveals the pivotal role this concept played in the making of the international order. Rather than being a primordial or natural phenomenon, ethnicity is a contingent product of the twentieth-century transition from a world of empires to a world of nation-states. As nineteenth-century concepts such as 'race' and 'civilisation' were repurposed for twentieth-century ends, ethnicity emerged as a 'filler' category that was plugged into the gaps created in our conceptual organisation of the world. Through this comprehensive conceptual reshuffling, the governance of human cultural diversity was recast as an essentially domestic matter, while global racial and civilisational hierarchies were pushed out of sight. A massive amount of conceptual labour has gone into the 'flattening' of the global sociopolitical order, and the concept of ethnicity has been at the very heart of this endeavour.

JAAKKO HEISKANEN is Lecturer in International Relations at Queen Mary University of London. His research is located at the intersection of international relations, nationalism studies, and conceptual history.

Ethnos of the Earth

International Order and the Emergence of Ethnicity

JAAKKO HEISKANEN
Queen Mary University of London

Shaftesbury Road, Cambridge CB2 8EA, United Kingdom

One Liberty Plaza, 20th Floor, New York, NY 10006, USA

477 Williamstown Road, Port Melbourne, VIC 3207, Australia

314–321, 3rd Floor, Plot 3, Splendor Forum, Jasola District Centre, New Delhi – 110025, India

103 Penang Road, #05-06/07, Visioncrest Commercial, Singapore 238467

Cambridge University Press is part of Cambridge University Press & Assessment, a department of the University of Cambridge.

We share the University's mission to contribute to society through the pursuit of education, learning and research at the highest international levels of excellence.

www.cambridge.org
Information on this title: www.cambridge.org/9781009512442

DOI: 10.1017/9781009512459

© Jaakko Heiskanen 2025

This publication is in copyright. Subject to statutory exception and to the provisions of relevant collective licensing agreements, no reproduction of any part may take place without the written permission of Cambridge University Press & Assessment.

When citing this work, please include a reference to the DOI 10.1017/9781009512459

First published 2025

A catalogue record for this publication is available from the British Library.

A Cataloging-in-Publication data record for this book is available from the Library of Congress

ISBN 978-1-009-51244-2 Hardback
ISBN 978-1-009-51243-5 Paperback

Cambridge University Press & Assessment has no responsibility for the persistence or accuracy of URLs for external or third-party internet websites referred to in this publication and does not guarantee that any content on such websites is, or will remain, accurate or appropriate.

isille ja äidille

Contents

Acknowledgements	*page* viii
Note on Style	xi
List of Abbreviations	xiii
Introduction	1
1 Nation	29
2 Race	79
3 Tribe	165
Conclusion	229
References	245
Index	302

Acknowledgements

This book is a revised version of my PhD dissertation, which I completed at the University of Cambridge in 2020. The year of completion was rather fitting, marking 100 years since the first written appearance of the word 'ethnicity' in its modern sense. Both during and after the PhD, I have benefitted immensely from the guidance of my wonderful supervisors, Ayşe Zarakol and Duncan Bell. They commented on multiple drafts at various stages of the project, and I am incredibly grateful for their kindness, generosity, and support. I also had the privilege to defend the thesis against Jens Bartelson and David Sneath, two brilliant scholars whose work I greatly admire. They offered plenty of constructive feedback, which I have attempted to incorporate into the book as best I can.

Over the course of the project, I have accumulated a debt of gratitude to innumerable friends and colleagues. Lucas de Oliveira Paes, Marie Prüm, Zeynep Gülşah Çapan, and Adam B. Lerner provided helpful feedback on early chapter drafts. Joanne Yao generously read the entire manuscript in its near-final state. Timo Aava, David G. Anderson, Malena Müller, and Volker Prott pointed me to sources I might have otherwise missed. The development of the book's argument also benefitted from the Introduction to Conceptual History summer school that I attended at the University of Helsinki in 2019. I am grateful to the organisers and participants of the summer school for the conversations they enabled, with special thanks to Evgeny Roshchin and Sophy Bergenheim for their discussant comments on parts of what would become Chapter 1 of the book. Courtesy of the CamPo exchange scheme, I was able to spend a semester at Sciences Po in the fall of 2019, which provided me with invaluable access to libraries and archives in Paris. I want to thank Alain Dieckhoff, Astrid von Busekist, Riva Kastoryano, Sandrine Revet, Daniel Sabbagh, and Christine Laurière for taking the time to share their knowledge of French anthropology and conceptions of ethnie during my stay in

Paris; the sections of the book dealing with the French-speaking world would have been much poorer without their guidance. As the book was nearing completion, I had the privilege of presenting it to discerning audiences at the Norwegian Institute of International Affairs and the Catholic University of Lille, and I want to thank all the participants at those events for their thoughtful comments and questions.

This book is the result of many years of thinking about ethnicity, nationalism, and international order, and some of the ideas presented herein were first developed in other publications. Notably, some of the theoretical arguments presented in Chapter 1 previously appeared in the following outputs: 'Spectra of Sovereignty: Nationalism and International Relations', *International Political Sociology*, 13 (3) (2019); 'Nations and Nationalism in International Relations', in *The Routledge Handbook of Historical International Relations*, edited by Julia Costa López, Halvard Leira, and Benjamin de Carvalho (2021); and 'Mind the Gap: The Nation Form and the Kohn Dichotomy', *Nations and Nationalism*, 29 (3) (2023). I am grateful to everyone who commented on those pieces and the various other papers (published or not) that I have written over the years. I especially want to mention Paul Beaumont, Benjamin de Carvalho, Julia Costa López, Oliver Kessler, George Lawson, Halvard Leira, Anya Ce Liang, Dylan M. H. Loh, Pedro Mendes Loureiro, Emma Mackinnon, Naosuke Mukoyama, and Hakan Sandal-Wilson. They contributed to the development of the book in a variety of ways, directly or indirectly, and I am very grateful to all of them. I am also grateful for many other friends and colleagues in my academic community, but I cannot thank everyone by name.

I also want to express my sincere gratitude to the two anonymous reviewers from Cambridge University Press for their excellent advice on how to strengthen the manuscript and improve the flow of the argument. A generous grant from the Leverhulme Trust (ECF-2020-243) gave me the time to revise the manuscript along the lines suggested by the reviewers. The subsequent cuts and changes have, I believe, resulted in a much more coherent volume. I also want to thank my editors at Cambridge University Press, John Haslam and Carrie Parkinson, for their guidance and oversight during the publication process.

Reconstructing a transnational and interlingual conceptual history of ethnicity required access to primary and secondary sources in numerous libraries and archives. For making the book possible, I want to extend my appreciation to the helpful and knowledgeable staff at the Bibliothèque de Sciences Po, Bibliothèque nationale de France, Bibliothèque Sainte-Geneviève, British Library, Cambridge University Library, Haddon Library, League of Nations Archives, Mémorial de la Shoah, Musée du quai Branly – Jacques-Chirac, Seeley Historical Library, and The National Archives.

I reserve my deepest gratitude for my family and my partner. Thank you for everything.

Note on Style

It has become commonplace for academic works to add scare quotes around problematic terms such as 'primitive' and 'civilised'. By flagging the objectionable quality of the terms they enclose, these supplementary marks help to denaturalise categories that might otherwise be taken at face value. This practice certainly resonates with the spirit of this book, which aims to challenge the perceived naturalness of 'ethnicity'. Nevertheless, I have generally avoided using scare quotes in the text. This was partly a stylistic decision, given the sheer number of questionable categories that appear throughout the book. But no less significant was the difficulty of actually selecting which terms to enclose in quotation marks and which terms to leave unmarked.[1] The concept of ethnicity itself is a case in point: even when academics append scare quotes to problematic neighbours such as 'race' and 'tribe', they allow the seemingly neutral concept of ethnicity to circulate without such warning signs. The lack of scare quotes in this book should therefore not be interpreted as an endorsement of the vocabulary printed on the page, but rather as an insistence on the problematic and provisional quality of *all* our categories.

For similar reasons, I have not followed the standard practice of highlighting foreign words and phrases by placing them in italics. Such stylistic separation of English from other languages tends to perpetuate the myth of 'natural' languages and suggests that interlingual translation is fundamentally different from intralingual translation. Yet words like 'race' look identical in English and French, allowing them to move across linguistic boundaries with relatively little disruption. This does not mean that 'race' has exactly the same meaning in English and French, of course, but it does problematise any straightforward distinction between 'English' and 'French' words. The scientific term 'ethnos' (borrowed from ancient Greek) has also travelled back and

---

[1] See also the insightful discussion in Jacobson 1998, ix–x.

forth between English, French, Russian, German, and other texts without always being marked as foreign. On the flip side, there may also exist significant conceptual differences within or between communities that supposedly speak the same language. The contrast between French and Haitian applications of the term 'ethnie' during the 1930s and 1940s, discussed in Chapter 2, is one example of this. To avoid exaggerating interlingual differences or downplaying intralingual differences, the text is presented without any stylistic markers to distinguish what is English from what is not.

Abbreviations

CSCE	Conference on Security and Co-operation in Europe
HRAF	Human Relations Area Files
ICCPR	International Covenant on Civil and Political Rights
ILO	International Labour Organization
IR	International Relations
OSCE	Organization for Security and Co-operation in Europe
PCIJ	Permanent Court of International Justice
UN	United Nations
UNESCO	United Nations Educational, Scientific and Cultural Organization
WGIP	United Nations Working Group on Indigenous Populations

Introduction

Ethnicity appears at first sight a very obvious, even natural thing. References to ethnic minorities and ethnic conflicts saturate the media on a daily basis. Population censuses, opinion polls, and diversity monitoring forms habitually include questions about the ethnic identity of the respondent. Innumerable scholars across the social and political sciences have dedicated their careers to understanding the mysteries of inter-ethnic relations. Politicians decry the horrors of ethnic cleansing abroad while grappling with the dilemmas of ethnic diversity at home. All around us, we are confronted by a world ordered on the basis of ethnic differences. And yet, for something that seems so ubiquitous and ordinary today, ethnicity is a surprisingly recent coinage: the first known use of the word 'ethnicity' in its modern sense is from 1920, and it did not acquire widespread currency until the second half of the century. As late as 1975, two leading American scholars remarked that ethnicity 'seems to be a new term'.[1]

What explains the remarkable rise of ethnicity in the twentieth century? The central argument of this book is that the emergence and popularisation of this new concept were symptomatic of a fundamental structural transformation of the global sociopolitical order: the dismantling of the European overseas empires and the consolidation of a postcolonial international system populated by formally equal and sovereign nation-states. Far from being a perennial or natural feature of the human condition, ethnicity is a contingent product of the specific constellation of historical forces that redefined conceptions of world order in the twentieth century. The world is not 'given' as ethnic; it is the international order that engenders the ethnicisation of the world.

In *Foundations of Modern International Thought*, David Armitage describes 'the long-drawn-out transition from a world of empires to a world of states' as 'the single most important shift in political

---

[1] Glazer and Moynihan 1975, 1.

consciousness of the last 500 years'.[2] This epochal shift was not only limited to the juridico-political process of decolonisation, but also entailed an epistemic transformation of how the world – and the people in it – were imagined. From the beginning of the nineteenth century to the middle of the twentieth, the Western imperial imaginary was characterised by a 'bifocal world-view' that segregated the global population into two main categories: the civilised and the primitive.[3] Within this binary framework, the peoples of the civilised world were typically classified into nations or nationalities, while primitive stateless societies were grouped into tribes. This civilisational hierarchy was often coupled to notions of superior and inferior races, with the implication that some peoples might be *inherently* incapable of becoming civilised.[4] In stark contrast to this bifurcated world view, the postcolonial world order that emerged from the ashes of the Second World War is imagined as a universalistic system of formally equal and sovereign nation-states. Civilisational and racial hierarchies have been expunged from the international realm, which is seen as a 'flat' and homogeneous plane – a timeless 'anarchy' of sovereign states, as scholars of International Relations (IR) like to describe it.[5]

In recent decades, the familiar conception of the international system as an anarchy of formally equal nation-states has come under attack from multiple fronts. On the one hand, new research into the intellectual origins of IR has foregrounded the centrality of race and empire for many of the field's pioneers: at the beginning of the twentieth century, the study of international politics was inseparable from the study of imperialism, race relations, and colonial administration.[6] On the other hand, there is a growing literature demonstrating the endurance of colonial structures into the postcolonial era: the unequal manner in which the non-Western world was incorporated into the international society ensured that the legacies of racial and civilisational hierarchies haunt world politics long after the demise of formal

---

[2] Armitage 2013, 13.   [3] Bell 2011, 867.
[4] Jacques 1997, 213–214; Lorimer 2005, 117; Mantena 2010, 5–6.
[5] The most systematic statement of this position is Waltz 1979. For critical analyses of the sovereignty/anarchy and inside/outside dichotomies, see especially Ashley 1988; Walker 1993.
[6] For example, Blatt 2018; Long and Schmidt 2005a; Olson and Groom 1991; Thakur, Davis, and Vale 2017; Thakur and Vale 2020; Vitalis 2000, 2010, 2015.

empires.[7] All in all, the assumption of anarchy that undergirds the work of realist, liberal, and even many constructivist IR theorists is predicated on a systematic amnesia regarding the global and imperial origins of the international order.[8]

A crucial yet unanswered question looms large over these debates: If deep-seated racial and civilisational hierarchies played a constitutive role in the formation of the states system and of IR as a discipline, and if the legacies of these undead hierarchies continue to haunt the theory and practice of world politics today, then how could they fall under the radar for most of the twentieth century? Put differently: How were theorists and practitioners of international affairs able to exorcise questions of race and empire so swiftly and easily? This book begins to answer this question by excavating the conceptual labour performed by ethnicity. Not only did the concept of ethnicity provide a seemingly egalitarian lens through which questions of human cultural diversity could be discussed, it partook in a veritable conceptual revolution that also reconfigured the meaning of existing categories such as 'nation', 'race', and 'civilisation'. Through this comprehensive conceptual reshuffling, racial and civilisational hierarchies were exorcised from the international plane, and the governance of human cultural diversity was recast as an essentially domestic matter – in John Ikenberry's words, 'cultural differences' were 'pushed down into civil society'.[9] A massive amount of conceptual labour has gone into the effacement of global racial and civilisational hierarchies, and the concept of ethnicity has been at the very heart of this endeavour, filling in the gaps created in our conceptual organisation of the world as nineteenth-century categories were repurposed for twentieth-century ends.

Yet, crucially, the emergence of ethnicity did not entail only the negation of imperial structures. As we shall see, the erasure of racial and civilisational hierarchies from the international plane went hand in hand with their internalisation under a new conceptual form that rendered them compatible with the ideological precepts of the emerging international order. The persistence of these imperial arrangements can be traced inside, outside, and between nations. Within nations, the seemingly innocuous distinction between the

---

[7] For example, Anievas, Manchanda, and Shilliam 2015; Barder 2021; Hobson 2014; Spanu 2020; Zarakol 2011, 2017.
[8] See especially Krishna 2001. [9] Ikenberry 2020, 138.

'national' majority and 'ethnic' minorities remains deeply indebted to the nineteenth-century standard of civilisation and associated contrasts between 'historical' and 'non-historical' peoples. A similar shift can be detected outside nations, on the international plane, where the emergence of ethnicity as a domestic container of cultural particularity facilitated the recoding of long-standing colonial distinctions in a seemingly culture-neutral register, with proxies such as 'development' and 'modernisation' replacing the old standard of civilisation. In this ostensibly egalitarian world order, boundaries between nations are reinforced and reified by new patterns of prejudice that differentiate groups from one another along a horizontal rather than a vertical axis: antiquated notions of superior and inferior races have given way to a new 'differentialist' racism that focuses on the incompatibility of different cultural traditions, or the importance of protecting the ethnic diversity of humankind.[10] This is one of the major paradoxes presented by the conceptual history of ethnicity: a concept that played a pivotal role in the dismantling of global racial and civilisational hierarchies is also deeply implicated in their reconfiguration and perpetuation.

Toward a Global Conceptual History of Ethnicity

The word 'ethnicity' was first used in its modern sense in 1920, but some of its cognates have a much longer history. The Greek 'ethnos', from which 'ethnicity' derives, was used to signify 'people' more than two millennia ago. During the medieval period, the terms 'ethnic' and 'ethnique' entered the English and French languages, respectively, to denote heathens or pagans; a text from 1772 also features the only recorded pre twentieth-century use of the word 'ethnicity' to refer to heathen or pagan superstition.[11] In the late eighteenth and nineteenth centuries, reflecting the rise of an increasingly nationalistic and racialised world order, the content of 'ethnic' and 'ethnique' shifted away from religious difference and more toward national or racial difference. It was also in this period that the sciences of ethnography and ethnology emerged as the study of peoples or races – but not yet ethnic groups.[12]

---

[10] Taguieff 2001, 4–6.   [11] Krieg-Planque 2005, 154–155; Sollors 1986, 25.
[12] On the conceptual history of 'ethnography' and 'ethnology', see Rohan-Csermak 1967; Stagl 1995, 1998; Vermeulen 1992, 1995, 2006, 2015.

It was not until the turn of the twentieth century that the ethnos-based vocabulary truly erupted: the French 'ethnie' was coined in 1896; the terms 'groupe ethnique' and 'ethnic group' received their first scholarly definitions in 1900; the French 'ethnicité' made its first written appearance in 1902; the English 'ethnocentrism' was coined in 1906; the term 'ethnos' started to gain traction as a scientific concept in Russia during the 1910s; the French 'ethnisme' appeared in print in 1916; and the earliest recorded use of the English 'ethnicity' in a non-religious sense came in 1920. At first relatively marginal, this new constellation of ethnos-based terms rapidly acquired prominence over the following decades: the United Nations officially adopted the term 'ethnic group' in 1950 and by the 1970s ethnicity seemed to be everywhere.

This book charts the historical trajectories of the cluster of ethnos-based words coined around the turn of the twentieth century.[13] Taken together, the emergence of these words indicates the emergence of a new concept. As Quentin Skinner observes, 'the surest sign that a group or society has entered into the self-conscious possession of a new concept is that a corresponding vocabulary will be developed, a vocabulary which can then be used to pick out and discuss the concept in question with consistency'.[14] Even if words and concepts are not entirely separable, the distinction between them is nonetheless important. 'A concept may be attached to a word', as Reinhart Koselleck explains, 'but it is simultaneously more than that word.'[15] A word becomes 'elevated to the status of a concept' when it 'bundles together the richness of historical experience and the sum of the theoretical and practical lessons drawn from it in such a way that their relationship can be established and properly understood only through a concept'.[16] The concept of the state, for example, knits together under a single word elements such as sovereignty, territory, citizenship, legislation, taxation, and military force. In the same way, the concept of ethnicity is embedded within a broader semantic field that includes not only cognates like 'ethnie' and 'ethnos', but also a variety of neighbours such as 'nation', 'race', 'tribe', 'culture', and 'civilisation'. It is this broader cluster of

---

[13] Conceptual history has already been productively applied to other key categories of international politics. See, for example, Bartelson 1995; Jordheim and Neumann 2011; Leira 2019; Roshchin 2017.
[14] Skinner 1979, 207.   [15] Koselleck 2011, 19.   [16] Koselleck 2011, 20.

supporting, cognate, and contrasting concepts that constitutes the meaning of ethnicity.[17]

Before discussing the conceptual history of ethnicity any further, I want to dispel the myth that concepts exist only in the mind, as ideational models or representations of social reality. Concepts and social reality are not external to one another; it is rather the case that 'concepts create, through their "topography," the reality to which we relate and attribute significance'.[18] In Foucauldian terms, we can say that concepts belong to the realm of discourse rather than language. Just as concepts are not reducible to words, discourse is not reducible to language: 'Of course, discourses are composed of signs; but what they do is more than use these signs to designate things. It is this *more* that renders them irreducible to the language (*langue*) and to speech. It is this "more" that we must reveal and describe.'[19] There is thus an 'excess' of discourse over language, of concepts over words. Discourses and concepts do not merely represent reality, but also partake in the constitution of that reality, constraining the avenues that social and political activity can take.[20] By assembling linguistic and extra-linguistic elements into larger discursive wholes, concepts create social order from experiences that would otherwise appear disorganised or unintelligible. 'Put metaphorically', Koselleck once mused, 'concepts are like joints linking language and the extra-linguistic world.'[21]

Due to their relationality and historicity, concepts can never be given a final definition. Whereas a technical term is a pure element of language that can be clearly defined, concepts are complex bundles of experiences and expectations that retain a degree of ambiguity.[22] The specific meaning of a concept will inevitably vary from context to context and person to person, as different actors deploy it with different intentions and for different purposes. Pushing this line of argument to the extreme, Skinner has even claimed that 'there can be no histories of concepts as such; there can only be histories of their uses in argument'.[23] Although Skinner is correct to highlight the ability of actors to mould the meaning of concepts to suit their own ends, his radically contextualist stance leads him to overlook the resistance of concepts to such moulding. All concepts carry semantic baggage that they inherit

---

[17] Berenskoetter 2017, 158. [18] Freeden 1996, 57. [19] Foucault 1972, 54.
[20] Koselleck 2004, 75–92. [21] Koselleck 1996, 61. [22] Koselleck 2011, 20.
[23] Skinner 1988, 283. See also Pocock 1996, 52–53.

from prior use, constraining the ability of actors to freely determine their meaning. Even if the meaning of a concept can never be definitively fixed, the repeated use of a concept over time will ensure that it acquires an irregular contour circumscribing the range of recognisable meanings that can be attributed to it. As Koselleck writes, 'the historical uniqueness of speech acts, which might appear to make any history of concepts impossible, in fact creates the necessity to recycle past conceptualizations'.[24] The range of meanings that a given concept may have is thus at least partly predetermined by the discursive web within which it has become embedded over time. To construct the conceptual history of ethnicity is therefore neither an attempt to arrive at a transhistorical definition nor a surrender to radical historicism. It is, instead, a serious attempt to establish the specific structure and function that this concept has acquired in modern social and political discourse.

Some excellent work on the conceptual history of ethnicity already exists. In particular, there is a robust literature on the emergence of ethnicity in the United States,[25] the history of the word 'ethnie' and its derivatives in France,[26] the development of ethnos-theory in Russia and beyond,[27] and the popularisation of ethnicity in the discipline of anthropology.[28] As yet, however, there has been no sustained attempt to connect these fragments into a general conceptual history that takes into account the systemic changes unfolding on the international level at the time. More broadly, there is a striking silence surrounding the concept of ethnicity when it comes to the study of politics. This is not to claim that political scientists have failed to talk about ethnicity – to the contrary, there are voluminous and ever-growing literatures on ethnic conflict, ethnic violence, and ethnic cleansing.[29] My point is, rather, that despite the omnipresent references to ethnicity in the political sciences, the political functions of this concept remain unexplored: the concept of ethnicity is treated as an apolitical analytical tool

---

[24] Koselleck 1996, 62.   [25] Hattam 2007; Rees 2007; Sollors 1986.
[26] Breton 1992; Krieg-Planque 2005; Martiniello 2013.
[27] Anderson, Arzyutov, and Alymov 2019; Anderson et al. 2019; Bassin 2016; Dragadze 1980; Skalník 1986, 1988.
[28] Amselle and M'Bokolo 1985; Banks 1996; Cohen 1978; Eriksen 2010; Jenkins 2008; Williams 1989.
[29] For example, Brown 1993; Harff and Gurr 2004; Horowitz 1985; Mann 2005; Taras and Ganguly 2010; Wolff 2006.

rather than a politically significant object of analysis in its own right.[30] What is lacking is a global conceptual history of ethnicity that seeks to understand the conditions of possibility of ethnicity as a concept and the ideological functions that this concept performs. Such a history would not merely ask questions about the construction of ethnic identities or the causes of ethnic violence, but would take *the concept of ethnicity itself* as a question in need of an answer.

This book is intended as a first step in mapping out the global conceptual history of ethnicity. By reconstructing a transnational and interlingual history of the concept, it departs from the traditional confines of national or disciplinary histories and embraces the recent turn toward 'connected' or 'entangled' histories. In the words of Sanjay Subrahmanyam, such histories are produced 'not by comparison alone but by seeking out the at times fragile threads that connected the globe'.[31] In this spirit, the book takes the reader on a series of transnational journeys from Paris to Port-au-Prince, from Makerere to Manchester, from St Petersburg to Shanghai, and many places in between. Importantly, this also means that the book is not a quest for the 'origin' of the concept.[32] Rather than originating at a singular source, ethnicity emerges from a multitude of heterogeneous beginnings, seeping through the gaps and fissures between existing categories until it saturates nearly the entirety of the conceptual field.

Inevitably, the spirit of transnational connectivity has been tempered by practical constraints of space and time, as well as the language skills of the author. Largely for these pragmatic reasons, the focus of the book is on the trajectories of ethnos-based terms in English and French, complemented by some discussion of their equivalents in other languages, notably German and Russian. While the selection of sources

---

[30] To take a salient example, the term 'ethnic cleansing' is widely used as a category of analysis in both quantitative and qualitative studies of violence, yet very little consideration is given to either the reasons for or the consequences of its popularisation since the end of the Cold War. Tracing the conceptual history of 'ethnic cleansing' reveals how this concept not only functions as a euphemistic alternative to 'genocide' that exculpates the international community from the burden of intervention, but also deflects attention away from the long history of racial and colonial violence through which the international order was forged. See Heiskanen 2021b.
[31] Subrahmanyam 1997, 761–762. See also Bhambra 2010; Pernau 2012; Werner and Zimmermann 2006.
[32] Foucault 1984; Said 1985.

has a Eurocentric quality, it is important to underline that languages do not necessarily correspond to geographical, political, or even cultural spaces. Focusing on so-called European languages is therefore not the same thing as focusing on Europe, and certainly does not entail positing Europe as the privileged site of historical progress. As the discussion of Haitian ethnie-theory in Chapter 2 demonstrates, one need neither reside in France nor identify as French in order to use the French language. Indeed, part of the reason why English and French are such a valuable starting point for constructing the global conceptual history of ethnicity is precisely because these languages dominated the global political economy of conceptual (ex)change in the period under scrutiny and were spoken across far-flung regions around the world.[33]

The above remarks are not intended to downplay the importance of studying other languages besides the European. Much more research is needed both on the translation of ethnos-based terms around the world and on alternative vocabularies of difference that may have existed or emerged around the same period. On this note, the turn-of-the-century coinage of 'minzoku' in Japanese and 'minzu' in Chinese is already worth noting: beginning their journeys as translations of European categories, these terms rapidly acquired social and political lives of their own and would go on to play pivotal roles in the Japanese and Chinese nation-building projects.[34] The contemporaneous emergence of such equivalents in a multitude of locations and languages around the world testifies not only to the interconnectedness of the twentieth-century world, but also to the subterranean conceptual and sociopolitical changes that were unfolding at the time – changes that would culminate in the end of empires and the birth of the international order.

From Expansion to Sublation: Theorising the Birth of the International Order

The birth of the international order was once recounted as a unilinear narrative of 'expansion' or 'diffusion' where European norms of mutual recognition and sovereign equality were adopted around the world. In this progressivist story, typified by Hedley Bull and Adam Watson's *The Expansion of International Society*, the emergence of a

---

[33] De Swaan 2001; Heiskanen 2021a.   [34] Doak 2007; Leibold 2007.

global international society was seen as a largely rational and rule-based process of voluntary incorporation whereby the non-European world was remade in the image of Europe.[35] The role of non-European states was reduced to that of passive consumers who 'played little role in shaping the foundations of the international society to which they now belong'.[36] Although this 'Eurocentric big bang theory'[37] has not entirely disappeared from IR scholarship, it no longer possesses the unquestioned authority it once did. For present purposes, it is helpful to divide the critiques of the expansion thesis into two main strands: those that foreground the experiences and agency of non-European states in the expansion process, and those that seek to do away with the metaphor of expansion altogether.

The first set of critiques has challenged the Eurocentric origin story by directing much needed attention to the experiences and agency of non-European states. In so doing, this critical scholarship has also exposed the manifold social hierarchies that stratify the supposedly egalitarian states system: non-European states joined a 'Janus-faced'[38] international society that not only promoted mutual recognition and cooperation among the civilised members of the club, but also practised coercive imperialism toward outsiders. The socialisation of non-European states into the European international society consequently went hand in hand with the institutionalisation of social hierarchies, as latecomers were burdened with the stigma of being developmentally behind Europe. Ensuing attempts by non-European states to prove their civilised status frequently entailed the adoption of an imperialistic posture toward their neighbours, leading to a multiplication of international hierarchies.[39] In the words of Edward Keene, the expansion of the international society was 'a two-way process' that entailed not only the extension of mutual recognition and sovereign equality to non-Europeans, but also, in tandem, the institutionalisation of standards of civilisation and sovereign inequality.[40]

Although the first strand of critical literature marks an important departure from the Eurocentric accounts of yore, it remains wedded to the metaphor of expansion and the idea of non-European states

---

[35] Bull and Watson 1984. See also Emerson 1960a; Plamenatz 1960.
[36] Bull 1984, 124.   [37] Hobson 2013, 32.   [38] Suzuki 2005.
[39] See especially Ejdus et al. 2014; Neumann 2011; Spanu 2020; Suzuki 2009; Zarakol 2011.
[40] Keene 2002, 8, 123, 126.

'entering' a pre-existing European international society. This leads to two limitations. First, by channelling the analysis toward European interactions with major non-European polities such as China, Japan, Russia, and Turkey, this literature overlooks broader systemic changes that were shaping the nascent international order at the time. Of particular significance are colonialism, which entailed the wholesale annexation of much of the world by the leading European powers, and nationalism, which entailed both the disintegration of multinational empires such as Austria-Hungary into smaller nation-states and the absorption of long-standing polities such as Bavaria into larger nation-states.[41] Taking colonialism and nationalism seriously requires shifting the focus of analysis from interactions between individual states to broader structures and processes. The second and related limitation of these critiques is the tendency to privilege continuity over change, especially the durability of imperial hierarchies before and after the 'entry' of non-European states into the expanding international society. While highlighting the existence and endurance of these hierarchies is a vital corrective to the progressivist story, what can be lost in this framing is how the expansion of the international society also entailed its fundamental reconfiguration on the basis of formal sovereign equality. As Christian Reus-Smit and Timothy Dunne note, the states system of today is 'a qualitatively different international society than its European progenitor'.[42]

To address these challenges, a second strand of the critical literature suggests abandoning the metaphor of expansion altogether. Thus, Reus-Smit and Dunne propose to replace 'expansion' with 'globalisation' to highlight not only the quantitative increase in the number of recognised sovereign states in the nineteenth and twentieth centuries, but also the qualitative transformation of the global sociopolitical order in the same period. The term 'globalisation', they add, also better captures how this transformation 'was the product of global social forces' rather than a purely European endeavour.[43] Along similar lines, Keene has proposed 'stratification' as a new 'master concept' for thinking about the history of international society. The goal of this terminological change, Keene explains, is to shift our focus from the 'entry' of non-European states into the European family of nations to a

---

[41] Keene 2014, 654–657.   [42] Reus-Smit and Dunne 2017b, 30.
[43] Reus-Smit and Dunne 2017b, 30.

more variegated exploration of 'who was where within international society'. In this way, the civilised family of nations is decentred and recast as 'merely a privileged group within a larger – indeed, effectively global – international social system'.[44]

Recent work on the globalisation or stratification of international society is to be commended for producing far richer historical accounts compared to what came before. Yet this literature, too, remains furtively beholden to the metaphor of expansion. Rather than jettisoning the expansion thesis altogether, what the metaphors of globalisation and stratification actually do is situate the process of expansion within a broader global context – what Bull himself called 'the world political system'.[45] This can be seen in Reus-Smit and Dunne's assertion that they take 'seriously the idea that international society emerged and globalized within a broader world political system'.[46] Even as the metaphor of globalisation directs our attention to a plurality of global forces, the underlying metanarrative is still that the European international society 'spread across the globe'.[47] Keene is even more explicit about his indebtedness to the metaphor of expansion, writing that the concept of stratification 'does not lose sight of the central theme of the expansion thesis, since it still allows us to ask how aspirants gained entry into the charmed circle of "civilised" nations'.[48] In the end, the familiar spatiotemporal frame of the expansion thesis is not so much reconfigured as buried under rich layers of historical detail. As a result, an unintended consequence of these studies has been to shift the focus of inquiry away from actually theorising the birth of the international order and more toward unpacking the complexities of the world political system within which this birth took place. Unwittingly or not, as Regan Burles observes, the revisionist literature ends up 'glossing over the distinction between before and after the globalisation of the international system'.[49] And whenever the question of the difference between before and after is raised, the expansion thesis remains the fallback position.

The challenge, then, is the following: How to theorise the historical novelty and specificity of the international order – the first truly global sociopolitical order – without resorting to the Eurocentric metaphysics

---

[44] Keene 2014, 652.   [45] Bull 1977, 266–271.
[46] Reus-Smit and Dunne 2017b, 34.   [47] Reus-Smit and Dunne 2017a, 6, 13.
[48] Keene 2014, 652–653.   [49] Burles 2023, 187.

Theorising the Birth of the International Order 13

of the expansion thesis? As we have seen, addressing this task requires not only the production of more detailed historical reconstructions of the past, but also the formulation of better theories capable of integrating those historical reconstructions into a grand narrative of the birth of the international order. 'If we dismantle Eurocentric grand histories that have animated our modern international order without replacing them with anything but micro-oriented work', Ayşe Zarakol writes, 'those macro-historical accounts that we think we have dismantled through our brilliantly devastating critiques of Eurocentrism will simply live on as zombie common-sense versions of themselves, filling in the blanks wherever there are some, and every account has blanks.'[50]

To get beyond the lingering influence of the expansion thesis, this book rethinks the birth of the international order through a scrutiny of its major concepts. Rather than being posited a priori, the theory of international order outlined in the following pages emerges inductively from the careful empirical analysis of the conceptual archive. By tracing how the concept of ethnicity arose and developed in relation to neighbouring categories, how it travelled from place to place, and how it was mobilised in practice by a variety of actors, a sociologically grounded theory of the birth of the international order gradually takes form. In other words, it is not a preformed metanarrative that dictates the direction of the analysis, but the 'self-movement' of the concept that gives shape to a speculative theory. This is G. W. F. Hegel's dialectical method applied to the conceptual history of ethnicity: the book takes up a concept as its object and 'lets it go its own way, while it simply watches the movement and development of it'.[51] Yet, as Hegel himself recognises, tracing the history of a concept can never be an entirely passive exercise. Even as this book takes the conceptual history of ethnicity as its object, it also forms part of that history.

---

[50] Zarakol 2022, 271. See also Saramago 2022.
[51] Hegel 1991b, 305. The self-movement of the concept is not a metaphysical fantasy, but a concrete sociological process that takes place within a political economy of conceptual (ex)change. As James (1980, 29) observes, Hegel 'takes time out to say, *and we will forget this at our peril*, that categories, the forms of logic, are in Desire, Will, etc., *human feelings and actions*. [...] This warns us that the whole magnificent structure is rooted in the concrete. We are going to think about it and analyse it and speculate, but every serious movement has come from below. Consciousness, logic as the science of thought, thought itself therefore is the link between us and *things*.' On the idea of a political economy of conceptual (ex)change, see also Heiskanen 2021a.

The speculative theory of international order that emerges from the conceptual history of ethnicity is anchored to the notion of Aufhebung – a German term usually translated into English as 'sublation'. In Hegel's work, this notion is elevated into the centrepiece of dialectical thought and given the status of 'one of the most important notions in philosophy'.[52] For Hegel, the dialectical moment is a moment of 'self-sublation' where concepts overturn themselves, pass into their opposites, and open themselves up to something new.[53] Of particular significance here is the dual meaning of sublation as both negation (to cancel, to put an end to) and preservation (to maintain, to take care of).[54] The concepts that undergo sublation are thus not simply overturned and erased, but also retained under a new form: 'The dialectic has a *positive* result, because it has a *determinate content*, or because its result is truly not *empty, abstract nothing*, but the negation of *certain determinations*, which are contained in the result precisely because it is not an *immediate nothing*, but a result.'[55] In simplest terms, the Hegelian insight into the birth of the international order is that this order did not emerge out of nothing, but from the concrete conditions that preceded it and that continue to haunt it from within.

Conceived as a moment of self-sublation, the birth of the international order takes the form not of a unilinear process of expansion or diffusion, but of a revolutionary double movement that turned the conceptual architecture of the bifurcated imperial order on its head. In Hegelian terms, the civilised world of the European metropole and the primitive world of the non-European periphery 'contradict themselves and pass over into their opposites'.[56] On the civilised side of the global divide, the key catalyst was the devastation brought about by the two world wars, which appeared to reduce the European family of nations to a condition of primitive anarchy – one English interwar commentator bluntly described the First World War as the 'Africanisation of Europe'.[57] Similar themes also inform the work of many twentieth-century anticolonial thinkers. According to Frantz Fanon, for example, the reason why the Second World War was so shocking to the European consciousness had less to do with the nature

---

[52] Hegel 1969, 106. [53] Hegel 1991b, 128.
[54] Hegel 1969, 106–108; Hegel 1991b, 154. [55] Hegel 1991b, 131.
[56] Hegel 1991b, 289. [57] Harrison 1920.

of the violence as such – concentration camps and genocide were the stock-in-trade of colonial rule – than with the fact that this violence was no longer confined to the colonial periphery.[58] As primitive savagery reared its head in the heart of civilised Europe, the global spatial divide between metropole and colony appeared to collapse.

Meanwhile, on the other side of the imperial divide, the implosion of the European family of nations was paralleled by the rise of anticolonial nationalism as an affirmative political force. As Dipesh Chakrabarty reminds us, the birth of the global order of nation-states is something that 'European imperialism and third-world nationalisms have achieved together'.[59] Beginning with the rise of transnational movements such as pan-Africanism and pan-Asianism in the last quarter of the nineteenth century, proceeding through debates over racial equality at Versailles, and culminating in a wave of decolonisation after the Second World War, non-European peoples staked their claim as full members of international society. In the 1950s and 1960s, it was the leaders of the newly independent postcolonial nations who spearheaded the universalisation of political concepts such as human rights and self-determination – concepts formerly seen as the preserve of civilised Europeans.[60] Anticolonial nationalists did not view these developments as the culmination of a unidirectional process of diffusion or expansion, but as 'a radical rupture' that entailed a fundamental reconfiguration of the global order on the basis of sovereign equality and non-domination.[61]

Taken together, this concurrent double movement – the becoming-primitive of the civilised and the becoming-civilised of the primitive – signalled the overturning of the bifurcated imperial order and its self-sublation into a global system of formally equal and sovereign nation-states. As the hegemonic Western gaze that had overseen the construction of the imperial world order ran up against its limits, this order was turned upside down and inside out. Instead of reproducing a Eurocentric expansion narrative or necessitating a false choice between continuity and change, the notion of sublation offers an elegant way of grasping the contradictions of this world-historical moment: the birth of the international order entailed *both* the negation of the old imperial order *and* the preservation of imperial hierarchies under a new

---

[58] Fanon 1956, 123. See also Hesse 2004, 19–20.   [59] Chakrabarty 2000, 41.
[60] Burke 2010, 114–121, 125–129; Getachew 2019, 71–106; Ravndal 2020.
[61] Getachew 2019, 17.

conceptual form. In a world of formally equal and sovereign nation-states, civilisational and racial hierarchies continue to matter, yet these hierarchies are not quite what they used to be.

Of Wholes and Holes: Sublation and Its Discontents

To invoke Hegel is to invite critique. The familiar objection to Hegel's logic is that it is a monological and totalising one, privileging identity over difference and silencing the voices of others. Differences are posited only to be overcome through sublation: 'when knowledge or theory comprehends the other, then the alterity of the latter vanishes as it becomes part of the same'.[62] In this way, the structure of Hegelian dialectics is said to mimic the structure of Western imperialism, which appropriates the non-Western other economically, politically, and culturally.[63] The 'assimilatory thrust'[64] of Hegel's logic also seems to be at odds with prevailing theoretical trends in IR. With the Eurocentrism of IR's theoretical apparatus laid bare, recent years have witnessed a proliferation of national and regional approaches to the study of world politics (Chinese IR, Indian IR, Japanese IR, African IR, Asian IR, and so on). By bringing a range of non-Western perspectives into view, this relativising and pluralising logic has sought to transcend the discipline's Eurocentric canon and pave the way for a 'Global IR'.[65] Against this backdrop, the monological and totalising tendencies of Hegelian dialectics may seem like a step backward rather than forward.

The relativising and pluralising logic that informs many recent critiques of Eurocentrism is normatively attractive and no doubt arises out of a genuine concern for the shortcomings of IR as a discipline. Yet closer scrutiny suggests that the narrative of European or Western dominance may in fact be entrenching the very Eurocentrism that it denounces.[66] After all, the distinction between the West and the non-West is itself a profoundly Eurocentric distinction: positing the non-West as something external to or separate from the West reduces the former into a residual container for everything that does not fit into the latter, while leaving the identity and coherence of the West itself largely

---

[62] Young 2004, 45.   [63] Young 2004, 34–35.   [64] Neumann 1999, 10.
[65] For example, Acharya and Buzan 2010, 2019; Tickner and Wæver 2009.
[66] Alejandro 2019, 12.

unquestioned. Rather than transcending the Eurocentric distinction between the West and the non-West, the relativist-pluralist approach merely reverses the hierarchy between the terms, now privileging the latter instead of the former. As Kimberly Hutchings warns, the category of the non-West 'always threatens to reinvent the binary oppositions that its use was intended to overturn'.[67]

Another way to put the issue is in terms of the relationship between the universal and the particular. Ironically, the quest for a 'Global IR' has often been characterised by a retreat from the global to the local, from the international to the national, from the universal to the particular: it is the particular ethnocultural traditions of the non-Western world that are seen as the source of redemption from the Eurocentric universalism of IR's theoretical toolkit. Although the recovery of alternative or forgotten perspectives can be a productive critical exercise, the mere addition of non-Western voices cannot break down the Eurocentrism of the disciplinary canon. To the contrary, this additive endeavour often ends up replicating the same ethnocentric logic that it seeks to overcome. In the same way that the Eurocentric logic grounds modern universals in the ethnocultural bloc known as the West, the relativist-pluralist approach retains a link between knowledge and ethnocultural particularity. Rather than offering a way out of the ethnocentric logic of Eurocentrism, therefore, the relativist-pluralist approach actually encourages the propagation of the same ethnocentric logic across the globe. The result is what Christopher Murray aptly describes as 'an ethnification of world political inquiry'.[68] Indeed, one of the central claims of this book is that the relativist-pluralist thrust of recent IR theory is inseparable from the emergence and popularisation of ethnicity as a new category for ordering the peoples of the world. Even as it appears directly opposed to IR's Eurocentrism, the relativist-pluralist agenda unwittingly functions as its 'underside and accomplice'.[69]

What all of this means is that the transcendence of IR's Eurocentrism cannot take the form of a retreat from the universal into the particular, from the West into the non-West. The mistake of the relativist-pluralist solution is to treat the Western perspective as if it were merely one

---

[67] Hutchings 2011, 645. See also Hobson and Sajed 2017, 551.
[68] Murray 2020, 420. See also Barkawi, Murray, and Zarakol 2023; Hutchings 2011; Matin 2011; Vasilaki 2012.
[69] Derrida 1978, 259.

perspective among a multiplicity of others. It is not. The Western perspective is not just one perspective among many, but also the hegemonic perspective that provides the conceptual form within which a multiplicity of non-Western perspectives can flourish. Amid a plurality of perspectives, the Western perspective stands out as an exceptional perspective that is internally split, divided not only from a range of other perspectives but divided also from itself. To ignore this structural asymmetry is to overlook the historical context of Western imperial rule and colonial domination within which the conceptual architecture of the international order – and the discipline of IR – was forged.[70] True universality is to be found neither in the hegemonic singularity of the West nor in the accumulation of ever more non-Western experiences from around the world, but in the contradictory complementarity of these two seemingly opposed moments.

'The task here, it seems, is not additive but reconstructive', Mustapha Kamal Pasha astutely remarks.[71] Rather than posit non-Western perspectives as something that exist outside or beyond the West – and that can therefore be 'added' to the Western canon – it is necessary to recognise how the non-West is continually interrupting the totalising thrusts of the West from within, preventing the West from constituting itself into a coherent totality.[72] Indeed, as soon as we pause to look more closely, we discover manifold discursive boundaries criss-crossing the imaginary terrain of the West, differentiating Western Europe from Eastern Europe, Northern Europe from Southern Europe, Europe in general from North America, white America from black America, and so on and so forth – not to even mention the miscellaneous assortment of other countries around the world, such as Australia and Japan, that are sometimes included in the elastic category of the West. Once the profound incoherence of the West is recognised, one is forced to grapple with the very real possibility that supposedly Western perspectives may already be suffused with non-Western ideas and experiences. The opposite, of course, may also

---

[70] Heiskanen 2021a; Shilliam 2011.
[71] Pasha 2011, 218. See also Bilgin 2016, 138; Chowdhry 2007, 105; Shilliam 2011, 24.
[72] The relationship between the West and the non-West is comparable to Dipesh Chakrabarty's distinction between 'History 1' and 'History 2'. See Chakrabarty 2000, 66.

be true: the much-coveted non-Western experiences may already be permeated by Western concepts and theories.[73]

Hegelian dialectics – epitomised by the notion of sublation – offer a fruitful yet largely untapped resource for working through the tensions that surround the relationship between Western and non-Western IR. In particular, it opens up the possibility of thinking complementarity despite contradiction: the possibility of thinking both the West 'within' the non-West and the non-West 'within' the West without dissolving the differential tension between them. From this perspective, the process of sublation is not about eliminating differences through their relentless synthesis, but about grappling with the undecidable play of identity and difference. The notion of the whole or the system that informs dialectical thought is not a self-enclosed totality, but a fractured collage shot through with fissures and contradictions.[74] The interesting question then becomes *how* – through what discursive manoeuvrings and conceptual tools – this fractured patchwork becomes imbued with an aura of fullness and coherence.

To tease out the productive tensions that underlie dialectical thought, I propose to read the notion of sublation through the philosophical oeuvre of Jacques Derrida. The dual meaning of sublation as negation and preservation lends itself especially well to this 'deconstructive' endeavour – indeed, Derrida himself designates the notion of sublation as the 'decisive target' of his work.[75] Sublation, as already noted, is characterised by a triadic structure where two concepts, through a double movement, overturn themselves and pass into their opposites, producing a third term that both encompasses and transcends the initial structure. Deconstruction mirrors this double movement exactly. As described by Derrida, deconstruction entails a 'double gesture' or 'double science' in relation to the system undergoing deconstruction. First, there is a phase of 'overturning' or 'reversal' that upends the hierarchical relationship between the two terms of a given

---

[73] Bilgin 2008, 5–6.
[74] See Brincat and Ling 2014; Ciccariello-Maher 2017. It is worth noting that Hegel himself did not always remain faithful to the insights of his dialectical logic. Especially his later lectures on the philosophy of history succumb to a profoundly Eurocentric and non-dialectical world view, epitomised by his infamous observation that Africa 'is no historical part of the World' (Hegel 2001, 117). Yet it is possible to take up the promise of Hegelian dialectics without subscribing to such monological readings of world history.
[75] Derrida 1981a, 248n53.

opposition while remaining within the terrain of the system.[76] The second phase then entails a more general displacement of the system itself: 'we must also mark the interval between inversion, which brings low what was high, and the irruptive emergence of a new "concept," a concept that can no longer be, and never could be, included in the previous regime'.[77] A moment of overturning coupled with the emergence of a new concept that transcends the existing system: Where is deconstruction located if not within the labour of sublation? In addition to this structural affinity, it is important to note the 'objective' quality of both processes: deconstruction, like sublation, is not an operation imposed by an acting subject from the outside, but an event that 'takes place'[78] or 'happens'[79] due to internal tensions within the system itself. Hence why Derrida refers to the 'auto-deconstruction' or 'self-deconstruction' of the system.[80] 'Deconstruction is not a philosophy or a method, it is not a phase, a period or a moment. It is something which is constantly at work and was at work before what we call "deconstruction" started', Derrida explains.[81] Any juxtaposition of 'deconstruction' to 'reconstruction' misses the point entirely.[82]

To read the notion of sublation through the lens of deconstruction requires neither the addition nor the subtraction of anything to or from this notion. All it entails is a meticulous reading of this notion on its own terms, a careful teasing out of the contradictions that animate it. Specifically, as noted above, deconstruction operates in the interval that differentiates the two moments of sublation: on the one side, concepts passing into their opposites; on the other side, these concepts being upended and transcended through the emergence of a third term. Deconstruction marks out and opens up this interval to closer scrutiny, foregrounding the undecidable play of negation and preservation that takes place at this critical juncture. In this way, deconstruction reveals *an inner undecidability within the logic of sublation itself*, an inner undecidability that 'can never be mediated, mastered, sublated, or dialecticized'.[83] The undecidable relationship between negation and preservation inserts a vital tension into the very core of the dialectical process, generating three distinct yet inseparable modalities of sublation: one where negation and preservation appear perfectly balanced,

---

[76] Derrida 1981c, 41; Derrida 1988, 21. [77] Derrida 1981c, 42.
[78] Derrida 1991, 274. [79] Caputo 1997, 9. [80] Caputo 1997, 9.
[81] Derrida 1999, 65. [82] Derrida 1999, 77. [83] Derrida 1981a, 221.

one where preservation trumps negation, and one where negation trumps preservation.

The first modality of sublation remains entirely compatible with the classic Hegelian understanding of the dialectical process as a linear movement. The new conceptual structures continue to reflect the conceptual structures that precede them, even as these earlier structures are negated. In Hegel's words, the sublated result 'still has ... *in itself* the *determinateness from which it originates*'.[84] What this means for IR is that the conceptual architecture of the international order does not emerge ex nihilo, but from the sublation of the bifurcated imperial order that preceded it. Hence, the conceptual opposition between the sovereign state and the anarchical international system, which has served as the foundation for IR's disciplinary identity, mimics the older distinction between civilised and primitive societies. Through a dialectical reversal, the hierarchical distinction between the civilised Western core and the primitive non-Western periphery is overturned into a seemingly universal and transhistorical distinction between the inside and the outside of the state. By extension, IR effectively accumulates the functions of colonial anthropology, emerging as the privileged scientific vehicle for the study of the modern state's 'other'.

The first modality of sublation, the strictly Hegelian one, presumes a balance between negation and preservation that allows the dialectical process to proceed smoothly. However, precisely because the tension between negation and preservation is the motor of the dialectical process, this tension can never cancel itself out: the two moments – negation and preservation – are always in excess of one another. Accordingly, the second modality of sublation entails an excess of preservation over negation: old imperial categories do not vanish into thin air, but continue to haunt the conceptual architecture of the new order. Some of these categories are rearticulated through 'pseudonyms'[85] or 'conceptual proxies'[86] that render them compatible with the universalistic pretensions of the states system. Thus, the nineteenth-century standard of civilisation is today perpetuated through discourses of 'development' and 'modernisation'.[87] Other imperial categories, such as the conceptual triad of 'nation', 'race', and 'tribe', endure as conflicting conceptual elements within the new

---

[84] Hegel 1969, 107. [85] Long and Schmidt 2005b, 11.
[86] Guilhot 2014, 702. [87] Gong 1984, 91–92; Zarakol 2011, 82–95.

system. These conceptual residues, which are never fully erased by the dialectical process, serve as ghostly vessels that carry the past into the present: they are the ineffaceable remainders and reminders of the nationalist, racist, and colonialist violences upon which the international order was founded and that always threaten to fracture its universalistic veneer. Due to this lingering threat, the undead remains of the imperial order require institutionalised management on the systemic level. In particular, we will see how the United Nations's three-pronged approach to the protection of minorities, the prevention of discrimination, and the promotion of indigenous rights maps seamlessly onto the imperial triad of nation, race, and tribe. The institutional form through which the United Nations approaches the governance of human cultural diversity is thus deeply influenced by the imperial foundations upon which the international order has been erected.

If the second modality of sublation entails an excess of preservation over negation, then the third modality entails an excess of negation over preservation: the silencing of voices, the denial of differences, that the system cannot incorporate in its form. This excess of negation, insofar as it entails a subtraction or erasure, leaves behind a blank space, a conceptual void, that must somehow be filled. There is a hole in the whole. The illusion that the dialectical reversal produces a sutured system therefore requires the production of a supplementary element that fills in this hole. Whereas the second modality of sublation entails the problematic presence of excessive elements within the system, the third modality entails the secretion of a supplementary element by the system itself in order to cover up a problematic absence or lack. It is worth quoting Derrida at length here:

The effect of focusing, in a text, around an impossible place. Fascination by a figure inadmissible in the system. Vertiginous insistence on an unclassable. And what if what cannot be assimilated, the absolute indigestible, played a fundamental role in the system, an abyssal role rather, the abyss playing an almost transcendental role and allowing to be formed above it, as a kind of effluvium, a dream of appeasement? Isn't there always an element excluded from the system that assures the system's space of possibility? The transcendental has always been, strictly, a transcategorial, what could be received, formed, terminated in none of the categories intrinsic to the system. The system's vomit.[88]

---

[88] Derrida 1986, 151, 162.

This 'inadmissible' or 'unclassable' element is a paradoxical one, falling both inside and outside the system. On the one hand, insofar as it fills in for a constitutive absence, the supplementary element is what makes it possible to think of the systematicity of the system in the first place: it provides the system with a semblance of coherence and totality. On the other hand, precisely because it appears as an extraneous addition to the system rather than as a feature of the system proper, this supplementary element also breaches the unity of the system and signals the system's inevitable opening to alterity. (In classificatory schemes, this residual category is often quite literally labelled 'other'.) Due to its contamination by alterity, by something external to the system, the supplementary element proves 'indigestible' to the system's operation and is ejected as 'vomit'. This element is the very condition of possibility of the system, yet it must also be expelled by that system. To quote Derrida again, the supplementary element is the symptom of 'an irreducible heterogeneity which cannot be eaten either sensibly or ideally and which – this is the tautology – by never letting itself be swallowed must therefore *cause itself to be vomited*'.[89]

In one of his essays on Hegel, Slavoj Žižek offers a similar digestive metaphor, writing that 'the standard critical reading constructs the Hegelian Absolute Substance-Subject as thoroughly *constipated* – keeping in itself the swallowed content'.[90] Distancing himself from this reading, Žižek joins Derrida in complementing the moment of consumption with a moment of excretion: 'Shitting is the immanent *conclusion* of the entire process: without it, we would be dealing with the "spurious infinity" of an endless process of sublation.'[91] The self-

---

[89] Derrida 1981b, 21. [90] Žižek 2011, 211.
[91] Žižek 2011, 223. In the cited passage, Žižek is drawing on the work of Catharine Malabou, a student of Derrida who challenged her teacher by arguing that the theme of abrogation or renunciation is already present in Hegel's logic. In Malabou's reading of Hegel, 'these two processes of sublation and abrogation are completely interdependent. [...] Speculative abrogation, in no way alien to the process of the *Aufhebung*, is indeed its fulfilment. Abrogation is a *sublation of sublation (relève de la relève)*, the result of the *Aufhebung*'s work on itself and, as such, its transformation' (Malabou 2005, 156). Whether or not the moment of excretion is already contained in Hegel's logic remains an open question, but either way there is no essential incompatibility between the Hegelian and the Derridean approaches. In one essay, Derrida (1978, 260) himself suggests that this might be a case of Hegel himself not being Hegelian enough: 'Hegel saw this without seeing it, showed it while concealing it. Thus, he must be followed to the end, without reserve, to the point of agreeing with him

sublation of the imperial order into the form of the international order thus depends on the secretion of a supplementary element that allows the new order to cohere. It is precisely at this point in the dialectical process that the conceptual birth of ethnicity takes place. As the international order devours its three-course meal of nations, races, and tribes, digesting them into formally equal and sovereign states, it also excretes the indigestible part of this meal as ethnicity. The concept of ethnicity is the excess or the waste – or, more graphically, the vomit or the excrement – of the international order.[92]

Three Chapters, Three Concepts

The main body of the book is organised into three chapters. Each chapter is anchored to a specific concept in relation to which the concept of ethnicity was articulated in the twentieth century: Chapter 1 focuses on 'nation', Chapter 2 on 'race', and Chapter 3 on 'tribe'. Of course, these were not the only concepts that shaped the meaning of ethnicity, and neighbouring terms such as 'civilisation' and 'culture' also feature prominently throughout the analysis. Nonetheless, it was the imperial trinity of nation, race, and tribe that served as the main point of reference for ethnicity's pioneers, and it is therefore this trinity that provides the book with its structure. It is also important to underline that the three chapters do not fall into a linear or chronological narrative. Instead, they are best understood in terms of a spiral radiating outward from a central problematique, or as a set of concentric circles nested one inside the other: each successive chapter is layered on top of and spills over from the previous one, broadening the spatiotemporal parameters of the analysis. In this

---

against himself and of wresting his discovery from the too *conscientious* interpretation he gave of it.'

[92] Reading Hegel's logic through Derrida's work overcomes the standard critique of the dialectical trinity as always-already reproducing the binary opposition between thesis and antithesis, which in turn reveal themselves as self-contained singularities. As Haraway (1991, 129) puts it, 'threes will always reduce to twos, which quickly become lonely ones in the vanguard. And no one learns to count to four.' Rather than wholly abandoning the triadic structure of Hegel's logic, the Derridean reading shows how the inner undecidability of the dialectic in fact entails the ejection of a residual fourth term as part of its operation. Reading Hegel together with Derrida, we can indeed learn to count to four.

way, the relatively simple and abstract concept of ethnicity articulated in the first chapter – ethnicity as depoliticised nationality – becomes increasingly refined and concrete over the course of the subsequent chapters. This spiral-like structure also means that there are certain tropes and themes that reappear, in different guises, over the course of the book. These include the passage from qualitative to quantitative understandings of concepts, the overturning of conceptual oppositions, and the reversal of causal chains. Such tropes are symptomatic of the work of sublation on the conceptual structures of the imperial order.

Chapter 1 shows how the politicisation of the nation concept – the equation of 'nation' with 'state' – created a terminological lacuna for ethnicity to occupy. The main cause of these conceptual changes was the nationalisation of European politics during the nineteenth century and the elevation of nationalism into the hegemonic source of state legitimacy. This produced a dialectical reversal, whereby nationalism ceased to be just one political ideology among many and instead established itself as the universal ground for all other political ideologies.[93] As the nationalist world view colonised the European socio-political imaginary, many commentators also noted a worrying transformation of nationalism from a constructive to a destructive force. Such anxieties were heightened by the First World War, which intensified nationalist competition among the great powers and catalysed the proliferation of competing claims to national self-determination. Against this backdrop, scholars and practitioners began to look for a less explosive vocabulary for addressing the so-called 'problem of minorities'. In effect, the sublation of the nation into the state had created a conceptual void: If the concept of the nation entailed an intrinsic link to statehood, then what term should be applied to those national groups or minorities that did not have a state of their own or even the aspiration to acquire one? It was amidst the ensuing attempts to fill this terminological vacuum that an embryonic concept of ethnicity was articulated as a depoliticised alternative to nationality. By avoiding any connotation of statehood, the depoliticised language of ethnicity allowed scholars and practitioners to discuss the problem of minorities without summoning the spectres of secession and irredentism that haunted the concept of the nation.

---

[93] Breuilly 2011, 102.

Chapter 2 zooms out from the European society of nations to the broader imperial order within which this society was embedded. Specifically, its focus is on the concept of race and what W. E. B. Du Bois famously described as 'the problem of the color-line, – the relation of the darker to the lighter races of men'.[94] By the second half of the nineteenth century, the concept of race had become a core component of European imperial ideology, linking supposed civilisational differences between peoples to innate physiological differences such as skin colour. The widespread appeal of the race concept stemmed from its malleability, allowing commentators to fuse social and cultural factors with notions of ancestry, biology, and blood in an incredibly flexible manner. By the dawn of the twentieth century, however, breakthroughs in physical anthropology and genetics meant that there was fast emerging a new conceptual divide between the biological and sociocultural spheres, differentiating what was 'inside us' and unchangeable from what was 'outside us' and malleable.[95] As the concept of race was torn between the biological and sociocultural spheres, the concept of ethnicity was proposed as a supplementary category to resolve these tensions: the concept of race was to be confined to biological or physical differences such as skin colour, while the concept of ethnicity was to be used for the sociocultural constitution of group identities. With regard to the constitution of the international order, the second chapter shows how the emergence of ethnicity and the reconfiguration of the race concept contributed to the effacement of the global or transnational stratum of race – in a word, ethnicity 'domesticated' race. Whereas the concept of race was centrally implicated in the hierarchical ordering of the imperial system, the concept of ethnicity entirely lacks this global or transnational dimension. Hence why there is no 'global ethnic line' comparable to the global colour line described by Du Bois.

Finally, Chapter 3 crosses over to the other side of the global imperial divide and tackles the concept of tribe. Traditionally used with reference to primitive non-European societies and contrasted to civilised European nations, the concept of tribe was rapidly

[94] Du Bois 1903, 13. See also Anievas, Manchanda, and Shilliam 2015.
[95] Meloni 2016, 65–66. See also Hattam 2007, 28–36; Lorimer 2009, 186–188; Stocking 1982, 253–267.

accumulating contradictions by the mid twentieth century. Most strikingly, the industrialisation and urbanisation of the African continent created a tension between rural and urban 'tribalisms' as rural tribespeople moved into towns in growing numbers. To defuse this tension, colonial anthropologists borrowed the concept of ethnicity from urban sociologists in the 1960s to differentiate urban ethnic groups from rural tribal populations. Almost immediately, however, the onset of decolonisation and the discrediting of Eurocentric civilisational hierarchies meant that the concept of tribe was ostracised on account of its colonial heritage. The concept of ethnicity again stepped in to fill the void, offering what seemed like a morally neutral category for describing the internal diversity of the new postcolonial states. In contrast to the hierarchical opposition between civilised (European) nations and primitive (non-European) tribes that structured anthropological knowledge production in the imperial era, the concept of ethnicity paved the way for a new kind of cultural relativism that conceded the formal equality of all peoples everywhere. Whereas the concept of tribe reinforced a bifurcated imperial order where the colonisers and colonised inhabited fundamentally different worlds, the concept of ethnicity suggests that 'we all live in one, "continuous" world'.[96]

In sum, the emergence of ethnicity in the twentieth century went hand in hand with a fundamental transformation of the global sociopolitical imaginary. The birth of ethnicity signalled the end of the great European nation-building projects, the delegitimation of the global racial hierarchy, and the dismantling of the European colonial empires: nationalism became associated with political extremism, racism came to be seen as an individual pathology, and colonialism was consigned to the past. Simply put, the emergence of ethnicity was the condition of possibility of the post-racial and postcolonial world order in which we find ourselves today. At the same time, however, the concept of ethnicity also belies the impossibility of this seemingly egalitarian order: in a Derridean twist, the condition of possibility turns out to be the condition of impossibility as well. Despite the repeated proclamations of national sovereignty and racial equality that have characterised world politics since 1945, the racial and civilisational

---

[96] Eriksen 2010, 14.

hierarchies of the imperial era did not vanish into thin air. As Johannes Fabian remarks, 'he who exorcises the devil must somehow believe in him'.[97] Precisely for this reason, the repeated attempts to exorcise nationalism, racism, and colonialism from the international plane deserve the most serious attention. The international plane is a haunted site where ghosts of orders past continue to roam.

---

[97] Fabian 2014, 56.

1 *Nation*

The word 'nation' today has two contrasting meanings, signifying both a community of people and a sovereign state. This dual meaning also informs IR's conceptualisation of nations and nationalism.[1] On the one hand, there is a widespread tendency among IR scholars to equate the nation with the state and to use terms like 'national interest' and 'national security' with reference to the interest and security of states. Nationalism, likewise, has been depicted as a 'centripetal force' that binds the state together: 'the better the state', Kenneth Waltz asserts, 'the more nationalistic' it is.[2] This conception of nationalism as the primary source of state legitimacy is rarely explicitly theorised, but instead serves as the unthinking background assumption that allows IR scholars to focus on what they are really most interested in: relations between pre-constituted nation-states. On the other hand, in the relatively few cases where IR scholars actually subject nations and nationalism to critical scrutiny, they tend to be pitted against the state in an antagonistic relationship. In the literature on nationalist conflict, for example, the 'state-to-nation balance' or 'nation-to-state ratio' is seen as a key variable in determining the likelihood of conflict in a given region.[3] In this antagonistic framing, nationalism is no longer the centripetal force that holds the state together, but a centrifugal one that threatens to pull it apart.

The contradictory uses of 'nation' and 'nationalism' have not gone unnoticed by scholars. The most common response has been to treat this as an unfortunate terminological muddle that could easily be avoided if political scientists just took more care to define their terms.[4] While terminological clarity is important, reducing the contradictions of the nation concept to a problem of definition tells us nothing about

---

[1] For a more detailed survey of the literature, see Heiskanen 2021c, 247–248.
[2] Waltz 1959, 177–178.
[3] Miller 2007, 20; van Evera 1994, 11. See also Mandelbaum 2013.
[4] For example, Barrington 1997; Connor 1978.

the sources or functions of these contradictions. In fact, the contradictory meanings of the word 'nation' are a reflection of the contradictory structure of the modern state, which is torn between universalism and particularism. The universalistic aspect of the state is evident in its claim to sovereignty, whereby the state effectively takes on the role of a secularised God. 'The state', as Hegel famously wrote, 'consists in the march of God in the world.'[5] Insofar as the state claims to be the sovereign guarantor of order and justice, it need only exist in the singular; the idea of an all-encompassing world-state is by no means conceptually incoherent.[6] At the same time, however, the state is also 'a bordered power-container' ruling over a finite portion of the earth's surface and population.[7] The universalistic claim of the state to be the sovereign guarantor of order and justice thus stands in fundamental contradiction with the inescapable territorial particularity of every actually existing state.[8]

It is the contradictory structure of the modern state that gives rise to nationalism as an ideology of state legitimacy.[9] Simply put, the nationalist solution to this contradiction is to insist that every state should represent a nation and that every nation should have a state of its own: 'let all nations have their own political roofs, and let all of them also refrain from including non-nationals under it', as Ernest Gellner memorably put it.[10] Or, in the more succinct formulation of Eric Hobsbawm, 'nation = state = people'.[11] By positing the existence of a pre-political nation as the foundation of the state, nationalism is able to conceal the arbitrariness of international borders and justify the territorial particularity of the state. Rather than stemming from a failure in conceptual precision, the dual meaning of the word 'nation' is a consequence of those specific historical circumstances that saw the triumph of the territorial state as the hegemonic form of political organisation.

Some obvious empirical barriers stand in the way of the nationalist solution to the problem of state legitimacy. To begin with, there are far more nations than states: the number of ethnically or culturally distinct human populations that exist on this planet is orders of magnitude

---

[5] Hegel 1991a, 279.   [6] Abizadeh 2005, 49–50.   [7] Giddens 1985, 120.
[8] See also Subotic and Zarakol 2013, 919–921.
[9] Breuilly 1993, 367–380; Connor 1981; Heiskanen 2021d.
[10] Gellner 1983, 1–2.   [11] Hobsbawm 1992, 19.

greater than the number of independent political units.[12] Granting statehood to every distinct group of people would necessitate a radical redrawing of international political boundaries and pave the way for a potentially endless process of political fragmentation. As Hans Morgenthau presciently observed in 1957, the only thing that can halt the proliferation of competing nationalist claims is state power.[13] The result is the 'A-B-C paradox' where 'nation B invokes the principles of nationalism against nation A, and denies them to nation C – in each case for the sake of its own survival'.[14] This institutionalised state of hypocrisy is further exacerbated by the continual intermingling of populations through migration and intermarriage, which makes it impossible to apply the principle of national self-determination consistently.

Yet, crucially, the shortcomings of the nationalist solution are not limited to these empirical obstacles. Even if all human migration were to cease and the political map were to be redrawn from scratch, the nationalist solution would still fall short of its aspirations. No amount of ethnic cleansing can ever ensure the congruence of national and political boundaries, for the limit of the nationalist solution is internal rather than external, logical rather than empirical. This is because, contrary to what nationalist ideologues claim, the nation is not a natural organism but a social construct that has to be continually reproduced through daily rituals and cultural practices.[15] And, as Aamir Mufti points out, this process of constructing a majoritarian national culture necessarily produces national minorities.[16] Counterintuitively, it is not the ethnic diversity of the world that frustrates the pursuit of nation-state congruency, but the pursuit of nation-state congruency that produces the ethnic diversity of the world. Due to this constitutive impasse, nationalism ultimately proves to be both cure and poison to the state: curative because it justifies the boundedness of the state with reference to a pre-political nation, yet poisonous because it opens the door to a never-ending series of secessionist and irredentist claims.

The central claim of this chapter is that the emergence of ethnicity in the twentieth century was, in part, an attempt to solve the contradictions of nationalism by articulating an alternative vocabulary to

---

[12] Connor 1972; Walby 2003. [13] Morgenthau 1957, 485.
[14] Snyder 1968, 17. [15] Billig 1995; Hobsbawm and Ranger 1983.
[16] Mufti 2016, 200–201.

describe stateless nations and national minorities. Simply put, safeguarding the international order from the destabilising force of nationalism requires the hierarchisation of two kinds of nation: those that possess or deserve statehood and those that do not. This, precisely, is the basic difference between a nation and an ethnic group: 'An ethnic group is distinguished from a nation, including an ethnic nation, by being a group with a common culture that does not seek to be a political community, does not seek self-governance, and certainly does not seek to constitute themselves into a state.'[17] If an ethnic movement claims the right to statehood, that movement 'by definition becomes a nationalist movement'.[18] It is this 'apolitical concept'[19] of ethnicity that underpins the ontology of the international order and the legitimacy of the nation-state. By serving as a residual or 'filler' category, the concept of ethnicity absorbs the surplus of nations that violate the principle of nation-state congruency. In contrast to the politically explosive vocabulary of nationality, which today is inextricably intertwined with notions of sovereignty and statehood, the vocabulary of ethnicity offers a depoliticised medium through which minority rights can be addressed without placing into question the existing arrangement of international borders.

To develop this argument, the remainder of the chapter proceeds in four sections. The first section provides a brief history of modern nationalism, focusing on the perceived transformation of nationalism from a constructive to a destructive force around the turn of the twentieth century. In Hegelian terms, the nationalisation of European politics produced a dialectical reversal that turned the relationship between nationalism and international order on its head: at the very moment that an international order of nation-states coalesced in Europe, nationalism turned against its own creation. Building on this analysis, the second and third sections show how the politicisation of the nation concept – the sublation of the nation into the state – opened up the conceptual space for ethnicity in academic and political discourse, respectively: the second section focuses on the conceptual frameworks deployed in academic studies of nationalism and international relations around the turn of the century, while the third section looks at the conceptualisation of national minorities in political negotiations and international treaties, focusing on the minority rights

[17] Nielsen 1999, 123.   [18] Eriksen 2010, 10.   [19] Woodwell 2007, 13.

regime set up at the end of the First World War. The fourth section wraps up the chapter by demonstrating how the conceptual hierarchy between nationality and ethnicity has been projected onto the international plane through the elaboration of a contrast between 'Western' or 'civic' nationalism on the one hand and 'non-Western' or 'ethnic' nationalism on the other.

Nationalism and International Order

The conceptual entanglement of 'nation' and 'state' was a long and drawn-out process that can be traced back to the late medieval period.[20] However, it was not until the French Revolution that nationalist ideas were first put into practice and the concept of the nation was redefined 'from a diffuse sentiment to a specific program for political and constitutional action'.[21] The Declaration of the Rights of Man and of the Citizen, promulgated by the French National Constituent Assembly in 1789, loudly proclaimed to the world that 'the source of all sovereignty resides essentially in the nation'.[22] In addition to this reconfiguration of domestic authority structures, the ensuing Revolutionary and Napoleonic wars also spurred the reconfiguration of external relations among European polities from a dynastic to a national model.[23] Indeed, the world-historical significance of these events lies precisely in their transnational scope. What the French Revolution inaugurated was not only a politicised concept of the nation, which had arguably existed for a century or two, but a *modular* conception of the nation that could be propagated around the world.[24]

During and after the French Revolution, the concept of the nation was not primarily defined in opposition to other nations or foreigners, but in opposition to the ancien régime and the conservative doctrine of divine right.[25] The concept of the nation thus acquired a distinctly liberal and progressive orientation that would remain with it for most of the nineteenth century. What made the 'principle of nationality' so

---

[20] On the conceptual history of 'nation', see Gorski 2000; Greenfeld 1992, 6–7; Hirschi 2012; Kemiläinen 1964, 13–59; Zernatto 1944.
[21] Sewell 2004, 96.
[22] Declaration of the Rights of Man and of the Citizen, quoted in Connor 1978, 382.
[23] Bukovansky 1999.
[24] Gorski 2000, 1458. See also Matin 2020; Sewell 2004.   [25] Sewell 2004, 109.

attractive to nineteenth-century liberals was precisely the fact that the political concept of the nation was historically novel and that it was opposed by the conservative segments of society. So long as nationalist discourse remained the preserve of a relatively small liberal-bourgeois elite, those 'ethnic' elements that would later become key features of nationalist discourse did not matter very much politically.[26] Even in the Germany of the Romantics, traditionally seen as the wellspring of ethnic nationalism, 'it was a liberal fusion of progress and cultural nationality that dominated nationalist discourse for much of the century'.[27]

Alongside its universalistic orientation and liberal character, another defining feature of nineteenth-century nationalism was its adherence to what Eric Hobsbawm calls the 'threshold principle'. By and large, nineteenth-century commentators assumed that the principle of self-determination was only applicable to nations that were culturally and economically of a 'viable' size. The construction of nations was generally seen as a process of unification into larger entities, typified by the experiences of Italy and Germany, rather than a process of fragmentation into smaller ones.[28] The threshold principle was politically significant because it ensured that nationalism did not threaten the universalistic narrative of progress that characterised nineteenth-century liberalism. An evolutionary understanding of human development toward ever-larger communities – from families to clans, from clans to tribes, and from tribes to nations – reinforced this alliance of nationalism and liberalism.[29] When the preeminent English liberal thinker John Stuart Mill discussed Irish nationalism in 1861, for example, he acknowledged that the Irish 'are sufficiently numerous to be capable of constituting a respectable nationality by themselves'.[30] In contrast, he believed that smaller 'half-savage' groups such as the Bretons and the Welsh should assimilate into the French and English nations, respectively.[31] Mill's characterisation of the smaller European nationalities as 'half-savage' also underlines how the requirement of size was coupled to a requirement of civilisation. As Mill put it in 1859, 'barbarians have no right as a *nation*, except a right to such treatment as may, at the earliest possible period, fit them for becoming one'.[32]

[26] Hobsbawm 1992, 40–44.   [27] Breuilly 2011, 81–82.
[28] Hobsbawm 1992, 31–33.   [29] Hobsbawm 1992, 38.   [30] Mill 1861, 295.
[31] Mill 1861, 293.
[32] Mill 1859, 772. See also Mehta 2012, 237–247; Pitts 2005, 133–162.

The Transformation of Nationalism

The period between 1871 and 1914, known as 'la belle époque', marked the high point of the alliance between nationalism, liberalism, and imperialism. In 1871, the great European nation-building projects of the nineteenth century culminated in the national unifications of Italy and Germany. Over the following decades, the nationalisation of European politics reached a point where every state was cultivating for itself a national base from which it could draw its legitimacy.[33] Even autocratic multinational empires such as Austria-Hungary and Russia began articulating 'official' nationalisms to prop up their regimes.[34] Formerly just one political position among many, nationalism now established itself as the universal ground for all political ideologies. In parallel, a new wave of European imperial expansion overseas meant that virtually the entirety of the earth's surface was divided up among a handful of imperialistic nation-states. As the blank spaces on European maps were filled in, the number of independent polities in the world sunk to an all-time low.[35] By the turn of the century, the ardent proponent of British imperialism Cecil Rhodes observed with equal pride and sadness that the 'world is nearly all parcelled out, and what there is left of it is being divided up, conquered and colonised'.[36] The sense of culmination and finality that defined the turn-of-the-century zeitgeist was eloquently captured by the American political scientist Paul S. Reinsch in 1900: 'The nations, having passed through their historical evolution, stand now, with fully developed individualities, face to face.'[37]

Precisely at its moment of triumph, nationalism shed its liberal-universalistic orientation and took on an increasingly ethnic-particularistic guise. In many ways, this dialectical reversal was the logical corollary of nationalism's own success. As national consciousness penetrated wider and deeper into European society, it became increasingly important for elites to understand how ordinary people felt about the nation in order to mobilise public opinion behind political decisions. Language and other 'ethnic' criteria of nationhood thus

---

[33] Breuilly 2011, 102. [34] Anderson 2006, 83–112; Seton-Watson 1977, 148.
[35] Osterhammel 2013, 697. [36] Rhodes, quoted in Stead 1902, 190.
[37] Reinsch 1900, 8. See also Reinsch 1902, 9–10. Reinsch's *World Politics at the End of the Nineteenth Century* has been said to indicate the 'first glimmerings of international relations as a discipline' (Olson and Groom 1991, 47).

acquired greater salience.[38] At the same time, the intensification of imperial rivalry among the great powers catalysed the division of Europe into competing transnational blocs centred on racialised ideologies such as pan-Germanism and pan-Slavism.[39] The combined effect of these developments was the rise of an ethnocentric cult of the nation-state, exemplified by the establishment of the French right-wing political movement *Action française* in 1899. Charles Maurras, a leading figure of the movement, defined the new 'integral nationalism' as 'the exclusive pursuit of national policies, the absolute maintenance of national integrity, and the steady increase of national power'.[40] Numerous turn-of-the-century commentators noted this 'exaggeration'[41] or 'perversion'[42] of nationalism with trepidation. In the midst of the First World War, which seemed to validate these fears, one British author lamented that the principle of nationality had 'changed in character with its success'. Nationalism was no longer 'the cry of an oppressed people' but had instead 'become allied with national pride, and with the wish to acquire power and territory'.[43] The word 'nationalism' itself was popularised in the last decade of the nineteenth century precisely as a term of abuse to denounce the new ethnocentric and power-hungry cult of the nation-state.[44]

The exaggeration of nationalism in international politics was accompanied by a second closely related shift: the transformation of nationalism from a unifying into a disintegrating force. At the very moment that the European nation-building projects seemed complete,

---

[38] Hobsbawm 1992, 43–45, 101–130.
[39] Arendt 1976, 222–266; Bell 2020; Younis 2017. These European developments were paralleled by the emergence of other transnational ideologies such as pan-Africanism and pan-Asianism outside Europe (see Chapter 2).
[40] Maurras, quoted in Hayes 1931, 165.   [41] Reinsch 1900, 6–7.
[42] Hobson 1902, 9–10.
[43] Urquhart 1916, 59. See also Rosenthal and Rodic 2015.
[44] In the French language, the term 'nationalisme' was coined in 1798 by the exiled French priest Augustin Barruel, who defined it as egotism practised by a nation. The English 'nationalism' first appears in a translation of Barruel's memoirs published in the same year. In both languages, the term was rarely used and it remained absent from lexicographies until the last quarter of the nineteenth century. It was only in the 1890s that the term was popularised, principally as a term of disapproval that was used to criticise ideas and practices that broke with what was considered the legitimate role of the nation. On the conceptual history of 'nationalism', see de Bertier de Sauvigny 1970, 155–161; Kettunen 2018, 344–347.

nationalism turned against its own creations. With an ever-growing number of 'new' or 'unhistorical' nations in Central and Eastern Europe asserting their right to self-determination, the 'threshold principle' of the nineteenth century was effectively abandoned.[45] E. H. Carr captured this transformation in his 1945 book *Nationalism and After*, where he divided the history of nationalism into three stages. The first stage comprised the gradual dissolution of the feudal system in the early modern period, while the second stage stretched from the end of the Napoleonic Wars to the outbreak of the First World War.[46] Carr was sympathetic toward this early form of nationalism, describing the nineteenth-century balance between nationalism and internationalism as 'the work of art rather than of nature'.[47] By the last quarter of the century, however, 'the first subterranean rumblings began to shake this splendid edifice' as nationalism entered its third and most recent phase: 'After 1870 the constructive work of nation-building seemed complete. Nationalism came to be associated with "the Balkans" and with all that the ominous term implied.'[48] Over the following years, the exemplary case of nationalism would increasingly shift from the national unifications of Italy and Germany to the fragmentation associated with the Balkans.

The dual transformation of nationalism in the last quarter of the twentieth century reflected the underlying contradiction between universality and particularity that cuts through the modern territorial state. On the one hand, nationalism turned out to be *not particular enough*: the legitimacy issues of the state can never be fully relieved through recognition by its national citizenry. As Ayşe Zarakol observes, the legitimacy of the state derives from it being sovereign *for* its citizens as well as *over* its citizens. This claim to universality cannot be assuaged by the essentially domestic and particularistic operation of nationalism. As a result, the state's search for ontological security must turn outward into the international realm: 'It must be sovereign *in the world*.'[49] The inadequacy of nationalistic particularism as the state's foundation thus generates a nationalistic universalism

---

[45] Hobsbawm 1992, 102. [46] Carr 1945, 2–7. [47] Carr 1945, 15.
[48] Carr 1945, 17. During the First World War, the British historian Toynbee (1915, 7) likewise identified the year 1870 as the decisive watershed after which the 'National State' ceased to be 'the ultimate ideal of European politics' and became increasingly bankrupt as a political concept.
[49] Zarakol 2018, 861. See also Zarakol 2011, 71–82.

or nationalistic imperialism that 'glows with the animus of greed and self-aggrandisement at the expense of others'.[50] This 'brutal egotism' and 'narrow chauvinism' among nation-states, as one commentator remarked in 1923, is 'the basic fact of international society'.[51]

On the other hand, nationalism also turned out to be *too particular*: by grounding the legitimacy of the state in particular ethnocultural characteristics, nationalism always-already – also threatens the unity of the state by paving the way for secessionist claims. If nationalistic universalism constitutes an international source of conflict, then nationalistic particularism constitutes a domestic one. This particularistic threat is ineradicable because, contrary to the claims of nationalists themselves, the nation is not given by nature but a historically contingent ideological construct. By the end of the First World War, it was becoming increasingly evident that nationalist claims for independence would not exhaust themselves. 'If the right of every group, however small, which may happen to be ethnically and linguistically distinct from the rest of the population, to separate and organize itself into a new state, were admitted and exercised in practice, it would lead to chaos and anarchy', the American political scientist James Wilford Garner wrote in 1928.[52] An important corollary to this was the foregrounding of the problem of national minorities as a pressing international concern. 'In the last resort there must always be minorities that suffer', the British historian Arnold Toynbee concluded in 1915. 'We can only secure that the minorities are as small and the suffering as mild as possible.'[53]

The dual threat that nationalism posed to international order was at the forefront of Hans Morgenthau's pioneering work on international politics. The particularistic or domestic aspect of the new nationalism was the focus of his 1957 article on 'The Paradoxes of Nationalism', where he described nationalism as 'a principle of disintegration and fragmentation' that culminated in 'anarchy'.[54] For Morgenthau, the disintegrative force of twentieth-century nationalism represented a stark departure from the unificatory nation-building projects of the previous century: 'No longer are national minorities to be protected against the state; it is now the state which must be protected against the

---

[50] Hobson 1902, 9.   [51] Brown 1923, 3.   [52] Garner 1928, 135.
[53] Toynbee 1915, 17.   [54] Morgenthau 1957, 484–485.

minorities.'[55] Echoing Carr's aforementioned linkage of twentieth-century nationalism with the Balkans, Morgenthau feared that the proliferation of nationalist claims would lead to 'Balkanization, demoralization, and barbarization on a world-wide scale'.[56] Given that the logic of nationalist fragmentation had 'no inherent limits', the only thing that could put a stop to it was state power: 'the process of national liberation must stop at some point, and that point is determined not by the logic of nationalism, but by the configurations of interest and power between the rulers and the ruled and between competing nations'.[57]

State power may have been seen as the antidote to nationalism's drive toward fragmentation, but in solving one problem it also created another: the assertion of state power transformed nationalism into a political religion that claimed for one nation-state the right to impose its will upon others. This was the universalistic or international dimension of the new nationalism. 'Traditional nationalism sought to free the nation from alien domination and give it a state of its own', Morgenthau explained in *Politics among Nations*. 'Once a nation had united its members in one state, national aspirations were satisfied, and there was room for as many nationalisms as there were nations which wanted to establish or preserve a state of their own.' Nationalist conflicts in the nineteenth century had been either conflicts between a subject nationality and its alien master or conflicts between two nations over the delimitation of their respective territories.[58] In contrast, nationalism in the twentieth century took the form of a 'nationalistic universalism' where 'the nation is but the starting point of a universal mission whose ultimate goal reaches to the confines of the political world'.[59] The emergence of the new nationalism was foreshadowed by the Napoleonic Wars and the First World War, but Morgenthau saw the 1930s and 1940s as the decisive break.[60] 'While the old nationalism seeks one nation in one state and nothing else', he wrote, 'the new one claims for one nation and one state the right to impose its own values and standards of action upon all other nations.'[61] The dangers of nationalistic universalism were multiplied by the advent of the atomic age, which heralded the possibility of

---

[55] Morgenthau 1957, 495. [56] Morgenthau 1957, 491.
[57] Morgenthau 1957, 485. [58] Morgenthau 1948, 268.
[59] Morgenthau 1948, 269. [60] Morgenthau 1957, 488–489.
[61] Morgenthau 1957, 488.

mutually assured destruction and rendered the protective functions of the nation-state obsolete.[62] 'If the West cannot think of something better than nationalism', rang Morgenthau's sombre conclusion, 'it may well lose the opportunity to think at all.'[63]

The Neutralisation of Nationalism

Insofar as the twin threats that nationalism poses to international order stem from the contradictory structure of the modern territorial state, they can never be fully eradicated. Yet their worst destabilising effects can be alleviated through a double move. The first part of this double move is well-known to IR theorists and entails displacing the 'problem of difference'[64] from the domestic to the international realm. This is achieved through the construction of a spatial distinction between the inside and the outside of the state, whereby the sovereign national identity is located within the bounds of the state territory and difference is projected out onto the international plane.[65] 'This demarcation and policing of the boundary between the "inside" and the "outside" of the political community', as David Blaney and Naeem Inayatullah explain, 'defines the problem of difference as *between and among* states; difference is marked and contained as *international* difference.'[66] By constructing an idealised global grid of internally homogeneous nations, the inside/outside framework avoids the overlap of 'self' and 'other'. The contradiction between universality and particularity is thus seemingly resolved: the identity of the nation appears universal domestically, but particular internationally. This is the culmination of the nationalist fantasy where, as Ernest Gellner famously put it, 'all nations have their own political roofs'.[67]

Of course, the ideal of the homogeneous nation-state remains forever an aspiration rather than a reality. In 1972, Walker Connor noted that only twelve of the world's states could be considered ethnically homogeneous to any significant degree, and the situation has hardly 'improved' since then – if anything, the international migration fuelled by globalisation has led to even greater heterogeneity.[68] Every state contains within its borders national minorities that governments must

---

[62] Morgenthau 1957, 490.   [63] Morgenthau 1957, 496.
[64] Inayatullah and Blaney 2004.   [65] Walker 1993.
[66] Inayatullah and Blaney 2004, 6.   [67] Gellner 1983, 1.
[68] Connor 1972, 320. See also Walby 2003.

seek to manage through policies ranging from assimilation and toleration to expulsion and extermination.[69] Crucially, however, such incongruencies are not reducible to a purely empirical issue: it is not simply the case that the ineradicable diversity of humankind makes it impossible to segregate national communities into distinct political units, or that realities of migration and intermarriage undercut attempts to achieve ethnic homogeneity within the state's territory. In fact, the situation is precisely the opposite: it is not the purported ethnocultural diversity of the world that prevents the construction of homogeneous nation-states, but the attempts to construct homogeneous nation-states that produce the ethnocultural diversity of the world.[70] The nationalist fantasy of the congruent nation-state is thus a fantasy in the strictest sense of this word: an impossible project that is not only destined to fail, but that can only exist through its very failure.[71] In the final analysis, the 'excess' of nations over states is a necessary consequence of nationalism itself.

While the discursive construction of the inside/outside dichotomy has become a familiar trope of IR theory, the second part of the double move has received less attention: the problem of difference has to be erased not only from the domestic realm, but also from the international realm. Otherwise, international politics would appear as a chaotic realm of pure difference and particularity that universal reason could not tame. For many of IR's pioneers, the experience of two world wars and mass genocide certainly seemed to validate such a pessimistic assessment. Prominent figures such as Hans Morgenthau and John Herz had emigrated to the United States from Germany in the 1930s and were acutely aware of nationalism's dangers.[72] Morgenthau, for example, worried that the exaggerated nationalism of the Second World War had dealt 'the final, fatal blow' to international restraints on destructive power politics.[73] At the same time, these traumatic experiences underlined the vital importance of bringing the chaotic international realm within the grasp of reason. Thus, it was against a backdrop of extreme nationalist violence that the first attempts to develop 'scientific' theories of international relations emerged in the late 1940s and 1950s, superseding the rather eclectic IR scholarship of

---

[69] Rae 2002. [70] Mufti 2016, 200–201. [71] Mandelbaum 2020.
[72] Rösch 2014. [73] Morgenthau 1948, 269.

the early twentieth century.⁷⁴ If there was any chance of formulating a rational theory of politics among nations, Morgenthau believed, such a theory could not begin from the particularistic logic of nationalism, but had to take as its starting point a universal understanding of power grounded in human nature: 'the struggle for power is universal in time and space'.⁷⁵

If the first part of the double move exorcises the problem of difference from the domestic realm, then the second exorcises the problem of difference from the international realm. To achieve this, the nation can appear on the international plane only in its universalistic capacity and not in its particularistic capacity: only the abstract and transposable form of the nation can be present; the concrete ethnocultural contents that make each individual nation unique must be discarded. Strictly speaking, therefore, a nation can no longer appear on the international plane as a nation at all, but must instead appear as a state. The difference between nation and state thus collapses as the former is sublated into the latter. Pushed to its logical conclusion, this conceptual short circuit extinguishes all qualitative differences between nations and transforms them into those 'black boxes' or 'billiard balls' that IR theorists are so fond of: nations become 'like units' devoid of qualitative differences. All that remains of the particularity of nations is their spatial aspect – territorial boundedness – as well as quantitative differences that can be captured through abstract and universally applicable categories such as 'power' or 'capabilities'.⁷⁶ Through this process of abstraction, which subordinates quality to quantity and difference to identity, the international realm is made accessible to reason.⁷⁷ This glorious triumph of universal reason reaches its climax when the term 'anarchy' ceases to indicate 'disorder and chaos' and transforms instead into an 'ordering principle' that allows the IR theorist to 'explain important aspects of social and political behavior'.⁷⁸

International Relations's resolution of the contradictions of nationalism is thus more intricate than usually recognised. It is not simply a case of displacing the problem of difference from the domestic realm to the

---

[74] Guilhot 2011a, 2017; Williams 2013.   [75] Morgenthau 1948, 16–17.
[76] Waltz 1979, 95–99. See also Jahn 2000, 13–15. The process of abstraction described here is analogous to Marx's (1976, 128) analysis of commodity exchange, where the 'sensuous characteristics' of commodities are 'extinguished' and qualitative differences are reduced to a quantitative equation.
[77] Jahn 2000, 1–29.   [78] Waltz 1979, 114–116.

international plane, but also of then erasing the problem of difference from the international plane as well. Through this double move, which collapses the nation into the state, the domestic political system and the international political system are made accessible to the universalistic pretences of political theory and international theory, respectively. Meanwhile, nationalism comes to be seen as a political pathology and banished to the discipline's peripheries.[79] All that remains of the nation's particularistic constitution is an ethereal spectre that makes itself felt through banal phrases such as 'national interest', 'national security', 'national defence', and, of course, the term 'international' itself. This haunting presence of the nation is an inexorable remainder and reminder of the nationalist forces that constructed the international order and that may at any moment erupt once again to obliterate it.[80]

But what happens to difference? What happens to the ineradicable kernel of ethnocultural particularity that fractures the nationalist fantasy from within? As the remainder of this chapter demonstrates, the consolidation of a system of nation-states in Europe was paralleled by the invention of a new concept that helped to neutralise the internal contradictions of nationalism: the concept of ethnicity. Through the elaboration of ethnicity as a depoliticised alternative to nationality, the particularistic dimension of the nation was given a separate conceptual existence from those universal categories that were applied to domestic and international politics. As the nation was sublated into the state and international anarchy metamorphosed into international order, the element of particularity inhabiting the nation 'dropped out' – was excreted, vomited, expelled – in the form of ethnicity. Although this conceptual separation of the universal and the particular components of the nation can never eliminate the contradictions of nationalism, it nevertheless provides these contradictions with a form in which they have 'room to move'.[81]

---

[79] Lerner 2022. [80] Heiskanen 2019.
[81] Marx 1976, 198. See also Markell 2003, 109–111. The logic that leads to the emergence of the concept of ethnicity is analogous to Marx's description of how a 'universal equivalent' or 'money commodity' emerges out of the process of commodity exchange: the underlying contradiction between the particular use-values of commodities and their universal exchange-values impels the designation of a particular commodity as the embodiment of exchange-value. Similarly, the contradiction between the universal conception of the nation as a state and the particular conception of the nation as a distinct community of people impels the coinage of a new concept – ethnicity – as the embodiment of the latter. The key difference is that the money commodity emerges as the

To substantiate this argument, the next two sections trace how a conceptual space for ethnicity opened up in academic discourse, and international legal and political practice, respectively.

Conceptualising the Non-political Nation

By the dawn of the twentieth century, the nationalisation of European politics had made the words 'nation' and 'state' interchangeable. The obvious problem that this posed to political commentators was how to refer to those stateless national groups that did not have a state of their own and perhaps did not even seek to acquire one. This section traces how turn-of-the-century scholars grappled with this conceptual puzzle, and how these definitional dilemmas eventually paved the way for a new conceptual distinction between nations and ethnic groups. In terms of source material, the focus is primarily on British, French, and American scholars who engaged with questions of international order and nationalism in the late nineteenth and early twentieth centuries. Together with encyclopaedia entries, two bibliographical compilations provided a helpful starting point: Parker Thomas Moon's *Syllabus on International Relations* from 1925 and Koppel S. Pinson's *A Bibliographical Introduction to Nationalism* from 1935.[82] Additional texts were then added through a 'snowball' approach (consulting the references of known works to find new works) to arrive at a corpus of well over fifty texts spanning the period from 1885 to 1945, although not all have been cited. Many of the texts were written by political scientists, but the authors also include historians, sociologists, lawyers, and philosophers, among others. This disciplinary heterogeneity is hardly surprising, given IR's interstitial and embryonic state. At the turn of the century, as Nicolas Guilhot observes, 'IR was generally considered to be an interdisciplinary field

---

particular form of universality, whereas the concept of ethnicity emerges as the universal form of particularity. See Marx 1976, 157–163.

[82] Moon 1925; Pinson 1935. The encyclopedias consulted were: *La grande encyclopédie: inventaire raisonné des sciences, des lettres et des arts* (1882–1902); *Cyclopædia of Political Science, Political Economy, and the Political History of the United States* (1899); *Encyclopædia of Religion and Ethics* (1908–1927); *The Encyclopædia Britannica: A Dictionary of Arts, Science, Literature and General Information* (1911); *The Encyclopedia Americana* (1918–1920); and *Encyclopaedia of the Social Sciences* (1930–1935).

located on the margins of political science, with no method of its own – a sort of commons, as it were, plowed by various disciplines ranging from economics to geography'.[83]

State versus Nation

Perhaps the most straightforward way to deal with the conceptual issues generated by the conflation of nation and state was simply to reject this conflation. While this had become a minority position by the beginning of the twentieth century, a handful of important scholars continued to oppose the interchangeable use of the two terms.[84] Foremost among them was Alfred Zimmern, a pioneer in the study of international affairs who became the first Woodrow Wilson Chair of International Politics at Aberystwyth in 1919 and the first Montague Burton Professor of International Relations at Oxford in 1930.[85] In Zimmern's view, nationality and statehood belonged to categorically different realms:

> Nationality, like religion, is subjective; Statehood is objective. Nationality is psychological; Statehood is political. Nationality is a condition of mind; Statehood is a condition in law. Nationality is a spiritual possession; Statehood is an enforceable obligation. Nationality is a way of feeling, thinking and living; Statehood is a condition inseparable from all civilized ways of living.[86]

For Zimmern, therefore, internationalism was not about relations between states or nation-states, not even about the interactions of diplomats, but about relations between nations as cultural or spiritual entities.[87] 'The true contact between the West European national triangle', he explained in 1923, 'must be a contact, not between trust-magnates or labor-leaders or even statesmen from the three countries, but, so to speak, between Shakespeare, Molière and Goethe.'[88] Zimmern's argument was partly motivated by a desire for terminological clarity, but political and ethical considerations were also central. During the First World War, he drew a distinction between 'true' and 'false' nationalism, aligning the former with a benign cultural or spiritual conception of nationhood and the latter with the political

---

[83] Guilhot 2011b, 128.   [84] For example, Beer 1917, 43; Leacock 1906, 17.
[85] Baji 2021; Markwell 1986.   [86] Zimmern 1918a, 51.   [87] Baji 2016.
[88] Zimmern 1923, 126.

ideal of the nation-state.[89] Restraining international competition and conflict required disentangling 'the problems of nationality' on the one hand from 'the problems of statehood and citizenship' on the other. 'It is from their century-old confusion that so much mischief and bloodshed have arisen', he concluded.[90]

Unsurprisingly, protestations such as Zimmern's were unable to reverse the growing tendency to substitute nation for state, epitomised by the establishment of the League of Nations – in fact, an inter-*state* organisation – in 1919. James Wilford Garner, Professor of Political Science at Illinois, was among a slew of prominent authors to point out this trend during the inter-war years: 'the term "nation" as used to-day by most writers connotes a political organization; that is, a nation is not only an association of which the bonds of union are cultural and spiritual, but it is also a politically organized aggregation. In short, it is a state.'[91] For many scholars, the equivalence of nation and state was especially apposite when it came to international politics. Thus, one early study of the relationship between nationalism and war explained that the word 'nation' could refer specifically to 'a state in which there is one *nationality*, a national-state', before specifying that 'in *international* relations' even a multinational polity such as Austria-Hungary 'is considered a *nation* like every other'.[92] Another commentator noted that both 'nation' and 'state' could be used 'to signify politically organized communities which enter into international relations'.[93] Stephen Haley Allen's *International Relations*, among the earliest books explicitly dedicated to the study of international politics, unapologetically used 'nation' and 'state' as synonyms.[94] For all of these scholars and the innumerable others who accepted the equivalence of nation and state, there was a need to coin another term to describe those national minorities and stateless nations that did not partake in international relations – entities that contemporaries sometimes described as 'repressed', 'oppressed', or 'submerged' nations.[95]

Nation versus Nationality

The first candidate to occupy the terminological vacuum created by the politicisation of the nation concept was 'nationality'. As one scholar

---

[89] Zimmern 1918a, 61–86.   [90] Zimmern 1923, 125.   [91] Garner 1928, 113.
[92] Krehbiel 1916, 1n1.   [93] Hicks 1920, 3.   [94] Allen 1920, 10–44.
[95] For example, Barnes 1920, 169; Brown 1923, 2; Hughan 1924, 122.

noted in 1916, it was due to the increasing use of the term 'nation' in a 'political sense' in the nineteenth century that 'nationality' came to be employed as a concrete noun with reference to ethnocultural groups.[96] In the French language, too, the word 'nationalité' was introduced in the early nineteenth century to describe various forms of spiritual, religious, or ethnocultural (but never legal or political) attachment.[97] Among the earliest works to explicitly discuss the distinction between 'nation' and 'nationality' was Henry Sidgwick's *The Elements of Politics* in 1891:

> by 'a nationality' we usually mean a body of human beings united by the kind of sentiment of unity or fellow citizenship that is required to constitute a nation, but not possessing in common an independent government which they alone permanently obey: being either divided among several governments, or united under one government along with persons of a different nationality.[98]

The key factor that differentiated a nation from a nationality was thus political unity. This point was echoed by other influential scholars of the time. In 1912, the British historian and politician James Bryce wrote that 'a Nation is a nationality, or a subdivision of a nationality, which has organized itself into a political body, either independent or desiring to be independent'.[99] Two decades later, the American pioneer of nationalism studies Carlton Hayes suggested that a nationality became a nation 'by acquiring political unity'.[100]

Recalling the 'threshold principle' that had regulated the recognition of new nations in the nineteenth century, the requirement of political organisation was usually coupled to notions of rank and size: a nationality was typically believed to be smaller and less accomplished than a nation proper, and thus equated with minorities rather than majorities. For example, commenting on groups such as the Scots in Britain and the Slovenes in Yugoslavia, the American political scientist James Wilford Garner claimed that it 'would be excessive flattery to their pride to call them "nations"; the term "nationality" more nearly corresponds to their importance'.[101] Echoing this sentiment, Pablo de Azcárate, a Spanish diplomat who worked for the League of Nations Minorities Section in the 1920s, opined that a nationality and a minority were 'in the last resort ... one and the same'.[102]

[96] Buck 1916, 46. [97] Noiriel 1995, 7–10. [98] Sidgwick 1891, 215.
[99] Bryce 1912, 424. [100] Hayes 1933, 5. [101] Garner 1928, 116.
[102] de Azcárate 1945, 5.

Not all scholars resorted to the word 'nationality' to defuse the contradictions of the nation concept. The American historian Harry Elmer Barnes, for example, preferred to differentiate between a 'nation' and a 'national state'.[103] So did Arthur Holcombe, Professor of Government at Harvard.[104] In such instances, it was 'nation' that was the ethnic or cultural category and 'national state' that was the legal or political category. Yet the legal or political dimension was not so easy to isolate from the nation concept. Thus, even as Holcombe insisted that a nation was a cultural rather than a political unit, he conceded that there was a 'tendency on the part of members of a nation to wish to dominate the state of which they happen to be a part or, failing that, to organize a state of their own'.[105] The same line of argument can be found in the work of John William Burgess, Professor of Political Science and International Law at Columbia and a key figure behind the establishment of the American Political Science Association in 1903.[106] Echoing Barnes and Holcombe, Burgess defined a nation principally in ethnocultural terms: not all nations were 'endowed with political capacity or great political impulse' and that it was 'therefore not to be assumed that every nation *must* become a state'.[107] Specifically, he believed that it was 'the Teutonic nations' that were 'particularly endowed with the capacity for establishing national states'.[108] Nonetheless, like Holcombe, he felt compelled to add a caveat: 'Where the geographic and ethnic unities coincide, or very nearly coincide, the nation is almost sure to organize itself politically, – to become a state.'[109] Having acknowledged the tendency of nations to seek statehood, Burgess was obliged to refer to nations that lacked this political capacity as 'unpolitical nations'.[110] This contrast between 'unpolitical' and 'political' nations achieved the same purpose as Barnes and Holcombe's distinction between 'nations' and 'national states' or the more widespread distinction between 'nationalities' and 'nations'. In each pairing, the first term designated an ethnocultural community, while the second referred to a similar community that was also politically organised.

---

[103] Barnes 1919, 744; Barnes 1920, 165–166. [104] Holcombe 1923, 134–136.
[105] Holcombe 1923, 135. [106] Schmidt 1998, 44.
[107] Burgess 1890, vol. I, 4.
[108] Burgess 1890, vol. I, 44. On Burgess's racialised conception of the nation-state, see also Blatt 2014.
[109] Burgess 1890, vol. I, 2–3. [110] Burgess 1890, vol. I, 4.

Table 1.1 *Splitting the nation concept*

Author	Date	Non-political category	Political category
James Bryce	1912	Nationality	Nation
John Holland Rose	1916	Nationality	Nation
Théodore Ruyssen	1917	Nationality	Nation
Harry Elmer Barnes	1919	Nation	National state
Arthur Holcombe	1923	Nation	National state
James Wilford Garner	1928	Nationality	Nation

Some of the binary frameworks elaborated by early twentieth-century scholars of nationalism and IR are summarised in Table 1.1 above. By making it possible to conceptually differentiate nation-states from stateless nations and national minorities, these distinctions enabled a partial resolution of the definitional dilemmas posed by the dual meaning of the word 'nation'. In parts of Central Europe, these conceptual distinctions were even developed into legal categories that justified the subordination of lesser nationalities under a dominant national identity.[111] The Hungarian Nationality Law of 1868, for example, granted some language rights to non-Magyar groups but reserved the term 'nation' or 'nemzet' to Hungary alone. Non-Magyar communities within the Hungarian part of the Austro-Hungarian Dual Monarchy were instead described as 'nationalities' or 'nemzetiség', a term adopted from Austrian legal terminology. In political terms, all nationalities belonged to the unitary Hungarian nation.[112]

The splitting of the political and non-political halves of the nation concept did not necessarily require a dichotomy; the same effect could also be achieved through the articulation of multiple neighbouring categories. In 1929, for example, Bernard Joseph proposed a tripartite framework consisting of national groups, nationalities, and nations. Each step along the sequence was also a step toward statehood, culminating in the nation, which was defined as 'a group of persons who constitute the population of a single state'.[113] What distinguished a nationality from a national group was a 'will to live' as a nation.[114] A national group was thus a potential nationality and a nationality was

---

[111] Seton-Watson 1977, 4.   [112] Seton-Watson 1977, 164.
[113] Joseph 1929, 23.   [114] Joseph 1929, 24–25.

a potential nation. In a similar vein, the influential French jurist Louis Le Fur developed a four-tiered framework consisting of 'race', 'nation', 'patrie', and 'état'. The first of these was of no political importance, but merely one possible contributing factor to a sense of nationality. The second tier was 'nation' or 'nationalité' (Le Fur used these terms interchangeably) and referred to an 'entité moral' with significant political potential.[115] The third tier represented the fulfilment of this political potential: 'La patrie, c'est la nation ayant pris conscience d'elle-même et devenue, de la part de ses membres, l'objet d'une sorte de culte, d'un sentiment spécial, le patriotisme, à base de reconnaissance et d'amour.'[116] Both 'patrie' and 'état' entailed political authority over a territory, but the latter was distinguished from the former by the possession of absolute sovereign authority over its lands.[117] For Le Fur, this fourth and final stage was the logical culmination of the lower terms in the framework.[118] Every nation or nationality was thus a potential state: 'la nationalité, c'est avant tout une virtualité, un État en germe, – comme inversement l'État c'est la nation juridiquement organisée'.[119]

Le Fur's characterisation of statehood as the natural culmination of nationality was widely shared by his contemporaries. In 1916, the English historian John Holland Rose defined a nation as 'a people which has attained to state organization' and a nationality as a people which had 'not *yet* attained' such organisation.[120] In 1928, James Wilford Garner approvingly cited Le Fur's characterisation of a nationality as 'a state *en germe*' and described political independence as 'the natural fruit of nationality where the population is sufficiently numerous and capable of maintaining a separate state existence'.[121] In the same vein, the French pacifist philosopher Théodore Ruyssen argued that 'the nation is the complete form – or, as we should say in philosophy, the *idea* or final cause – which the nationality desires to realize'.[122] Ruyssen sketched out a three-tiered framework whereby an ethnic group could develop, via a nationality, to a full member of international society: 'La nationalité, c'est le groupe ethnique privé de l'indépendance politique et qui aspire à la conquérir ... ; c'est, si l'on veut, la nation en puissance, mais assez consciente de cette puissance pour tendre de toutes ses forces au droit de prendre rang, en pleine

---

[115] Le Fur 1922, 98.   [116] Le Fur 1922, 99.   [117] Le Fur 1922, 104–105.
[118] Le Fur 1922, 106–108.   [119] Le Fur 1922, 153.
[120] Holland Rose 1916, viii–ix, italics added.   [121] Garner 1928, 120.
[122] Ruyssen 1917, 73.

égalité, dans la Société des Nations libres.'[123] All in all, there was a widespread sense that a nationality was somehow unfulfilled without development into a nation-state. Nationalities were seen as 'des êtres jeunes, voire même enfants' that would blossom into nations once they reached 'pleine maturité'.[124] In this unilinear temporal sequence, the 'possible' was understood as an 'unrealized actual' that remained somehow 'lacking' or 'incomplete' until it had been fully actualised.[125]

An especially influential German-language text is also worth mentioning here: Johann Kaspar Bluntschli's *Lehre vom modernen Staat*. Originally published in German in 1851, the book was translated into French in 1871 and into English in 1885. The English translation, titled *The Theory of the State*, was widely read, reissued in numerous editions, and served as the main political theory textbook in Cambridge and Oxford in the late nineteenth century.[126] By the 1910s, Bluntschli's works were circulating as far as East Asia, informing the development of Japanese and Chinese conceptions of the nation.[127] The book is structured around familiar conceptual distinctions, with the German 'Volk' possessing a political connotation that the word 'Nation' lacked. Thus, as Bluntschli himself noted, it was 'Volk' and not 'Nation' that corresponded to the English and French 'nation'.[128] The translators heeded Bluntschli's recommendation, rendering 'Volk' as 'nation' and 'Nation' as 'people' or 'peuple'.[129] The latter category was defined as 'a union of masses of men of different occupations and social strata in a hereditary society of common spirit, feeling and race, bound together, especially by common language and customs, in a common civilisation which gives them a sense of unity and distinction from all foreigners, quite apart from the bond of the State'.[130] For Bluntschli, a people was therefore

---

[123] Ruyssen 1919, 780. [124] Brunhes and Vallaux 1921, 625.
[125] Chakrabarty 2000, 249–250. A report on nationalism by the Royal Institute of International Affairs (1939, xvii) published on the eve of the Second World War described a nationality as 'a people, potentially but not actually a nation'.
[126] Bell 2014, 693. [127] Bastid-Bruguière 2004.
[128] Bluntschli 1886, vol. I, 91.
[129] Bluntschli 1877, 70; Bluntschli 1885, vi–vii, 82.
[130] Bluntschli 1885, 86. For the German text, see Bluntschli 1886, vol. I, 96: 'die erblich gewordene Geistes-, Gemüts- und Rassegemeinschaft von Menschenmassen der verschiedenen Berufszweige und Gesellschaftsschichten, welche auch abgesehen von dem Staatsverbande als kulturverwandte Stammesgenossenschaft vorzüglich in der Sprache, den Sitten, der Kultur sich verbunden fühlt und von den übrigen Massen als Fremden sich unterscheidet'.

'not a political society; but if it is really conscious of its community of spirit and civilisation, it is natural that it should ask to develop this into a full personality with a common will which can express itself in act; in fact, to become a State'.[131] At the same time, Bluntschli sought to maintain some kind of threshold principle to such development, asserting that 'only a people of political capacity can claim to become an independent nation'.[132] It was precisely the acquisition of an independent state that marked the transformation of a people into a nation: 'By a Nation (*Volk*) we generally understand a society of all the members of a State as united and organised in the State. The Nation comes into being with the creation of the State. It is the consciousness, more or less developed, of political connection and unity which lifts the Nation above the People.'[133]

Nationality versus Ethnic Group

In their efforts to distinguish between the political and non-political meanings of the word 'nation', turn-of-the-century commentators produced a cacophony of conceptual frameworks. These frameworks were mostly populated by nation-based words such as 'nation', 'nationality', 'national group', and 'national state', complemented by a smattering of other terms such as 'race' and 'people'. The most popular distinction was no doubt the binary contrast between nations and nationalities, but other conceptual schemas could serve the same purpose equally well. Through such distinctions, it became possible for authors to

---

[131] Bluntschli 1885, 95. For the German text, see Bluntschli 1886, vol. I, 107: 'Zunächst freilich ist die Nation nur Kultur- und nicht Staatsgemeinschaft. Aber wenn sie sich ihrer Geistesgemeinschaft recht lebendig bewusst wird, dann liegt der Gedanke und das Verlangen nahe, dass sie diese Gemeinschaft auch zu voller Persönlichkeit ausbilde, dass sie auch einen gemeinsamen Willen hervorbringe und ihren Willen machtvoll bethätige, d. h. dass sie den Staat bestimme oder zum Staat werde'.

[132] Bluntschli 1885, 98. For the German text, see Bluntschli 1886, vol. I, 111: 'nur eine politisch befähigte Nation kann berechtigt sein, ein selbständiges Volk zu werden'.

[133] Bluntschli 1885, 86. For the German text, see Bluntschli 1886, vol. I, 97: 'Unter Volk verstehen wir in der Regel die zum Staate geeinigte und im Staate organisierte Gemeinschaft aller Staatsgenossen. Die Entstehung des Volkes kommt zugleich mit der Schöpfung des Staates zur Wirksamkeit. Das Gefühl, in höherer Stufe das Bewusstsein politischer Zusammengehörigkeit und Einheit hebt das Volk über die Nation empor'.

acknowledge the 'excess' of nations over states while also maintaining a threshold principle that limited the number of nations destined for statehood.

The gatekeeping function of the nation/nationality distinction was soon undermined by two interrelated factors. First, the presupposed temporal link between nationalities and nations presented a problem: given that nationalities were widely expected to mature into politically independent nations, the nationalist threat to the international order was not so much neutralised as merely deferred into the future. Recognising this issue, James Bryce lamented the failure of existing terminology 'to distinguish a Nationality which, like the Scottish, does not seek to be politically independent from a Nationality which, like the Lithuanian, does so desire'.[134] The second and related problem was that the terms 'nationality' and 'national' were increasingly equated with 'citizenship' and 'citizen', respectively.[135] Carlton Hayes explained the situation in 1933 as follows:

> It was in part to atone for the abuse of the word 'nation' that the word 'nationality' was coined in the early part of the nineteenth century and speedily incorporated into most European languages. Thenceforth, while 'nation' continued to denote the citizens of a sovereign political state, nationality was more exactly used in reference to a group of persons speaking the same language and observing the same customs. The jurists have done their best to corrupt the new word 'nationality,' just as they had corrupted the old word 'nation'; they have utilized 'nationality' to indicate citizenship.[136]

In this way, much like the word 'nation' before it, the word 'nationality' also acquired a 'political' meaning alongside its 'ethnic and cultural' meaning.[137] By the beginning of the twentieth century, there was fast emerging a conceptual lacuna that these nation-based words were struggling to fill. Ultimately, it was the language of ethnicity that was inserted into this void. Faced with the politicising and temporalising thrust of modern nationalism, the popularisation of ethnos-based terms represented an attempt to depoliticise and detemporalise nationality and thus freeze the political map.

---

[134] Bryce 1922, 118.   [135] Holcombe 1923, 128; Joseph 1929, 19.
[136] Hayes 1933, 4–5.
[137] Boehm and Hayes 1933, 231–232. See also Flournoy 1933; Garner 1919; Smith 1899.

In turn-of-the-century discussions of nationalism and international relations, ethnos-based words make sporadic appearances but receive little conceptual development. As early as 1890, John William Burgess explained that 'the word nation is a term of ethnology, and the concept expressed by it is an ethnological concept'. He accordingly defined the nation as a 'population of an ethnic unity, inhabiting a territory of a geographic unity'.[138] When clarifying what he meant by 'ethnic unity', Burgess explained that this referred to 'a population having a common language and literature, a common tradition and history, a common custom and a common consciousness of rights and wrongs'.[139] During the inter-war years, Louis Le Fur referred to 'minorités ethniques' and Raymond Leslie Buell to 'ethnic minorities', but neither offered a definition.[140] Others noted in passing that the term 'nation' was etymologically an 'ethnic'[141] or 'ethnical'[142] concept. Another brief but illuminating distinction between ethnicity and nationality can be found in a two-volume study on civilisation and nationhood by the French philosopher and sociologist Joseph Thomas Delos from 1944. Delos equated a 'communauté ethnique' or 'groupe ethnique' with a 'communauté de conscience' and described this as a preliminary stage to the emergence of a 'communauté nationale':

Le passage de la *communauté de conscience* à la *conscience de former une communauté* est une transformation de la plus haute importance. Au moment où s'éveille la conscience de son unité et de son individualité et où s'affirme la volonté de continuer cette vie commune, le groupe ethnique franchit une étape, et il serait souhaitable, croyons-nous, de lui réserver alors le nom de communauté *nationale*. Grâce à cet élément subjectif, – conscience et vouloir-vivre commun, – la nation apparaît distincte du milieu ethnique, au sens strict du mot, tout en lui restant liée comme un stade postérieur est lié au stade antérieur.[143]

Delos thus considered a national community to be a higher or more developed form of an ethnic group, with the passage from the latter to

---

[138] Burgess 1890, vol. I, 1.
[139] Burgess 1890, vol. I, 2. In his subsequent discussion of European nations and nationalities, Burgess refers to 'ethnical varieties', 'ethnical composition', 'ethnically different populations', 'ethnical fact', 'ethnical conflict', 'ethnical character', and 'ethnographical lines'. See Burgess 1890, vol. I, 13–21 passim.
[140] Buell 1926, 172–173; Le Fur 1922, 62.   [141] Garner 1928, 110.
[142] Beer 1917, 43; Herbert 1920, 16.
[143] Delos 1944, vol. I, 89, 93–94. The term 'groupe ethnique' is also found in Delos 1928.

the former entailing the emergence of a shared desire to live together as an independent community.

The general impression that emerges from these early twentieth-century texts is an understanding of ethnicity as a foundation of nationhood, but without the subjective or political dimension of the latter. In this sense, the concept of ethnicity was almost indistinguishable from the non-political meaning of nationality. Indeed, the French author René Johannet pointed out in 1918 that most contemporary definitions of 'nationalité' were identical to the French anthropologist Joseph Deniker's definition of 'groupe ethnique'.[144] In an influential study published in both French and English in 1900, Deniker had proposed a new conceptual distinction between races and ethnic groups: whereas races were theoretical abstractions based on physical traits, ethnic groups were 'real and palpable groupings ... formed by virtue of community of language, religion, social institutions, etc.'[145] Among some anthropologists, then, the concept of ethnicity was already emerging as a relatively coherent and well-defined alternative to the concept of race (see Chapter 2). In the early twentieth-century literature on nations and nationalism, by contrast, the embryonic concept of ethnicity still lacked a clear definition and remained jumbled up with older conceptions of race and nationality. In the relatively few cases where ethnos-based terms such as 'ethnic' and 'ethnical' do make an appearance, they did not yet possess the status of a distinct concept, but functioned instead as a supplementary vocabulary that helped to qualify or specify other (typically nation-based) terms. It was not until the second half of the twentieth century – when the concept of race was pushed aside – that the ethnos-based vocabulary would move from the margins of social and political discourse to centre stage.

Minority Rights

In international political and legal practice, the mismatch between national and political boundaries is managed through minority rights provisions. The first time that minorities were described as 'national' rather than religious communities was in 1815 at the Congress of Vienna. Although several subsequent nineteenth-century treaties also contained clauses pertaining to minority rights, it was not until after

---

[144] Johannet 1918, 24–25.   [145] Deniker 1900b, 2–3.

the First World War that an international regime of minority protection was put into practice. Set up under the auspices of the newly formed League of Nations, the international minority rights regime was chiefly a response to the proliferation of nationalist claims in Central and Eastern Europe after the disintegration of the Ottoman, Habsburg, and Romanov multinational empires. Against this backdrop, minority rights essentially functioned as a 'substitute' for national self-determination in those instances where statehood was considered either unfeasible or undesirable by the great powers.[146]

There are substantial connections between the scholarly debates discussed in the previous section and the political negotiations that produced the minority rights regime at the end of the First World War. Not only was national self-determination a central issue in both settings, but the Allied Powers' reliance on expert commissions to produce empirical data for the peace talks also meant that there were significant overlaps in personnel. The British Political Intelligence Department included historians Arnold Toynbee and Alfred Zimmern, both of whom had produced influential scholarly works on nationalism, while the French Comité d'Études featured renowned geographers such as Jean Brunhes and Emmanuel de Martonne.[147] The American expert commission, known as 'the Inquiry', was the largest of all. Set up by Woodrow Wilson in September 1917, it numbered some 150 scholars and collected or produced nearly 2,000 separate reports and documents, plus at least 1,200 maps.[148] At the end of the war, numerous members of the Inquiry served as advisors to the American plenipotentiaries attending the peace conference and as negotiators on international commissions.[149] Although nearly every major international conference since 1815 had provided some role for experts and advisers, this was the first time that the major powers sought to formulate a clear and systematic approach ahead of time.[150] The emphasis on calculation and classification in the reordering of the international system was a significant break with the tradition of rule by right or warfare, signalling the triumph of 'population politics' on the international plane.[151] Informed by a wealth of empirical data, the work of the Allied preparatory commissions reconceptualised political

---

[146] Kunz 1954, 282. See also Jackson Preece 1998.
[147] Goldstein 1991; Kitsikis 1972; Palsky 2002; Prott 2014.
[148] Gelfand 1963, x–xi. [149] Gelfand 1963, 150–151.
[150] Gelfand 1963, 34; Smith 2003, 135. [151] Weitz 2008.

and ethnographical boundaries as measurable and manipulable objects that could be rationally arranged to create ethnically homogeneous nation-states.[152] In the words of Hannah Arendt, 'the nation had conquered the state'.[153]

The bulk of this section is concerned with the negotiations over the wording of the minority rights treaties that were imposed on several Eastern European states at the conclusion of the First World War. In addition to the treaty documents themselves, the key primary sources include the minutes of the Committee on New States and the Protection of Minorities, which was responsible for the drafting of the minorities treaties; the minutes of the Greco-Bulgarian Mixed Commission, which oversaw the subsequent exchange of populations between Greece and Bulgaria; the diaries of David Hunter Miller, an American lawyer who served on the Inquiry and the Committee on New States and the Protection of Minorities; and the published records of the United States Department of State. The section concludes with a brief discussion of the development of minority rights since 1945.

The Problem of Minorities after the First World War

The so-called 'problem of minorities' was among the central issues facing the peacemakers at the end of the First World War. For the advocates of national self-determination, the solution to this problem was territorial readjustment: the state should be made to fit the nation by redrawing existing political boundaries. By contrast, the advocates of minority protection prioritised maintaining the territorial status quo even if this entailed the co-presence of multiple national groups within the same state. As C. A. Macartney explained in 1934, the idea of minority protection was premised on the assumption 'that it is possible to put an end to the whole movement towards so-called national self-determination'.[154]

The development of Woodrow Wilson's drafts for the Covenant of the League of Nations during the peace process reveals a shift in emphasis from territorial readjustment to minority protection. His first draft made no reference to minority rights, embracing instead the principle of national self-determination. Thus, Article III of the draft

---

[152] Crampton 2006, 731–736.   [153] Arendt 1976, 275.
[154] Macartney 1934, 278.

made provisions for 'territorial readjustments' if these were to become necessary 'by reasons of changes in present racial conditions and aspirations or present social and political relationships, pursuant to the principle of self-determination'. In a revolutionary proposal, contracting parties were required to 'accept without reservation the principle that the peace of the world is superior in importance to every question of political jurisdiction or boundary'.[155] Unsurprisingly, Wilson's draft met with heavy protest. In his commentary on the proposal, David Hunter Miller underlined the practical difficulties of drawing political boundaries in accordance with 'racial or social conditions' and noted that the provisions suggested by Wilson would merely 'legalize irredentist agitation'.[156] The idea of territorial readjustment was thus swiftly abandoned. Instead, Wilson's subsequent drafts required all new states 'to accord to all racial or national minorities within their several jurisdictions exactly the same treatment and security, both in law and in fact, that is accorded the racial or national majority of their people'.[157] Miller applauded the shift in favour of minority protection, noting that 'protection of the rights of minorities and *acceptance of such protection by the minorities* constitute the only basis of enduring peace'.[158]

Despite featuring prominently in the drafting process, all clauses pertaining to minority protection were dropped from the final text of the Covenant. This was done at the behest of the British delegation, which preferred to settle the provisions of the territorial treaties before considering the minorities question.[159] As a result, the inter-war minority protection regime comprised a motley collection of international instruments, eighteen in all: five minorities treaties concluded with Poland, Yugoslavia, Romania, Czechoslovakia, and Greece; special minorities provisions in the four peace treaties imposed on Austria, Bulgaria, Hungary, and Turkey; four subsequent conventions pertaining to Danzig, Memel, Upper Silesia, and the Åland Islands; and five unilateral declarations by Albania, Estonia, Latvia, Lithuania, and Iraq upon their entry into the League of Nations. The wording of these

---

[155] Miller 1928, vol. II, 12–13. [156] Miller 1928, vol. II, 71.
[157] Miller 1928, vol. II, 91. The quote is from Wilson's second draft. The wording was largely unchanged in the third draft. See Miller 1928, vol. II, 105.
[158] Miller 1928, vol. II, 71.
[159] Macartney 1934, 219. See also Headlam-Morley 1972, 112–113; Miller 1928, vol. I, 60.

instruments was schematic, with the Polish treaty serving as a model for the others.[160] The proceedings of the Committee on New States and the Protection of Minorities, hastily created on 1 May 1919 to undertake the drafting of the minority rights provisions, offers valuable insights into the negotiations behind the wording of these instruments. The Committee initially consisted of Philippe Berthelot of France, David Hunter Miller of the United States, and James Headlam-Morley of the United Kingdom, with E. H. Carr as secretary. It was later enlarged to include five more representatives from France, the United States, Italy, and Japan; Robert Cecil also attended several meetings as a representative of the League of Nations.[161] In total, the Committee held sixty-four meetings between May and November 1919.[162]

National Minorities versus Racial, Religious, or Linguistic Minorities

The starting point of the deliberations of the Committee on New States and the Protection of Minorities was two statements drafted by Woodrow Wilson. One of these was a general statement on religious liberties and will not be discussed here. The other concerned 'racial or national minorities' and read as follows:

The State of   covenants and agrees that it will accord to all racial or national minorities within its jurisdiction exactly the same treatment and security, alike in law and in fact, that is accorded the racial or national majority of its people.[163]

It is important to note the reference to 'national minorities' here, given that the phrase was subsequently dropped from all official documents. Several references to 'national minorities' can also be found in early drafts of the minority rights clauses and in the correspondence of the Committee. For example, the initial draft clauses for the protection of minorities in Poland, put forth by David Hunter Miller at the Committee's first meeting, made reference to 'the several national minorities' in Poland and stated that 'the Jewish population of Poland shall constitute a national minority'.[164] These clauses were based on Jewish proposals for the protection of minorities that had

---

[160] League of Nations 1927, 6–8; Thornberry 1991, 41–42.
[161] Macartney 1934, 224–225.   [162] Miller 1924, vol. XIII.
[163] Miller 1924, vol. XIII, 15.   [164] Miller 1924, vol. XIII, 17.

been given to Miller by Julian Mack and Louis Marshall of the American Jewish Congress.[165] In the end, however, the term 'national minority' is nowhere to be found in the League of Nations treaties or declarations.[166] Instead, the minority rights instruments referred to 'racial, religious or linguistic minorities'.

Why was the term 'national minorities' dropped? Pablo de Azcárate, a Spanish diplomat and the third director of the minorities section of the League of Nations, ventured the following explanation in 1945:

[T]he expression 'national minority' refers to a more or less considerable proportion of the citizens of a state who are of a different 'nationality' from that of the majority. The objection to this definition of a minority is that it involves such an indefinite, and probably indefinable, concept as that of nationality. It was doubtless in order to overcome this objection that the treaties ending the 1914–1918 war, in their provisions relating to the protection of minorities by the League of Nations, did not speak of 'national' minorities, but of minorities of 'race, language and religion.'[167]

De Azcárate is no doubt correct when he describes the concept of nationality as 'indefinite' and 'probably undefinable'. However, an analysis of the correspondence and documents of the Committee on New States and the Protection of Minorities suggests that the word 'national' was dropped for more specific reasons than. In an illuminating report to the Council of Four – composed of Georges Clemenceau of France, David Lloyd George of the United Kingdom, Vittorio Emanuele Orlando of Italy, and Woodrow Wilson of the United States – on 14 May 1919, the Committee made some observations on the status of the Jews and concluded that they were a 'racial' and 'religious' minority but not a 'national' minority: 'The other minorities differ from the Jews in that they are national minorities inhabiting in more or less compact bodies certain specified areas. [...] The Jews are both a religious and a racial minority, and special questions therefore arise in their case which do not arise in the case of other minorities.'[168]

---

[165] Miller 1924, vol. I, 261–268; Miller 1924, vol. VIII, 422–424; Miller 1924, vol. IX, 7–8. The most influential Jewish delegation at the peace conference was the American Jewish Congress. During the war years, there was debate among Jewish representatives about whether the phrase 'national rights' or 'group rights' should be used. The American Jewish Congress eventually settled on 'national rights'. See Janowsky 1933, 161–190, 263.

[166] Macartney 1934, 4.   [167] de Azcárate 1945, 3.

[168] Miller 1924, vol. XIII, 55.

The report then went on to state that Jewish demands to be 'recognized as a definite nationality which would have separate electoral curias in the Diet and other electoral bodies' had been unanimously rejected on the grounds that this would amount to 'setting up a State within a State, and would very seriously undermine the authority of the Polish government'.[169] Even James Headlam-Morley, a vocal advocate of Jewish rights, resisted Jewish demands for national autonomy, noting in his diary in May 1919 that he 'could not support any claim to "national" rights' on the part of the Jews.[170]

The views of the Committee were reflected in the Council of Four, where both Woodrow Wilson and David Lloyd George expressed the opinion that nothing could be more dangerous than the creation of a Jewish state within Poland.[171] Paul Mantoux, the interpreter of the French Prime Minister Georges Clemenceau at the peace conference, also recorded the following comment by Arthur Balfour: 'Nous ne devrions rien stipuler pour les Juifs, mais seulement pour les personnes de religion juive. Il est dangereux de paraître légiférer en faveur d'une race.'[172] Unsurprisingly, similar protestations were raised by the Polish delegate Ignacy Jan Paderewski, who expressed concern that meeting the Jewish demands 'would transform the Jews into an autonomous nation'.[173] To allay these fears, the final draft of the Polish treaty was accompanied by a letter from Clemenceau to Paderewski explicitly stating that the clauses relating to the Jews 'do not constitute any recognition of the Jews as a separate political community within the Polish State'.[174]

In sum, the decision to adopt the phrase 'racial, religious or linguistic minorities' instead of 'national minorities' was motivated by two inter-related considerations. First, due to the association of nationhood with statehood, the term 'national minorities' seemed to justify the creation of states within states – something that the peacemakers desperately wished to avoid. The 'trinity' of race, religion, and language was seen to encompass the same content as the term 'nationality', minus the dangerous political component.[175] The desire to prevent minority groups from becoming states within states was also reflected in the individualistic wording of the treaties, which referred to 'members of

---

[169] Miller 1924, vol. XIII, 56.   [170] Headlam-Morley 1972, 117.
[171] Mantoux 1955, vol. I, 440.   [172] Mantoux 1955, vol. II, 490.
[173] Miller 1924, vol. XIII, 175.
[174] Miller 1924, vol. XIII, 221. See also Temperley 1921, vol. V, 137.
[175] Macartney 1934, 4–10.

minorities' rather than 'minorities'.[176] The second and related factor behind the decision to avoid the phrase 'national minorities' was the lack of clarity about whether the Jews could be considered a 'national' minority, given their geographical dispersion and the centrality of religion to their common identity. As a result, the peacemakers were concerned that the term 'national minorities' could be exploited by governments to exclude the Jews from protection.[177]

Racial Minorities versus Ethnic Minorities

The word 'ethnic' is nowhere to be found in any of the English language versions of the treaties. However, it was not entirely absent from deliberations. For example, the records of the United States Department of State use phrases such as 'ethnic composition'[178] and 'ethnographic map'[179] on multiple occasions. The French 'ethnique' is also widely used in relevant documents, and early French plans for the organisation of the peace conference referred to the rights of 'ethnical and religious minorities'.[180] Moreover, the records of the Committee on New States and the Protection of Minorities show that correspondence translated from French into English usually rendered the French 'ethnique' as 'ethnic' or 'ethnical'. In the final version of the Polish treaty, there is some inconsistency: the adjective 'racial' in Articles 8 and 9 was translated into French as 'ethnique', but 'racial minorities' in Article 12 was translated as 'minorités de race'. It is unclear why the French text varies between the two formulations while the English text only uses the term 'racial', but the most likely explanation is simply that the French language had lacked a direct equivalent of 'racial' until just a few years prior. Whereas in the English language the word 'racial' had been in use since the mid nineteenth century, the first definition of 'racial' in the French language did not appear until 1911.[181] In practice, this meant that the French 'ethnique' served as the equivalent of the English 'racial' until the early decades of the

---

[176] Fink 2004, 389; Macartney 1934, 283.   [177] Shaw 1992, 20.
[178] United States Department of State 1919, vol. I, 64, 67.
[179] United States Department of State 1919, vol. VI, 140, 142.
[180] Baker 1923, vol. III, 62; Janowsky 1933, 320; Tardieu 1921, 88–89.
[181] See the entries for 'racial' in the *Oxford English Dictionary* and the *Trésor de la langue française*, available online at www.oed.com and http://atilf.atilf.fr/tlf.htm, respectively (last accessed 21 February 2020).

twentieth century. The subsequent separation of race and ethnicity can be seen in Louis Le Fur's coinage of 'racique' as an alternative to 'ethnique' in 1921: 'J'emploi ce néologisme car le terme "ethnique," qui vient de *ethnos* (peuple), est ambigu, la notion de peuple se rapprochant plus de celle de nation que de celle de race.'[182]

Some insight into the meaning of the word 'race' in the English language is provided by the proceedings of a General Conference held by the Inquiry on 2 August 1918, which included fifteen of the commission's senior members. When the definition of 'race' was brought up, Isaiah Bowman stated that the term should be used 'only in its ethnological meaning'. The conference subsequently adopted a formulation for 'boundaries' that included 'linguistic, religious, racial, historical, strategic, etc.' factors.[183] Among scholars, there is some disagreement over how these statements should be interpreted. According to Volker Prott, the separation of linguistic and religious criteria from racial ones in the formulation for 'boundaries' suggests a hereditary understanding of race among members of the Inquiry.[184] By contrast, Jeremy Crampton claims that the deliberations exemplify a 'socio-cultural' rather than a 'hereditary' conception of race.[185] Both interpretations can be justified and the best explanation is quite simply that a clear distinction between the biological and the sociocultural spheres did not yet exist (see Chapter 2). The question of whether 'race' was used in a sociocultural or hereditary sense is thus somewhat misleading.

The uses of the term 'ethnic' in these discussions were even more varied than the uses of 'race'. In a letter to the Greek delegation, for example, the French delegate Berthelot referred to 'ethnic minorities, such as Mussulmans, Albanians, Bulgarians, Koutzo-Valachs, the Jews of Salonika, and the monks of Mount Athos'.[186] Similarly, the Greek delegate Eleftherios Venizelos wrote of 'the scholastic liberty of the ethnic minorities' including 'Jews and Mussulmans'.[187] From these examples, it is clear that the meaning of 'ethnic minorities' was not limited to racial characteristics (however defined) but could also encompass linguistic and religious differences. Insofar as race, religion, and language were viewed as the key components of national identity,

---

[182] Le Fur 1921, 217n1. See also Taguieff 2001, 87.
[183] Proceedings of a General Conference held by the Inquiry on 2 August 1918, quoted in Prott 2014, 745–746.
[184] Prott 2014, 746.   [185] Crampton 2006, 739.
[186] Miller 1924, vol. XIII, 293.   [187] Miller 1924, vol. XIII, 396.

this suggests that the phrase 'ethnic minorities' effectively served as the depoliticised equivalent of 'national minorities'.

The language of ethnicity also appears in the documents concerning the reciprocal exchange of populations between Bulgaria and Greece after the war. The idea for the 'racial adjustment' of populations originated with the Greek delegate Venizelos.[188] At the peace conference, Venizelos circulated draft clauses proposing the establishment of a mixed commission to oversee the population exchange. The matter was eventually referred to the Committee on New States and the Protection of Minorities, which accepted Venizelos's proposal to insert a clause into the Treaty of Neuilly to bind Bulgaria to accept forthcoming provisions for a voluntary exchange of populations.[189] Thus, the second paragraph of Article 56 of the Treaty required Bulgaria 'to recognise such provisions as the Principal Allied and Associated Powers may consider opportune with respect to the reciprocal and voluntary emigration of persons belonging to racial minorities'. In the French version, 'racial minorities' was rendered 'minorités ethniques'. Some of the correspondence of the Committee on New States on this matter also refers to 'ethnic minorities', usually in translations of French-language documents.[190]

The Treaty of Neuilly was later supplemented by the Convention of Neuilly, which contained the specific provisions for the population exchange. The first draft of the Convention, prepared in French by the Greek delegation and translated into English, referred to the rights of 'ethnic minorities'.[191] The Italian delegation noted the discrepancy between the Greek draft and the other minorities treaties and proposed the following amendment: 'In order to avoid all ambiguity, it would be preferable to retain, for all alien minorities, the same expression that we find in the treaties for the protection of minorities. It would thus be preferable, instead of speaking simply of ethnic minorities, to say: Minorities of race, religion, or language.'[192] The Committee on New States and the Protection of Minorities promptly accepted the Italian

---

[188] Ladas 1932, 28–29. [189] Miller 1924, vol. XIII, 306–317, 461–474.
[190] For example, a report of the Committee on New States to the Secretary-General of the Peace Conference from September 1919 has the following wording of the clause: 'Bulgaria undertakes to recognise the dispositions which the Principal Allied and Associated Powers may judge advisable relative to the reciprocal and voluntary emigration of ethnic minorities' (Miller 1924, vol. XIII, 472).
[191] Miller 1924, vol. XIII, 499–503. [192] Miller 1924, vol. XIII, 523.

delegation's suggestion and brought the text of the Convention in line with the other minorities treaties. Article 1 of the final draft accordingly read as follows: 'The High Contracting Parties recognise in favour of their nationals belonging to racial, religious, and linguistic minorities the right to emigrate freely into their respective territories.'[193]

The Convention of Neuilly was drawn up rather hastily and left many questions to be decided by the Mixed Commission that would oversee the exchange of populations. In 1922, the Commission drew up the Rules on the Reciprocal and Voluntary Emigration of Greek and Bulgarian Minorities.[194] The working language of the Commission was French and the Rules were accordingly written in French.[195] The generic phrase for a minority in the Rules was 'minorité ethnique'. For example, Article 34 of the Rules required that persons seeking to emigrate acquire 'un certificat de minorité ethnique'.[196] This ethnic minority certificate, provided by the mayor of the locality where the applicant was domiciled, would serve as evidence that the applicant belonged 'ethniquement' to the nationality of the country to which they sought to emigrate. On the model template of the ethnic minority certificate, the Mixed Commission included the following explanatory note: 'Indiquer la nationalité à laquelle le requérant appartient au point de vue ethnique, religieux, linguistique.'[197] What is interesting here is the reappearance of the two other elements of the trinity (religion and language) alongside ethnicity. This suggests that the meaning of ethnicity oscillated between a broad and a narrow interpretation. Ethnicity in the broad sense encompassed all three qualities of national minorities (race, religion, and language), whereas ethnicity in the narrow sense effectively functioned as a synonym of race, possibly excluding religion and language. However, given the looseness with which the terms 'race' and 'racial' were used, this distinction was by no means clear-cut. The Mixed Commission appears to have resolved the issue in

---

[193] Miller 1924, vol. XIII, 546.
[194] Ladas 1932, 44–45. For the text of the Rules, see Ladas 1932, 744–770. The text of the Rules including the Annexes can be found in box C147 at the League of Nations Archives in Geneva.
[195] Commission Mixte d'Émigration Gréco-Bulgare 1921, vol. I, 5.
[196] Ladas 1932, 757.
[197] 'Formulaire Modèle N° 2.A. Certificat de membre de minorité ethnique', Annex to *Règlement sur l'émigration réciproque et volontaire des minorités grecques et bulgares*, box C147, League of Nations Archives, Geneva.

favour of a broad interpretation when it determined that whenever there was doubt as to whether a person was akin by their race, religion, or language to the people of a country, this doubt should be resolved in favour of the person in question.[198] This flexibility could be taken to mean that the Commission sought to encourage the greatest possible amount of migration so as to achieve homogeneous nation-states and a definitive resolution of the problem of minorities in this region. However, it can also be seen to reflect the importance of the 'subjective criterion' in ethnic belonging, thus distancing ethnicity from a biological understanding of race.[199]

To sum up, the conceptualisation of minority rights in the aftermath of the First World War was dominated by the trinity of race, religion, and language. Use of the word 'national' was almost entirely avoided due to its association with statehood. In this sense, the end of the First World War signalled the moment when the concepts of nationhood and statehood were decisively collapsed into one another in international political discourse – a conceptual union consecrated by the establishment of the League of Nations as an organisation of territorial states. This discursive institutionalisation of the legal-political definition of the nation created a pressing need for an alternate term to designate those stateless nations and national minorities that disrupted the territorial grid of purportedly congruent nation-states. The rather unwieldly phrase 'racial, religious or linguistic minorities' was the official name given to the category of non-political nations in the inter-war minority rights treaties, but references to 'minorités ethniques' were commonplace in French and the term 'ethnic minorities' also makes occasional appearances in English during the drafting process. In this context, ethnicity functioned as a 'filler' category, operating in the interstices of race, religion, and language to provide a depoliticised alternative to the language of nationhood and nationality. By allowing statesmen and their advisors to conceptualise minority groups without evoking the spectres of irredentism or secession, the concept of ethnicity was inaugurated as the guarantor of the nation-state and the gatekeeper of international order.

---

[198] Commission Mixte d'Émigration Gréco-Bulgare 1921, vol. I, 22–24; Ladas 1932, 77.
[199] Ladas 1932, 77–78, 168; Nestor 1962, 178–179.

The Problem of Minorities after the Second World War

At the end of the Second World War, the defunct League of Nations was supplanted by the United Nations. Although the language of self-determination was repeatedly invoked during the First World War and the inter-war years, it was never actually incorporated into positive international law. In 1945, by contrast, the principle of self-determination was expressly enshrined in the Charter of the United Nations.[200] Thus, Article 1 of the Charter proclaimed that a principal aim of the organisation was to 'develop friendly relations among nations based on respect for the principle of equal rights and self-determination of peoples'. Unsurprisingly, the United Nations has run into many of the same conceptual conundrums that plagued the architects of the League of Nations minority rights regime. In particular, the references to 'nation' and 'people' in the Charter provoked controversy due to concerns that they might legitimate secession.[201] At the time, the use of these terms was justified on the grounds that they encompassed colonies, mandates, and protectorates that did not qualify as states but nevertheless fell within the remit of the United Nations.[202]

Like the Covenant of the League of Nations, the Charter of the United Nations does not contain any specific provisions for the protection of minorities. The question of minority rights was instead passed to the Sub-Commission on the Prevention of Discrimination and Protection of Minorities, which published a memorandum on the definition and classification of minorities in 1949. The memorandum emphasised that the term 'minority' should not be interpreted in its broad or literal sense to include any social class or cultural group that was dominated by another class or group, but should be applied 'especially to a national or similar community'.[203] Invoking Ferdinand Tönnies's influential distinction between Gemeinschaft and Gesellschaft, the memorandum defined a nation as a 'community' united by affective factors such as culture or descent, and a state as a 'society' or 'organisation' united by interest.[204] While asserting that 'most nations have their own State', the memorandum recognised that

---

[200] Thornberry 1991, 15.   [201] United Nations 1954, vol. XVII, 142.
[202] United Nations 1954, vol. XVIII, 657–658. See also Quane 1998, 539–547.
[203] UN Doc. E/CN.4/Sub.2/85, paras. 37–38.
[204] UN Doc. E/CN.4/Sub.2/85, paras. 13–27.

the boundaries of nations and states did not always coincide.[205] It was precisely to these incongruences between national communities and state boundaries that the category of the minority was to be applied.

Echoing the interwar debates surveyed above, there has been repeated controversy over the use of the phrase 'national' minorities' in international treaties since the Second World War. A very clear example is the drafting of Article 27 of the International Covenant on Civil and Political Rights (ICCPR). The debate that erupted during the drafting process in 1953 centred on the use of the word 'national' to describe minorities, with delegates coalescing into three camps: those who favoured the phrase 'ethnic, religious or linguistic groups within States'; those who favoured 'national minorities'; and those who proposed 'national, ethnic, religious and linguistic minorities' as a compromise.[206] The term 'national minorities' was backed by the Soviet delegate, who defined a nation as 'an historically formed community of people characterised by a common language, a common territory, a common economic life and a common psychological structure manifesting itself in a common culture'.[207] According to the Soviet delegate, 'an ethnic or linguistic group could form a national minority, but a group could be called an ethnic or linguistic group long before it had reached the stage of becoming a national minority'.[208] Ethnicity was thus understood conceived as something broader than nationality – or, to put it the other way round, nationality added an extra (political) layer to ethnicity.[209] The Soviet proposal was met with strong objections from delegates of states that refused to recognise the existence of rival national groups within their territories. According to the French delegate, for example, the Soviet proposal 'affected only countries where the minorities possessed national characteristics; such cases were not commonly met with in other countries'.[210] Likewise, the Indian delegate claimed that 'the Soviet Union proposal created certain difficulties for her country which, while composed of a number of different linguistic groups, had no national minorities'.[211] Representing the compromise position, the delegate from the Philippines was willing to accept the inclusion of the word 'national' into the text, but 'only on the

---

[205] UN Doc. E/CN.4/Sub.2/85, para. 30.
[206] UN Doc. E/CN.4/689, paras. 51–56. [207] UN Doc. E/CN.4/SR.369, 16.
[208] UN Doc. E/CN.4/SR.369, 13.
[209] Henrard 2000, 53–55; Ramaga 1992, 421–423; Thornberry 1991, 160–161.
[210] UN Doc. E/CN.4/SR.370, 7. [211] UN Doc. E/CN.4/SR.369, 7.

understanding that it would not prejudge the application of the principle of self-determination to the new article'.[212] In the end, recalling the outcome of the debates in 1919, the controversial term was left out of the ICCPR and the less politicised expression 'ethnic, religious or linguistic minorities' was used instead. The ICCPR was adopted by the United Nations General Assembly in 1966.[213]

Although it was left out of the ICCPR, the term 'national minorities' can be found in a plethora of other international agreements relating to minority issues. These include the Convention against Discrimination in Education, adopted by the United Nations Educational, Scientific and Cultural Organization (UNESCO) in 1960; the Helsinki Final Act, adopted by the Conference on Security and Co-operation in Europe (CSCE) in 1975; the Copenhagen Document, adopted by the Organization for Security and Co-operation in Europe (OSCE) in 1990; and the Framework Convention for the Protection of National Minorities, adopted by the Council of Europe in 1994.[214] Significantly, the word 'national' was also inserted into the first international instrument exclusively devoted to minority rights: the Declaration on the Rights of Persons Belonging to National or Ethnic, Religious and Linguistic Minorities, adopted by the United Nations General Assembly in 1992.[215]

The idea of a United Nations declaration on minority rights had initially been floated by Special Rapporteur Francesco Capotorti's *Study on the Rights of Persons Belonging to Ethnic, Religious and Linguistic Minorities* in the 1970s.[216] In response, the United Nations Human Rights Commission set up a working group to draft a declaration and Jules Deschênes, a Canadian member of the Sub-Commission on the Prevention of Discrimination and Protection of Minorities, was asked to prepare a report on the definition of 'minority'.[217] The Deschênes report, submitted in 1985, recommended that the word 'national' be left from any declaration out due to its lack of clarity.[218] The controversial nature of this term was also reflected in the fact that it was suspended in square brackets for most of the drafting process. In the end, however, the working group decided to ignore Deschênes's advice, drop the brackets, and include the word

---

[212] UN Doc. E/CN.4/SR.370, 8.   [213] UN Doc. A/RES/2200(XXI).
[214] Shaw 1992, 20–22; Wheatley 2005, 45–62.
[215] UN Doc. A/RES/47/135. See also Henrard 2000, 185–193; Thornberry 1995b.
[216] UN Doc. E/CN.4/Sub.2/384/Rev.1, para. 617.
[217] Thornberry 1995b, 25–27.   [218] Thornberry 1995b, 33.

'national' in the declaration.[219] In 1991, the working group published the following summary of the discussions:

Concern was voiced about the addition of national minorities to those listed in article 27 of the International Covenant on Civil and Political Rights. On the one hand, a preference was expressed for focusing on guarantees for national minorities only, because members of ethnic, religious and linguistic minorities should as a matter of existing principles enjoy equality with other citizens of States. It was also stated that there was need to expand article 27. On the other hand, it was said that it would be difficult or even impossible to set up legal distinctions between national and ethnic groups, that the term 'ethnic' probably encompassed 'national' and that, in order to avoid confusion in different jurisdictions, a formulation including all these elements should be prepared by the Working Group.[220]

Further clarity on the choice of terminology came in 2005, when the working group published a commentary on the declaration. Notably, the commentary emphasised that the addition of 'national' minorities to the list of minorities to be protected 'does not extend the overall scope of application beyond the groups already covered by article 27. There is hardly any national minority, however defined, that is not also an ethnic or linguistic minority'.[221] The commentary also took care to point out that minority rights were individual rather than collective rights.[222]

All in all, the protection of minority rights accomplishes in international political and legal practice what 'ethnicity' accomplishes in conceptual terms. Taken together, the articulation of the concept of ethnicity and the institutionalisation of international minority protection absorb the 'excess' of nations that cannot be accommodated within the ontological gridwork of the states system. The international minority rights regime thus functions as a 'safety valve' that helps to minimise the threat of secession.[223] However, precisely by foregrounding the existence of subordinated national communities within states, the discourse of minority rights also serves as a reminder of the nationalist violence that forged the present boundaries of the international order and that may at any moment return to pulverise them

---

[219] UN Doc. E/CN.4/1991/53, para. 28.
[220] UN Doc. E/CN.4/1991/53, para. 10.
[221] UN Doc. E/CN.4/Sub.2/AC.5/2005/2, para. 6.
[222] UN Doc. E/CN.4/Sub.2/AC.5/2005/2, para. 15.
[223] Shahabuddin 2016, 106.

again. This ominous underside of minority protection is manifest in the controversies that have surrounded the phrase 'national minorities' throughout the twentieth century. In many ways, these terminological difficulties would be simplified if the term 'national' were dropped completely – and yet, stubbornly, this term 'refuses to fade away'.[224] A symptom of nationalism's internal contradictions, the spectre of the nation haunts the discourse of minority rights.[225]

From the Standard of Civilisation to the Standard of Congruency

The preceding sections have shown how the concept of ethnicity and the international minority rights regime emerged in tandem as a means of neutralising the threat that nationalism poses to the international order. As discussed in more detail earlier in the chapter, this neutralisation entails a double move: first, the problem of difference is displaced from the domestic to the international plane such that difference becomes located between (rather than within) nation-states; second, any qualitative differences between nation-states are erased as the concept of the nation is sublated into the concept of the state. Through this double move, nation-states come to be seen as congruent 'like units' differentiated from one another only by quantitative factors such as their territorial size and material capabilities. The concept of ethnicity emerges as the particularistic residue of this dialectical process, an undialecticisable kernel excreted by the process of sublation. For the international order, however, this residual difference presents an intractable problem: given that an ethnic group is in essence a depoliticised nation, the nationalist threat is not so much eliminated as merely deferred into the future. There is always the possibility that an ethnic group might become politicised at some later date, leading to new secessionist or irredentist claims. Due to this lingering threat, the double move outlined above has to be supplemented with a third gesture: the displacement of the concept of ethnicity from the 'self' to the 'other', historically from the West to the non-West. In this way, the domestic hierarchy between the majority nation and ethnic minorities

---

[224] Shaw 1992, 21.
[225] In a fascinating article on the conceptualisation of 'spectral' legal personality in inter-war international law, Wheatley (2017, 58) notes that national minorities were 'likened to slaves and ghosts'. See also Heiskanen 2019.

is transferred onto the international plane, producing an international hierarchy between a civic West and an ethnic non-West.

The contrast between the civic West and the ethnic non-West can be traced back to nineteenth-century distinctions between civilised and uncivilised peoples. Among the most influential of these was the contrast between 'historical' and 'non-historical' peoples that can be found in the works of G. W. F. Hegel, Karl Marx, and Friedrich Engels, among others. In this context, 'historical' peoples were conceived as civilised nations that either already possessed a state of their own or had the political capacity to acquire one, and that were destined to play a major role in world history. By contrast, 'non-historical' peoples were smaller ethnic units that lacked the capacity to develop into civilised states and were consequently destined to be colonised, assimilated, eradicated, or reformed. Engels notoriously described these uncivilised populations as 'Völkerabfälle', loosely translated as 'ethnic trash'.[226] Analogous distinctions can be found in the works of many other nineteenth-century scholars. John Stuart Mill contrasted 'civilized' and 'backward' peoples, asserting that only the former were capable of becoming political nations.[227] Similarly, Johann Kaspar Bluntschli argued that only those peoples with 'manly qualities' had the capacity to form national states of their own: 'The incapable need the guidance of other and more gifted nations; the weak must combine with others or submit to the protection of stronger powers.'[228] Despite their individual nuances, what all of these nineteenth-century frameworks had in common was their grounding in a unilinear metanarrative of civilisational progress where nationhood represented the highest stage of civilisation. In the words of Prasenjit Duara, 'to be a nation was to be civilised and vice versa'.[229] The operative distinction was not (yet)

---

[226] Coakley 2012, 149. See also Herod 1976; Nimni 1989; Rosdolsky 1986.
[227] Mill 1861, 293.
[228] Bluntschli 1885, 98. For the German text, see Bluntschli 1886, vol. I, 111: 'Die unfähigen bedürfen der Leitung durch andere, begabtere Völker. Die schwachen sind genötigt, sich mit anderen zu verbinden oder sich dem Schutze stärkerer Mächte unterzuordnen [...] Die volle Geistes- und Charakterkraft, um einen nationalen Staat zu schaffen und zu erhalten, haben strenge genommen nur die Nationen, in welchen die männlichen Seeleneigenschaften (wie Verstand und Mut) überwiegen. Die mehr weiblich gearteten werden schliesslich immer durch andere, ihnen überlegene Mächte staatlich beherrscht werden'.
[229] Duara 2001, 100.

between two different kinds of nation, but between civilised nations and various uncivilised peoples that were denied the status of nations proper.

The link between nationalism and civilisation was broken around the turn of the twentieth century. On the one hand, the dark side of nationalism was made plain by the upsurge of nationalist violence between 1914 and 1945 that has been labelled the 'European civil war'.[230] Against the backdrop of total war and genocide, it became clear that nationalism did not necessarily go hand in hand with civilisational progress, but could also run counter to it. As Western commentators sought to make sense of these contradictions, binary distinctions between 'good' and 'bad' nationalisms began to proliferate: Alfred Zimmern distinguished 'true' from 'false' nationalism in 1918, while Carlton Hayes contrasted 'original' to 'derived' nationalism in 1928.[231] For both scholars, the first type of nationalism remained compatible with the universal values of Western civilisation, while the second entailed its degeneration into mysticism and violence. On the other hand, at the same time that the civilised European nations appeared to descend into a state of primitive anarchy, the supposedly 'non-historical' or 'backward' peoples were asserting their right to national self-determination ever more forcefully. At the end of the First World War, the disintegration of the Ottoman, Habsburg, and Romanov multinational empires signalled the definitive collapse of the 'threshold principle' that had limited the recognition of new nations during the nineteenth century. Henceforth almost any group of people, regardless of its size or perceived civilisational standing, could claim for itself the status of nationhood.[232] The non-European world, too, saw the proliferation of new anti-imperial national and transnational movements at the turn of the twentieth century. By challenging prevalent narratives of racial hierarchy and foregrounding the civilisational achievements of non-European peoples, these movements dismantled the Eurocentric standard of civilisation that had restricted the concept of the nation to a select group of white Europeans.[233] It was also in reaction to this anti-imperial groundswell that there also emerged, for the first time, a distinct notion of 'the West' as a distinct geocultural entity.[234]

---

[230] Preston 2000. [231] Hayes 1928; Zimmern 1918b.
[232] Hobsbawm 1992, 102.
[233] Aydin 2007b, 2013; Manela 2007; Younis 2017.
[234] Bonnett 2004; GoGwilt 1995; Leigh 2021.

The turn-of-the-century crisis spurred a fundamental rethinking of the relationship between nationalism and civilisation. With regard to the typologisation of nations, the most important upshot of this crisis was a rotation of the primary axis of comparison by ninety degrees: the vertical distinction between civilised nations and their various uncivilised 'others' was now supplanted by a horizontal distinction between Western and non-Western nations. To be clear, this conceptual reorientation did not entail a wholesale erasure of the civilisational hierarchy so much as its internalisation: as the non-historical or backward peoples were belatedly granted the status of nations, these newcomers were also cast as developmentally behind the established nations of the West. One of the most salient manifestations of their developmental backwardness was the supposed mismatch between national and political boundaries. 'The superiority of Western culture arises from the fact that Western Europe has larger compact ethnological masses, while the East is the classic soil for the fragments of nations', the eminent German historian and politician Heinrich von Treitschke explained in 1916.[235] Similar distinctions between an ethnopolitically congruent West and a fractured or incongruent non-West can be found in the writings of British, French, and Italian scholars from the same period, although ongoing geopolitical rivalries ensured that they typically excluded Germany from the West.[236] During the First World War, for example, the French philosopher Théodore Ruyssen described Germany, Austria-Hungary, and Turkey as 'conglomerations of imperfectly absorbed and unequally treated nationalities'.[237]

The incipient contrast between Western and non-Western nationalism was systematised and popularised by Hans Kohn's *The Idea of Nationalism* in 1944. In chapter VII of this landmark work, Kohn distinguished nationalism 'in the Western world' from nationalism 'outside the Western world, in Central and Eastern Europe and in Asia'. Western nationalism, Kohn explained, was 'a predominantly political occurrence' that either preceded or coincided with the formation of the state. As a political project led by a strong bourgeoisie, Western nationalism remained aligned with the liberal – universal values of the Enlightenment. In the non-Western world, by contrast,

---

[235] Treitschke 1916, vol. I, 273. [236] Sluga 2002.
[237] Ruyssen 1916, 311. See also the Royal Institute of International Affairs 1939, 43.

nationalism emerged at a later stage of development and 'found its first expression in the cultural field'. Non-Western nationalism therefore 'grew in protest against and in conflict with the existing state pattern – not primarily to transform it into a people's state, but to redraw the political boundaries in conformity with ethnographic demands'.[238] Because it was rooted in traditional ties of kinship and status rather than a rational social contract, non-Western nationalism also 'lent itself more easily to the embroideries of imagination and the excitations of emotion'.[239] Kohn's distinction between the civic West and the ethnic non-West was subsequently taken up by numerous influential scholars and still serves as a touchstone for nationalism studies today. In testimony to Kohn's lasting influence, the framework is widely known as the 'Kohn dichotomy'.[240]

Significantly, the distinction between the civic West and the ethnic non-West is not merely an academic abstraction, but has also informed international political and legal practice. During the inter-war years, this can be seen in the limitation of the League of Nations minority rights instruments to the new states of Eastern Europe. The exclusion of Western states from the burden of minority protection was based on the assumption that they were sufficiently 'civilised' to be able to integrate any existing minorities into their national cultures.[241] Proposals by Latvia, Finland, and Lithuania in the 1920s to generalise the minority protection regime to include all member states were met with stiff opposition and never made any headway.[242] The eastward displacement of ethnicity during the inter-war years is even more explicit in the advisory opinion of the Permanent Court of International Justice (PCIJ) on the Greco-Bulgarian Communities Case in 1930. Although most of the inter-war minority rights instruments were written in individualistic language, the Convention of Neuilly that regulated the exchange of populations between Greece and Bulgaria exceptionally referred to 'communities'. When Greece and Bulgaria were unable to agree on the meaning of this term, the Mixed Commission overseeing the population exchange sought an

---

[238] Kohn [1944] 2005, 329.   [239] Kohn [1944] 2005, 331.
[240] See, for example, Gellner 1983, 99–100; Greenfeld 1992, 1–26; Ignatieff 1994, 1–11; Kemiläinen 1964, 111–142; Plamenatz 1973; Smith 1986, 138–144; Snyder 1954, 117–122.
[241] Mazower 1997, 53.   [242] League of Nations 1927, 17–19.

advisory opinion from the PCIJ.[243] The PCIJ's opinion was given in both English and French, with French as the authoritative language.[244] In its definition of communities, the PCIJ established an explicit link between the concept of ethnicity and the concept of minority: 'les communautés ont un caractère exclusivement minoritaire et ethnique'. The English version of the advisory opinion rendered 'ethnique' as 'racial' throughout. Thus, the above sentence was translated as: 'communities are of a character exclusively minority and racial'.[245] Significantly, the PCIJ's opinion also referred to a 'tradition' of collective identity 'which plays so important a part in Eastern countries'.[246] In this way, the PCIJ projected the concept of ethnicity onto Eastern Europe and excused Western European states from the burden of protecting ethnic minority communities within their territories.

When nationalism returned to European frontpages at the end of the Cold War, so did the practice of imposing unequal responsibilities for minority protection upon Western and Eastern European states. Thus, the universal justice-based track championing individual rights was supplemented by a security-based track that places special obligations on Eastern European states on the grounds that minorities in those states constitute a security threat to the continent. Security was also understood differently for Western and Eastern Europe, with a narrow interpretation of war between states applying to the former and a much broader conception applying to the latter, legitimating Western intervention in Eastern European countries even when there was little or no prospect of outright war. The resultant contrast between an 'ethnic' Eastern Europe and a 'non-ethnic' or 'post-ethnic' Western Europe can be seen in the tendency of some Western European states – notably France – to deny the existence of any ethnic minorities on their national territory.[247] 'Although it has no national minorities on its territory, France, conscious of the importance which this question has for many participating States and of many populations, is ready to participate in the elaboration of conclusions which would be inspired by these ideas and to give them its accord', the French delegate announced at the CSCE Meeting of Experts on National Minorities in 1991.

---

[243] See Ladas 1932, 157–179.   [244] PCIJ 1930, 36.   [245] PCIJ 1930, 30.
[246] PCIJ 1930, 21.
[247] Kymlicka 2001, 369–387. See also Jutila 2009; Kymlicka 2015; Shahabuddin 2016, 136–216.

More specifically, the French delegate distinguished between those states 'which have been constructed, founded, assembled through a slow economic, social, cultural, and political process' and those 'where the entanglement of peoples remains extreme and is the sometimes recent reminder of tumultuous upheavals'. Minority rights, the French delegate insisted, were only relevant for the latter.[248] More generally, the externalisation of ethnicity beyond the West is manifest in how phenomena such as 'ethnic cleansing' and 'ethnic conflict' are primarily associated with Eastern Europe and the Global South.[249]

The construction of an international hierarchy between the civic West and the ethnic East is the final step through which the phantasmatic ideal of the congruent nation-state is made present in the West.[250] Thus, even when Western nations are described as multicultural societies that encompass a plurality of ethnic groups, they are simultaneously presented as well-integrated communities bound together by an overarching civic culture. Meanwhile, non-Western nations are said to be plagued by a perennial mismatch between the boundaries of the nation and the boundaries of the state. The most salient manifestation of this imputed incongruence is the tendency to characterise many non-Western countries – especially those of postcolonial Africa – as 'artificial states' without 'natural boundaries'.[251] The dangers and shortcomings of non-Western nationalism are thus perceived to stem not simply from its backward-looking attachment to an ethnic or organic conception of the nation, but more specifically, from the alleged mismatch between political and ethnographical boundaries. It is this lack of congruence – the gap between the nation and the state – that is said to produce the emotional and violent tendencies of non-Western nationalism by pushing non-Western nations to 'compensate by overemphasis and overconfidence' for their developmental backwardness.[252] In the final analysis, the 'ethnic' quality of non-Western nationalism does not refer to a positive presence, but to a constitutive gap, a traumatic fissure, that fractures

---

[248] Dejean de la Batie, quoted in Berman 1998, 40.
[249] Heiskanen 2021b; Malešević 2010.
[250] For a more detailed analysis, see Heiskanen 2023. On nationalism as a phantasmatic project, see also Mandelbaum 2013, 2020.
[251] Fall 2010.   [252] Kohn [1944] 2005, 330.

the nationalist project from within: the gap between the universalistic conception of the nation as a legal or political unit, on the one hand, and the particularistic conception of the nation as an ethnic or cultural community, on the other. The international hierarchy between the civic West and the ethnic non-West emerges when this inner contradiction of the nation concept is captured, reified, and projected onto the international plane.

2 Race

On the subject of race, Robert Vitalis writes, the discipline of IR is defined by a 'norm against noticing'.[1] Others have gone further, arguing that the field's silence on race amounts to a 'wilful amnesia' or 'calculated forgetting' that deliberately obscures the racialised constitution of the international order.[2] IR's neglect of race is, however, a relatively recent development. At the beginning of the twentieth century, as Duncan Bell notes, 'race was widely and explicitly considered a fundamental ontological unit of politics, perhaps the most fundamental of all'.[3] For many of the earliest self-declared IR scholars, the study of international affairs was inseparable from, even synonymous with, the study of race relations and racial hierarchies.[4] It was only after the Second World War, with the delegitimation of scientific racism and the break-up of the European colonial empires, that the concept of race was shunted to the margins of the discipline and the literature on the topic dried to a trickle.[5] Since the end of the Cold War, the tide has turned once again: informed by a range of theoretical traditions ranging from historical sociology to decolonial thought, a new wave of scholarship has set out to uncover the persistent influence of race and racism in the theory and practice of world politics.[6]

Any rigorous discussion of race and racism in world politics has to navigate the perilous waters between two seemingly opposed positions. On the one side, there is the well-known liberal story about

---

[1] Vitalis 2000, 333. [2] Krishna 2001, 403; Thompson 2013, 135.
[3] Bell 2013, 1.
[4] Bell 2020; Blatt 2004, 2014, 2018; Long and Schmidt 2005a; Thakur, Davis, and Vale 2017; Thakur and Vale 2020; Vitalis 2000, 2010.
[5] Füredi 1998. For exceptions, see Mazrui 1968; Rosenau 1970; Shepherd and LeMelle 1970; Tinker 1977; Vincent 1982.
[6] For example, Acharya 2022; Anievas, Manchanda, and Shilliam 2015; Barder 2021; Doty 1993; Gruffydd Jones 2008; Hobson 2022; Mittelman 2009; Nisancioglu 2020; Persaud and Sajed 2018; Persaud and Walker 2001; Sabaratnam 2020; Vucetic 2011.

international progress on the problem of racism since the end of the Second World War. While the liberal story is both protracted and complex, the highlight reel includes the disgrace of scientific racism, the end of colonial rule, and the recognition of the racial unity of humankind. At the end of the day, discourses of racial inequality no longer serve as explicit organising principles of the global political order. Opposed to this progressivist narrative stands a more critical reading of twentieth-century history that foregrounds the 'sublimated'[7] presence of race and racism in international affairs. Even if explicitly racist tropes have been largely eliminated from mainstream political discourse, the theory and practice of world politics remain profoundly influenced by race and racism: racialised Orientalist and Eurocentric assumptions still animate many strands of IR theorising, and global inequalities in wealth and power retain a profoundly racialised character. In the words of Errol Henderson, race and racism are 'hidden in plain sight'.[8]

This chapter explores the seemingly contradictory possibility that both of these narratives are, in their essentials, correct.[9] Recognising rupture and reinscription as two sides of the same dialectical coin, I propose to take both the liberal and critical positions equally seriously: an overdue recognition of the ongoing significance of race and racism in world politics must be accompanied by an equally sincere acknowledgement of the thoroughgoing reorganisation of the international order on the basis of formal racial equality. Even if race and racism continue to inform international politics today, this reorganisation means that they have nonetheless taken on a very different guise compared to the late nineteenth or early twentieth centuries. The challenge for critical work is therefore not merely to show that race and racism continue to matter, but more precisely, as Ann Laura Stoler puts it, to excavate 'the discursive bricolage whereby an older discourse of race is "recovered," modified, "encased," and "encrusted" in new forms'.[10] Heeding Stoler's advice, the goal of this chapter is to unearth the conceptual labour through which the category of race was extracted from the study of world politics and repackaged in a conceptual form that rendered it compatible with post-war liberal ideology.

[7] Hobson 2022, 10.   [8] Henderson 2013.
[9] This line of inquiry is inspired by Anderson's (2019b, 7) insightful analysis of race and racism in American anthropology.
[10] Stoler 1995, 61.

A key contributing factor to the erasure of race from the purview of IR was the conceptual separation of the ethnocultural and political spheres, outlined in Chapter 1, and the widespread tendency to view race as belonging to the former rather than the latter. Framed this way, race either appears as something entirely removed from politics or its significance is reduced to that of 'an exogenously generated independent variable'.[11] Building on this argument, the present chapter demonstrates how the invention and popularisation of the concept of ethnicity in the twentieth century contributed to the 'domestication' of race. This idea of domestication should be understood in two senses at once. First, it refers quite literally to the rearticulation of race as a domestic issue rather than a global one, as a matter of internal state administration rather than a structuring principle of the international order. After the emergence of ethnicity and the domestication of race, it was no longer the case that 'international relations meant race relations'.[12] Yet the notion of domestication also comes with a second and more metaphorical sense that evokes a process of taming, of bringing race under control, as one might domesticate a wild animal. This sense of the term captures how the domestication of race was a process of sublation rather than mere erasure, combining negation with internalisation. Race and racism were not so much expunged from international relations as given a new conceptual form that rendered them compatible with the ontological and ideological assumptions of the emerging post-racial order of formally equal and sovereign nation-states.

The emergence of ethnicity and the reconfiguration of the race concept were intertwined with two other conceptual innovations which, taken together, allowed for the consolidation of a 'flat' or 'anarchical' understanding of international order. The first was the coinage of the term 'racism' in the early twentieth century, a conceptual innovation that worked in tandem with the concept of ethnicity to discredit ideologies of global racial hierarchy. As we shall see, the concept of racism that came to dominate international political discourse after 1945 was an exceptionalist and Eurocentric one: informed by the European experience of the Second World War and the Holocaust, racism came to be understood as a form of political extremism, an individual pathology grounded in bad science. The

---

[11] Smith 2004, 44. [12] Vitalis 2015, 1.

implication was that this pathology could be expunged through proper education and the spread of liberal-democratic norms. The systematic practices of racial exclusion and exploitation that defined the experiences of black Americans and colonial subjects were little more than an afterthought, obfuscating the global or transnational stratum of race that had underpinned the imperial world order. The second and closely related conceptual innovation was the relativisation and pluralisation of the concept of civilisation. Formerly understood as a singular process and standard centred on European achievements, the word 'civilisation' could now also be used to designate a multiplicity of different yet formally equal cultural blocs. It is this relativised and pluralised concept of civilisation that has filled in for the global or transnational dimension of race that was silenced by the twin concepts of ethnicity and racism.

The remainder of this chapter is organised into four sections. The first section offers a brief conceptual history of race in the modern era. In particular, it highlights the disjuncture between domestic and global meanings of race and the emergence of a new conceptual distinction between race and culture by the second decade of the twentieth century. As the concept of race was torn apart along these fault lines, the concept of ethnicity was inserted into the gaps. Accordingly, the second and by far the longest section of the chapter traces the articulation of ethnicity at the intersection of race and culture through four vignettes, each following the history of an influential ethnos-based term: 'ethnic group', 'ethnicity', 'ethnie', and 'ethnos'. The third section complements this conceptual history of ethnicity by tracing how the concept of racism was invented and popularised in the same period. Taken together, the second and third sections argue that the concept of ethnicity and the concept of racism have jointly accomplished the domestication of race. The fourth and final section shows how a relativised and pluralised concept of civilisation has subsequently filled in for the effaced global or transnational stratum of race.

Contradictions of the Race Concept

By the close of the eighteenth century, 'race' had established itself as a core concept in many European languages. Still, the term bore little resemblance to the way in which it is used or understood today. Rather than being limited to the categorisation of people on the basis of physical differences such as skin colour, race in the eighteenth century remained an incredibly multifaceted category. It was used interchangeably with the equally malleable term 'nation' to refer to all kinds of human groups, regardless of whether these groups were differentiated by phenotype, language, culture, religion, class, or gender. 'In its most common usage,' Roxann Wheeler summarises, '*race* simply meant group.'[13] It was only in the nineteenth century that this omnibus category acquired somewhat clearer boundaries as two key fault lines opened up: first, a split between national and global meanings of race that reflected the internal contradictions of the nation-state and second, a conceptual separation of the biological and sociocultural spheres.

Race versus Nation

The emergence of the modern concept of race is inseparable from the consolidation of a global order of imperialistic nation-states in the nineteenth century. As detailed in Chapter 1, the modern state is characterised by a constitutive tension between universality and particularity. On the one hand, the sovereign state functions as the secularised equivalent of God, claiming to embody universal values such as order and justice. On the other hand, every actually existing state occupies only a finite portion of the earth's surface. Nationalist ideology helps to ease this tension by grounding the abstract political concept of the state upon an inherently particularistic concept of the nation. Nationalism thus operates at the intersection of politics and culture, bringing about what Umut Özkirimli describes as the 'culturalisation of politics' and the 'politicisation of culture'.[14] Yet the supplementary concept of the nation always proves to be both too little and too much: too little, because it does nothing to guarantee the sovereignty of the state in the face of geopolitical rivals; and too much, because it opens the door to secessionist and irredentist claims. No sooner has a nation-state been established that its claim to sovereignty is subjected to contestation from both within and without.

It is the inability of nationalism to fully overcome the internal contradictions of the modern state that gives rise to racism as a further

[13] Wheeler 2000, 31.
[14] Özkirimli 2005, 20–22. See also Yack 2001, 523–530.

supplementary logic. Just as the state calls for nationalism to supplement itself, so nationalism, in turn, calls for racism as its own supplement. Mirroring the dual logic of nationalism that it supplements, the logic of racism splits into two contrasting strands. The first of these strands is particularistic, arising from the need to fix the boundaries of the nation in space and explain the persistence of the nation across generations through time. To this end, racism as a supplement of particularity seeks to identify some hereditary, pseudo-biological, or even cultural 'essence' that can serve as the transhistorical foundation of the national identity.[15] If nationalism operates at the intersection of politics and culture, bringing about the politicisation of culture and the culturalisation of politics, then racism operates at the intersection of culture and nature, bringing about the 'naturalisation of culture' and the 'culturalisation of nature'.[16] By grounding the cultural concept of the nation in an imaginary nature – defined in terms of ancestry, biology, blood, and so on – racism is able to find a seemingly unshakeable foundation for the particularity of the modern state. The modern state is thus not only a national state: it is also a racial state.[17]

As a supplement of particularity, racism takes the form of a 'supernationalism' that seeks to fulfil the nationalist fantasy through the creation of an internally homogeneous and congruent nation-state. 'You need more nationalism. You need a nationalism which is, so to speak, more nationalistic than nationalism itself', as Étienne Balibar writes.[18] Operating within the territorial frame of the state, this 'internal racism' is geared toward the 'permanent purification' of the social body 'against its own elements and its own products'.[19] Pierre-André Taguieff describes this as a logic of 'self-racialization' where the identity of the nation is aligned with a particular racialised identity while the figure of the other is coupled to the empty place of the universal. Precisely because it occupies the position of the universal, the figure of the other comes to be seen as an omnipresent and unnatural threat to the national body, above all through the prospect of racial intermixing and degeneration.[20] In a desperate attempt to save

[15] Abizadeh 2012, 868–873; Balibar 1991b, 59–60. [16] Wade 2002, 15.
[17] Goldberg 2002. [18] Balibar 1994, 203.
[19] Foucault 2003, 62. On Foucault's analysis of racism, see also Rasmussen 2011; Stoler 1995, 55–94.
[20] Taguieff 2001, 122–125.

the nation from this ethereal menace, the self-racialising logic directs itself against 'the alleged, quasi-hallucinatory visibility of the "false nationals"' that are seen to sap the power of the nation from within.[21] Historically, the most salient target of European self-racialising projects has been the diasporic figure of the Jew, which disrupts the neat spatial distinction between insiders and outsiders. Prior to the establishment of the state of Israel in 1948, as Zygmunt Bauman notes, the Jews 'were the ultimate incongruity – a *non-national nation*. Their strangeness was not confined to any particular place; they were *universal strangers*'.[22] However, precisely because the self-racialised national identity can only be defined negatively, this identity 'remains constantly in doubt and in danger; the fact that the "false" is too visible will never guarantee that the "true" is visible enough'.[23] Consequently, rather than guaranteeing a congruent nation-state, the self-racialising project produces the opposite result: by seeking to identify 'the *ideal nation* inside the nation', racism as a supplement of particularism ends up constructing an internal racial hierarchy that 'segregates the nation itself' and fractures the illusion of national homogeneity.[24]

The failure of racist supernationalism to guarantee the internal unity of the nation-state leads us to the second strand of racism's dual logic: a universalistic form of racism that flows outward from the nation and onto the international plane. Indeed, the vast majority of modern racial theories have been centred on communities that do not coincide with the boundaries of nations but instead refer to transnational groupings of people. This transnational stratum of race first emerged during the European exploratory voyages, which entailed an enormous increase in the perceived size and diversity of the world. In this context, racial classifications functioned as a pragmatic way for European thinkers to group the innumerable peoples of the world into a more manageable number of categories and halt the 'kaleidoscopic multiplication of ever more nations and tribes'.[25] Although racial classifications varied greatly in form and content, they were typically centred on no more than a handful of major groups. These major groups were defined primarily with reference to physiological characteristics such as skin colour or skull shape, and associated with large continental land masses.

---

[21] Balibar 1991b, 60.
[22] Bauman 1991, 85. See also Barnett 2020; Bauman 1989.
[23] Balibar 1991b, 60.   [24] Balibar 1994, 194.   [25] Stuurman 2000, 16.

If the particularistic strand of racism is about demarcating the frontiers of an ideal nation, then the universalistic strand of racism is about determining 'the frontiers of an ideal humanity'.[26] Inevitably, however, any attempt to define the frontiers of an ideal humanity also entails an 'infinite process of demarcation between the human, the more-than-human, and the less-than-human'.[27] The universalistic strand of racism thus not only entails the grouping of peoples into a handful of racial categories, but also the production of a hierarchical gradation of these races based on their level of cultural achievement. As European imperial expansion continued into the second half of the nineteenth century, racial classifications were increasingly mapped onto narratives of civilisational development, whereby different races were understood to possess different capacities for progress.[28] In this global hierarchy, the less civilised races were deemed to be not only closer to nature, but also, by implication, closer to animality.[29] Thus, in the same way that the particularistic strand of racism ends up stratifying the nation domestically, the universalistic strand of racism ends up constructing a global hierarchy of races. This universalistic logic of racism corresponds to what Taguieff calls 'other-racialization', where racialised others are marked as members of particular races while the identity of the self is equated with an ideal humanity and remains racially unmarked.[30] Because this ideal remains racially unmarked, it 'is always glimpsed only negatively: it is what allows us to see the deficient and the abnormal without itself being seen'.[31] The paradigmatic example of this other-racialising logic is the colonial relationship and the white/black dichotomy, where whiteness functions as the invisible standard relative to which the cultural achievements of other races are measured.[32] By the end of the nineteenth century, this racial hierarchy had hardened to the point where civilisation was widely deemed 'the exclusive property of whites'.[33] If there exists an 'inner contradiction'[34] or 'inner incompatibility'[35] between nation-state and

---

[26] Balibar 1991b, 61. [27] Balibar 1994, 197.
[28] Adas 1989, 194–198, 271–275, 338–342; Jacques 1997, 213–214; Mantena 2010, 5–6.
[29] On the entanglement of the culture/nature and human/animal distinctions, see Horigan 1988.
[30] Taguieff 2001, 121–122. [31] Montag 1997, 291.
[32] Taguieff 2001, 121–122. [33] Lorimer 2005, 117. [34] Arendt 1945, 441.
[35] Anderson 2006, 93.

empire as political forms, then the universalistic logic of other-racialisation was the critical link that allowed them to coexist in relative harmony. By arranging the peoples of the world into a hierarchy of races, the universalistic strand of racism legitimated the practice of nationalistic imperialism in perpetuity.

On the conceptual level, the tension between the particularistic and universalistic strands of racism's dual logic was manifest in the splitting of the race concept in two. On the one hand, reflecting the particularistic strand, the word 'race' was widely used to refer to a nation in the ethnocultural and non-political sense of the latter. In 1908, for example, the British historian Robert Seton-Watson published a book on nationalist tensions in the Habsburg empire under the title *Racial Problems in Hungary*.[36] Likewise, as seen in Chapter 1, the minority rights treaties signed at the end of the First World War referred to persons belonging to 'racial' rather than 'national' minorities due to the political connotations of the nation concept.[37] On the other hand, reflecting the universalistic strand of racism's dual logic, the entrenchment of European imperialism and the popularisation of global racial classifications imbued the race concept with a transnational dimension that broke the equivalence of nation and race: there could be significant 'national' variation within each of the major 'racial' groups.[38] In this way, by the dawn of the twentieth century, two contrasting meanings of 'race' came to exist side by side: a particularistic or local meaning where 'race' was a synonym of 'nation' in the ethnocultural and non-political sense of the latter, and a universalistic or global meaning where 'race' was associated with a handful of major human groups defined primarily by physical characteristics such as skin colour.

Race versus Culture

The second key development in the conceptual history of race in this period was the changing relationship between race and culture. For most of the nineteenth century, race was understood as 'an integrated physical, linguistic, and cultural totality'.[39] This omnibus concept of race was informed by a Lamarckian understanding of heredity, according to which acquired characteristics such as religion, language, political institutions, and social practices could also become

---

[36] Seton-Watson 1908.   [37] Stourzh 1994, 79.   [38] Hudson 1996, 254–255.
[39] Stocking 1994b, 15.

hereditary.[40] In an attempt to impose greater clarity and precision on this vast subject, nineteenth-century scholars often distinguished between 'true' or 'natural' races on the one hand and 'historical' or 'artificial' races or 'nations' on the other. This corresponded to the distinction between the universalistic and particularistic meanings of race outlined above: the 'true' or 'natural' were associated with the major continental land masses and usually numbered no more than three or four, while the 'historical' or 'artificial' races or 'nations' consisted of countless smaller groups such as the English, the French, and the Jews. The distinction between these two kinds of races was often understood to be one of degree rather than kind, whereby the historical or artificial races were 'true races in the process of formation'.[41]

In the second half of the nineteenth century, the omnibus concept of race came under challenge from two fronts. Among anthropologists, the adoption of statistical methods rapidly undermined the conception of race as a real phenomenon. As more and more ethnographical data was gathered and processed, it became clear that different physical traits did not necessarily correlate with one another and that many human populations did not fit into established racial typologies. Contrary to their intentions, the attempts of anthropologists to empirically measure and correlate different physical characteristics ended up reducing the concept of race to a statistical ideal type that had no concrete referent in the real world.[42] By the last quarter of the century, the influential French anthropologist Paul Topinard was arguing that there were no pure races and that the anthropological concept of race was a theoretical abstraction that existed only in the mind of the scholar. In practice, Topinard claimed, anthropological fieldwork was concerned with peoples rather than races: 'les races sont des conceptions, les peuples sont des réalités.'[43]

Meanwhile, in the biological sciences, Charles Darwin's studies on natural selection, Gregor Mendel's research on genetics, and Francis Galton's distinction between nature and nurture challenged the Lamarckian assumption that socially or culturally acquired characteristics could be inherited. The decisive break came at the turn of the twentieth century, following the publication of August Weismann's theory of

---

[40] Hattam 2007, 21–44; Stocking 1982, 234–269; Stocking 1994b.
[41] Stocking 1982, 245.   [42] Barkan 1992, 2; Stocking 1982, 57–58.
[43] Topinard 1885, 207. See also Topinard 1879.

the continuity of the germ plasm in 1892 and the rediscovery of Mendel's work on genetics in 1900. Over the following years, an ever clearer set of conceptual distinctions emerged to differentiate the biological and sociocultural spheres.[44] By the second decade of the twentieth century, the 'soft' Lamarckian paradigm had been supplanted by a 'hard' conception of heredity according to which 'the hereditary material is *fixed once and for all at conception* and *unaffected by changes* in the environment'.[45]

The displacement of the Lamarckian paradigm was accompanied by a transformation of the concept of culture. For most of the nineteenth century, 'culture' was used as a synonym of 'civilisation' and conceived as a singular standard against which the accomplishments of different races could be measured. Now, this unilinear understanding of culture-as-civilisation was replaced by a relativistic understanding of cultures or civilisations in the plural. A key figure behind this shift was the German-born Jewish-American anthropologist Franz Boas, widely regarded as the 'father' of modern American anthropology. For Boas, civilisation was not an absolute standard but something relative: there was neither scientific nor moral justification for the 'civilised' nations to look down upon the 'primitive' tribes. On the relationship between race and culture, Boas's position was equally unwavering: '[A]ny attempt to explain cultural form on a purely biological basis is doomed to failure.'[46] Not only was Boas one of the most influential scholars of his generation, he was also a devoted teacher whose work was taken up by a talented cohort of students.[47] Boas's first doctoral student, Alfred Kroeber, was one of the first scholars to articulate an explicit conceptual separation of the biological and sociocultural spheres, publishing several articles on heredity in the 1910s before proposing a distinction between the 'organic' and 'superorganic' levels in 1917.[48] Other influential Boasians, including Ruth Benedict and Margaret Mead, helped popularise the view that anthropologists should study cultures in the plural, thereby displacing the singular understanding of culture-as-civilisation.[49]

Taken as a whole, these conceptual changes constituted a moment of sublation that turned the relationship between race and culture or

---

[44] Hattam 2007, 28–36; Lorimer 2009, 186–188; Stocking 1982, 253–267.
[45] Meloni 2016, 62.
[46] Boas 1940, 265. See also Barkan 1992, 76–90; Stocking 1982, 195–233.
[47] Barkan 1992, 90–95.   [48] Kroeber 1917. See also Kronfeldner 2009.
[49] Kuper 1999, 60–67. See, for example, Benedict 1934; Mead 1937.

civilisation on its head. This dialectical reversal was elegantly captured by Alexander Goldenweiser, yet another student of Boas, in 1921:

> [T]he view still generally held of the relation between race and civilization may well be reversed. According to the prevailing view, man is many and civilization one, meaning by this that the races differ significantly in potential ability and that only one, the white race, could have and actually has achieved civilization. The reverse view, forced upon the ethnologist and the historian by a more critical and open-minded survey of the facts, reads thus: *man is one, civilizations are many*, meaning by this that the races do not differ significantly in psychological endowment, that the variety of possible civilizations is great and of the actual ones, considerable, and that many civilizations other than ours have achieved things of genuine and unique words.[50]

This dialectical reversal may have resolved some of the contradictions that plagued the race concept in the early twentieth century, but in doing so it also created a new conceptual lacuna: If 'race' now referred to the human species as a whole, and if 'civilisation' was to step in for the transnational stratum of race, then what term should be used for the local or particularistic meaning of race? What name should be given to those historical or artificial races that lacked the physical distinctiveness and transnational spread of the natural races, but instead seemed more like stateless nations or nationalities? The following section traces the histories of four key terms that were coined at the turn of the twentieth century to fill precisely this void: 'ethnic group', 'ethnicity', 'ethnie', and 'ethnos'.

The Emergence of Ethnicity: Race and/or Culture

As race and culture drifted apart, the concept of ethnicity was inserted into the gap thus created. This section traces the popularisation of this new concept through four detailed vignettes, each following the history of a different ethnos-based term. The first vignette looks at the dissemination of the term 'ethnic group', exploring how this term emerged in early twentieth-century scholarly literature before being incorporated into the vocabulary of the United Nations after the Second World War. The second vignette focuses on the popularisation of the term 'ethnicity' in the United States, from Jewish-American attempts to redefine their group

---

[50] Goldenweiser 1921, 14–15.

identity at the beginning of the twentieth century to the 'ethnic revival'[51] of the 1970s. The third vignette turns to the Francophone world, focusing on the varied uses of the term 'ethnie' in France and Haiti. Finally, the fourth vignette looks at the transnational travels of the term 'ethnos', an especially nomadic category that takes us on a meandering journey from imperial Russia to China and South Africa.

Ethnic Group: Replacing Race at the United Nations

The terms 'ethnic', 'ethnical', and 'ethnique' entered the English and French vernaculars in the early modern period, when they were used to describe heathens or pagans. With the ascendancy of an increasingly racialised worldview in nineteenth-century Europe, this religious connotation was largely forgotten and the ethnos-based terms instead became associated with the amorphous notion of race. Use of the term 'ethnique' with reference to racially defined communities was especially common in the French language, where the terms 'racial' and 'racique' remained rare until the early twentieth century.[52] Hence, for example, why the minority rights treaties concluded at the end of the First World War often referred to 'racial minorities' in English but 'minorités ethniques' in French (see Chapter 1).

The conceptual separation of 'race' and 'ethnic group' began around the turn of the twentieth century. The earliest definition of the latter can be found in Joseph Deniker's *Les races et les peuples de la terre*, published in 1900 and translated into English as *Races of Man* the same year. Born in 1852 to French parents in Astrakhan in the Russian Empire, Deniker studied in St Petersburg and travelled extensively across Europe before settling in Paris in 1876. He acquired a doctorate in natural science from Sorbonne in 1886 and was appointed chief librarian of the Musée National d'Histoire Naturelle in Paris in 1888. In *Les races et les peuples de la terre*, Deniker objected to the widespread use of zoological terms such as 'race' with reference to real

---

[51] Smith 1981.
[52] See the entries for 'race' and 'racial' in the *Trésor de la langue française*, available online at http://atilf.atilf.fr/tlf.htm (last accessed 1 January 2023). The term 'racique' was apparently first used by the French jurist Louis Le Fur in 1921. He justified his coinage on the basis that the older term 'ethnique' was ambiguous and more closely aligned with 'peuple' or 'nation' rather than 'race' (Le Fur 1921, 217n1).

human groups and proposed 'groupe ethnique' or 'ethnic group' as an alternative. He defined ethnic groups as 'real and palpable groupings [...] formed by virtue of community of language, religion, social institutions, etc., which have the power of uniting human beings of one or several species, races, or varieties, and are by no means zoological species; they may include human beings of one or of many species, races, or varieties'.[53] What Deniker called 'ethnic groups' thus encompassed all 'sociological units' including peoples, nations, and tribes.[54] In contrast, races were 'somatological units' that could only be deduced from the statistical analysis of physical traits; races were 'theoretic types' or 'approximations' whose applicability to real human groups was prevented by the continual intermingling of populations.[55]

Another early discussion of the concept of ethnic group can be found in Max Weber's renowned *Wirtschaft und Gesellschaft*, published posthumously in 1922, which contains a short chapter on 'Ethnische Gemeinschaften'.[56] The chapter title was translated into English as 'Ethnic Groups', but a more literal rendering would be 'Ethnic Communities'.[57] The chapter was based on a manuscript that Weber wrote in 1911, making it one of the earliest scholarly engagements with the concept of ethnic group.[58] In the essay, Weber took care to distinguish an ethnic community from racialised notions of kinship community. Even if discrimination based on outward appearance could play a role in the formation of ethnic communities, what mattered was the social process of group closure rather than the physical characteristics themselves: 'We shall call "ethnic groups" those human groups that entertain a subjective belief in their common descent because of similarities of physical type or of customs or both, or because of memories of colonization and migration; this belief must be important for the propagation of group formation; conversely, it does not matter whether or not an objective blood relationship exists.'[59] Weber

---

[53] Deniker 1900b, 2–3. For the French text, see Deniker 1900a, 3: 'constitués en vertu de la communauté de langue, de religion, d'institutions sociales, etc., et nullement des espèces zoologiques; ils peuvent englober des êtres humains d'une seule ou de plusieurs espèces, races ou variétés.'
[54] Deniker 1900b, 281, 293.   [55] Deniker 1900b, 3–4.
[56] Weber 1922, 216–226.   [57] Weber 1978, 385–398.   [58] Banton 2007, 20.
[59] Weber 1978, 389. For the German text, see Weber 1922, 219: 'Wir wollen solche Menschengruppen, welche auf Grund von Aehnlichkeiten des äußeren Habitus oder der Sitten oder beider oder von Erinnerungen an Kolonisation und Wanderung einen subjektiven Glauben an eine Abstammungsgemeinsamkeit

complained about the ambiguity of the German word 'ethnisch', asserting that any rigorous sociological analysis would require this 'collective term' or 'Sammelbegriff' to be thrown overboard. This critique is significant insofar as it suggests that the word was already circulating in German intellectual circles at the time, even if it did not yet have the status of a distinct scientific concept. The ambiguity of the term also led Weber to draw parallels between ethnicity and nationality: 'The concept of the "ethnic" group, which dissolves if we define our terms exactly, corresponds in this regard to one of the most vexing, since emotionally charged concepts: the *nation*, as soon as we attempt a sociological definition.'[60] For Weber, the difference between ethnicity and nationality was that the latter had a more explicit connection to political power and statehood.[61] Ultimately, despite Weber's intellectual prominence and the chapter's conceptual clarity, his essay on ethnic communities was rarely cited, even by German sociologists and ethnologists who were using neighbouring terms such as 'Ethnos' or 'Volk' in their own work. Only with the meteoric rise of ethnicity's popularity in the second half of the century did Weber's forgotten chapter begin to receive more sustained attention.[62] Weber's influence on the development of modern sociology may have been immense, but he seems to have had little impact on the conceptual history of ethnicity.

Despite the seminal interventions of Deniker and Weber, it was through the medium of the English language that the term 'ethnic group' eventually gained popularity. The first sustained discussion of the term by Anglophone thinkers came in 1935, when biologist Julian Huxley and anthropologist Alfred Cort Haddon published *We Europeans: A Survey of 'Racial' Problems*. It is likely that the two British scholars borrowed the phrase 'ethnic group' from Deniker, whose work was readily available in English translation and who had delivered the Huxley Memorial Lecture at the Royal

---

  hegen, derart, daß dieser für die Propagierung von Vergemeinschaftungen wichtig wird, dann, wenn sie nicht "Sippen" darstellen, "ethnische" Gruppen nennen, ganz einerlei, ob eine Blutsgemeinsamkeit objektiv vorliegt oder nicht.'
[60] Weber 1978, 395. For the German text, see Weber 1922, 224: 'Der bei exakter Begriffsbildung sich verflüchtigende Begriff der "ethnischen" Gemeinschaft entspricht nun in dieser Hinsicht bis zu einem gewissen Grade einem der mit pathetischen Empfindungen für uns am meisten beschwerten Begriffe: demjenigen der "Nation", sobald wir ihn soziologisch zu fassen suchen.'
[61] Weber 1922, 226; Weber 1978, 398.   [62] Raum 1995, 74–76.

Anthropological Institute of Great Britain and Ireland in 1904.[63] Haddon the anthropologist was certainly familiar with Deniker's work, having cited him in previous publications.[64] In any case, *We Europeans* became one of the most influential interwar critiques of scientific racism, lambasting the imprecise manner in which the word 'race' was being used in both scientific and popular parlance.[65] Huxley and Haddon's solution to the prevailing conceptual ambiguity was to replace the term 'race' with 'ethnic group' when actually existing social groups were involved: 'For existing populations, the word *race* should be banished, and the descriptive and non-committal term *ethnic group* should be substituted.'[66] In proposing this terminological change, Huxley and Haddon were inspired by the way in which the term 'ethnos' was used by the ancient Greek historian and ethnographer Herodotus: '[H]is *ethnos* is at times a tribe, at times a political unit, at times a larger grouping, and in using the word he guards himself against treating either type of unit as necessarily or even probably of common descent. It is, in fact, what we in this volume label, non-committally, an "ethnic group".'[67] As far as the problematic term 'race' was concerned, Huxley and Haddon argued that this should be limited to those 'sub-species' of *Homo sapiens* that could be differentiated on the basis of biological characteristics. Echoing Deniker's earlier description of 'races' as 'theoretic types' that existed only in the mind of the scholar, Huxley and Haddon emphasised that such 'races' or 'sub-species' were 'purely hypothetical' due to the continuous migration and crossing of human populations.[68] These conceptual proposals garnered attention from the broader scientific community, with one reviewer praising the term 'ethnic group' as 'an advance on Professor Boas's proposal to substitute "populations" for "race"'.[69] Huxley returned to the subject in 1941, arguing that that the 'qualitative' concept of race as a discrete type of people should be replaced by a 'quantitative' or 'statistical' concept based on gene frequencies.[70] He also reiterated his belief that it was desirable to 'banish the question-begging term "race" from all discussions of human affairs and substitute the noncommittal phrase "ethnic group"'.[71]

---

[63] Deniker 1904. [64] For example, Haddon 1909, x.
[65] Barkan 1992, 296–310. [66] Huxley and Haddon 1935, 268.
[67] Huxley and Haddon 1935, 31. [68] Huxley and Haddon 1935, 136.
[69] Dover 1935, 736. [70] Huxley 1941, 123–124. [71] Huxley 1941, 126.

The term 'ethnic group' was next picked up by Ashley Montagu, a British-American anthropologist who had trained under Franz Boas and Ruth Benedict.[72] Montagu's first major salvo against the race concept came in 1941, when he delivered a now-famous lecture to the American Association of Physical Anthropologists. Drawing on recent findings in genetics, Montagu argued that the prevailing anthropological concept of race was an ambiguous 'omelet' that had 'no existence outside the statistical frying-pan in which it has been reduced by the heat of the anthropological imagination'.[73] The following year Montagu published *Man's Most Dangerous Myth*, a bestseller in which he identified two concepts of race, one anthropological and the other sociological, both of which he considered deeply problematic. Regarding the former, Montagu reiterated the criticisms he had voiced in the 1941 lecture, asserting that the anthropological concept of race was 'meaningless' insofar as it was based on statistical averages and thus 'inapplicable to anything real'.[74] This statistical concoction, Montagu argued, should be replaced by a new genetic concept of race to which he now, inspired by Huxley and Haddon, gave the name 'ethnic group'. Montagu defined an ethnic group as 'one of a number of populations, comprising the single species *Homo sapiens*, which individually maintain their differences, physical and cultural, by means of isolating mechanisms such as geographic and social barriers'. In short, an ethnic group was 'part of a species population in the process of undergoing genetic differentiation'.[75] Given that there were no 'hard and fast genetic boundaries between any groups of mankind', ethnic groups were dynamic and processual formations rather than static types.[76] In addition to this anthropological concept of race, Montagu also identified a sociological concept of race based on 'social factors alone'.[77] He again proposed eradicating the problematic term, this time replacing it with 'caste': 'Negroes, Jews, Japanese, and Indians are in actual practice treated by dominant white groups as if they were members of specific castes. [...] There can be no cultural "races," there can only be cultural castes.'[78] As a result of all this conceptual restructuring, Montagu concluded that the term 'race'

---

[72] Brattain 2007, 1393. [73] Montagu 1941b, 245. [74] Montagu 1942, 32.
[75] Montagu 1942, 44. [76] Montagu 1942, 46. [77] Montagu 1942, 70.
[78] Montagu 1942, 72. See also Montagu 1941a. The understanding of race as a kind of caste relationship was commonplace in American sociological discourse during the 1930s and the 1940s. See Rees 2007, 86–114.

should only be used with reference to 'the five or six large divisions of man'.[79] In the revised and expanded second edition of the book, published in 1945, he abandoned the word 'race' entirely and suggested that these large groups of mankind be referred to as 'divisions' instead.[80]

The scientific campaign to replace 'race' with 'ethnic group' bore fruit in 1950. In January, the United Nations Sub-Commission on the Prevention of Discrimination and Protection of Minorities took the decision to systematically replace 'racial' with 'ethnic' in all official documentation:

The groups to be protected are 'ethnic, religious or linguistic groups'. The term 'racial' was eliminated because the Sub-Commission considered that so-called racial groupings are not based upon scientific facts and tend to become indistinct as a result of evolutionary processes, intermarriage, and changes in ideas or beliefs about race. The term 'ethnic' was considered to refer to the whole of a group's physical, cultural and historical heritage; hence specific mention of 'cultural characteristics' was considered unnecessary.[81]

The term 'ethnic' was thus deemed the broadest term available, encompassing both 'racial' and 'cultural' factors.

In July of the same year, the United Nations Educational, Scientific and Cultural Organization (UNESCO) issued a statement on 'the race question' prepared by a committee of experts that included Ashley Montagu. Julian Huxley, who served as the first Director-General of UNESCO from 1946 to 1948, was also among a dozen scholars to provide feedback on a draft. The final version of the statement defined the concept of race in genetic terms: '[T]he term "race" designates a group or population characterized by some concentrations, relative as to frequency and distribution, of hereditary particles (genes) or physical characters, which appear, fluctuate, and often disappear in the course of time by reason of geographic and or cultural isolation.'[82] The UNESCO statement thus embodied the passage from a 'typological' to a 'population' concept of race,[83] or what Huxley had in 1941 described as a shift from a 'qualitative' to a 'quantitative' concept of race.[84] However, the authors of the statement recognised that 'when most people use the term "race" they do not do so in the sense above

---

[79] Montagu 1942, 74. [80] Montagu 1945, 5.
[81] UN Doc. E/CN.4/Sub.2/119, para. 31. See also UN Doc. E/CN.4/Sub.2/SR.48, paras. 11–16.
[82] UNESCO 1969, 30–31. [83] Gannett 2001. [84] Huxley 1941, 123–124.

defined'.⁸⁵ For this reason, no doubt reflecting Montagu and Huxley's influence, paragraph six recommended replacing the word 'race' with 'ethnic group':

National, religious, geographic, linguistic and cultural groups do not necessarily coincide with racial groups: and the cultural traits of such groups have no demonstrated genetic connection with racial traits. Because serious errors of this kind are habitually committed when the term 'race' is used in popular parlance, it would be better when speaking of human races to drop the term 'race' altogether and speak of ethnic groups.⁸⁶

The statement also recognised the existence of three 'major divisions' of mankind based on physical differences: the Mongoloid, the Negroid, and the Caucasoid. Ethnic groups were described as 'sub-groups' within these major divisions.⁸⁷ The overarching conclusion of the experts was that race was biologically a 'fact' but sociologically a 'myth'.⁸⁸

UNESCO's 1950 statement on race provoked criticism from physical anthropologists and geneticists who felt that they had not been adequately represented. In response, the UNESCO project director Alfred Métraux organised a new meeting of experts consisting entirely of physical anthropologists and geneticists, following which a second statement was issued in 1951.⁸⁹ The new statement was more equivocal than its predecessor on the question of whether races existed. In line with the first statement, the preamble of the second statement noted that the experts had sought to 'avoid dogmatic definitions of race' and that race was 'a dynamic rather than a static concept'. Immediately thereafter, however, the preamble continued as follows: 'The physical anthropologist and the man in the street both know that races exist; the former, from the scientifically recognizable and measurable congeries of traits which he uses in classifying the varieties of man; the latter from the immediate evidence of his senses when he sees an African, a European, an Asiatic and an American Indian together.'⁹⁰ On the distinction between race and culture, however, the second statement was in agreement with the first: 'National, religious, geographical, linguistic and cultural groups do not necessarily coincide with racial groups; and the cultural traits of such groups have no demonstrated

---

[85] UNESCO 1969, 31. See also UNESCO/SS/Conf.1/SR.1–6.
[86] UNESCO 1969, 31. See also UNESCO/SS/Conf.1/SR.1–6.
[87] UNESCO 1969, 31–32. [88] UNESCO 1969, 33–34.
[89] Brattain 2007, 1399; Selcer 2012, S174. [90] UNESCO 1969, 37.

connexion with racial traits. [...] The use of the term "race" in speaking of such groups may be a serious error, but it is one which is habitually committed.'[91]

The term 'ethnic group' does not appear anywhere in the second UNESCO statement, but the concept received further elaboration later the same year when both statements were published with annotations by Montagu intended to clarify their meaning to the broader public.[92] In his commentary on UNESCO's first statement from 1950, Montagu justified the replacement of 'race' by 'ethnic group' on the grounds that 'it is easier to re-educate people by introducing a new conception with a new term'.[93] Whereas the word 'race' had all manner of erroneous assumptions associated with it, the term 'ethnic group' was 'noncommittal' and implied 'a question mark, *not* a period. [...] Each time it is used it is likely to elicit the question, "What do you mean by *ethnic group*?"'[94]

> One may use it [ethnic group] as equivalent to the definition of race in the biological sense, but one can use it also of groups which are less clearly defined, which may or may not be races and hence which should not be called races in the absence of the necessary scientific demonstration. All that we say when we use the term *ethnic group* is that here is a group of people who physically, and perhaps in other ways, may be regarded as a more or less distinct group. Until we know what they really are, and until we understand thoroughly what we are talking about with respect to this and all other groups, let us call all such groups *ethnic groups*.[95]

In a paper presented at Columbia University in 1959 and published in the journal *American Anthropologist* in 1962, Montagu reiterated his preference for a 'noncommittal' understanding of ethnic groups, stating that such groups could be differentiated by both 'physical or genetic and cultural' factors.[96] Whereas 'race' was 'a trigger word' from which 'a whole series of emotionally conditioned responses follow', the 'intentionally vague' meaning of 'ethnic group' provided 'a stimulus to rethink the foundations of one's beliefs' and thus

---

[91] UNESCO 1969, 39.
[92] Montagu 1951. A reworked edition of the volume was published in 1972, also incorporating two subsequent UNESCO statements on the topic. See Montagu 1972.
[93] Montagu 1951, 71. [94] Montagu 1951, 72. [95] Montagu 1951, 72.
[96] Montagu 1962, 927.

encouraged 'the passage from ignorant or confused certainty to thoughtful uncertainty'.[97]

Given Montagu's insistence on the 'intentionally vague' and 'non-committal' meaning of 'ethnic group', it is hardly surprising that the new term came up against criticism. In 1943, the geneticist J. H. McGregor voiced his concern that the new term 'would soon come to be as badly misused'. Theodosius Dobzhansky, another prominent geneticist and critic of scientific racism, raised similar concerns in more figurative language. In a letter to Montagu written in 1944, Dobzhansky wrote that scientists could claim to have proven 'the non-existence of races but demonstrated the existence of several glof glubs'. From here, however, it would only be a short step to 'glof glub discrimination, glof glub pride, and glof glub conflicts'. The zoologist Ernst Mayr was more sympathetic to Montagu's proposal, but recommended that another term be used, such as 'section, division, series, set, array, [or] group'. Mayr himself preferred 'subspecies' as he believed that this term would have 'only the meaning [...] given to it by those who have first defined it'.[98] Similar objections to the phrase 'ethnic group' recurred over subsequent decades, especially after the promulgation of UNESCO's first statement on race in 1950,[99] and again after the publication of Montagu's Columbia University seminar in *American Anthropologist* in 1962.[100] Critics repeatedly pointed out that Montagu's 'intentionally vague' definition left the new term open to exactly the same kind of abuse from which the word 'race' already suffered.

Montagu's rather unconvincing answer to these criticisms was to insist that the development of 'ethnic group prejudice' was 'quite impossible' because 'ethnic group' was 'a noncontaminating neutral concept'.[101] To claim that 'race prejudice' would be replaced by 'ethnic group prejudice' was 'to miss the point'.[102] Whereas the meaning of 'race' was taken for granted, 'ethnic group' was a 'suspense account' phrase.[103] In Montagu's view, the expression 'ethnic group' served a kind of terminological placeholder, remaining in a state of

---

[97] Montagu 1962, 926.
[98] McGregor, Dobzhansky, and Mayr, all quoted in Brattain 2007, 1395.
[99] For example, Hager et al. 1951; Montagu 1950; Vallois et al. 1951.
[100] For example, Brace et al. 1964; Martin 1963; Polgar 1964.
[101] Montagu 1972, 70–71.   [102] Montagu 1950, 319.
[103] Montagu 1950, 334.

superposition between race and culture until the true nature of the group could be determined through scientific methods.

'I am merely suggesting that, where there is no doubt, we continue to use the term "race," but that where there is any doubt whatever we, as scientists, use the phrase "ethnic group." And I am suggesting that in popular parlance it would be better that the term "race" be dropped altogether, because it has, as it were, been so badly compromised,'

he explained to his critics in 1950.[104]

For Montagu, the need to supplement the concept of race with the 'noncommittal' and 'intentionally vague' concept of ethnic group stemmed from the distinctiveness of the human condition, specifically from the fact that 'man is uniquely the *cultural* animal'.[105] Although evolutionary biological factors were involved in the 'raciation' of both animals and humans, the latter were distinguished from the former by 'man's entry into that unique zone of adaptation in which he excels beyond all other creatures, namely *culture*, that is to say, the man-made part of the environment'. Given that 'man's cultural activities' played a central role in the constitution and evolution of human groups, Montagu considered the biological or zoological concept of race to be 'inapplicable to most human populations as we find them today'.[106] In contrast, the 'noncommittal' and 'intentionally vague' quality of 'ethnic group' made this 'a uniquely appropriate phrase' by which to describe human populations.[107] Faced with the drifting-apart of race and culture, Montagu proposed 'ethnic group' as a 'filler' category that could bridge both sides of the new conceptual divide.

Ethnicity: Melting the Pot in the United States

The only known appearance of the term 'ethnicity' prior to the twentieth century dates from 1772, when it was used to translate the Spanish 'etnicidad'. The relevant passage is from *The History of the Famous Preacher Friar Gerund de Campazas*, originally written in Spanish by the celebrated Jesuit preacher and satirist José Francisco de Isla and translated into English by the Irish travel writer Thomas Nugent: 'From the curling spume of the celebrated Egean waves fabulous

---

[104] Montagu 1950, 336. [105] Montagu 1950, 335.
[106] Montagu 1962, 919. [107] Montagu 1950, 335.

ethnicity feigned Venus their idolatress conceived.'[108] This use of 'ethnicity' to indicate heathen or pagan superstition was consistent with the early modern practice of using 'ethnic' and 'ethnicism' with reference to heathens or pagans.[109] When the first edition of the *Oxford English Dictionary* was published in 1897, it still defined 'ethnicity' as 'heathendom, heathen superstition'. By then, however, the term was marked as 'obsolete' and 'rare'.[110]

After Nugent's eighteenth-century translation, the next recorded appearance of the word 'ethnicity' is not until 1920, when it appears in Isaac Berkson's *Theories of Americanization*. By this time, the term had lost its religious connotations and was instead closely associated with race and culture. Berkson refers to 'ethnicity' only once in the book, does not provide a definition, and indeed gives no indication that he was coining a new concept: 'To regard every individual of an ethnic group as having primarily the characteristic nature of that group, as if affiliation with it invested him with a particular kind of *ethnicity* which then determined his nature, is contrary to the doctrine that each individual structure is primary.'[111] Berkson also sporadically used the term 'ethnos' as an alternative to 'ethnic group' or 'race'.[112] While 'ethnos' failed to catch on in this context, the following decades saw 'ethnic group' and 'ethnicity' gain widespread currency across the United States.

Berkson, a Jewish-American educator and philosopher, belonged to a group of New York-based Zionist intellectuals that also included the renowned theorist of cultural pluralism Horace Kallen. Both Berkson and Kallen contributed articles to the *Menorah Journal*, a Zionist organ published by the Intercollegiate Menorah Association and dedicated to the promotion of Jewish culture in the United States. For present purposes, what was significant about this circle of Zionist thinkers was their desire to conceive of Judaism as something more than just a religion. In the last quarter of the nineteenth century, the preferred vocabulary for capturing Jewish group identity beyond

---

[108] See the entry for 'ethnicity' in the *Oxford English Dictionary*, available online at www.oed.com (last accessed 22 February 2020).
[109] See the entries for 'ethnic' and 'ethnicism' in the *Oxford English Dictionary*, available online at www.oed.com (last accessed 23 July 2020).
[110] Murray 1897, vol. III, 314. See also Dike 1935, 360.
[111] Berkson 1920b, 89, italics added.
[112] Berkson 1920b, 53, 88, 92, 93, 98, 102, 103, 106, 113, 117, 163.

religious identity was that of race, and references to the 'Jewish race' were common among Jews and non-Jews alike.[113] By the beginning of the twentieth century, however, two developments combined to make 'race' a problematic term for Jewish-Americans. First, the massive social dislocation brought by industrialisation, urbanisation, and immigration led to the entrenchment of a white/black dichotomy in the United States as people searched for some kind of fixity in a society that appeared increasingly fluid. The growing racialisation of minority groups was epitomised by the Immigration Acts of 1917 and 1924, which aimed to restrict immigration from Eastern and Southern Europe as well as Asia. In this uncertain climate, the racial peculiarity of the Jews 'threatened to cast them beyond the pale of whiteness'.[114] Jewish-Americans of a Zionist persuasion were thus torn between the longing for a distinct racial identity of their own, on the one hand, and the desire to be seen as members of white America, on the other. The second development that rendered the word 'race' problematic for Jewish-Americans was the discrediting of the 'soft' Lamarckian understanding of heredity and the emergence of a much sharper conceptual divide between race and culture. Thus, the expert of Jewish physical anthropology Maurice Fishberg concluded in 1911 that the Jews could not be considered a 'race' in the anthropological sense of the term.[115] In Zionist circles, however, the reduction of Jewish identity to religious identity was unacceptable and Fishberg's conclusions were strongly criticised.[116]

The conundrum of Jewish group identity was eventually solved by switching from a racial to a cultural register. In the work of Horace Kallen, this shift can be detected as early as 1910. In an article published in the Zionist journal Maccabaean in 1906, Kallen still described the Jews as a 'race'.[117] Four years later, however, he placed the emphasis squarely on 'history' and 'culture'. In a revealing passage, Kallen noted that it was inappropriate to describe the Jews as a race or even as a nationality: 'That they have racial unity is properly enough disputed; that they have nationality the "diaspora" would seem to preclude.'[118] On the next page, he wrote that 'the Jews, as an *ethnic*

---

[113] Goldstein 2006, 16–17; Greene 2011; Korelitz 1997. See also Leff 2005.
[114] Goldstein 2006, 31. See also Rees 2007, 50–57.   [115] Fishberg 1911.
[116] Goldstein 2006, 114.   [117] Kallen 1906.
[118] Kallen [1910] 1932, 38. Kallen made the same point about Jewish nationality in a speech at the dinner of the Second Menorah Convention in 1914, when he

group, were the great middlemen of mediaeval times'.[119] The fact that 'ethnic group' was italicised could indicate that Kallen was self-consciously introducing a new concept. However, he did not define ethnicity and instead switched back to the language of nationality, asserting that 'Jewish religion is a function and an expression of nationality and depends on nationality for life'.[120] Kallen's preference for the language of nationality is evident in his subsequent elaboration of the theory of cultural pluralism, which characterised the United States as a federation of multiple nationalities.[121]

Kallen's theory of cultural pluralism bears a close affinity to the liberal internationalism of Alfred Zimmern. Both Kallen and Zimmern were deeply influenced by the cultural Zionism of Asher Ginsberg and the two men forged a lifelong friendship during Zimmern's visit to the United States in 1911–1912. Kallen's vision of the United States as a federation of multiple nationalities mirrors, on a national scale, Zimmern's aspiration for a global commonwealth of formally equal cultural nations. Both men sought to banish the concept of race from political debate and, in doing so, elevated a depoliticised concept of nationality into the cornerstone of their respective theories.[122] This depoliticisation of nationality set Kallen and Zimmern apart from their contemporaries, most of whom accepted the politicised definition of nationality as either a synonym of citizenship or indicating a potential nation-state (see Chapter 1). By contrast, Kallen and Zimmern saw no necessary or desirable link between nationality and statehood. This depoliticised understanding of nationality helps to explain why neither thinker needed the concept of ethnicity to express their arguments: for both Kallen and Zimmern, the depoliticised concept of nationality already served the function of ethnicity.

Although Kallen questioned the appropriateness of describing the Jews as a race, his writings exhibit a residual Lamarckism. Thus, he continued to invoke a wide range of criteria, including ancestry, as the basis of nationality and liked reminding his audience that the etymological roots of 'nationality' lay in the Latin 'natio', signifying birth.[123] A more decisive break with the Lamarckian paradigm can be found in

noted that the Jews, unlike other immigrant groups, did not have a 'national center'. See Intercollegiate Menorah Association 1914, 85.
[119] Kallen [1910] 1932, 39.   [120] Kallen [1910] 1932, 41.
[121] Kallen 1915a, 1915b, 1915c.   [122] Baji 2016; Pianko 2009.
[123] Pianko 2008, 301–313.

the work of Isaac Berkson, who explicitly called for a 'change of emphasis from race to culture'.[124] According to Berkson, Jewish identity was 'cultural and spiritual' and could not be grasped in terms of race or religion.[125] Although Berkson emphasised the importance of endogamy for the maintenance of Jewish identity, the reasoning behind this was not racial but thoroughly sociocultural: 'Unless the family preserves the ethnic affiliation, the child is extremely unlikely to come under the group influences of school and synagogue. [...] The marriage within the group would be the result of free choice to preserve the cultural inheritance, not the impulse of racial clannishness or the dictates of a superstitious tribalism.'[126]

Like Kallen, Berkson described the Jews as a 'nationality' on several occasions.[127] He also echoed Kallen's qualms regarding the difficulty of applying this term to the Jews: '[T]he Jew does not owe an allegiance to the nation from which he has emigrated in the same way that a German or an Italian might; the Jews do not come from their own land.'[128] But whereas Kallen persisted with the language of nationality despite the difficulties, Berkson opted to describe the Jews as a 'minority ethnic community' or simply as an 'ethnic group'.[129] Berkson's linkage of ethnicity with minority status imbued this concept with a distinct connotation of otherness: the 'supreme difference' between ethnic classifications and political or economic classifications, Berkson explained, was that 'the former is foreign and the latter are indigenous. These ethnic distinctions – Jew, Italian, Pole – were formed under the conditions of other times and other places'.[130]

The embryonic concept of ethnicity that was emerging in the works of these Jewish-American scholars was bounded by the concept of race. More precisely, their understanding of ethnic difference was limited to the white side of the emerging white/black divide. In *Culture and Democracy in the United States*, Kallen's most detailed exposition of the theory of cultural pluralism, the status of black Americans was reduced to a single footnote: 'I do not discuss the influence of the negro [...]. This is at once too considerable and too recondite in its processes for casual mention. It requires separate analysis.'[131] For all its merits, Kallen's theory of cultural pluralism remained 'encapsulated in white

[124] Berkson 1920a, 311.   [125] Berkson 1920a, 312–313.
[126] Berkson 1920a, 316.   [127] Berkson 1920a, 313; Berkson 1921, 50.
[128] Berkson 1920b, 52.   [129] Berkson 1920b, 49–55.
[130] Berkson 1920b, 50.   [131] Kallen [1924] 1998, 218n1.

ethnocentrism'.[132] Berkson, likewise, did not refer to black Americans a single time when describing his community theory of American life. For these Zionist thinkers, the depoliticised concept of nationality or ethnicity promised Jewish-Americans a distinct group identity of their own while also enabling them to present themselves as loyal members of white America. Simply put, the concept of ethnicity allowed the Jews to appear 'both white and different'.[133] The flipside to this 'whitening' of Jewish-Americans and other European immigrant populations was the hardening of the colour line. As white minority 'races' were being redefined as 'ethnic groups', the meaning of 'race' was also being restabilised around the white/black binary.[134]

Despite Kallen and Berkson's elision of the black American experience in their writings, the problems they were grappling with were not entirely alien to the dilemmas faced by contemporary black American scholars. From different sides of the colour line, both communities were trying to negotiate the difficulties of dual identification, or what W. E. B. Du Bois – the first black American to receive a PhD from Harvard University – described as the problem of 'double-consciousness'.[135] Du Bois himself never used the concept of ethnicity to make sense of this dilemma, relying instead on the established concepts of race and nation. In testimony to the malleability of these terms at the turn of the century, Du Bois frequently slipped between them, describing black Americans at times as a 'race' and at other times as a 'nation'. Central threads running through his work were a critique of scientific racism and a refusal to reduce racial or national cohesion to physical likeness. Even when Du Bois conceded that physical characteristics 'play a great part' in binding a race or nation together, he also insisted that 'the deeper differences are spiritual, psychical, differences – undoubtedly based on the physical, but infinitely transcending them'.[136] In addition to sharing a physical resemblance, Du Bois argued that black Americans were also united by common historical and cultural traditions, especially slave religion. It was precisely this reconceptualisation of the black American population, not only as a biological category but as 'a separate nation within a nation', that laid

---

[132] Higham 1984, 210. See also Hattam 2007, 54–62, 73–76.
[133] Goldstein 2006, 166. See also Rees 2007, 6.   [134] Jacobson 1998.
[135] Du Bois 1903, 3.   [136] Du Bois 1897, 8. See also Appiah 2014, 83–117.

the foundations for the rise of black ethnicity as a political force later in the twentieth century.[137]

The first black American scholar to use the language of ethnicity was the writer and philosopher Alain Locke, another graduate of Harvard. Locke was deeply influenced by the work of Franz Boas and believed that biology had no influence on the actually existing 'racial' groups that could be observed in society. However, in contrast to many other critics of scientific race theory, Locke did not want to abandon the concept of race completely.[138] He considered race to be such a central category that it was unlikely to be 'superceded [sic] except by some revised version of itself. Too much social thinking has gone into it for it to be abandoned as a center of thought or of practice. To redeem, to rescue, or [to] revise that thought and practice should be the aim of race theorists and those who want to educate people into better channels of group living'.[139] It was during his ensuing attempts to redefine the race concept that Locke tentatively adopted the language of ethnicity. In the first of a series of five lectures delivered at Howard University in 1916 (unpublished in his lifetime), Locke argued that race was a product not of nature or biology, but of culture and history: '[W]hen the modern man talks about race he is not talking about the anthropological or biological idea at all. [He is really talking about the historical record of success or failure of] an ethnic group.'[140] In a subsequent article, Locke described this reconfigured conception of race as an 'ethnic race' or 'social race'.[141] On the one hand, he emphasised that 'these groups, from the point of view of anthropology, are ethnic fictions' insofar as they 'have neither purity of [blood] nor purity of type'.[142] On the other hand, he was equally adamant that 'race is a fact in the social or ethnic sense'.[143] The crucial upshot of Locke's two-pronged argument was to turn relationship between race and culture on its head: 'Instead therefore of regarding culture as expressive of race, race by this interpretation is regarded as itself a culture product.'[144]

Du Bois and Locke's reconceptualisation of black American racial identity in cultural rather than merely biological or physical terms

---

[137] Du Bois [1936] 1985, 144. See also Henderson 2019, 73–78, 152–173.
[138] Henderson 2019, 121–129; Stewart 1992, xxiii–xxv.
[139] Locke [1916] 1992, 85.   [140] Locke [1916] 1992, 11.
[141] Locke [1924] 1989, 190, 192.   [142] Locke [1916] 1992, 11.
[143] Locke [1924] 1989, 192.   [144] Locke [1924] 1989, 193.

echoes the attempts by Zionist scholars such as Kallen and Berkson to ground Jewish-American identity on a cultural basis. Indeed, it was during conversations with Locke at Harvard around 1906–1907 that Kallen first came up with the term 'cultural pluralism' to describe his theory of American group life.[145] It is also likely that Du Bois's theorisation of 'double consciousness' was prompted by his exposure to German antisemitism while studying at the University of Berlin between 1892 and 1894.[146] Despite these connections, however, Jewish-Americans and black Americans approached the problem of double consciousness from quite different perspectives: whereas the most pressing problem for Jewish-Americans was the threat of assimilation into the white majority, for black Americans it was the perpetuation of racial segregation.[147] While the likes of Kallen and Berkson could 'pass' for white men and espouse a pluralist vision of American society, on the darker side of the colour line there was far less room for manoeuvre: '[E]verything was either black or white.'[148]

References to 'ethnic groups' and 'ethnic communities' begin to appear with some regularity in American social science during the 1930s.[149] The word 'ethnicity' itself can be found in the context of W. Lloyd Warner's Yankee City project, a community study of Newburyport, Massachusetts, conducted during the 1930s and published in five volumes between 1941 and 1959. The first volume identifies ten ethnic groups in the city and notes in passing that these groups construct social barriers 'on the basis of ethnicity'.[150] The second volume, published in 1942, offers a more detailed explication of the term: 'Ethnicity may be evaluated almost entirely upon a biological basis or upon purely social characteristics. Negroes tend to be at the first extreme, since they are most physically variant of all groups in the community, and the Irish at the other extreme, since they are most like the native white stock.'[151] The third volume of the series, published in 1945 and titled *The Social Systems of American Ethnic Groups*, makes frequent use of the adjective 'ethnic' but not 'ethnicity'.[152] There is also a notable discrepancy between the number of ethnic groups discussed in the first two volumes and the third

---

[145] Kallen 1957. [146] Thomas 2020. [147] Higham 1984, 210–213.
[148] Higham 1984, 212.
[149] Ware 1931, 1935, 127–234; Wessel 1931; Woofter 1933.
[150] Warner and Lunt 1941, 211–212. [151] Warner and Lunt 1942, 73.
[152] Warner and Srole 1945.

volume. In volumes one and two, ethnicity is treated as a universal category that all individuals possess, akin to age or sex.[153] On this basis, the authors identify a total of ten ethnic groups in the city: '(1) Native or Yankee; (2) Irish; (3) French (French Canadians); (4) Jewish; (5) Italian; (6) Armenian; (7) Greek; (8) Polish; (9) Russian; and (10) Negro'.[154] In contrast, volume three considers only eight of these groups. The two omissions are the 'Native or Yankee' and the 'Negro'.[155]

Concerning the exclusion of the 'Native or Yankee' from the third volume, it appears that the authors adopted a popular conception of ethnicity according to which the dominant group in society has no ethnic identity.[156] This question of whether or not the majority group of a society constitutes an ethnic group has been a recurring one. If an ethnic group is simply an identity group with a shared culture, then 'not only the French-Canadians or the Pennsylvania Dutch would be ethnic groups but also the French of France or the Irish in Ireland'.[157] Or, as Everett and Helen Hughes succinctly put it, 'we are all ethnic'.[158] In practice, however, there has been a widespread tendency among American scholars to reserve the concept of ethnicity to designate minority groups only. As noted above, Berkson described ethnic groups as being of 'foreign' origin. Likewise, the third volume of the Yankee City series defined 'ethnics' as persons of 'foreign culture'.[159] This has been described as the 'minus one' model of ethnicity insofar as it implies that a state always contains one community – the majority nation – that is not considered an ethnic group.[160] The *Harvard Encyclopedia of American Ethnic Groups*, published in 1980, still vacillated on this question. On the one hand, the editors identified three 'ethnic' sub-types within the white Anglo-Saxon Protestant majority nation: 'Appalachians', 'Southerners', and 'Yankees'. On the other hand, they still maintained that there existed a large number of 'plain' or 'nonethnic' Americans.[161]

As regards the exclusion of the black American population from the third volume of the Yankee City series, this was consistent with the

---

[153] Warner and Lunt 1942, 66.
[154] Warner and Lunt 1941, 211. See also Warner and Lunt 1942.
[155] See Warner and Srole 1945.   [156] Banton 1983, 146; Sollors 1986, 23–26.
[157] Francis 1947, 395n13.   [158] Hughes and Hughes 1952, 7n1.
[159] Warner and Srole 1945, 28.   [160] Banton 1983, 63–67.
[161] Thernstrom, Orlov, and Handlin 1980, vi–vii.

restabilisation of the race concept around the white/black dichotomy and the consequent tendency to discuss ethnic minority relations and race relations in separate spheres. In the middle decades of the twentieth century, there was a clear division of labour in American social science between scholars who studied European immigrants and those who studied slavery and black American history, with the concept of ethnicity reserved for the former and the concept of race for the latter.[162] This divide was also reflected in the prevalent 'melting pot' ideology: whereas ethnic groups of European origin were expected to assimilate into the American majority culture, racial differences were seen as 'a near-absolute barrier to assimilation'.[163] Thus, the Yankee City project concluded that the assimilation of racially distinct populations such as "Negroes" would be 'slow and usually painful'.[164] Within this binary framework, Hispanics, Asians, and Native Americans had an ambiguous status and were often omitted from discussion altogether.[165]

Even as the adjective 'ethnic' began to spread, take-up of the word 'ethnicity' itself seems to have been slow. David Riesman's use of the term in 1953 has gained some fame, as it has been erroneously credited as the first written appearance of the term.[166] A handful of other passing references to 'ethnicity' can be found in the 1950s, but none give it detailed consideration.[167] Instead, the popularisation of the term had to wait until the discrediting of the melting pot ideology in the 1960s and 1970s. The first salvo was fired in 1963, when Nathan Glazer and Daniel Patrick Moynihan published their hugely influential book *Beyond the Melting Pot*, arguing that the melting pot 'did not happen'.[168] Reconceptualising ethnicity as a dynamic and ongoing phenomenon, the authors claimed that 'even after distinctive language, customs, and culture are lost', ethnic groups 'are continually recreated

---

[162] Halter 2006, 161–163; Mason 1999, 14–15. There are some exceptions to this pattern, with a handful of American scholars using the term 'ethnic' to encompass racial as well as cultural differences. For example, Bloom 1948; Cox 1948, 317–319.
[163] Banks 1996, 68.   [164] Warner and Srole 1945, 286.
[165] Halter 2006, 161; Mason 1999, 21.
[166] Riesman 1953, 15. See, for example, Chapman 1993, 19; Eriksen 2010, 4; Glazer and Moynihan 1975, 1.
[167] For example, Braithwaite 1953, 140, 143; Broom 1954, 115; Smith 1955, 47; Smith 1957, 443, 444, 445; Vreeland 1958, 88.
[168] Glazer and Moynihan 1963, v.

by new experiences in America'.[169] Nevertheless, the book still contained strong assimilationist undertones. Echoing an older notion of a 'triple-melting-pot' structured along religious lines,[170] Glazer and Moynihan predicted that ethnic identities based on national origin would be subsumed under broader religious and racial categories. This would ultimately lead to the consolidation of four major groups in American society: 'Catholics, Jews, white Protestants, and Negroes'.[171] A similar argument was made by Milton Gordon a year later, when he depicted the United States as a 'multiple melting pot' wherein religious, racial, and even some national divisions were expected to persist.[172]

A more radical critique of the melting pot ideology required a reconfiguration of the relationship between ethnicity and race. An early step in this direction had been the theorisation of race as a particular kind of caste relationship during the late 1930s and 1940s. Although this approach was swiftly dismantled by critics, it was significant for rearticulating race in social rather than biological terms.[173] The most influential statement along these lines was Gunnar Myrdal's *An American Dilemma*, published in 1944, which conceptualised racial categories as products of social prejudice: it was racism that produced race and not the other way round. 'The definition of the "Negro race" is thus a social and conventional, not a biological concept', Myrdal concluded.[174] While challenging the prevalent grounding of racial identities in biology or nature, the race-as-caste literature still remained firmly entrenched within the melting pot paradigm. According to Myrdal, for instance, the principal purpose of overcoming white prejudice was to facilitate the full assimilation of the black population into mainstream American culture. Indeed, Myrdal was the main authority responsible for popularising the view that the black population did not have an ethnic or cultural identity of its own, but merely a 'distorted' or 'pathological' mutation of mainstream American values.[175] Even Glazer and Moynihan's *Beyond the Melting Pot*, known for its rejection of the melting pot ideology, still

---

[169] Glazer and Moynihan 1963, 17.
[170] For example, Herberg 1960; Kennedy 1944.
[171] Glazer and Moynihan 1963, 314.   [172] Gordon 1964, 130–131.
[173] Rees 2007, 86–114.
[174] Myrdal 1944, vol. I, 115. See also Omi and Winant 1994, 16–17.
[175] Myrdal 1944, vol. II, 928. See also Blauner 1972, 125; Rees 2007, 117.

held on to this view: 'It is not possible for Negroes to view themselves as other ethnic groups viewed themselves because – and this is key to much in the Negro world – the Negro is only an American, and nothing else. He has no values and culture to guard and protect.'[176]

The situation changed dramatically in the mid-1960s with the rise of the Black Power movement. In contrast to the integrationist philosophy of the Civil Rights movement, the Black Power movement drew on a long tradition of black nationalist thought. Echoing Du Bois's aforementioned work, the Black Power movement conceived of black Americans as 'a nation within a nation' and advocated for this nation's right to autonomy and self-determination.[177] This nationalist approach to black American identity was epitomised by the Republic of New Africa, a black nationalist organisation formed in 1968 that called for the creation of a sovereign black-majority nation to be carved out of several southern states.[178] In conceptual terms, the vocalisation of black nationalism catalysed the reformulation of race as a particular form of ethnicity rather than a wholly separate phenomenon. An early indication of this shift can be found in a 1962 article by Lester Singer, which proposed the term 'ethnogenesis' to describe the processes through which new ethnic groups emerge. Instead of limiting this concept to white minority groups, Singer suggested that it could also be used to analyse the changing status of black Americans. Nevertheless, Singer's argument remained tentative: '[W]hile it is proper to regard the Negroes as an ethnic group, it is also proper to say that they are still in the *process of becoming* an ethnic group, that is, their ethnicity is still *developing*.'[179] Even many leaders of the Black Power movement, including Malcolm X, subscribed to the popular view that black Americans lacked a cultural heritage of their own. Instead of drawing inspiration from the cultural traditions and historical struggles of black Americans – as Du Bois and Locke had done earlier in the century – the Black Power movement privileged African anticolonial movements as referents.[180]

The first full-fledged articulation of black ethnicity can be found in *The Crisis of the Negro Intellectual*, an influential text published in

---

[176] Glazer and Moynihan 1963, 53.   [177] Henderson 2019, 43–94.
[178] Henderson 2019, 311–329.   [179] Singer 1962, 430.
[180] Henderson 2019, xi.

1967 by the social critic and black nationalist Harold Cruse. Rejecting the view that black Americans had no values or tradition of their own, Cruse pointed to the existence of a vibrant and distinct black American cultural heritage: black Americans were an 'ethnic group' or 'ethnic minority' like any other. One of the consequences of this reframing was a fracturing of the white/black dichotomy into a plurality of ethnic communities. 'American group reality demands a struggle for democracy among ethnic groups, rather than between two races', Cruse argued. 'What is called a racial struggle over civil rights is, in reality, the contention in America among several different ethnic groups, of which Anglo-Saxon Protestants and American Negroes are only two.'[181] The salience of the white/black dichotomy in the popular imaginary, Cruse maintained, should not be allowed to mask the fact that 'Indians, Mexicans, and other non-white hyphenated-Americans at the bottom of the ethnic totem pole are also involved'.[182] What differentiated black Americans from these other ethnic groups was the paradoxical fact that they were 'the ethnic source of America's only native and original artistic ingredients' and yet, at the same time, also 'this country's most culturally deprived minority'.[183] Specifically, Cruse suggested that the experience of the black American population should be understood as a form of 'domestic colonialism'.[184] Due to its unique social position as a domestic colony, the black American population was to play the 'pivotal' role in the liberation struggle.[185]

Following Cruse's seminal work, many other black nationalist authors took up the lens of 'domestic colonialism' to theorise the status of black Americans in the United States.[186] In his history of ethnicity in the United States, Richard Rees has also highlighted the role of Robert Blauner, a sociologist based at the University of California, in articulating the link between domestic colonialism and black ethnicity.[187] Building on Cruse's insights, Blauner detailed how the suppression of particularistic black ethnic identities under conditions of slavery and

---

[181] Cruse 1967, 458.   [182] Cruse 1967, 317.   [183] Cruse 1967, 223.
[184] Cruse [1962] 1968, 75–76. The idea of 'domestic' or 'internal' colonialism originated with Latin American dependency theorists in the 1950s, although the terms themselves do not appear until the 1960s. The term 'domestic colonialism' was first used by Harold Cruse in 1962, while 'internal colonialism' was coined by the Mexican sociologist Pablo González Casanova in 1963. See Gutiérrez 2004.
[185] Cruse 1967, 318.   [186] For example, Carmichael and Hamilton 1968.
[187] Rees 2007, 115–149.

institutionalised racism 'ironically created the conditions for a more unified regrouping and a new sense of peoplehood unimpaired by ethnic division'.[188] It was thus the homogenising experience of domestic colonialism that, according to Blauner, laid the groundwork for the emergence of black ethnicity as a political force in the 1960s and 1970s. Under the influence of black nationalism, an externally imposed racial category was dialectically reappropriated and reformulated as a subjective ethnic identity.

The rise of the Black Power movement in the mid-1960s was paralleled by the rise of the Red Power movement. In much the same way that the Black Power movement sought to overturn the prevailing conception of the black American population as devoid of cultural identity, the Red Power movement sought to overturn the prevailing conception of Native American communities as stagnant relics of history.[189] There was substantial cross-fertilisation and cooperation between the two movements, but also points of difference and conflict. For instance, the Native American author and activist Vine Deloria Jr sought to carve out a separate conceptual space for the Red Power movement by sharply distinguishing its tribal nationalism from what he viewed as the 'anti-white reaction' of the Black Power movement.[190] For the purposes of this chapter, however, the most salient point is how the political activism of the Red Power movement fostered a more positive conception of pan-Indian identity that transcended local tribal affiliations and paved the way for an 'Indian ethnicity'.[191] As one commentator put it in 1968, 'Pan-Indianism is the creator of a new identity, a new ethnic group, if you will, a new "nationality" in America'.[192]

The success of the Black Power and Red Power movements during the 1960s prompted the creation of a series of affirmative action programmes designed to neutralise the situation. Ironically, however, these programmes ended up inspiring new claims to ethnic status: 'Since the best way to get a share of federal funds and to be heard was to activate an ethnic constituency and to claim "minority" status, it paid everyone to try to get into the ethnic act.'[193] For many commentators, it seemed as if the United States had been swept by an 'ethnic

---

[188] Blauner 1972, 18. [189] Nagel 1996.
[190] Deloria 1969, 182. See also Bruyneel 2007, 124–169.
[191] For example, Lurie 1965, 37. [192] Thomas 1968, 139.
[193] van den Berghe 1978, xxix. See also Rees 2007, 143–144; Smith 1982, 1–2.

fever'.[194] The late 1960s and 1970s thus witnessed a veritable subjectification of ethnicity, as different groups appropriated the concept of ethnicity as a tool of identity politics. Indeed, it was at this juncture that the concept of identity burst onto the scene in American social science. As Philip Gleason explains in his semantic history of identity, social and political developments in these decades 'affirmed the durability of ethnic consciousness, gave it legitimacy and dignity, and forged an even more intimate bond between the concepts of ethnicity and identity'.[195] Recast as a subjective identity category, the referents of the ethnicity concept were no longer limited to white minority groups of foreign origin. Instead, the concept now became universalised and 'freely applicable to the analysis of virtually all national and tribal groups'.[196]

The universalisation of ethnicity heralded by the Black Power and Red Power movements marked the definitive collapse of the melting pot ideology – this was *The Rise of the Unmeltable Ethnics*, to borrow the evocative title of Michael Novak's 1972 book.[197] The following year, the sociologist Harold Abramson declared that assimilationist predictions had not been fulfilled and that even the major religious groups remained internally divided along ethnic lines.[198] Glazer and Moynihan returned to the topic in 1975 and likewise concluded that both the 'liberal expectancy' and the 'radical expectancy' had been disappointed: neither liberal predictions about the assimilation of ethnic groups into the majority nation nor Marxist predictions about the subordination of ethnic ties to class loyalties had come true.[199] Instead, Glazer and Moynihan pointed to 'the steady expansion of the term "ethnic group" from minority and marginal subgroups at the edges of society – groups expected to assimilate, to disappear, to continue as survivals, exotic or troublesome – to major elements of society'.[200] The old assimilationist paradigm thus gave way to a new emphasis on pluralism and autonomy. By the close of the 1970s, ethnicity had metamorphosed from an 'antechamber to assimilation' into an enduring feature of American society.[201]

Regarding the relationship between the concept of ethnicity and the concept of race, one of the most important consequences of these

[194] Steinberg 1989, 3. [195] Gleason 1983, 929. [196] Rees 2007, 145.
[197] Novak 1972. [198] Abramson 1973, 172–182.
[199] Glazer and Moynihan 1975, 6–7. [200] Glazer and Moynihan 1975, 5.
[201] Rees 2007, 138.

developments was the recasting of race as a particular form of ethnic identity. In 1973, for example, Abramson suggested that even if 'race is the most salient ethnic factor, it is still only one of the dimensions of the larger cultural and historical phenomenon of ethnicity'.[202] Numerous other statements to this effect could be cited, but perhaps the best evidence for this conceptual shift is the fact that even the sociobiologist Pierre van den Berghe, who resisted the subsumption of race under ethnicity throughout the 1970s, came to view race as 'a special case of ethnicity, rather than a categorically discrete phenomenon', by 1983.[203] More recently, Stuart Hall has described this conceptual transformation as 'the end of the essential black subject'.[204] 'If the black subject and black experience are not stabilized by Nature or by some other essential guarantee,' Hall writes, 'then it must be the case that they are constructed historically, culturally, politically – and the concept which refers to this is "ethnicity".'[205]

Ultimately, the rearticulation of race as a special case of ethnicity does not negate the fact that physical characteristics matter for boundary-construction and group-formation. This inscribes an inherent asymmetry into the position of white and non-white groups in the United States. For those individuals who are fortunate enough to 'pass' as white, ethnic affiliation becomes a symbolic choice, a supplementary characteristic that can be added to the identity-repertoire of the individual as and when desired. On the darker side of the colour line, by contrast, there is much less flexibility as 'the racialization of groups of color continues to take precedence over their ethnicity and ascribes positionality without option'.[206] Even as racial identities have come to be recognised as socially constructed categories rather than purely biological ones, they cannot be entirely assimilated under the heading of culture. Race haunts ethnicity from within.[207]

---

[202] Abramson 1973, 175.
[203] van den Berghe 1983, 222. For his earlier views on race and ethnicity as distinct phenomena, see van den Berghe 1970, 10–11; van den Berghe 1978, xv, 9–10.
[204] Hall 1996, 444.   [205] Hall 1996, 446.   [206] Rees 2007, 145.
[207] To capture the interplay of race and ethnicity, a number of scholars have used compound terms such as David Theo Goldberg's 'ethnorace' and Alain Locke's 'ethnic race'. See, for example, Alcoff 2000; Bernasconi 2007; Goldberg 1993, 1997.

Ethnie: Reconfiguring Race in the Francophone World

The word 'ethnie' was coined by the French anthropologist Georges Vacher de Lapouge in 1896. Politically, Vacher de Lapouge strikes a rather confusing figure: an active socialist and member of the Parti ouvrier français until the turn of the twentieth century, he is mostly remembered for his promotion of scientific racism and influence on Nazi race theory. He was also one of the earliest Francophone proponents of eugenics and is credited with introducing the term 'eugénique' into the French language. From the 1880s, Vacher de Lapouge advocated for the establishment of 'anthroposociologie' as a new scientific discipline, the purpose of which would be the application of anthropological insights to social policy, and called on the French government to control breeding practices. In 1897, he proposed replacing the national slogan 'Liberté, Égalité, Fraternité' with 'Déterminisme, Inégalité, Sélection!'[208]

Although Vacher de Lapouge's thought was steeped in scientific racism, he was also very aware of the ongoing conceptual separation of race and culture. In view of this, he believed that the word 'race' should be restricted to the zoological sphere and that a new word was needed to describe historically formed human populations. The two words that Vacher de Lapouge proposed for this purpose in 1896 were 'ethne' and 'ethnie':

> Il faudrait lui trouver un autre nom, car ce mode de groupement, à la fois naturel et factice, est à peu près l'opposé de ce que les zoologistes appellent race; il y a antagonisme de la race et de cela. Peuple, nation, nationalité sont des termes également impropres; ils ont, comme celui de race, un sens exact, préexistant, qu'il n'est pas permis de détourner de sa valeur primitive, sous peine de confusion. J'ai proposé ethne ou ethnie, vocables dont le premier est plus correct, le second plus facile à prononcer.[209]

This passage, found in *Les sélections sociales*, seems to be the only time that 'ethne' and 'ethnie' appear in Vacher de Lapouge's work. The new coinages were briefly acknowledged in Alfred Fouillée's *Psychologie du peuple française*, an influential and popular book published in eight editions between 1898 and 1927.[210] Despite an initially positive reception, the

---

[208] Vacher de Lapouge 1897, 2. See also Béjin 1982; Hecht 2000; Noiriel 2007, 272–275; Quinlan 1998; Schneider 1990, 59–62; Staum 2011, 54–55; Taguieff 2000.
[209] Vacher de Lapouge 1896, 10.   [210] Fouillée 1898, 27.

views that Vacher de Lapouge expounded in *Les sélections sociales* came to be almost unanimously rejected by the French academic community by the turn of the century.[211] Although he maintained an international correspondence with prominent eugenicists such as Madison Grant in the United States and Hans Günther in Germany, Vacher de Lapouge remained a marginal figure in French science until his death in 1936.[212]

Meanwhile, in Switzerland, the word 'ethnisme' was introduced into the French language by the founder of structuralist linguistics Ferdinand de Saussure. This independent coinage – typically rendered into English as 'ethnic unity' or 'ethnicity' – appears in Saussure's lectures at the University of Geneva between 1906 and 1911, posthumously assembled and published as *Cours de linguistique générale* in 1916. At the beginning of the chapter in which the word 'ethnisme' appears, Saussure asserts that race and language are distinct phenomena and 'have no necessary connection'. 'But there is another type of unity,' he continues, 'which is of infinitely greater importance and which is constituted by the social bond: *ethnic unity* [*ethnisme*].'[213] The 'mutual relation' that Saussure posited between language and ethnicity introduced a circularity into his argument, whereby language and ethnicity reproduced and reinforced one another: 'The social bond tends to create linguistic community and probably imposes certain traits on the common idiom; conversely, linguistic community is to some extent responsible for ethnic unity. In general, ethnic unity always suffices to explain linguistic community. [...] Reciprocally, on the question of ethnic unity, we must first consult language.'[214] As Robert Young points out, the seemingly marginal and insignificant concept of ethnisme, which only appears toward the end of the *Cours de linguistique générale*, in fact designates the limit of Saussure's theoretical edifice: 'His deliberately vague definition of "*ethnisme*"

---

[211] Taguieff 2000, 23–24.   [212] Taguieff 2000, 39–49.
[213] de Saussure 1959, 223. For the French text, see de Saussure [1916] 1995, 305: 'mais il y a une autre unité, infiniment plus importante, la seule essentielle, celle qui est constituée par le lien social: nous l'appellerons *ethnisme*.'
[214] Saussure 1959, 223. For the French text, see Saussure [1916] 1995, 305–306: 'le lien social tend à créer la communauté de langue et imprime peut-être à l'idiome commun certains caractères; inversement, c'est la communauté de langue qui constitue, dans une certaine mesure, l'unité ethnique. En général, celle-ci suffit toujours pour expliquer la communauté linguistique. [...] Réciproquement, sur la question de l'unité ethnique, c'est avant tout la langue qu'il faut interroger; son témoignage prime tous les autres.'

betrays the moment in which his account of language has to encounter the "social bond" that gives it the unity to make up a *langue*. At this point, the purely formal analysis of "abstract objectivism" has to encounter what, after Saussure, we might call "the positive fact".[215] The ambiguous concept of ethnisme thus signals the critical point where Saussure's abstract account of language 'has to touch upon the problematic realm of materiality and the social foundation of language which otherwise he wishes to deny'.[216]

Saussure's 'ethnisme' seems to have been a nonce word. Even so, it offers an interesting parallel to the use of the term 'ethnie' by the French physician and anthropologist Félix Regnault. Although he subsequently fell into obscurity, Regnault was a well-connected figure in his time, serving as president of the Société d'Anthropologie de Paris in 1926 and as president of the Société Préhistorique Française from 1928 until his death in 1938.[217] During a meeting of the Société d'Anthropologie de Paris in 1919, Regnault proposed the term 'glossethnie' or simply 'ethnie' to describe a social group speaking the same language.[218] Regnault seems to have come up with the term independently, as he does not reference Vacher de Lapouge's earlier use of the term. In other writings, Regnault cites Joseph Deniker's distinction between races and social groups, but he does not specifically mention Deniker's use of the phrase 'groupe ethnique' to designate the latter.[219] Echoing Saussure's sociolinguistic definition of ethnisme, Regnault's primary objective in (re)introducing the word 'ethnie' into the French language was to differentiate between the biological and linguistic meanings of 'race' that were so often confused by his contemporaries: 'Cette distinction permettra d'opposer l'ethnie à la race avec laquelle on la confond si souvent. En anthropologie comme en histoire naturelle et en zootechnie, race est un terme anatomique. Ethnie sera un terme psychique.'[220] Regnault promoted his new coinage throughout the 1920s, notably at a conference of the Institut International d'Anthropologie held in Amsterdam in 1927.[221] In a subsequent article on the disciplinary classification of the anthropological sciences published in 1931, Regnault expanded the meaning of 'ethnie' beyond linguistic groups to encompass any human community held together

---

[215] Young 2002, 68. [216] Young 2002, 75.
[217] On Regnault, see Desoille 1938; Rony 1996, 25–30. [218] Regnault 1919.
[219] Regnault 1931, 124. [220] Regnault 1919, 55.
[221] Regnault 1920, 1921, 1928.

by 'psychic' ties. He thus redefined 'glossethnie' or community of language as a sub-type rather than a synonym of 'ethnie'. The other sub-type that he proposed was 'iéroethnie' or community of religion.[222]

Regnault's concept of ethnie was quickly picked up by the physician and anthropologist George Montandon.[223] Born in Switzerland in 1879, Montandon trained and practised as a medical doctor before setting off to explore remote parts of Ethiopia in 1909. After returning to Europe two years later, he gave a number of guest lectures at prestigious geographical societies across the continent and published his first travelogue in 1913. At the outbreak of the First World War, Montandon initially volunteered as a surgeon, but returned to writing by 1917. His few publications from this period suggest that he was influenced by the racial theories of Arthur de Gobineau and harboured antisemitic views. Between 1919 and 1921, Montandon served as a delegate of the International Committee of the Red Cross and was sent on a fact-finding mission to Siberia, where he met his pro-Bolshevik wife and converted into an enthusiastic communist. Upon his return to Switzerland, he joined the Communist Party in Lausanne and was active in spreading pro-Bolshevik propaganda. After failing to secure an academic post in Switzerland, Montandon abandoned his political activism and moved to France in 1925. There he began to study anthropology in earnest and took up a position at the École d'Anthropologie in Paris in 1931. He quickly moved up the academic ranks and gained a permanent professorship after acquiring French citizenship in 1936. By the end of the decade, Montandon would become one of the leading proponents of antisemitic thought in France.[224]

Montandon was the key figure behind the dissemination of the term 'ethnie' during the 1930s and 1940s. He first used the term in a footnote in his 1928 book *L'ologenèse humaine*, where he mentions that 'ethnie' had been proposed as an alternative to 'race' at the Amsterdam conference of the Institut International d'Anthropologie in 1927. (It is obvious that Montandon is referring to Regnault's aforementioned conference paper, even if he does not mention Regnault by name.) Although Montandon did not elaborate on the

---

[222] Regnault 1931, 126–127. [223] Montandon 1931.
[224] Conklin 2013, 91–97; Knobel 1988; Piana 2016; Reynaud-Paligot 2010.

meaning of the term in any detail, it is already clear that his understanding of 'ethnie' differed markedly from that of Regnault. Whereas Regnault's conference paper had clearly distinguished the 'psychic' concept of ethnie from the 'anatomical' concept of race, Montandon suggested that the term 'ethnie' referred to groups defined by somatic, linguistic, and cultural factors simultaneously.[225]

Montandon's first in-depth engagement with the concept of ethnie was in a commentary on Regnault's aforementioned article on the classification of the anthropological sciences from 1931. This was followed two years later by a revised popular version of *L'ologenèse humaine*, titled *La race, les races*. When elaborating on the concept of ethnie in these texts, Montandon compared it to several neighbouring terms, including Joseph Deniker's 'groupe ethnique' and Arthur Keith's 'ethnos' (more on Keith in the next vignette). Interestingly, even though Montandon was inspired by Georges Vacher de Lapouge's social Darwinism, he never mentioned Vacher de Lapouge's earlier use of the word 'ethnie' and instead credited Regnault with coining the term.[226] However, Montandon considered the omission of physical characteristics from Regnault's 'psychic' definition of ethnie problematic as it entailed, for example, the conflation of the black and white populations of the United States into a single ethnie. Instead, Montandon argued that an ethnie should be understood as any distinguishable human group, regardless of whether this group was defined by physical, linguistic, religious, cultural, or mental characteristics.[227] Whereas the concept of race was a scientific abstraction based on the measurement of physical traits, the concept of ethnie was a 'natural' human group that could be identified without scholarly intervention: 'ce groupe est un groupe *naturel*, défini par ceux qui en font partie et par ceux qui ne lui appartiennent pas, sans l'ingérence du savant.'[228] These views were reiterated in Montandon's 1935 book *L'ethnie française*, which opened in a provocative manner: 'Parler de *race* française, c'est ne pas savoir ce qu'est une race. Il n'y a pas de *race* française. Il y a une *ethnie* française, dans la constitution somatique de laquelle entrent les éléments de plusieurs races.'[229] At first glance, this statement would appear to establish a clear distinction between race

[225] Montandon 1928, 344n1.
[226] Montandon 1931, 128; Montandon 1933, 15–16.
[227] Montandon 1931, 129; Montandon 1933, 18.   [228] Montandon 1933, 14.
[229] Montandon 1935b, 9.

and ethnie. Upon closer reading, however, it is clear that the incorporation of physical characteristics in the definition of ethnie left the door open for its racialisation. Rather than separating race and ethnie, Montandon subsumed the concept of race under the more expansive concept of ethnie. As he exclaimed in 1941, 'l'ethnie ne s'oppose pas à la race: *elle l'englobe*; l'ethnie englobe la race!'[230]

Montandon's conceptual framework enabled him to espouse a racist and antisemitic line of thinking while avoiding outdated notions of racial types that were by now coming under attack. In fact, Montandon's ethnie-theory did nothing less than turn the prevailing understanding of racial purity on its head. Through the lens of ethnie, Montandon recast racial purity not as a feature of the past that ought to be maintained, but as something that lay in the future and ought to be achieved: 'la race pure ne représente pas un passé, mais un devenir.'[231] Although racist and antisemitic motifs recur throughout Montandon's writings, he was skilled at hiding his more extremist ideas in footnotes. As a result, some of his publications from the early 1930s actually received praise from critics of scientific racism.[232] In a review of *La race, les races*, for example, the prominent French ethnographer Arnold van Gennep commended Montandon for his 'systematic elimination of those confusions between people, language, and race [...] that we see [...] being resuscitated to Hitler's great benefit'.[233] It was only after the German occupation of France in 1940 that Montandon's true colours were laid bare, as he began to actively collaborate with the Vichy regime and publish increasingly radical material.[234]

In addition to popularising the word 'ethnie', Montandon elaborated two other ethnos-based words during the 1940s: 'ethnisme' and 'ethnicité'. As noted above, the term 'ethnisme' had already been used by the Swiss linguist Ferdinand de Saussure several decades earlier to indicate a social bond. By contrast, Montandon compared 'ethnisme' to 'racisme' and used it interchangeably with 'ethnoracisme' (another new coinage).[235] If Saussure's 'ethnisme' can be translated as 'ethnic unity' or 'ethnicity', then Montandon's 'ethnisme' is perhaps best rendered as 'ethnism' or 'ethnicism'. Montandon's rationale

---

[230] Montandon 1943, 3.
[231] Montandon 1933, 112. See also Conklin 2013, 175–176.
[232] Conklin 2013, 177–179.   [233] van Gennep, quoted in Conklin 2013, 178.
[234] Conklin 2013, 308–324.
[235] Knobel 1988, 108–110; Staum 2011, 201–204.

for coining this term was that most cases of racism had the natural human group or ethnie, rather than the abstract biological concept of race, as their point of reference. Due to the currency that the word 'racisme' had acquired by the 1940s, Montandon did not insist on his new coinage except in technical usage: 'Quant au terme de *racisme*, qui est un mot du langage courant, et signifie la reconnaissance, la mise en valeur, voire l'exaltation de la notion raciale, on l'emploiera aussi bien s'il s'agit de racisme proprement dit que s'il s'agit d'ethnisme.'[236] As regards the term 'ethnicité', it seems that Montandon was the second person to use this word in print and the first to explain its meaning.[237] In the same way that he saw 'ethnisme' as a supplement to 'racisme', Montandon saw 'ethnicité' as a supplement to 'nationalité'. Simply put, ethnicité was to ethnie what nationalité was to nation:

'Comme ils ne disposaient pas du terme d'ethnie pour le groupe humain naturel, les Napoléons, Napoléon Ier puis Napoléon III, ont appelé "nationalité" ce qui devait être qualifié d'ethnie ou d'*ethnicité*. Il importe de rendre au terme de nationalité son sens logique et l'on dira d'un Français du centre, Basque, Corse, Breton ou Flamand, tandis qu'on dira d'un Basque que c'est un homme de nationalité française, mais d'ethnicité basque, etc.'[238]

The term 'nationalité' thus encompassed all members of the French nation-state, whereas 'ethnicité' referred to linguistic, cultural, or racial belonging.

Another important text to use the term 'ethnie' in the 1930s was René Martial's *La race française*, published in 1934. Martial was a prominent French physician and immigration specialist whose political views – akin to those of Vacher de Lapouge and Montandon – moved between socialism and scientific racism.[239] Given the similarities in their training and thinking, Martial and Montandon engaged with each other's writings surprisingly little, possibly due to mutual rivalry.[240] When Martial introduced the term 'ethnie' in *La race française*, he avoided any reference to Montandon and credited Regnault as its originator. Following Regnault's 'psychic' conception

---

[236] Montandon 1943, 3. See also Montandon 1941, 3.
[237] The first person to use 'ethnicité' in print was the French philosopher Jules de Gaultier in his 1902 novel *Le Bovarysme*, but he does not define or develop the concept. See the entry for 'ethnique' in the *Trésor de la langue française*, available at http://atilf.atilf.fr/tlf.htm (last accessed 2 January 2023).
[238] Montandon 1943, 4. See also Montandon 1944.   [239] Larbiou 2005.
[240] Taguieff 1994, 182.

of ethnie, Martial described ethnies as 'des entités psychologiques nettement différenciées'. These psychologically differentiated entities were produced through the mixture of multiple races or parts of races; there was no such thing as a racially pure ethnie.[241] The key concept for Martial was, however, 'race' rather than 'ethnie'. Whereas Regnault erected a clear-cut division between race and ethnie, and Montandon subsumed race under ethnie, Martial subsumed ethnie under race. Placing special emphasis on blood types, Martial argued that an ethnie was not only a psychological unit, but also constituted 'un substratum biologique : le groupement sanguin'.[242] This line of argument led Martial to propose a new 'synthetic' definition of race that encompassed the concept of ethnie: 'On appelle la race l'ensemble d'une population dont les caractères psychologiques latents ou manifestes (langue en particulier) et les traits anthropo-biologiques constituent, dans le temps (histoire), une unité distincte.'[243]

In a rare instance of direct engagement between the two authors, Montandon published a brief review of Martial's *La race française* in 1935. Unsurprisingly, Montandon complained about Martial's elastic use of the word 'race' and suggested that he should have stuck with the word 'ethnie' to avoid confusion.[244] Instead of heeding his rival's suggestion, however, Martial opted to discard the word 'ethnie' entirely in favour of his new 'synthetic' concept of race, which he now began to call the 'race-résultat' – the word 'ethnie' is nowhere to be found in Martial's subsequent writings. To clarify what he meant by a 'race-résultat', Martial offered the metaphor of felt-making:

Lorsqu'on veut faire un feutre, on prend les poils de beaucoup de lapins: des noirs, des blancs, des épais, des minces, etc. Lorsqu'ils sont tous bien amalgamés, ils constituent un tissu, un feutre, solide, indéchirable, inusable, que l'on ne peut que détruire mais pas diviser. Même si des poils sont d'une couleur quelque peu différente, ils sont si bien incorporés qu'ils ne peuvent être extraits du feutre. Ce feutre, ce feutrage, c'est la race-résultat.[245]

The study of these race-résultats would be the task of a new synthesising science that Martial christened 'anthropo-biologie'. Its three core

---

[241] Martial 1934, 8.   [242] Martial 1934, 14.
[243] Martial 1934, 317. See also Martial 1938, 9–10; Martial 1939, 39; Martial 1942b, 9; Martial 1943, 9.
[244] Montandon 1935a.
[245] Martial 1938, 26. See also Martial 1939, 36–37; Martial 1942a, 45.

pillars were history, psychology, and biology, of which the first two were more important than the third. Although an ethnie or race-résultat could usually be identified by its physical characteristics, the psychology of the group was the key differentiating factor.[246] In the end, there was very little to separate Martial's 'synthetic' conception of race from Montandon's 'natural' definition of ethnie. Both scholars were looking for a way to supplement Regnault's purely 'psychic' understanding of ethnie with some kind of racial dimension, but whereas Montandon retained the word 'ethnie' for this purpose, Martial opted for 'race-résultat' instead.

Another parallel between Montandon and Martial concerns their understanding of racial purity. The two men approached this question from very different theoretical perspectives – Martial focusing on blood types while Montandon drew on the hologenetic theory of evolution – yet they reached some strikingly similar conclusions. As noted above, Montandon denounced the idea of originary pure races and instead located racial purity in the future. Martial, likewise, emphasised that all existing human populations were racially mixed: 'Il n'existe aujourd'hui que des races-résultats, les plus homogènes elles-mêmes n'étant pas restées pures.'[247] This led Martial to criticise contemporary German race-theorists who sought to attain racial purity through elimination: 'Si les hommes d'Etat allemands persévèrent dans leurs méthodes de purification par élimination, méthode spécifiquement raciste et s'opposant, par définition, au métissage, ils doivent, après avoir expulsé les Juifs, expulser ceux des Aryens qui ont subi le métissage mongol : entre 10 et 20 % suivant les rameaux.'[248] Although Martial privileged métissage over elimination, he believed that too much racial mixing would be detrimental and that a careful process of social selection was desirable. He likened this to the breeding of animals, where the goal was to maximise positive traits and minimise negative ones.[249] What differentiated human from animal breeding was the need to consider psychological traits as well as physical ones.[250] Through a judicious process of selection, Martial suggested, it was theoretically

---

[246] Martial 1934, 13–14, 245–246. [247] Martial 1938, 10.
[248] Martial 1938, 25–26. [249] Martial 1938, 106–107.
[250] Martial 1938, 108.

possible to recreate pure racial types: 'La race pure peut donc se reconstituer.'[251]

Similar themes arise in Jacques Boulenger's *Le sang français*, published in 1943. A French writer and journalist, Boulenger contributed to collaborationist periodicals during the German occupation and shared Montandon and Martial's antisemitism. In the introduction to *Le sang français*, Boulenger offers a useful survey of some of the key terms floating around in French academia at the time. These included the well-established 'race historique' and 'nationalité' as well as two ethnos-based terms: Joseph Deniker's 'groupe ethnique' and Sergei Shirokogoroff's 'ethnos' (more on Shirokogoroff in the next vignette). Boulenger quickly dismissed any variant of 'race' or 'nationalité' for having too many different connotations that obfuscated their meaning. However, the alternatives proposed by Deniker and Shirokogoroff did not satisfy Boulenger either: Deniker's 'groupe ethnique' he considered too cumbersome, while Shirokogoroff's recourse to the Greek 'ethnos' he deemed unnecessary when an equivalent already existed in the French language. The equivalent Boulenger had in mind was, of course, Montandon's concept of ethnie: 'nous pouvons si bien dire en français *ethnie*, comme le demande Montandon.'[252]

Following in Montandon's footsteps, Boulenger defined an ethnie as a natural or actually existing grouping of people sharing certain affinities: 'L'ethnie est un groupement que les hommes ont formé d'eux-mêmes en vertu de leurs affinités réciproques.'[253] In contrast, the concept of race was a scientific abstraction that could only be identified by scholars through the study of hereditary characteristics. This led Boulenger to quickly dismiss the idea of racially pure ethnies. With the possible exception of some isolated primitive groups, racial intermixing was the norm.[254] Some ten pages later, however, Boulenger appears to contradict himself when he asserts that the ideal ethnie would be formed of one race only: 'L'ethnie parfaite serait celle dont tous les membres seraient de la même race.'[255] The explanation for this apparent contradiction – on the one hand, the recognition that ethnies were racially mixed; on the other hand, the idealisation of racially pure ethnies – is that Boulenger's concept of ethnie was not opposed to the concept of race in a binary fashion. Instead, following Montandon,

---

[251] Martial 1934, 291. [252] Boulenger 1943, 12. [253] Boulenger 1943, 66.
[254] Boulenger 1943, 66–68. [255] Boulenger 1943, 77.

ethnie encompassed race as one of its determinants. For Boulenger, the global dominance of the white race was proof of the inequality of races; by extension, it could be assumed that there were inequalities between the sub-types of different races. And given that ethnies were formed out of the mixture of different races and sub-types of races, this implied that different ethnies had different capacities for civilisation that reflected the capacities of the different races and sub-types of races out of which they were formed. Consequently, even if a racially pure ethnie was little more than a myth, the racial refinement of ethnies was nonetheless desirable.[256]

A recurring feature in the writings of Montandon, Martial, and Boulenger is the preoccupation with the figure of the Jew. Between 1941 and 1944, Montandon published a review called *L'Ethnie Française* in which he publicised his increasingly radical ideas, authoring an article on the 'ethnie Juive' for each issue.[257] He also wrote a ninety-page illustrated booklet explaining how the Jewish physical type could be recognised.[258] Martial was less confident about the possibility of identifying a Jew based on their physical characteristics, writing that there was no 'type Juif' but only 'le paradoxe du type juif'. The paradox here was the fact that an individual with ostensibly Jewish features was not necessarily a Jew and, inversely, that a Jew did not necessarily possess Jewish features.[259] This points to an important tension that runs through modern antisemitic discourse more generally. On the one hand, the inconspicuous and diasporic nature of the Jews rendered them a seemingly omnipresent threat to the purity of the nation, or in this case, the French ethnie. By 1939, Montandon was advocating for a vigorous policy of 'ethnisme' or 'ethnoracisme' as the best way to combat the Jewish peril and protect France from unchecked miscegenation.[260] On the other hand, precisely because of their diasporic history, the Jews also represented the foremost example of racial self-conservation in the face of external pressures. According to Boulenger, for instance, the Jews had only been able to retain a distinct identity and acquire global influence thanks to their 'foi raciste' and practice of endogamy.[261] As Pierre-André Taguieff notes, modern

---

[256] Boulenger 1943, 77–86. [257] Archives d'Histoire de l'Ethnologie 1993.
[258] Montandon 1940. [259] Martial 1934, 241.
[260] Knobel 1988, 108–110; Staum 2011, 202–203. [261] Boulenger 1943, 159.

antisemitism is animated not only by fear or hatred, but also contains a hint of jealousy: 'dans la haine moderne visant les Juifs, il y a de la peur, de la phobie et de l'admiration'.²⁶²

There are substantial parallels and connections between French ethnie-theory and German race-theory in this period. Both Vacher de Lapouge and Montandon corresponded with the leading German race-theorist Hans Günther – known to his colleagues as 'Rassen-Günther' – who in turn referenced their work with admiration.²⁶³ It is also likely that Montandon's conceptualisation of the relationship between 'race' and 'ethnie' was influenced by Günther's distinction between 'Rasse' and 'Volk' in the 1920s.²⁶⁴ Both Montandon and Boulenger noted the equivalence between the French 'ethnie' or 'groupe ethnique' and the German 'Volkstum', which encapsulated a racialised understanding of nationality or national character under the Third Reich.²⁶⁵ During the German occupation of France, Montandon actively collaborated with the Vichy regime, using his expertise to decide on indeterminate cases of 'Jewishness' and making a profit of several million francs in the process.²⁶⁶ In view of this dark history, it seems fitting that the liberation of France went hand in hand with the downfall of French ethnie-theory, symbolised by the assassination of Montandon and his wife by the French resistance on 3 August 1944.²⁶⁷

Despite their influence, Montandon and his acolytes never acquired a monopoly on the term 'ethnie' and alternative definitions continued to circulate during the war. In 1943, for example, Henri Vallois's *Anthropologie de la population française* made the case for a mutually exclusive distinction between race and ethnie reminiscent of Regnault's earlier work. For Vallois, as for Regnault, the word 'race' referred to groups united by hereditary physical characteristics, whereas an 'ethnie' was a community formed of civilisational or cultural characteristics only.²⁶⁸ In the book's bibliography, Vallois included the following critical note after Montandon's *L'ethnie française*: 'Malgré l'ambigu de son titre, ce volume ne traite que l'anthropologie physique.'²⁶⁹ Nonetheless, partly due to its close association with the likes of

---

²⁶² Taguieff 1994, 214.   ²⁶³ Hecht 2000, 293; Knobel 1988, 108.
²⁶⁴ Conklin 2013, 179.
²⁶⁵ Boulenger 1943, 12; Montandon 1935b, 26. See also Krieg-Planque 2005, 147.
²⁶⁶ Conklin 2013, 308.   ²⁶⁷ Knobel 1988, 112.   ²⁶⁸ Vallois 1943, 13.
²⁶⁹ Vallois 1943, 127.

Montandon and partly due to the colourblind ideology of the post-war French republic, the word 'ethnie' fell out of favour. A few exceptions notwithstanding,[270] use of the word 'ethnie' in the 1950s and 1960s was restricted to anthropological studies of non-European societies, where 'ethnie' displaced older colonial concepts such as 'tribu' and 'peuplade' (see Chapter 3). In this way, the French 'ethnie' became roughly equivalent to the English 'tribe'.[271]

Although the word 'ethnie' is still widely shunned in French academia, other ethnos-based terms have made a tentative comeback. The word 'ethnicité', used by Montandon in the 1940s, began to make sporadic appearances again in the 1960s and 1970s to translate the increasingly popular 'ethnicity' from English to French.[272] However, it was not until Françoise Morin convened a roundtable of the Association Française des Anthropologues in November 1981 that this concept received an official welcome (back) into French academic circles.[273] Faced with a global upsurge of ethnic and nationalist movements, Morin lambasted French anthropologists for failing to develop adequate concepts to theorise such phenomena: 'Certains mots comme groupe ethnique, tribu, nationalité sont devenus insolites et désuets, d'autres comme ethnicité sont directement traduits de l'anglais sans définition préalable.'[274] In subsequent decades, the concept of ethnicity has gained some ground in Francophone scholarship and a number of major studies have been published on the topic.[275] Still, their historical links to scientific racism and colonialism have ensured that the ethnos-based terms have not gained anywhere near the kind of popularity they enjoy in the Anglophone world.[276]

An interesting countermovement is also worth noting here: at the same time that the English 'ethnicity' is creeping into the French language in the form of 'ethnicité', the French 'ethnie' is moving in the opposite direction. Seemingly unaware of its racist and colonialist baggage, a number of Anglophone scholars have adopted the French

---

[270] For example, Becquet 1963; Heraud 1963.   [271] Cahen 1994, 12.
[272] For example, Bernier, Elbaz, and Lavigne 1978; Boyon 1963, 1006; Douglass and Lyman 1976, 197; Nicolas 1973, 105, 122; Raveau 1976; Rousseau 1978; UNESCO 1971; Wallerstein 1972, 227.
[273] Poutignat and Streiff-Fenart 1995, 21–22.   [274] Morin 1981, 17.
[275] For example, Amselle 2011; Breton 1992; Cahen 1994; Gosselin and Lavaud 2001; Martiniello 2013; Poutignat and Streiff-Fenart 1995.
[276] Martiniello 2013, 19–25.

'ethnie' as an alternative to the rather cumbersome and problematic 'ethnic group'. Besides being shorter and pithier, the word 'ethnie' has been praised for avoiding the potentially misleading connotation of social cohesion implied by the word 'group'.[277] Other Anglophone scholars have proposed the neologism 'ethny' for similar reasons.[278] However, neither 'ethnie' nor 'ethny' has gained much currency, and 'ethnic group' remains the hegemonic term in the English-speaking world.

Although it failed to make a lasting impression in Western academia, the term 'ethnie' enjoyed transnational circulation during the 1930s and 1940s. An especially interesting connective thread takes us across the Atlantic, from metropolitan France to the Caribbean island of Haiti, where a group of black nationalist thinkers known as the 'Griots' developed their own brand of ethnie-theory. The Griots group had its origins in the meetings of three young men known as 'les trois D' during the late 1920s: the journalist Louis Diaquoi, the lawyer Lorimer Denis, and the medical student François Duvalier. They first met at the Lycée Pétion in Port-au-Prince, where they studied under the renowned Haitian ethnographer Jean Price-Mars, and began to meet regularly to discuss the significance of his work for their generation. Shortly before his premature death in 1932, Diaquoi announced the formation of the Griots group, whose name was inspired by the traditional West African word for a storyteller or poet. In 1938, they set up the quarterly review *Les Griots: La Revue Scientifique et Littéraire d'Haïti* as an outlet for their ideas.[279]

The Griots movement promoted an assertive brand of black nationalism known as 'noirisme'. Their political theory possessed a distinctly authoritarian strain, depicting liberal institutions such as free elections and freedom of the press as 'sordid tinsel designed to mislead the masses'.[280] The group presented the history of Haiti as a struggle between the black masses and an exploitative mixed-race elite that sought to impose a foreign European culture on the country with the help of the Catholic Church. Fusing the ethnographical work of Haitian scholars such as Price-Mars with novel theories of ethnicity emanating from France, the group formulated a racialised

---

[277] Petersen 1980, 234; Smith 1986, 21–22.
[278] McDonald 2007, 4; van den Berghe 1983, 222.
[279] Nicholls 1996, 167–169; Smith 2009, 23–24.   [280] Nicholls 1996, 172.

understanding of the Haitian nation centred on folklore and vodou.[281] Denis and Duvalier, the two ringleaders of the movement after Diaquoi's death, readily admitted that the concept of race was a scientific abstraction and that the Haitian population was racially mixed. Nonetheless, they insisted on the reality of race as a social phenomenon and borrowed Montandon's concept of ethnie to make their case: the Haitian ethnie, Denis and Duvalier argued, was formed historically out of the mixture of European and African racial and cultural heritage, with the African heritage being dominant.[282] A 'Declaration' published in the first volume of *Les Griots* announced the strengthening of the Haitian ethnie as one of its key objectives: 'aider à renforcer l'unité de l'ethnie haïtienne'.[283]

Les Griots closed down in 1940 due to a lack of funds and Duvalier left Haiti in 1944 to pursue a two-year course in public health at the University of Michigan. Yet the splintering of the group's leadership did not reduce the influence of its noiriste ideology, which was starting to take hold across Haitian society more broadly.[284] In this period, the most detailed exposition of Haitian ethnie-theory can be found in the work of the lawyer and ethnographer Kléber Georges-Jacob. A protégé of Price-Mars and affiliate of the Griots group, Georges-Jacob published two book-length studies of the Haitian ethnie during the 1940s: *L'ethnie haïtienne* in 1941 and *Contribution à l'étude de l'homme haïtien, au service de l'histoire ethno-sociale de l'ethnie haïtienne* in 1946.[285] Although he credited Regnault with coining the term, Georges-Jacob embraced Montandon's definition of an ethnie as a 'natural' grouping formed through the fusion of somatic, linguistic, and cultural factors over time.[286] The scientific study of the Haitian ethnie thus required the simultaneous consideration of three factors: race, history, and culture.[287] The social cohesion of the Haitian ethnie, Georges-Jacob argued, was sustained through a non-hierarchical or

---

[281] Birkenmaier 2016, 86–93; Nicholls 1996, 167–172; Smith 2009, 23–28.
[282] Denis and Duvalier 1936, 12; Denis and Duvalier 1938b, 151; Denis and Duvalier 1939, 304. In formulating these ideas, Denis and Duvalier also cite the work of René Martial and Sergei Shirokogoroff. See, for example, Denis and Duvalier 1938a, 4; Denis and Duvalier 1939, 306–307.
[283] Brouard et al. 1938, 1.   [284] Smith 2009, 28.
[285] Georges-Jacob 1941, 1946. See also Nicholls 1996, 170–171; Verna 2017, 83–84.
[286] Georges-Jacob 1941, 13; Georges-Jacob 1946, 66–67, 202.
[287] Georges-Jacob 1946, 10, 14, 18, 201.

differentialist form of racism that had striking echoes of Montandon's notion of 'ethnisme' or 'ethnoracisme'. At the same time, Georges-Jacob was careful to distinguish this affirmative form of racism from Nazi race-theory and notions of superior and inferior races. 'Notre racisme,' he explained, 'est plus une attitude de dignité et de prestige qu'un sentiment de blancophobie.'[288]

While explicating the nature of the Haitian ethnie, Georges-Jacob heaped praise on the American writer and philosopher Alain Locke, who had delivered and published a series of six lectures at Port-au-Prince in 1943.[289] Locke likely would have been uncomfortable with the Griots group's authoritarian political theory, but what they both had in common was the valorisation of black cultural traditions – Locke, too, cited the ethnographical work of Price-Mars with admiration. There are also substantial similarities between Haitian ethnie-theory and Locke's reflections on the concept of 'ethnic race' discussed in the previous vignette. In different ways, all of these authors were grappling with the undeniable social and political significance of racial identities, while also seeking to challenge notions of pure racial types and racial hierarchies that were being used to justify discrimination against black Americans. During his Port-au-Prince lectures, titled *Le rôle du nègre dans la culture des Amériques*, Locke affirmed the equality of all races, placed African civilisation on par with the European, and argued that the diasporic black population of the Americas possessed a rich cultural heritage of its own – a heritage scholars were only just starting to excavate. Locke concluded the final lecture with a call for social and cultural exchange amid the black diaspora, with the goal of fostering an inclusive pan-American dialogue about democracy.[290]

Three years after Locke's lectures, the election of the black nationalist politician Dumarsais Estimé to the Haitian presidency catapulted the Griots authors to the corridors of power: Georges-Jacob was brought on as an assistant to the secretary of state for education in 1946, while Duvalier – who had by now returned from the United States – was made minister of health and labour in 1949.[291]

---

[288] Georges-Jacob 1946, 202. See also Georges-Jacob 1941, 13–16.
[289] Georges-Jacob 1946, 12–14.
[290] For the French text of the lectures, see Locke [1943] 2009. For the English text of the lectures, see Carter 2016. On Locke's visit to Haiti, see also Stewart 2018, 826–835.
[291] Nicholls 1996, 189; Smith 2009, 146.

Meanwhile, Denis and Duvalier had begun work on what would become the most important treatise of Haitian noiriste ideology, *Le problème des classes à travers l'histoire d'Haïti*. The study initially appeared in serial form in the noiriste journal *Chantiers* in 1946, with an updated version published in book format two years later. Denis and Duvalier also collaborated with Georges-Jacob and others to revive *Les Griots* as a weekly newspaper in 1948, now with the subtitle *Hebdomadaire Politico-Social*. The change in subtitle reflected a shift in the journal's focus: whereas its first incarnation had been primarily dedicated to science and literature, the new version was 'a political and social organ that dealt explicitly with the practice and application of Haitian black power'.[292] In their writings from this period, Denis and Duvalier articulated in radicalised form what David Nicholls has called the 'black legend' of the Haitian past, namely, the view that the black masses had been divided and exploited by a small mixed-race elite since the country's independence. The only solution to this state of affairs, Denis and Duvalier claimed, was the creation of a powerful and unified black class to control all areas of political and social life.[293]

In 1950, the noiristes were forced out of power by a coup d'état that ousted Estimé, sent Duvalier into hiding, and installed Paul Magloire as president. Following several years of economic hardship and political instability that undermined the authority of the Magloire regime, Duvalier made a successful return to the political stage and, after a fiercely contested election, was installed as president of Haiti in 1957. Duvalier held the presidency until his death in 1971, when he was succeeded by his son Jean-Claude. Even if many of the authoritarian policies that characterised the Duvalier years were little more than self-serving attempts to concentrate political power in the hands of his family, he did not entirely abandon the noiriste values that he had formulated together with Denis. In particular, his conflict with the Catholic Church and promotion of vodou traditions were entirely in line with the tenets of the Griots group.[294] As Nicholls suggests, Duvalier's 'general aim' once in power was 'to translate into practical policy that ideology which he had helped to develop' over the preceding decades.[295]

---

[292] Smith 2009, 105.
[293] Nicholls 1996, 194–196. See also Smith 2009, 105–106.
[294] Nicholls 1996, 212–238.   [295] Nicholls 1996, 212.

Ethnos: Travels of a Concept across Eurasia (and Beyond)

The Greek word 'ethnos' makes sporadic appearances in nineteenth-century texts that seek to define or explain the etymology of 'ethnography' and 'ethnology'. Prominent scholars to use the term include the Italian geographer Adrien Balbi in 1826,[296] the American archaeologist Daniel Brinton in 1890,[297] and the German ethnologist Adolf Bastian in 1893–1894.[298] However, it was not until the early twentieth century that the term 'ethnos' was incorporated from Greek into other European languages and elevated into a scientific concept in its own right. The key figures behind this new concept were three scholars working in the Russian Empire: Nikolai Mogilianskii, Sergei Rudenko, and Sergei Shirokogoroff.

Circumstantial evidence suggests a possible connection between Russian ethnos-theory and French ethnie-theory surveyed in the preceding vignette. To begin with, Mogilianskii, Rudenko, and Shirokogoroff were all mentored by Fiodor Volkov, a Ukrainian anthropologist who lived in Paris from 1887 to 1906. During this time, Volkov acted as a medium between French and Russian anthropology and came into contact with prominent French anthropologists such as Joseph Deniker, the first scholar to define 'groupe ethnique' in 1900.[299] Mogilianskii, Rudenko, and Shirokogoroff themselves also studied in Paris around the turn of the century, and Shirokogoroff later corresponded with Félix Regnault, the main propagator of the word 'ethnie' during the 1920s.[300] In their recent study on the development of ethnos-theory, David Anderson and Dmitry Arzyutov also point out that the term 'ethnos' was used by the French anthropologist Georges Papillault in 1908. Shirokogoroff was studying in Paris at the time and it is likely that Papillault was one of his lecturers at the École d'Anthropologie.[301] However, closer inspection of Papillault's text suggests that this link is more apparent than real: although Papillault does use the term 'ethnos' in passing, his aim was not to coin a new concept but to criticise the disciplinary labels 'ethnologie' and 'ethnographie'. Specifically, Papillault pointed out that neither discipline

---

[296] Fischer 1970, 177. [297] Brinton 1890, 100–101.
[298] Köpping 1995, 83. [299] Alymov 2019, 89–90; Richard 2012.
[300] Alymov 2019, 79; Alymov and Podrezova 2019, 175; Arzyutov 2019, 256–259; Sirina and Zakurdaev 2016, 15.
[301] Anderson et al. 2019, 743; Arzyutov 2019, 258–259.

actually had 'ethnos' or 'peuple' as its object: ethnologie was the study of 'races' while ethnographie was the study of 'civilisations'. He accordingly proposed that 'ethnologie' be renamed 'somatologie' and 'ethnographie' be renamed 'ethologie'. This last neologism Papillault derived not from 'ethnos' but from 'ethos', the Greek term for mores and customs.[302] All in all, while substantial connections and parallels do exist between French and Russian theories of ethnicity, there is no evidence of a direct link leading from one to the other. Developments in the two countries appear to have been, as Thomas Schippers puts it, 'très similaire, mais indépendant'.[303]

As with the popularisation of other ethnos-based words such as 'ethnicity' and 'ethnie', the emergence of the term 'ethnos' in the Russian Empire was closely connected to changing conceptions of race. The word 'rasa' had entered Russian academic discourse in the second half of the nineteenth century, whereafter it was used interchangeably with 'plemia' – typically rendered into English as 'tribe'.[304] Like the word 'race' in Western Europe, 'rasa' and 'plemia' had both a global and a local meaning in turn-of-the-century Russia. In the global or universalistic sense, these terms referred to human groups differentiated by physical characteristics such as skin colour, thus dividing humanity into a handful of racial or tribal groups associated with the major continental land masses. In contrast, the local or particularistic meaning of these terms was more ambiguous and flexible, encompassing a broad range of groups of various sizes such as the Slavs, the Poles, the Ukrainians, or the Jews.[305]

Against this backdrop, two contrasting approaches to the race concept emerged among Russian scholars at the beginning of the twentieth century, one developed by anthropologists based in Moscow and the other by ethnographers based in St Petersburg. According to the Moscow-based group, the polyvalence of the terms 'rasa' and 'plemia' called for a much clearer distinction between the biological and sociocultural spheres.[306] The following statement from Dmitrii Anuchin – the most prominent member of the group – is exemplary:

Race indicators do not coincide with tribal or national ones (language, religion, mode of life, belonging to a particular state); among the same

---

[302] Papillault 1908, 127, 131.   [303] Schippers 2009, 29.
[304] Mogilner 2013, 8.   [305] Avrutin 2007, 15.
[306] Mogilner 2013, 8–9, 133–164.

people there can be representatives of different race types, or representatives of another race can be part of different tribes and peoples (narodnostei). Race types are more or less abstract concepts of [physical] traits.[307]

Meanwhile, in St Petersburg, a very different understanding of the race concept was emerging under Fiodor Volkov's influence. After returning from Paris in 1906, Volkov worked at the Russian Museum in St Petersburg and from January 1907 lectured in anthropology and ethnography at St Petersburg University. Whereas the Moscow-based anthropologists wanted to clearly distinguish races from nations and tribes, the ethnographers associated with the Russian Museum tended to conflate these categories; by the same token, they were sceptical of any disciplinary hierarchy between anthropology and ethnography. For example, Volkov's own research focused on his native Ukraine and used ethnographical data to theorise a pure and homogeneous Ukrainian anthropological type.[308] To justify his approach, Volkov invoked the authority of the Société d'Anthropologie de Paris, which likewise subsumed the study of human culture under the physical study of the human species.[309] Unsurprisingly, Volkov's work was criticised by Anuchin for 'mixing up *narodnost* (or *narod*), tribe, and race – notions that differ significantly'.[310]

Charged with a lack of terminological rigour by their Moscow-based rivals, a number of ethnographers associated with Volkov and the Russian Museum sought to develop a more 'scientific' conceptualisation of their object of study. It was against this backdrop that 'ethnos' emerged as an alternative to existing categories such as 'narod' (people) and 'narodnost' (nationality). The new term was first proposed by Nikolai Mogilianskii, a Ukrainian ethnographer and archaeologist working as curator at the Russian Museum, during a meeting of the Anthropological Society of St Petersburg University in 1902.

---

[307] Anuchin, quoted in Mogilner 2013, 133.
[308] Mogilner 2013, 93–98, 213–216.
[309] Alymov, Anderson, and Arzyutov 2019, 32–33.
[310] Anuchin, quoted in Mogilner 2013, 214. See also Alymov 2019, 117–121. The Russian 'narod' is typically rendered into English as 'people' or 'nation'. The Russian 'narodnost' corresponds to the old meaning of the English 'nationality' and the French 'nationalité' before these terms became synonymous with citizenship; the term 'narodnost' thus refers primarily to linguistic or cultural identity and is often translated as 'ethnicity' today. See Cadiot 2007, 13–14; Knight 2000; Miller 2008.

Mogilianskii's lecture, published in 1908, did not contain a detailed explication of the term.[311] A fuller elaboration of the concept had to wait until 1916, by which time Mogilianskii had become head of ethnography at the museum:

> The ἔθνος concept – is a complex idea. It is a group of individuals united together as a single whole by [...] common physical (anthropological) characteristics; a common historical fate, and finally a common language – which is the foundation upon which, in turn [an ethnos] can build a common worldview [and] folk-psychology – in short, an entire spiritual culture.[312]

Mogilianskii spelt the term 'ethnos' in Greek letters to emphasise its scientific credentials and the need for trained experts to identify and investigate ethnoses. Like Volkov, with whom he had become close friends during their time in Paris, Mogilianskii rejected any clear-cut distinction between the biological and sociocultural spheres. An ethnos was to be understood as a biosocial totality, and studying an ethnos therefore required the consideration of physical and biological alongside social and cultural factors.

The nascent development of ethnos-theory in the Russian Empire was stumped by the Bolshevik Revolution of 1917. Mogilianskii himself went into exile, moving first to Kiev in 1918, then to Paris in 1920, and finally to Prague in 1923. Although he continued to teach and publish until his death in 1933, he seems to have become a marginal figure in the subsequent dissemination of the ethnos concept.[313] With Mogilianskii out of the country, it was Sergei Rudenko – another Ukrainian anthropologist and student of Volkov – who became the main advocate of ethnos-theory in the 1920s.[314] After the Stalinist clamp-down on ethnography in 1928, however, the concept of ethnos came under ideological criticism for divorcing ethnic phenomena from the socioeconomic base and thus precluding the historical-materialist analysis of human societies.[315] Many leading ethnographers were purged and Rudenko himself was arrested in 1930, although there is no direct evidence that the arrest was linked to his scholarly views.[316] The ethnos concept was subsequently kept alive in oral discussions

---

[311] Alymov, Anderson, and Arzyutov 2019, 30–33; Cadiot 2007, 104–109.
[312] Mogilianskii, quoted in Alymov 2019, 103.   [313] Alymov 2019, 79.
[314] Hirsch 2005, 196–197, 206.
[315] Alymov, Anderson, and Arzyutov 2019, 39–40; Sirina et al. 2016, 35.
[316] Alymov and Podrezova 2019, 183.

The Emergence of Ethnicity 137

during seminars and private conversations, but it disappeared from printed texts and would not resurface in the Soviet Union until the 1960s (see Chapter 3).[317]

With the exile of Mogilianskii and the marginalisation of Rudenko, the subsequent propagation of ethnos-theory primarily took place through the work of the Russian anthropologist Sergei Shirokogoroff. Mentored by Volkov at the Russian Museum, Shirokogoroff first began to develop the ethnos concept around 1912 while conducting ethnographical research in Siberia.[318] With the escalation of political instability in St Petersburg, Shirokogoroff relocated permanently to the Far East in 1917. He initially found work as a lecturer and anti-Bolshevik political activist in Vladivostok, where he resided from 1918 to 1922, before moving briefly to Japan and finally settling in China.[319] In a curious coincidence, the Swiss medical doctor and amateur anthropologist George Montandon – who would later become the most prominent ethnie-theorist in France – also spent time in Vladivostok between 1919 and 1922 as a delegate of the International Red Cross.[320] However, there is no evidence that the two men had any contact.

Shirokogoroff first outlined his theory of ethnos in a pamphlet published in Vladivostok in 1922, followed by a book-length study published in Shanghai in 1923, both written in Russian.[321] He subsequently also published extracts and summaries of his theory in English and French.[322] Echoing Mogilianskii's definition of ethnos, Shirokogoroff incorporated both biological and sociocultural criteria into his theory. In 1924, Shirokogoroff's first English-language publication on the topic offered the following definition of an ethnos: 'a unit in which all processes of cultural and somatological variations of man as species (or genus) operate and which is understood by itself as a group of people united by the idea of unity of origin, customs, language and technical culture'.[323] Shirokogoroff described an ethnos as a 'biological species' comparable to animal species and referred to its 'biological power' as a key factor in its survival.[324] Although he viewed an ethnos as a concrete biosocial entity, Shirokogoroff did not

[317] Alymov, Anderson, and Arzyutov 2019, 44.
[318] Anderson 2019a, 206–208.   [319] Arzyutov 2019, 259–281.
[320] Piana 2016.   [321] Anderson et al. 2019, 745.
[322] Shirokogoroff 1924, 1931, 1933, 1935, 1936.   [323] Shirokogoroff 1924, 27.
[324] Shirokogoroff 1924, 7.

succumb to simplistic typological thinking. He repeatedly emphasised that an ethnos was a dynamic entity that emerged out of biological and sociocultural processes of differentiation and that experienced periods of growth and decline. 'Although the ethnos as a unit may be a concrete physical phenomenon, consisting of physical individuals, where the processes are going on it is not a static phenomenon, and thus it cannot be expressed in static terms', Shirokogoroff explained. 'The conception of this phenomenon must be as one of a process covering more or less numerous units and is thus dynamic and not static.'[325]

Shirokogoroff's 1931 publication, *Ethnological and Linguistical Aspects of the Ural – Altaic Hypothesis*, is significant as it is the only text (published or unpublished) where he compares his concept of ethnos to Félix Regnault's concept of ethnie and Ferdinand de Saussure's concept of ethnisme.[326] Shirokogoroff emphasised two key differences between himself and the Francophone theorists. First, in contrast to Regnault and Saussure's emphasis on language as the key differentiating factor, Shirokogoroff conceived of an ethnos as a biosocial totality. Second, Shirokogoroff considered Regnault and Saussure's definition of ethnic units to be much too static and proposed his own processual understanding of ethnos as a dynamic alternative.[327] 'These two instances suffice to show that such a term was needed,' Shirokogoroff explained, 'but it ought to be given a more elastic, more definite, dynamic meaning, and it ought not to be confined to the language or ethnographic complex only.'[328] Shirokogoroff also compared his theory to French ethnologist Arnold van Gennep's work on 'nationalité', but concluded that the terms 'nationalité' and 'nationality' should be reserved for phenomena relating specifically to the nation, as opposed to ethnic phenomena in general.[329]

From 1922 until his death in 1939, Shirokogoroff lived and worked in China, moving from university to university on short-term contracts.[330] His ethnos-theory thus matured in an unstable political context in which China was transforming from an empire into a nation-state. Part and parcel of this transformation was the translation of European political and scientific concepts into Chinese, often via

---

[325] Shirokogoroff 1931, 12.   [326] Anderson 2019a, 207.
[327] Shirokogoroff 1931, 12–14.   [328] Shirokogoroff 1931, 14.
[329] Shirokogoroff 1931, 14–15.   [330] Arzyutov 2019, 274–281.

The Emergence of Ethnicity

Japanese. Of particular significance was the coinage of the term 'minzu' in the 1890s as the Chinese equivalent of the Japanese 'minzoku', which was itself a neologism coined to translate the German 'Volk'.[331] Akin to the amorphous concept of Volk from which they derived, 'minzoku' and 'minzu' were highly malleable terms that could be used in a number of different ways. James Leibold explains:

> Much like minzoku in Japan, minzu provided a linguistic 'chameleon' in China, coming to index a 'surplus of meanings' related to group identity. In early twentieth-century China (and arguably today), minzu connoted a cluster of meanings and associations similar to those captured in English by race, nation, people, ethnic group, and nationality.[332]

Shirokogoroff played an important role in the development of early Chinese anthropology and, by implication, also in the articulation of the minzu concept. His most prominent student was the pioneer of Chinese anthropology Fei Xiaotong, who drew on Shirokogoroff's ethnos-theory to argue for a dynamic and situational definition of minzu.[333] Through these intellectual exchanges, the concepts of ethnos and minzu became inextricably entangled. By the 1930s, as Anderson and Arzyutov observe, 'it is no longer quite clear whether Shirokogoroff imported his romantic ideas of ethnic equilibrium to China or whether he became one of the most prominent exporters of early *minzu*-talk to Western Europe'.[334]

Shirokogoroff also cultivated connections in Japan, where he had briefly resided in 1922, and visited the country again in 1933 and 1935. The most prominent Japanese theorist of minzoku or ethnos was Oka Masao, a leading figure in the establishment of ethnology in Japan. Oka had studied in Vienna from 1929 to 1935 and came into contact with Shirokogoroff's ethnos-theory indirectly through the work of the German ethnologist Wilhelm Mühlmann.[335] In addition to these concrete historical entanglements between ethnos, minzu, and minzoku, there is also an interesting etymological parallel worth noting: the root of both the Japanese 'minzoku' and the Chinese 'minzu' is the ancient Chinese 'min', which – akin to the ancient

---

[331] Bastid-Bruguière 2004; Leibold 2007, 8.   [332] Leibold 2007, 8.
[333] Guldin 1994, 44–46; Leibold 2007, 132; Sirina and Zakurdaev 2016, 18–22.
[334] Anderson et al. 2019, 745.
[335] Anderson et al. 2019, 765–766. See also Steger 2019.

Greek 'ethnos' – signified 'people' in the broadest sense of this term.[336] The turn-of-the-century emergence of ethnos-based words in the West thus finds a counterpart in the rise of min-based words in the East.

Shirokogoroff's ideas were widely disseminated through his multilingual publications and lively correspondence. He even sent unsolicited copies of his work to Franz Boas, hoping to find work in the United States.[337] In the Francophone world, as we have seen, Shirokogoroff's publications were read and cited by ethnie-theorists ranging from George Montandon and Jacques Boulenger in France to Lorimer Denis and François Duvalier in Haiti. In the United Kingdom, Shirokogoroff's most prominent correspondents were Arthur Keith and George Pitt-Rivers – the former a Scottish anatomist and proponent of scientific racism, the latter an English eugenicist and Nazi sympathiser. It seems likely that the occasional use of the term 'ethnos' by these two British scholars was due to their exchanges with Shirokogoroff.

In the writings of Arthur Keith, the term 'ethnos' can be found in the title of his 1931 book *Ethnos: Or the Problem of Race Considered from a New Point of View*. This is the only written appearance of 'ethnos' in Keith's work: throughout the main body of the book as well as in his other publications, Keith opted for 'race' and 'nation' instead. It is interesting to see, however, that his understanding of these terms changed substantially over time. In his early work, Keith adopted a restrictive definition of race as an anthropological category that had little or no overlap with the concept of the nation. 'In the strict sense in which the anthropologist uses the term "Race" there is in Europe no racial problem', he explained in 1919. 'Our universal disturbances are those of nationality.'[338] By the beginning of the 1930s, however, Keith had shifted his position to the point where he viewed race and nation as a continuum. 'Nation-building is the first step in race-building', he explained in *Ethnos*.[339] Race prejudice, Keith argued, was an evolutionary mechanism intended to encourage 'the production of higher and better races of Mankind'.[340] It is likely that the broadening of Keith's conception of race during the late 1920s and 1930s was due to Shirokogoroff's influence, with whom Keith had initiated a

---

[336] Burtscher 2012, 47. [337] Anderson et al. 2019, 748; Arzyutov 2019, 266.
[338] Keith 1919, 18. [339] Keith 1931a, 83. [340] Keith 1931b, 35.

correspondence from 1925.[341] Thereafter, Keith's flexible concept of race began to function as an equivalent of Shirokogoroff's biosocial concept of ethnos. Shirokogoroff himself was proud of the recognition he received from the Scotsman and valued Keith's opinion highly.[342] He did, however, criticise Keith for conflating the ethnical concept of race with the political concept of the nation: '[I]n the hands of Sir A. Keith, the application of the theory of ethnos to nations was a source of some defects in his outline of the process of evolution of human races. When one wants to use the theory of ethnos, the distinction between the ethnical units and nations must be very sharp.'[343]

The other prominent British scholar with whom Shirokogoroff exchanged letters was the notorious English eugenicist George Pitt-Rivers. Akin to Keith, Pitt-Rivers seems to have preferred a flexible definition of 'race' over Shirokogoroff's 'ethnos', as the latter makes only a handful of appearances in his writings. In a paper read out during a meeting of the Royal Anthropological Institute in 1926, for example, Pitt-Rivers used the word 'ethnos' twice to refer to the racial and cultural constitution of a population.[344] The views he expressed in the paper resonated with those of Keith, who was sitting in the audience, and the two men subsequently became lifelong friends.[345] The following year Pitt-Rivers published *The Clash of Culture and the Contact of Races*. Although the book featured a reference to Shirokogoroff's *Ethnical Unit and Milieu* in a footnote,[346] the word 'ethnos' only appears in the index and redirects the reader to 'race'. The term 'race' was defined broadly as 'ethnic identity and distinction – however determined – without necessarily involving the difficult and uncertain question of ethnic origin'.[347] Pitt-Rivers also cited Shirokogoroff in support of his proposals to set up an international eugenicist organisation under the auspices of the League of Nations.[348] Although Pitt-Rivers's thought was animated by a virulent strain of antisemitism, this did not stop him from achieving considerable academic success during the 1920s. It was only in the 1930s, when he began to fraternise with the British Union of Fascists and publicly endorsed Adolf Hitler, that his reputation

---

[341] Anderson et al. 2019, 748.
[342] Anderson et al. 2019; Arzyutov 2019, 277–278.
[343] Shirokogoroff 1935, 20.   [344] Pitt-Rivers 1927b, 3, 4.
[345] Hart 2015, 58–59.   [346] Pitt-Rivers 1927a, 101n.
[347] Pitt-Rivers 1927a, 5.   [348] Anderson et al. 2019, 748.

crumbled.[349] Although there are some indications of antisemitism in Shirokogoroff's own writings, these pale in comparison to Pitt-Rivers. And while Shirokogoroff did express an interest in translating his theory into practice, he seems to have remained reticent about embracing eugenics.[350]

The unsavoury linkages between ethnos-theory and scientific racism continue through Shirokogoroff's correspondence with a number of German ethnologists in the Third Reich, culminating in an invited visit to Berlin in the winter of 1935–1936.[351] Among his contacts in Germany was the aforementioned ethnologist Wilhelm Mühlmann, who has been described as 'the most influential and most intelligent Nazi ideologist of academic *Völkerkunde*'.[352] The main objective of Mühlmann's work was to engender a paradigm shift in German ethnology by overcoming the distinction between nature and culture. This was to be accomplished through the multivalent concept of 'Volk' or 'Ethnos' (terms that he used interchangeably).[353] Although Mühlmann emphasised that the biological concept of race was very different from the ethnological concept of Volk or Ethnos, he also maintained that these concepts could not be fully separated. Echoing George Montandon's subsumption of race under ethnie, Mühlmann insisted that the concept of race was to be incorporated into the totalising concept of Volk or Ethnos: 'Der Vorgang der Rassenbildung verläuft innerhalb des Ethnos.'[354] In addition to developing his own racialised version of ethnos-theory, Mühlmann also translated a chapter of Shirokogoroff's *Psychomental Complex of the Tungus* into German and published a high-profile obituary for his pen pal in 1940.[355] He would continue to draw on Shirokogoroff's ethnos-theory in his post-war works.[356]

Finally, through its impact on German ethnology, Shirokogoroff's ethnos-theory also indirectly contributed to the development of South African anthropology under the apartheid regime. Many South African anthropologists studied in Germany during the 1930s, where they were exposed to the work of Mühlmann and his contemporaries.

---

[349] Hart 2015, 4–5.
[350] Anderson et al. 2019, 748, 758, 768; Arzyutov 2019, 259, 279–280.
[351] Anderson et al. 2019, 748, 768. [352] Gingrich 2005, 131–132.
[353] Mühlmann 1938, 1–8, 227–240. See also Gingrich 2005, 132–133.
[354] Mühlmann 1938, 236. [355] Anderson et al. 2019, 748.
[356] For example, Mühlmann 1964.

In Afrikaans-medium universities, many South African anthropologists adopted the ethnos as their primary unit of analysis, conceptualising it as a 'social-organic' entity united by common descent as well as culture.[357] In a unique twist, South African scholars infused Mühlmann's ethnos-theory with theological ideas, whereby 'God brings each ethnos into being in particular historical and geographical circumstances and gives to each a calling'.[358] As Shirokogoroff's ideas were translated via Mühlmann into the South African context, his original emphasis on the dynamism of the ethnos was almost entirely lost.[359] In the hands of South African anthropologists, an ethnos became 'an entity whose essential characteristics were fixed in time and space and could therefore be taken for granted'.[360] Politically, this static version of ethnos-theory served as a justification for the policy of separate development of South African ethnic groups.[361]

Summary

The trajectories of the ethnos-based terms recounted in the above vignettes are obviously very different, reflecting the particular historical context in which each of them was articulated. There is also substantial variation in the meaning of each individual word, depending on the author using it. Nevertheless, at least two important commonalities stand out. The first is the highly ambivalent position that all of these ethnos-based terms occupied between race and culture. The relationship between these terms is reducible neither to a binary logic of either/or nor to a synthesising logic of both/and: the former would imply that ethnicity is *either* race *or* culture, while the latter would imply that ethnicity is *both* race *and* culture. Instead, the concept of ethnicity follows a more complex logic of and/or that superimposes these alternatives over one another: ethnicity is *either* race *or* culture while simultaneously being *both* race *and* culture.[362] Hence why ethnicity tends to be read as a synonym of race when compared to culture, but as a synonym of culture when compared to race. This polysemy of ethnicity reflects its historical and structural function as a residual category that was devised to plug the emerging rift between

---

[357] Sharp 1980, 4. See also Sharp 1981; Skalník 1988. [358] Sharp 1981, 23.
[359] Sharp 1981, 32–33. [360] Evans 1997, 228. [361] Evans 1997, 225–234.
[362] On the plural logic of and/or, see Weber 2016, 40–41.

race and culture. On the one hand, due to its liminal position between race and culture, the concept of ethnicity contains an excess of meaning that problematises any straightforward either/or choice between these concepts. On the other hand, given that the concept of ethnicity emerges precisely at the moment where race and culture are coming apart, it cannot be understood as a simple amalgam of the two either. Ethnicity is the bridge that links race and culture together while also marking out their separation.

The plural logic of and/or complicates the familiar antiracist narrative, which takes the adoption of the term 'ethnic group' by the United Nations to symbolise the triumph of liberalism over racism, of good over evil. By juxtaposing the new concept of ethnicity to the problematic and controversial concept of race, the post-war liberal consensus sought to present ethnicity, in the words of Ashley Montagu, as 'a noncontaminating neutral concept'.[363] While this antiracist reading of ethnicity's history is not entirely wrong, it glosses over the racist applications of ethnos-based terms throughout the 1930s and 1940s. Situated ambiguously between race and culture, the concept of ethnicity could be mobilised not only to dismantle, but also to reinforce and rearticulate racist theories and practices. In this regard, the connections between the new ethnos-based terms and conceptions of Volk in Nazi Germany are worth re-emphasising: Wilhelm Mühlmann explicitly equated Ethnos with Volk, while Hans Günther maintained a friendly correspondence with Georges Vacher de Lapouge and George Montandon. In Montandon's hands, the term 'ethnie' became not only an intellectual device for justifying discriminatory policies without resorting to outdated notions of racial types, but also a practical tool in aiding the Vichy regime's persecution of Jews. Although further research is needed into the entanglement of ethnicity and Volk in the German context, these examples are already sufficient to invalidate any simplistic equation of ethnicity with antiracism. The connections between ethnicity and racism run much deeper than the liberal orthodoxy of the post-war era would like to admit.

The second important commonality among the new ethnos-based terms that emerged in the early twentieth century is that they were all articulated with reference to the particularistic or domestic meaning of race qua nationality, while neglecting the universalistic or global

---

[363] Montagu 1972, 71.

meaning of race as a major division of humanity. This is evidenced by the silence over colonialism in all four vignettes, as well as the overriding preoccupation with the status of the Jews at the expense of black Americans or colonial subjects. Indeed, many of the key figures behind the dissemination of the ethnos-based words were either Jewish themselves, as were Isaac Berkson and Ashley Montagu, or of antisemitic bent, as were George Montandon and George Pitt-Rivers. Even in the relatively few cases when the concept of ethnicity was taken up by black authors or activists, such as the Black Power movement in the United States or the Griots group in Haiti, this tended to be in the service of nationalist projects: the Black Power movement's reconceptualisation of black American identity as a form of ethnic identity underpinned claims for the creation of an autonomous black-majority nation, while the Griots group reappropriated French ethnie-theory to promote a racialised understanding of the Haitian nation. Time and again, the concept of ethnicity was understood in local and particularistic terms, having little or no relation to the global stratification of the human species. This pattern is also reflected in the discrepancy between the number of races and the number of ethnic groups that are said to inhabit the world: whereas theorists of race rarely invoked more than a handful of major categories, the corresponding figure for ethnic groups is easily in the hundreds. The *Harvard Encyclopedia of American Ethnic Groups*, for instance, identifies over 100 ethnic groups in the United States alone.[364] The concept of ethnicity was invented in the twentieth century with an eye on managing the nation-state's internal others, while eliding imperial hierarchies and global racial inequalities.

Conceptualising Racism

'It might be said,' George Fredrickson writes, 'that the concept of racism emerges only when the concept of race, or at least some of its applications, begin to be questioned.'[365] The same, as we have seen, can also be said about ethnicity: the concept of ethnicity emerges only when the concept of race, or at least some of its applications, begin to be questioned. In this sense, the concept of ethnicity is historically and logically coupled to the concept of racism. To explore

---

[364] Thernstrom 1980. [365] Fredrickson 2002, 156.

these connections further, this section traces how the critique of the race concept and its supplementation by the concept of ethnicity in the first half of the twentieth century were accompanied by the articulation of three distinct conceptions of racism: a liberal understanding of racism as an individual pathology, a systemic conception of racism as a structural feature of modern society, and a new cultural racism that no longer requires the concept of race as its ground.

The threefold conceptualisation of racism that emerged in the twentieth century was symptomatic of the aporetic double movement of sublation, where negation and preservation remain in an unresolved tension. In Hegelian terms, the liberal response to racism is the movement of negation, seeking to erase the stain of racism from civil society by marginalising the concept of race and adopting a colourblind approach to politics. The systemic conception of racism is the flipside of the liberal response, affirming the reality of race and racism as sociological phenomena even in the absence of outspoken racists: from the systemic perspective, racism cannot be eliminated through a colourblind approach alone but also requires policies of affirmative action to rectify deeply entrenched structural inequalities. Finally, from within the interstices of this double movement there emerges a new differentialist form of racism that eludes both the liberal and systemic conceptions. This 'ethnic' or 'cultural' conception of racism is neither the racism of racists denounced by liberals nor the racism without racists denounced by critics of systemic racism, but a racism without races that follows from the ethnicisation of the world.

The Liberal Concept of Racism

In the French language, the earliest uses of the terms 'racisme' and 'raciste' can be traced to the turn of the twentieth century. The meaning of these new terms was highly ambivalent, with French nationalists also using them as positive self-designators to underline their belief in the French race and the need to protect this race from degeneration.[366] From this perspective, 'to be "racist" was to be "truly French"'.[367] A more critical use of the new vocabulary began to take hold during

---

[366] Taguieff 2001, 85–87.   [367] Miles and Brown 2003, 58.

the 1920s with German nationalism as the main point of reference. Thus, in a lengthy study of the formation of races published in 1922, the librarian of the Belgian colonial ministry Théophile Simar used the term 'racisme' to denounce prevalent theories of Germanic superiority – an argument likely provoked by Germany's 'rape of Belgium' during the First World War.[368] Around the same time, the term 'raciste' was popularised as a translation of the German 'völkisch', serving as a derogatory label to denounce the extremist politics of the German nationalist right.[369] In this context, even the aforementioned French nationalists began to distance themselves from the concept of racism. Thus, an article published in the French right-wing newspaper *Action française* in 1927 equated 'racisme' with xenophobia, bellicosity, imperialism, and pan-Germanism. Through this 'polemical lumping together' of various derogatory designations, French nationalism came to be defined in opposition to German racism.[370] However, it would take another decade and a half for this antiracist discourse to establish itself as the hegemonic conception of racism. During the Second World War, as we saw in the previous section, French collaborationists such as George Montandon still advocated for a vigorous French 'ethnoracisme' as the best way to protect the French nation from unchecked miscegenation.[371] It was only through the work of UNESCO in the post-war years that the meaning of 'racisme' was finally stabilised as a misguided prejudice that could be overcome through individual education and a universal politics of humanity.[372]

In the English language, a number of precursors to 'racism' also appear around the turn of the century, including 'race-pride', 'race-rivalry', and 'race-antagonism'.[373] Of particular note here is the term 'racialism', which began to make regular appearances during the 1910s and was used by British writers to describe a dangerous form of nationalism associated with German militarism and the outbreak of the First World War.[374] This meaning of 'racialism' persisted into the

---

[368] Fredrickson 2002, 158–159.
[369] Taguieff 2001, 88–90. For example, Lichtenberger 1923, 53.
[370] Taguieff 2001, 93.   [371] Knobel 1988, 108–110; Staum 2011, 202–203.
[372] Balibar 2008, 1633.   [373] Lorimer 2005, 123–124.
[374] For example, Muir 1919, 45; Toynbee 1918, 557; Urquhart 1916, 59. Lorimer (2005, 124–125) has also noted an earlier use of 'racialism' in South Africa in 1907, when the term was used by British settlers to denounce Afrikaner nationalism. The earliest recorded appearance of the term is from the late

inter-war years. In 1935, for example, Julian Huxley and Alfred Cort Haddon denounced the 'violent racialism' spreading through Europe as 'a myth, and a dangerous myth at that'.[375] In 1926, the derivative 'racialist' was used by the American sociologist Frank Hankins in a book titled *The Racial Basis of Civilization*. Like many of his contemporaries, Hankins attacked theories of Germanic superiority, yet failed to extend this egalitarian ethos to black Americans or colonial subjects. Thus, even as he criticised the claims of racial purity put forward by the so-called 'racialists', Hankins also objected to 'the equally perverse and doctrinaire contentions of the race egalitarians'.[376]

The word 'racism' itself began to make regular appearances in the English language during the 1930s and 1940s, primarily in response to the racial policies implemented by the Third Reich. It was against this backdrop, for example, that the Jewish-German sexologist Magnus Hirschfeld used the word 'racism' in the title of a book manuscript written in 1933–1934. An outspoken advocate of gay liberation and critic of scientific racism, Hirschfeld was stripped of his German citizenship in 1934 and exiled to France, where he died of a stroke a year later.[377] His book manuscript, titled *Rassismus* in German, was translated into English as *Racism* and published posthumously in 1938. The terms 'racism' and 'racist' can be found interspersed throughout the text, which also called for the establishment of a 'League for the Prevention of Racism'.[378] Echoing contemporaries such as Julian Huxley and Ashley Montagu, Hirschfeld emphasised the unsound scientific basis of the race concept as well as its 'multifarious' and 'conflicting' meanings.[379] 'If it were practicable,' Hirschfeld wrote, 'we should certainly do well to eradicate the use of the word "race" as far as subdivisions of the human species are concerned.'[380]

Hirschfeld's book failed to garner a wide readership.[381] Still, the liberal concept of racism that he helped to articulate in the 1930s would gain widespread currency with the outbreak of the Second World War. Especially significant for the dissemination of the new

nineteenth century. See the entry for 'racialism' in the *Oxford English Dictionary*, available online at www.oed.com (last accessed 6 July 2023).
[375] Huxley and Haddon 1935, 287. [376] Hankins 1926, ix.
[377] Dose 2014; Mancini 2010. [378] Hirschfeld 1938, 263.
[379] Hirschfeld 1938, 54. [380] Hirschfeld 1938, 57.
[381] Dose 2014, 10; Fredrickson 2002, 163.

concept was Ruth Benedict's *Race: Science and Politics*, an influential and popular book published in numerous editions during and after the war. Trained as an anthropologist under Franz Boas, Benedict's scholarship on race was defined by a critique of racial hierarchy and a clear separation of hereditary biological traits from acquired cultural characteristics. By the time Modern Age Books approached Benedict to write an accessible book on race in the late 1930s, she had already established a reputation as a leading American anthropologist and advocate of cultural tolerance. Benedict initially wanted to call the book *Race and Racism*, but the publisher asked her to change the title, noting that 'racism' was not a commonly known term. In defending her original title, Benedict underlined that the 'special point of the book' was 'its complete separation of Race from Racism'.[382] This was reflected in the organisation of the book into two sections, the first on 'Race' and the second on 'Racism'. The former, Benedict argued, was 'a scientific field of inquiry' whose 'special problem is that of genetic relationships of human groups'.[383] Racism, by contrast, was a 'superstition' or 'dogma' centred on a belief in the inequality of races and the idealisation of racial purity: 'Racism is essentially a pretentious way of saying that "I" belong to the Best People.'[384] Benedict's critique of racism was echoed by other influential thinkers and public intellectuals during and after the war, entrenching the concept in the wider social consciousness.[385]

A salient and recurring theme in all of the above examples is the association of racism with an aggressive version of German nationalism and doctrines of Germanic superiority. Put bluntly, racism was conceptualised as an intra-white issue. One of the few scholars to apply the concept more broadly was the French-born American-educated historian Jacques Barzun in his 1938 book *Race: A Study of Modern Superstition*. Although Barzun described the Third Reich as 'the most blatant apostle of racialism', he recognised that the phenomenon of was not limited to German attitudes toward Jews; it also lay behind the assumption that 'the whites are unquestionably superior to the colored races' and that 'the great American problem is to keep the

---

[382] Benedict, quoted in Anderson 2019b, 95. See also Caffrey 1989, 282–301. The version of the book published in the United Kingdom in 1942 used Benedict's original title. See Benedict 1942.
[383] Benedict 1940, 151.   [384] Benedict 1940, 152–153.
[385] For example, Arendt 1944; Montagu 1945.

Anglo-Saxon race pure from the contamination of Negro (or Southern European, or Jewish) "blood".[386] Yet Barzun belonged to a small minority of Western scholars who appreciated the full scale of the subject. Advocates of global racial equality remained few and far between, even among outspoken critics of the Third Reich, and the treatment of non-white groups and colonial subjects generally fell beyond their purview.[387] During the inter-war years, it was just as common for the term 'racialism' to be used with reference to anti-imperialist movements as European imperialism. 'Virtually every anti-imperialist outburst,' as Frank Füredi reminds us, 'would be interpreted through the vocabulary of anti-white racialism.'[388]

After 1945, the Holocaust became the paradigmatic case for bounding the concept of racism. Racism thus came to be understood as an extreme phenomenon, an aberration in the fabric of the international order rather than an integral feature thereof. This exceptionalist and Eurocentric definition of racism was reinforced by the work of UNESCO, which opted to challenge the scientific concept of race on its own terms, criticising it for being unscientific and thus positing 'an *a priori* separation between "race" and politics'.[389] By conceptualising racism as an individual pathology based on pseudoscientific knowledge, the UNESCO approach implied that racism could be addressed through education at the level of the individual, without questioning the role of national or global structures of power.[390] Once this exceptionalist and Eurocentric concept of racism was established with the Holocaust as its privileged point of reference, it could subsequently be expanded to encompass other experiences, such as racial segregation in the United States and the apartheid in South Africa. Through a process of often retrospective incorporation, these other experiences of racism were moulded to fit the template provided by the paradigmatic case of the Holocaust: the exception rather than the norm. Overcoming each of these particular instances of racism in turn justifies the liberal narrative of progress toward a 'post-racial' world. Like the concept of ethnicity to which it is historically and logically coupled, the liberal concept of racism is directed at the particularistic logic of self-racialisation, of which the Jewish experience and the Holocaust are paradigmatic, while

---

[386] Barzun 1938, 6–7. See also Fredrickson 2002, 163–165.
[387] Füredi 1998, 6–9.   [388] Füredi 1998, 131. See also Tinker 1977, 131.
[389] Lentin 2005, 383.   [390] Lentin 2005, 383–389.

neglecting the universalistic logic of other-racialisation, of which the black experience and colonial rule are paradigmatic. In this way, as Barnor Hesse writes, 'the concept of racism is doubly-bound into revealing (nationalism) and concealing (liberalism), foregrounding (sub-humanism) and foreclosing (non-Europeanism), affirming (extremist ideology) and denying (routine governmentality)'.[391]

The Systemic Concept of Racism

The liberal concept of racism, which views racism as an exception or pathology, was subjected to criticism from its inception. Already in the 1940s, the Trinidadian-American sociologist Oliver Cox challenged Ruth Benedict's conceptualisation of 'racism' as 'a racial ideology or philosophy of racial superiority'. The problem with Benedict's definition, Cox argued, was that it focused on 'an idea' rather than 'social facts and situations'.[392] 'This is the kind of approach,' Cox wrote, 'which unwittingly deflects the view from the real impersonal causes of race prejudice.'[393] In particular, the understanding of racism as an ideological dogma overlooked how 'modern race relations developed out of the imperialistic practices of capitalism'.[394] For these reasons, Cox preferred to stick to older terms such as 'race relations' and 'race antagonism' – terms that he deemed more attuned to the social and material substratum of racism.[395]

Meanwhile, other black antiracist thinkers such as W. E. B. Du Bois, Aimé Césaire, and Frantz Fanon underlined the parallels between the atrocities committed by the Third Reich and those sanctioned by European colonial powers: dehumanisation and slavery were recurring features of colonial rule, while concentration camps were first used on the African continent.[396] According to these scholars, the reason why the experience of the Second World War was so shocking for the European consciousness had less to do with the horrific practices themselves than with the fact that these practices were now being carried out on European soil: '[T]hey tolerated that Nazism before it was inflicted on them,' Césaire wrote in 1955, 'they absolved it, shut their eyes to it, legitimized it, because, until then, it had been applied only to non-European peoples.'[397] The following year, Fanon described the racial

---

[391] Hesse 2004, 14. [392] Cox 1948, 482. See also Cox 1944.
[393] Cox 1948, 480. [394] Cox 1948, 483. [395] Anderson 2019b, 20.
[396] Hesse 2004, 19–20. [397] Césaire 1955, 36.

policies of the Third Reich as the establishment of a colonial regime in the heart of Europe: 'l'institution d'un régime colonial en pleine terre d'Europe'.[398] With the persistence of European colonial rule into the post-war years, Césaire denounced the 'pseudo-humanism' of the victors as 'narrow and fragmentary, incomplete and biased and, all things considered, sordidly racist'.[399] Crucially, the goal of these anticolonial thinkers was not simply to incorporate colonial rule into the Eurocentric concept of racism as yet another particular case, but to challenge the very concept of racism by foregrounding how racism was constitutive of modern society. 'Le racisme n'est jamais un élément surajouté découvert au hasard d'une recherche au sein des données culturelles d'un groupe', Fanon insisted. 'La constellation sociale, l'ensemble culturel sont profondément remaniés par l'existence du racisme.'[400]

Against the liberal desire to purify modern universals by extracting and expunging racism therefrom, the systemic conception views racism as constitutive of those universals. On the semantic level, this is manifest in the critical practice of appending 'racial' to supposedly universal and culture-neutral categories. Thus, the social contract is shown to be underpinned by a 'racial contract',[401] the modern territorial state is unmasked as a 'racial state',[402] capitalism is recast as 'racial capitalism',[403] and sovereignty is rethought through the lens of 'racial sovereignty'.[404] A similar emphasis on the constitutive power of racism informs Eduardo Bonilla-Silva's influential conception of 'systemic racism' as a set of 'practices and behaviors that produce a racial structure – *a network of social relations at the social, political, economic, and ideological levels that shapes the life chances of the various races*'.[405] What all of these arguments have in common is a refusal to reduce racism to an individual pathology and a desire to come to grips with racism as a constitutive logic that structures the social, political, economic, and cultural landscape of modernity from within. Systemic racism, to borrow Bonilla-Silva's evocative metaphor, is not merely the product of a few 'rotten apples' (the racists), but is ingrained in the body of the apple tree itself.[406]

---

[398] Fanon 1956, 123. There is substantial evidence that German racial policies were inspired by European colonial practices and the Jim Crow laws in the United States. See Whitman 2017; Zimmerer 2005.
[399] Césaire 1955, 37.   [400] Fanon 1956, 125–126.   [401] Mills 1997.
[402] Goldberg 2002.   [403] Robinson 2020.   [404] Nisancioglu 2020.
[405] Bonilla-Silva 2022, 21.   [406] Bonilla-Silva 2022, 20.

To recap, the first half of the twentieth century witnessed the articulation of two contrasting conceptions of racism that continue to inform contemporary understandings of the phenomenon. On one side stands the liberal tradition, epitomised by the work of UNESCO, which understands racism in particularistic terms as the pathology of individual racists. Racism, in this account, is an excess or aberration in the fabric of the international order rather than an integral feature thereof. The liberal solution to racism is accordingly located on the side of the universal, in the promotion of abstract and ostensibly culture-neutral ideals of individualism, education, and human rights; the aim is to purge race from written and spoken language in the hopes of eventually achieving a 'colourblind' world. Almost diametrically opposed to the liberal tradition stands the work of the antiracist tradition outlined above. Despite manifold differences between the authors surveyed here, all of them locate racism on the side of the universal rather than the particular. For these antiracist thinkers, racism is not an aberrant excess of particularism that disrupts the normal operation of modern politics, but a systemic feature that functions as the constitutive underside of the international order. Whereas the liberal tradition sees racism as a function of racist individuals, the systemic approach unveils how the inequalities produced by centuries of subordination and discrimination generate a 'racism without racists' that structures society as a whole.[407] By extension, the systemic perspective contends that the problem of racism cannot be solved simply by eliminating the concept of race from political discourse. Taken by itself, this 'colourblind' approach merely obfuscates the underlying racial inequalities that structure the societal playing field. Instead, it is necessary to leverage the sociological reality of race in the fight against racism through race-conscious policies such as affirmative action.[408] In this spirit, the seminal works of Du Bois, Césaire, and Fanon do not negate or expunge black racial identity in favour of abstract universals, but to the contrary, invest this racial identity with a positive valence that colonial rule had denied it. If the liberal critique of racism entails a dialectical 'reversal' from an objectivist to a subjectivist understanding of race – a shift from the study of races or racial inequality to the investigation of racism or the *belief* in racial inequality – then the systemic approach entails 'a reversal of the reversal' that reaffirms

---

[407] Bonilla-Silva 2022.   [408] Bernasconi 2011, 92.

the social reality of race in order to problematise the colourblindness of the liberal approach.[409] It was this dialectical revindication of the depreciated black subject that the French philosopher Jean-Paul Sartre famously described as an 'anti-racist racism'.[410]

The New Differentialist Racism

The liberal movement of negation and the anti-racist movement of affirmation do not exhaust contemporary forms of racism. From between the cracks of this double movement, there emerges a new form of racism that eludes both the exceptionalist and the systemic conceptions. This is neither the racism of racists nor a racism without racists, but a racism without races – an 'ethnic' or 'cultural' racism that no longer requires the concept of race as its ground.[411] In effect, the invention of the concept of racism in the first half of the twentieth century not only heralded the end of racism as a legitimate political ideology, but also inaugurated a new and more insidious form of racism capable of disavowing its own racist properties. Born after the dismantling of explicitly racist ideologies, the new post-racial racism is a strange kind of 'meta-racism' that can also take the form of its opposite – a racism that can also take the form of antiracism.[412]

At the core of the new racism is a 'fundamentalism of difference' that idealises human cultural diversity and endeavours to protect this diversity from 'the devouring abstraction of the universal'.[413] Whereas the old racism invoked a hierarchy of races, the new racism is a 'differentialist racism' that limits itself to reifying the differences between formally equal cultures or ethnic groups.[414] In the words of Étienne Balibar, the new racism 'does not postulate the superiority of certain groups or peoples in relation to others but "only" the harmfulness of abolishing frontiers, the incompatibility of life-styles and traditions'.[415] The French anthropologist Claude Lévi-Strauss has the questionable honour of playing a pivotal role in both dismantling the old hierarchical paradigm and constructing its differentialist successor: Lévi-Strauss's *Race et*

---

[409] Balibar 2008, 1635–1637.
[410] Sartre 1951, 244. See also Fanon 2002, 133.
[411] See especially Ansell 1997; Balibar 1991a; Barker 1981; Gilroy 1987; Havertz 2023; Taguieff 2001.
[412] Balibar 1991a, 21–23. [413] Taguieff 2001, 6.
[414] Taguieff 2001, 5–6. See also Stolcke 1995. [415] Balibar 1991a, 21.

histoire, published by UNESCO in 1952, presented a thorough critique of essentialist theories of racial inequality, while his *Race et culture*, published by UNESCO in 1971, forcefully argued against the mixing of cultures in order to safeguard human cultural diversity.[416] This emphasis on the protection of distinct cultures or ethnic groups subsequently became a core feature of right-wing parties and movements opposed to immigration.[417]

The rise of the new differentialist racism is inextricably intertwined with the conceptual history of ethnicity. Indeed, it is the emergence of ethnicity as the universal ground of human difference that is the condition of possibility of this racism without races. Rather than grounding itself upon the concept of race, the new racism thrives upon an ethnicised understanding of difference. More fundamentally, both the emergence of ethnicity and the rise of the new racism are inseparable from the consolidation of a global international system populated by formally equal and sovereign nation-states. With this passage from a world of empires to a world of nation-states, vertical narratives of racial inequality are displaced by horizontal and seemingly egalitarian narratives of ethnic or cultural difference that naturalise the territorial divisions of the international order. The postcolonial world order, as Nandita Sharma writes, 'not only produces but also normalizes a racism in which political separations and segregations are seen as the natural *spatial* order of nationally sovereign states'.[418] Whereas the primary ideological function of the old hierarchical racism was to legitimate European imperial rule over non-European peoples, the primary ideological function of the new differentialist racism is to segregate migrants and foreigners from the 'natives' inhabiting the national territory.

From the Clash of Races to the Clash of Civilisations

Ethnicity is often described as a 'euphemism' for race.[419] There is a grain of truth to this claim, insofar as both concepts can function as markers of differences that are perceived to be somehow innate or natural. Yet the conceptual shift from race to ethnicity in the twentieth

---

[416] Balibar 1991a, 22. [417] Havertz 2023.
[418] Sharma 2020, 4. See also Balibar 1991a, 21; Gilroy 1987, 43–69.
[419] For example, Allen and Eade 1999, 2; Ballard 1996, 3.

century also entailed an important structural change: whereas the nineteenth-century concept of race had possessed both a national and a transnational dimension, the concept of ethnicity was articulated with reference to the national dimension only. Hence why there is no 'global ethnic line' comparable to the global colour line famously described by W. E. B. Du Bois at the beginning of the twentieth century. The emergence of ethnicity went hand in hand with the erasure of racial hierarchies from the international plane and the institution of the racial unity of mankind as a foundational norm of the post-war global order. This erasure of race from the international plane was, however, more apparent than real: insofar as the universalistic dimension of race is a corollary of the aporetic structure of the modern state, the transnational stratum of the race concept could not simply disappear. Indeed, even as the concept of race was being cast aside, a relativised and pluralised concept of civilisation was being articulated in its place. In the same way that the concept of ethnicity functions as a proxy for the particularistic dimension of race in the domestic sphere, a relativised and pluralised concept of civilisation functions as a proxy for the universalistic dimension of race on the international plane.

Recent decades have seen civilisational labels such as 'Western', 'Christian', 'Slavic', 'Asian', 'Confucian', 'Muslim', and 'Islamic' acquire a new-found salience in academic and popular discourse alike.[420] Existing work has investigated the construction of civilisational identities, explored relationships between different civilisations, and analysed how civilisational labels are invoked in political rhetoric.[421] As yet, however, there has been no systematic historical or structural explanation as to *why* the theory and practice of international politics are characterised by such rhetoric in the first place: Where did this pluralised concept of civilisation come from? In the relatively few cases where this question is raised at all, it tends to be casually attributed to Samuel Huntington's infamous predictions about a 'clash of civilisations' that would define the post-Cold War world – a prophesy that seemed to be vindicated by the onset of the war on terror in the early 2000s.[422] Yet a closer analysis of the historical record shows that this relativistic and pluralistic conception

[420] Bettiza 2014; Brubaker 2017; Kumar 2014.
[421] For example, Hall and Jackson 2007; Katzenstein 2010, 2012a, 2012b; Michael and Petito 2009; O'Hagan 2002.
[422] Huntington 1993.

of civilisations can be traced all the way back to the turn of the twentieth century. In fact, this new understanding of civilisations emerges precisely at the moment when old discourses of international racial hierarchy are being dismantled and cast aside. Contemporary anxieties about a clash of civilisations can thus be said to mark the return of the repressed transnational stratum of race. The discourse of civilisations is a remainder and reminder of the fact that inter-national relations not only once were, but in many ways still are, inter-racial relations as well.

Prior to the 1870s, the concept of civilisation referred to a singular process and standard, of which the European nations were believed to represent the highest and most advanced form.[423] The displacement of this singular Eurocentric standard by a relativised and pluralised conception of different-yet-equal civilisations was the result of a profound legitimacy crisis that rocked the Eurocentric world order around the turn of the twentieth century. At the heart of this legitimacy crisis was a growing awareness of a contradiction between the two key organising principles of the imperial system: the hierarchy of civilisation and the hierarchy of races.

The standard of civilisation, despite its Eurocentric applications, was fundamentally universalistic in nature. Even if different races were presumed to have different capacities for development, the idea of a civilisational hierarchy 'did not theoretically preclude the ability of a "race" to become civilized'.[424] The abstract and universalistic language of international law through which the standard of civilisation was articulated also helped to disassociate it from the white European nations and promulgate the idea that *any* nation or race could ascend to civilised status, so long as it conformed to certain legal and normative standards.[425] In stark contrast, the entrenchment of the global colour line in the second half of the nineteenth century posited the existence of essential differences between particular races.[426] Instead of merely lagging behind Europe, some primitive groups were deemed *inherently* incapable of attaining civilised status. Whereas the

---

[423] On the conceptual history of 'civilisation', see Benveniste 1971, 289–296; Bowden 2009, 23–46; Febvre 1973; Kuper 1999, 23–46; Stocking 1987, 8–45.
[424] Duara 2001, 101.
[425] In practice, of course, the integration of non-Western states into international society was an unequal process that entailed the perpetuation of sociocultural hierarchies. See especially Getachew 2019, 37–70; Zarakol 2011, 2014.
[426] Jacques 1997, 213–214; Mantena 2010, 5–6.

civilisational hierarchy merely deferred the attainment of equality into the future, the racial hierarchy legitimated imperial rule in perpetuity. With the racialisation of the imperial order, the 'not yet' of the European civilising mission transformed into a 'not yet forever'.[427]

The contradiction between the discourse of civilisation and the discourse of race was outlined by the French racial theorist Arthur de Gobineau as early as 1853.[428] On the one hand, the advance of civilisation was predicated upon ongoing processes of exchange and assimilation among different groups, and the subjugation of others was the measure of its success. This understanding of civilisation as a process of integration into ever-larger communities was reflected in prevalent evolutionary narratives about primitive bands merging into clans, clans fusing into tribes, and tribes ultimately uniting to form civilised nations.[429] On the other hand, in direct contrast, the ideal of racial purity depended on the segregation of different racial groups. This meant that only the most primitive and isolated communities could be considered to possess even a minimal degree of racial purity. Meanwhile, the spread of European civilisation and the exponential acceleration of global exchange seemed to be bringing about an irredeemable intermixture of races. Although both the concept of civilisation and the concept of race revolved around the nature/culture opposition, they pointed in diametrically opposite directions: the onward march of civilisation represented the triumph of culture over nature, whereas the cultivation of racial purity was about subordinating culture to nature. It was this contradiction between race and civilisation that underlay the legitimacy crisis of the Eurocentric world order around the turn of the twentieth century.

The crisis of the imperial order can be traced on both sides of the global imperial divide. In much of the non-Western world, a universalistic understanding of civilisation had gained widespread currency by the mid nineteenth century. It was the acknowledgement of the material superiority of the Europeans that underpinned the Tanzimat reforms in the Ottoman Empire and the Meiji reforms in Japan, for example. Such reform projects were, however, predicated upon the decoupling of the Eurocentric standard of civilisation from

---

[427] Ghosh and Chakrabarty 2002, 148, 151.   [428] Todorov 1993, 131–140.
[429] Connor 1991, 7.

particularistic notions of race, religion, or geography: the acceptance of European superiority in the material sphere did not translate into an acceptance of European superiority in the cultural sphere, and non-European powers expected that institutional reforms would allow them to enter the prestigious club of civilised nations. Disillusionment soon followed, as European colonial expansion continued and justifications for imperialism became increasingly racialised. The subsequent backlash against European hegemony saw the articulation of new self-assertive non-Western civilisational identities such as pan-Islamism, pan-Asianism, and pan-Africanism. From the 1870s, intellectuals associated with these transnational movements attacked the Eurocentric standard of civilisation and placed the achievements of Islamic, Asian, and African civilisations on an equal footing with those of Europe.[430] These themes were manifest in Du Bois's speech to the first Pan-African Conference in London at the turn of the century, when he also uttered his most famous phrase for the first time: 'The problem of the twentieth century is the problem of the color line.'[431]

Meanwhile, among the European imperial powers themselves, the contradiction between race and civilisation illuminates the otherwise puzzling appearance of narratives of racial decline in the late nineteenth century: at the very moment when European imperial dominance reached its zenith, there was a proliferation of anxiety over racial degeneration. By the last quarter of the nineteenth century, any European setbacks against non-European powers – such as the British defeat at Khartoum in 1885 or the Italian defeat at Adowa in 1896 – would provoke alarmist speculation about the future of the white race.[432] Japan's unprecedented victory over Russia in 1905 was especially striking, with Alfred Zimmern interrupting his lectures on Greek history at the University of Oxford to discuss 'the most important historical event which has happened, or is likely to happen, in our lifetime; the victory of a non-white people over a white people'.[433] The savage trench warfare of the First World War, often referred to as a 'fratricidal war' in the white crisis literature, further undermined European claims to civilised status and served to consolidate fears of

---

[430] Aydin 2007b, 2013; Younis 2017.
[431] Du Bois, quoted in Getachew 2019, 6.   [432] Füredi 1998, 25–78.
[433] Zimmern, quoted in Aydin 2007a, 216.

racial decline.[434] The perceived decline of the white race and the growing assertiveness of the non-white races constituted the two opposite yet complementary moments of an epochal revolution that would ultimately turn the imperial world order on its head. Taken together, they signalled the end of white man's monopoly on civilisation.

The charged international climate found expression in a number of arenas. The pages of the *Journal of Race Development*, established in 1910, were 'almost entirely devoted to minimizing or pre-empting the coming conflict between races'.[435] The journal would change its name to the *Journal of International Relations* in 1919 and finally to *Foreign Affairs* in 1922, making it one of the earliest recognisable IR journals.[436] A similar concern with the future of race relations prevailed at a number of international conferences, such as the Conference on Nationalities and Subject Races held in London in 1910.[437] 'The problem before us,' Gilbert Murray stated in his opening address, 'is, how two races, the one ruling and the other subject, can live together with advantage to both, each getting as far as possible good from the other and not injury.'[438] The more famous Universal Races Congress, held in London the following year and attracting over 1,000 participants, had a similar objective: 'to discuss [...] the general relations subsisting between the peoples of the West and those of the East, between so-called white and so-called coloured peoples, with a view to encouraging between them a fuller understanding, the most friendly feelings, and a heartier co-operation'.[439] Participants at the Universal Races Congress included prominent intellectual and political figures such as Mohandas Gandhi, W. E. B. Du Bois, Paul S. Reinsch, Israel Zangwill, H. G. Wells, and François Légitime, to name only a few; a paper by Franz Boas was also circulated although he was unable to attend the conference.[440] There was a general consensus among the participants that 'pure racial types'

---

[434] Bonnett 2004, 18. See also Adas 1989, 365–380.
[435] Füredi 1998, 47–48. See, for example, Blakeslee 1910.
[436] Blatt 2004, 691–692.
[437] For the proceedings of the Conference on Nationalities and Subject Races, see Dryhurst 1910.
[438] Murray 1910, 5.   [439] Spiller 1911, xiii.
[440] On the Universal Races Congress, see Geulen 2007, 82–85; Lake and Reynolds 2008, 241–262; Pennybacker 2005; Rich 1984; Tilley 2014.

and 'racial hierarchies' were outdated and inaccurate notions for understanding the relations between races.[441]

By the end of the First World War, the Eurocentric world order was teetering under the weight of its contradictions. The unmarked white gaze that had, over the course of the nineteenth century, constructed a gradated hierarchy of racialised others came up against its internal limit. At the very moment that European civilisation appeared to have triumphed in material terms, the threat of miscegenation and racial degeneration also reached its peak. The white gaze thus increasingly turned inward, becoming conscious of itself as merely one particular race among others and shattering the fantasy of universality.[442] The response to this new-found sense of vulnerability was the rise of a self-racialising discourse calling for white solidarity in the face of *The Rising Tide of Color against White World-Supremacy*, as the title of Lothrop Stoddard's influential book put it.[443] It was at this historical juncture, spurred by the logic of self-racialisation, that 'whiteness' as a racial identity acquired widespread currency for the first time.[444]

The self-racialising discourse of whiteness was, however, immediately undercut by the aporetic logic of self-racialisation itself, which operates from a position of 'absolute insecurity'.[445] As Étienne Balibar explains, the desperate attempt to define the 'true' or 'pure' members of the white race could only be achieved through their juxtaposition against those that were 'false' or 'impure'. The self-racialised identity therefore 'remains constantly in doubt and in danger; the fact that the "false" is too visible will never guarantee that the "true" is visible enough'.[446] The discourse of white supremacy and the crisis of whiteness were thus two sides of the same dialectical coin, unable to overcome the constitutive aporia around which they revolved. The self-propelled fragmentation of white supremacism was manifest in the emergence of a plurality of racialised transnational identities within the geography of whiteness, such as pan-Germanism, pan-Slavism, and the idea of Anglo-America.[447] After 1917, these intra-white divisions were amplified by the emergence of the Soviet Union as a potentially 'colour-blind' political rival, which created a new ideological rift within the West and compelled Western political and intellectual elites

---

[441] Tilley 2014, 775.   [442] See Montag 1997.   [443] Stoddard 1920.
[444] Lake and Reynolds 2008.   [445] Taguieff 2001, 123.
[446] Balibar 1991b, 60.
[447] See, for example, Bell 2007, 2012, 2020; Younis 2017.

to address the issue of racial discrimination.[448] In his contribution to the *Encyclopaedia of the Social Sciences* in 1934, for example, Hans Kohn claimed that 'the awakening of underprivileged races is stimulated by the equalitarian and humanitarian policies of the Soviet Union, where a determined stand has been taken against race discrimination'.[449] Ultimately, calls for white solidarity foundered on the suspicions that white supremacist authors continued to hold regarding 'the traitorous nature of huge swaths of white people, most notably the Russians and the working classes'.[450]

The nail in the coffin of the Eurocentric imperial order was the Second World War, which severed any remaining link between race and civilisation. On the Axis side, the self-racialising political ideology of the Third Reich pitted a racialised conception of the German Volk against the unbridled forces of civilisation: the separation of humanity from nature was deemed to have gone too far, undermining the process of natural selection and threatening the German Volk with degeneration. In this profoundly pessimistic ideological narrative, social life was depicted as an endless struggle for survival where 'it is not the fittest who survives, but the survivor who proves to be the fittest'.[451] The principal foil to this self-racialising project was the figure of the Jew, embodying the promiscuous excesses of civilisation that undermined the natural division of mankind into territorially rooted nations: 'Jews were not understood as conventionally inferior, but as radically unnatural.'[452] This antagonism between race and civilisation was mirrored in the Allied camp, but with the polarities reversed: whereas Nazi ideologues considered the racial purity of the German Volk to be under threat from the excesses of civilisation, in the Allied narrative it was civilisation that was under threat from German racism. As Edward Keene notes, the Allied campaign against the Third Reich was the first time that the concept of civilisation was 'explicitly being deployed *against* the scientific theories of race that had given it much of its legitimacy as a way of articulating the rationale behind the bifurcated nature of order in world politics'.[453] In the polarising furnace of the Second World War, the tension between race and civilisation grew into an unsustainable contradiction.

The defeat of the Third Reich in 1945 discredited the self-racialising discourse, which had sought to resolve the tension between race and

---

[448] Füredi 1998, 194.   [449] Kohn 1934, 40.   [450] Bonnett 2004, 18.
[451] Geulen 2017, 210.   [452] Hutton 2005, 16.   [453] Keene 2002, 121.

civilisation in favour of the former. At the same time, an alternative solution to this contradiction was already emerging among liberal internationalist figures such as Arnold Toynbee and H. G. Wells. In contrast to their white supremacist contemporaries, the likes of Toynbee and Wells did not view the national and racial awakenings taking place in the non-European world as an existential threat to Europe. To the contrary, they interpreted such developments as evidence of the convergence of other nations and races on a Eurocentric path to modernity. In the hands of these liberal internationalists, the relationship between Europeans and non-Europeans was understood 'less in terms of an essential *racial* supremacism than in terms of a belief in Europe's *civilizational* advancedness'.[454] Of course, this shift in perspective did not mean that racist baggage entirely disappeared. Toynbee, for instance, still claimed that the black race was the only race that had 'not made a creative contribution to any one of our twenty-one civilizations'.[455] The crucial point, however, is that Toynbee explained the alleged deficiency of the black race with reference to historical contingencies rather than racial essences: '[T]he so-called racial explanation of differences in human performance and achievement is either an ineptitude or a fraud.'[456] In the same vein, Wells grounded his ambitious designs for Anglo-American union in similarity of language rather than race. Although Wells believed that the peoples of the world could be arranged into a developmental hierarchy, he firmly rejected the notion of intrinsic differences between races: developmental discrepancies were the result of historical or structural factors and could therefore be overcome.[457]

In many ways, the liberal internationalist narrative of civilisational differences was a continuation of long-standing discourses. In nineteenth-century Britain, for example, the 'ladder of civilisation' had been 'the dominant metaphor' through which the peoples of the world were ordered.[458] In the midst of the turn-of-the-century crisis, however, the concept of civilisation also underwent a crucial transformation: formerly conceived as a singular process and standard, the concept of civilisation now became relativised, pluralised, and concretised. Toynbee's monumental *A Study of History*, conceived in the 1920s and published in twelve volumes between 1934 and 1961, was among the first texts to advocate for the comparative study of 'civilisations' in the plural, identifying twenty-one civilisations in total. Martin Wight, who worked

---

[454] Tonooka 2021, 110.   [455] Toynbee 1934, 233.   [456] Toynbee 1934, 245.
[457] Bell 2018.   [458] Mandler 2000, 233.

with Toynbee at Chatham House and wrote his obituary in 1976, would describe his colleague as 'the historian who was to teach the English-speaking world that there are other civilizations beside the Western'.[459] However, contrary to what Wight seems to imply, this was not simply a case of adding a range of new civilisations alongside a pre-existing notion of Western civilisation. Rather, it was only as a result of the relativisation and pluralisation of the concept of civilisation that the notion of 'the West' as a particular civilisational identity became conceivable in the first place.[460]

The relativisation and pluralisation of the concept of civilisation went hand in hand with the recasting of human difference in cultural rather than racial terms. While many aspects of Huntington's 'clash of civilisations' thesis have justifiably come under attack, few dispute his characterisation of a civilisation as 'a cultural entity'.[461] This understanding of a civilisation as a transnational cultural bloc has taken over many of the earlier functions of race, such as dividing humanity into a handful of major groups, but it is no longer mired by rigid typological thinking or outdated notions of pure racial types. As Alastair Bonnett notes, 'whiteness cannot be acquired but "Westernness" can'.[462] Put differently, the displacement of the concept of race by a relativised and pluralised concept of civilisation means that the superiority of the Western world is no longer seen to inhere in the West itself: rather than the West setting the international standard against which others are measured, it is now a seemingly autonomous and free-floating international standard that determines the ranking of particular nations or civilisations, including the West, on the developmental ladder.[463] If the West happens to be the best match to this seemingly abstract international standard, this tends to be attributed to a fortuitous accumulation of historical factors rather than to the innate superiority of Westerners. The effect of this conceptual restructuring is to flatten the global racial hierarchy and allow a multiplicity of different civilisations to flourish on the principle of formal equality. Recalling the words of Alexander Goldenweiser, this was a shift from the view that 'man is many and civilization one' to the view that 'man is one, civilizations are many'.[464]

---

[459] Wight, quoted in Mazower 2006, 564.
[460] Bonnett 2004; GoGwilt 1995; Leigh 2021. On earlier uses of the concept of 'the West' in the British context, see Varouxakis 2020.
[461] Huntington 1993, 23.   [462] Bonnett 2004, 27.
[463] Heiskanen 2021a, 251–252.   [464] Goldenweiser 1921, 14.

3 Tribe

'There are two kinds of colonial histories', Mahmood Mamdani writes. 'The grand narrative of colonialism, its meta-history, is written in bold within the frame of race. Its micro-histories are written in small script within the frame of tribe.'[1] Insofar as the previous chapter focused on the concept of race and the idea of the global colour line, it was concerned with what Mamdani calls the 'grand narrative' or 'meta-history' of colonialism. By contrast, this chapter shifts the attention to the second kind of colonial history identified by Mamdani: the 'micro-histories' articulated through the concept of tribe.

By the last quarter of the nineteenth century, the vast majority of European observers viewed the world through a 'bifocal lens' that lumped people into two basic categories: the civilised and the primitive.[2] 'Nineteenth-century authors vied with each other to coin the most compelling labels to capture this contrast,' Michael Adas writes, 'and there were many variations on the dichotomies of active and passive, male and female.'[3] Among the most influential were Henry Maine's contrast between 'status' and 'contract',[4] Ferdinand Tönnies's distinction between 'Gemeinschaft' and 'Gesellschaft',[5] and Émile Durkheim's opposition between 'organic' and 'mechanical' solidarity.[6] Besides structuring academic theories, such binaries legitimated the extension and perpetuation of European imperial rule over the rest of the world.[7] At the same time, European commentators were well aware of the countless distinct communities that inhabited either side of the global divide. Within Europe, as seen in Chapter 1, this diversity was typically captured by grouping people into nations or nationalities. Yet the concept of the nation – widely seen as the most advanced political form – was rarely extended to those non-Europeans that were deemed to reside beyond the pale of civilisation. Instead, it was the

---

[1] Mamdani 2012, 53.   [2] Bell 2011, 867.   [3] Adas 1989, 197.
[4] Maine 1861.   [5] Tönnies 1887.   [6] Durkheim 1893.   [7] Mantena 2010.

concept of tribe that served as the main category for describing and ordering smaller groupings of non-European people. Put bluntly, tribes were primitive nations.[8]

At first glance, the concept of tribe may seem tangential, perhaps even totally irrelevant, for the disciplinary concerns of IR. Whereas the centrality of the nation is written into the name of the discipline and the concept of race has generated substantial debate, the concept of tribe has simply been ignored.[9] And yet, the familiar depictions of the international system as a 'state of nature' or 'anarchy' owe a profound debt to colonial conceptions of primitive society, which, in turn, are deeply entangled with the concept of tribe. Indeed, one of the central arguments of this chapter is that many of the ideological functions of primitive society as the 'other' of the civilised state were transferred onto international society during the period of decolonisation in the 1960s and 1970s. Ironically, just as anthropologists were becoming more self-reflexive of their role in the European colonial project, leading IR scholars from Hedley Bull to Kenneth Waltz were borrowing anthropological categories left, right, and centre. All in all, the theoretical discourse of the 'anarchy problematique'[10] that came to dominate IR theory in the second half of the twentieth century owes a profound yet overlooked debt to anthropological discourses about primitive tribes.

'Anthropologists customarily use the term "tribe" to designate two realms of different yet connected facts', the French anthropologist Maurice Godelier wrote in 1973. On the one hand, the concept of tribe signified a particular *stage* in the evolution of human society: from this temporal or historical perspective, the concept of tribe belonged essentially to the past, representing a primitive stage of social development. On the other hand, the concept of tribe also signified a particular *type* of human society distinct from other types such as 'bands' or 'states'.[11] The first two sections of this chapter trace how, over the course of the twentieth century, both conceptions of the tribe came under attack. The first section shows how the conception of the tribe as a specific stage of human social evolution was rendered problematic by the rapid industrialisation and urbanisation of the colonies, which seemed to entail the 'detribalisation' of tribal societies.

---

[8] Hudson 1996, 257–258.   [9] For an exception, see Manchanda 2018.
[10] Ashley 1988.   [11] Godelier 1973, 1.

Combined with the delegitimation of imperial rule and the dismantling of Eurocentric metanarratives of civilisational progress, terms such as 'tribe' and 'tribalism' came to be seen not only as empirically inaccurate, but also as politically inappropriate. At the same time, as the second section of the chapter demonstrates, the conception of the tribe as a distinct type of society was coming under scrutiny through the popularisation of statistical methods for cross-cultural comparisons. Whereas the concept of tribe referred specifically to a primitive form of social organisation, the new cross-cultural comparisons required a culture-bearing social unit that was applicable to all societies around the world, regardless of their supposed stage of development. As both the historical and structural specificity of the tribe concept came to be seen as a hindrance, this colonial category was displaced by the more neutral and malleable concept of ethnicity. This conceptual shift entailed a fundamental transformation in anthropological perspectives: whereas tribes had been conceived as homogeneous and isolated communities beyond the pale of civilisation, the concept of ethnicity paved the way for a more dynamic conception of social differentiation that was deemed universally applicable to all societies.[12]

With regard to the book's theoretical argument about the dialectical constitution of the international order, the focus of the first two sections is on the moment of negation: the delegitimation of colonial rule and the dismantling of Eurocentric metanarratives of civilisational progress. By contrast, the third and fourth sections of the chapter focus on the moment of preservation and explore how the afterlives of the imperial order haunt the international order from within. To this end, the third section traces the conceptual entanglements between colonial anthropology and IR. Through a careful reading of IR's theoretical canon, it shows how the functions of primitive society as the 'other' of the civilised state were reinscribed into the idea of international anarchy. The fourth and final section moves from IR theory to international political and legal practice, analysing the rise of indigenous rights discourse from the late nineteenth century to the present. Building on Paul Keal's work, I show that the recognition of indigenous rights by the international community is largely about preserving the moral legitimacy of the states-system.[13] If minority rights function as a safety valve that sutures the future of the international order

[12] Cohen 1978, 384.   [13] Keal 2003.

against the future threat of nationalist secession, then indigenous rights suture the international order from its colonial past.

Temporal Limits of the Tribe Concept

As unilinear narratives of civilisational progress became entrenched in Western consciousness during the nineteenth century, the concept of tribe became coupled to notions of savagery and barbarism. From this point on, the word 'tribe' designated not only a particular type of society organised around kinship ties, but also an earlier or lower form of society that preceded the rise of civilisation. Western thinkers generally presumed that tribal groups had been left behind by the forward march of history and were destined to be reformed, protected, or eradicated by the more civilised nations.[14] In the emerging disciplinary division of labour, the task of studying these primitive societies largely fell on the shoulders of anthropologists.[15] Africa, in particular, came to be seen as a 'living laboratory'[16] ideally suited for anthropological fieldwork: 'a primitive, unchanging, ahistorical, isolated continent, fragmented into a multiplicity of self-contained, mutually antagonistic, but internally stable and harmonious "tribes"'.[17]

This section begins by tracing how ever-larger conceptual fissures began to emerge in the evolutionary narratives of Francophone and Anglophone colonial anthropology in the middle of the twentieth century, and how the concept of ethnicity was mobilised to paper over these cracks. Of particular significance here was the question of social change: as urbanisation and industrialisation gathered speed across the African continent, Western anthropologists believed they were witnessing the transformation of primitive tribespeople into civilised city dwellers before their very eyes. It was this dialectical reversal – the becoming-civilised of the primitive – that initiated the self-deconstruction of the civilised/primitive dichotomy and the supplementation of the existing vocabulary with ethnos-based terms, first in French and later in English. These conceptual shifts were accelerated by decolonisation, which transformed colonial territories into independent nations and delegitimised the global hierarchy between civilised and primitive peoples. By the end

[14] Fried 1975, 7–8; Sneath 2007, 39–64; Yapp 1983, 154.
[15] On anthropology and colonialism, see Asad 1973; Stocking 1991; Thomas 1994; Trouillot 2003.
[16] Tilley 2011.   [17] van den Berghe 1965, 1.

of the 1960s, the concept of tribe was widely considered outdated and offensive, with many anthropologists opting to describe their object of study through politically neutral alternatives such as 'ethnicity' and 'ethnic group' instead. At the end of the section, I also consider the simultaneous re-emergence of the term 'ethnos' in the Soviet Union. Despite obvious ideological differences between the two contexts, there is a striking resemblance in the function of 'ethnicity' in Western anthropology and 'ethnos' in Soviet ethnography: in the same way that 'ethnicity' served as a transhistorical category capable of bridging civilised/primitive dichotomy among Western colonial anthropologists, Soviet ethnos-theory posited the 'ethnos' as a stable core that survived across historical-materialist stages of social evolution. All in all, the popularisation of these ethnos-based terms entailed the displacement of temporalised metanarratives of civilisational or socioeconomic development with a seemingly transhistorical conceptualisation of culture difference.

The Rise of 'Ethnie' in Francophone Colonial Anthropology

When ethnos-based terms such as 'ethnie' and 'groupe ethnique' started to be applied to non-European peoples by French anthropologists, they displaced pejorative colonial concepts such as 'tribu' and 'peuplade'.[18] These colonial concepts had enjoyed widespread use in the early twentieth century,[19] before falling out of favour during the 1940s and 1950s. The earliest French-language text to apply 'ethnie' and 'groupe ethnique' to the colonised portion of the world appears to have been Georges van der Kerken's *L'ethnie Mongo*, a multivolume study of the Mongo people in the Belgian Congo commissioned by the Institut Royal Colonial Belge and published in 1944. Van der Kerken, a Belgian lawyer and colonial administrator, dedicated numerous pages to defining 'ethnie' or 'groupe ethnique' (he used these terms interchangeably). In clarifying their meaning, van der Kerken carefully differentiated them from a litany of neighbouring terms that included 'tribu', 'sous-tribu', 'groupe de clans', 'clan', 'groupe des familles', 'famille', 'race', and 'peuplade'.[20] He credited Félix Regnault with coining the term 'ethnie' in 1927 and George Montandon with further

---

[18] Breton 1992, 10; de Heusch 1997, 185; Gosselin 1985, 112; Nicolas 1973, 95–96.
[19] For example, Labouret 1931; Maitre 1912; Moret and Davy 1923.
[20] van der Kerken 1944, vol. I, 8, 505–516.

specifying its meaning in the 1930s (see Chapter 2).[21] Drawing on Montandon's understanding of the ethnie as a 'natural' human grouping, van der Kerken finally arrived at the following definition: 'L'*Ethnie*, constituant un *groupe naturel*, en ce sens qu'il est la *résultante de l'histoire*, se définit, en ordre principal, par des caractères *linguistiques, culturels* et *mentaux* et, en ordre accessoire, par des *caractères somatiques*.'[22]

By the 1950s, Francophone scholars studying non-European peoples were regularly using the terms 'ethnie' and 'groupe ethnique' without finding it necessary to specify their origin or meaning.[23] Although the exact reasons behind the proliferation of these terms in the post-war years remain unclear, several contributing factors can be identified. To begin with, there was the French experience of the Second World War: the decisive military defeat by Germany in 1940, the installation of a collaborationist regime in France proper, and the exile of the Free French leader Charles de Gaulle radically transformed the power relations between metropolitan France and its colonies. This change was recognised by the post-war French government, which sought to reconfigure the imperial framework on a more inclusive basis and rejected the name 'French Empire' in favour of 'French Union' at the end of 1945.[24] It seems likely that the new political climate contributed to the delegitimation of pejorative colonial categories such as 'tribu' and 'peuplade', and encouraged anthropologists to look for alternatives. The ethnos-based terms would then have been readily available for adoption, having been in circulation among French anthropologists for several decades already: 'groupe ethnique' had been defined by Joseph Deniker as early as 1900, while 'ethnie' was popularised by Félix Regnault and George Montandon during the inter-war years (see Chapter 2). Although all three men had 'race' rather than 'tribu' as their point of reference, the ethnos-based terms were malleable enough to be repurposed from physical anthropology to colonial anthropology without much difficulty.

Another key factor behind the popularisation of the ethnos-based terms was the rise of a new generation of French anthropologists

---

[21] van der Kerken 1944, vol. I, 8n1, 510n1.
[22] van der Kerken 1944, vol. I, 516.
[23] For example, Balandier 1951, 1953, 1955; Borde 1950; Mercier 1954; Nicolas 1952; Richard-Molard 1952; Rouch 1956.
[24] Cooper 2014, 7–8, 21.

interested in the study of social change in the colonies. Led by Georges Balandier, this emerging cohort of scholars challenged the prevailing structuralist-functionalist understanding of tribes as segregated and largely unchanging containers of primitive social organisation. Instead, Balandier urged anthropologists to reflect on the impact of ongoing social, cultural, political, and economic transformations in the colonies, having witnessed them first-hand during his stay in Gabon and Congo between 1948 and 1950.[25] Rather than viewing ethnies as isolated units, Balandier focused on the complex relations within which they were embedded and through which they were socially constituted. This required understanding them as part of a dynamic colonial context, or what he called 'la situation coloniale'.[26] Meanwhile, other young scholars such as Jean Rouch and Paul Mercier used terms such as 'de-tribalisation', 're-tribalisation', and 'super-tribalisation' to conceptualise how processes such as migration and urbanisation were affecting tribal identities.[27] The shift from 'tribu' to 'ethnie' in the post-war years was thus symptomatic of a more general reconfiguration of anthropological perspectives that problematised the established conceptual divide between primitive and civilised societies. To paraphrase Mercier, the birth of ethnicity went hand in hand with 'la mort du primitive'.[28]

In the English-speaking world, the terminological shift from tribes to ethnic groups and from tribalism to ethnicity had to wait until the late 1960s. 'Whereas in French anthropology, the term *tribu* has become obsolete, Anglophone scholars tenaciously cling to the words *tribe* and *tribal*', the American anthropologist Pierre van den Berghe complained in 1965.[29] The time lag is somewhat puzzling, given that British and American anthropologists were well versed in the works of their Francophone counterparts – Rouch and Mercier's analyses of de-tribalisation, re-tribalisation, and super-tribalisation were widely cited in the English-language literature, for example. The parallels between Balandier's research into the dynamism of the colonial situation and the relational – processual approach of Max Gluckman's 'Manchester School' are also striking, and were even noted by Balandier himself.[30] The texts published by Balandier and his colleagues were littered with

---

[25] Copans 2001, 36–37.   [26] Balandier 1951.
[27] Mercier 1961; Rouch 1956.   [28] Mercier 1951, 11–16.
[29] van den Berghe 1965, 3.   [30] Balandier 1960, 2. See also Agier 2017.

references to 'ethnies' and 'groupes ethniques', but for reasons unknown these terms were not picked up by the Anglophone scholars reading them. When the English terms 'ethnic group' and 'ethnicity' did finally break through in the late 1960s, they were imported from American sociology rather than French anthropology. Among Anglophone anthropologists the displacement of the concept of tribe also appears to have been a more deliberate and contested process than it was among their Francophone counterparts. At the heart of the resulting debates was, again, the problem of social change.

The Manchester School and the Problem of Social Change

Perhaps the greatest difficulty facing Anglophone anthropologists in the early twentieth century was explaining and conceptualising social change. The hegemonic structuralist-functionalist paradigm, propagated by revered scholars such as A. R. Radcliffe-Brown and E. E. Evans-Pritchard, 'recognized social process, yet only insofar as process was reducible to, and so in the service of, social stasis'.[31] Tribalism, for example, was understood as a primitive rural phenomenon that would disappear in the course of modernisation because it had no functional purpose in a modern urban setting.[32] At the same time, it was becoming increasingly evident that the societies studied by anthropologists were themselves experiencing profound transformations. Nowhere was this more apparent than on the African continent, where the spread of industrialisation and urbanisation was radically reshaping the social, economic, and cultural landscape. 'It is hardly surprising', Thomas Hylland Eriksen and Finn Sivert Nielsen observe, 'that the issue of social change first came to the fore in British anthropology among scholars studying people who were themselves undergoing rapid, unpredictable and irreversible change.'[33] Ultimately, it was the attempts to make sense of these processes that paved the way for the deconstruction of the concept of tribe and the emergence of ethnicity.

The first anthropological research centre on the African continent was the Rhodes-Livingstone Institute, founded by Godfrey Wilson in present-day Zambia in 1938.[34] The key question that animated Wilson's work was the transition from 'primitive' to 'civilised'

[31] Evens and Handelman 2006, 1. [32] Banks 1996, 29.
[33] Eriksen and Nielsen 2013, 108. [34] Eriksen and Nielsen 2013, 108.

society.³⁵ This distinction between primitive and civilised societies mirrored the distinction between tribes and nations: 'A tribe [...] was not a community like a nation state; it was a loosely linked system of similar, tiny and relatively autonomous local communities.'³⁶ For Wilson, the transformation of tribes into nations represented 'the process of civilization or the process of detribalization'. Detribalisation and civilisation were thus 'the same thing'.³⁷

When Max Gluckman succeeded Wilson as the director of the Rhodes-Livingstone Institute in 1941, Wilson's primitive/civilised dichotomy was relabelled tribal/industrial, but the underlying puzzle remained unchanged.³⁸ During his time at Oxford in the 1930s, Gluckman had been heavily influenced by the work of Radcliffe-Brown and Evans-Pritchard, and his intention was to further advance their structuralist-functionalist approach by incorporating into it the empirical study of concrete processes and conflicts.³⁹ Therefore, instead of taking the rural tribe as the starting point of his analysis, Gluckman opted to focus on the transformative power of the urban context.⁴⁰ In retrospect, this focus on social change was the 'Trojan horse' that would lead to the deconstruction of the structuralist-functionalist edifice.⁴¹

When Gluckman moved to the University of Manchester and set up the Department of Social Anthropology there in 1949, many of the leading figures of the Rhodes-Livingstone Institute, including A. L. Epstein and J. Clyde Mitchell, also became associated with the so-called 'Manchester School' of anthropology. Following Gluckman's lead, the main puzzle that these Manchester School anthropologists grappled with was the persistence of 'tribal' identities in urban areas. In effect, the process of 'detribalization' seemed to be accompanied by a seemingly contradictory process of 'retribalization'.⁴² 'The views expressed on the place of "tribalism" in the modern situation often appear to be diametrically opposed', Epstein observed in 1958. Anthropologists seemed to have arrived at the paradoxical conclusion that 'the urban African remains a tribesman, and yet is not a tribesman'.⁴³

Against this backdrop, the pioneering insight of the Manchester School anthropologists was to demonstrate that urban and rural

---

³⁵ Wilson 1941, 1942; Wilson and Wilson 1968.   ³⁶ Wilson 1941, 11.
³⁷ Wilson 1941, 12.   ³⁸ Asad 1991, 319.
³⁹ Evens and Handelman 2006, 1–2.   ⁴⁰ Gluckman 1960, 56–58.
⁴¹ Evens and Handelman 2006, 3.   ⁴² Cohen 1969, 1–2.
⁴³ Epstein 1958, 228–229.

'tribalism' were fundamentally different phenomena.[44] Rather than being a simple extension of rural tribalism into urban areas, the tribalism of the towns was a distinct phenomenon in its own right. By implication, urban tribalism was not a feature of primitive society but a consequence of modernisation. 'Tribalism in the Central African towns is, in sharper form, the tribalism of all towns', Gluckman explained.[45] To clarify this new-found distinction between rural and urban tribal identities, Mitchell referred to traditional rural associations as 'tribal structure' and reserved the term 'tribalism' for urban situations of inter-group contact.[46] Similarly, Epstein differentiated the 'tribal custom' of 'intra-tribal' settings from the 'tribalism' of urban contexts.[47] The influential British anthropologist Aidan Southall, who was teaching at Makerere University in Uganda at the time, arrived at the same conclusion: 'Urban is thus different from rural tribalism', he asserted in 1961.[48] A conceptual distinction between rural and urban tribalism was fast emerging.

The first scholar to use the word 'ethnicity' in this context was the American social scientist Immanuel Wallerstein in 1960. Building on the insights of Mitchell and Epstein, Wallerstein distinguished between 'tribes' in rural areas and 'ethnic groups' in towns. Reserving the term 'tribalism' for the former, Wallerstein defined 'ethnicity' as 'the feeling of loyalty to this new ethnic group of the towns'.[49] He further suggested that 'with increasing urbanization, loyalty to the ethnic community is coming to supersede loyalty to the tribal community and government'.[50] The next mention of 'ethnicity' came in 1967, when P. C. Lloyd pointed out that 'ethnicity' and 'tribalism' seemed to refer to the same phenomenon: the latter was commonly used 'to connote loyalty to an ethnic group (or tribe) which parallels or transcends loyalty to the new state. The term "ethnicity" is frequently used here by sociologists, though it has yet to find its way into colloquial usage in the English-speaking states'.[51] For Lloyd, as for Wallerstein, ethnicity was 'to a large extent an urban phenomenon, and one which develops with increasing modernization of the economy'.[52]

The first study by a Manchester School anthropologist to use the term 'ethnicity' was Abner Cohen's 1969 book *Custom and Politics in*

---

[44] Banks 1996, 29; Lentz 1995, 308.   [45] Gluckman 1965, 292.
[46] Mitchell 1956, 30.   [47] Epstein 1958, 231.   [48] Southall 1961, 35.
[49] Wallerstein 1960, 133.   [50] Wallerstein 1960, 133–134.
[51] Lloyd 1967, 289.   [52] Lloyd 1967, 290.

Urban Africa. Noting that the term 'tribalism' had been 'severely criticized in recent years',[53] Cohen adopted 'ethnicity' as a morally neutral alternative: 'The term "ethnicity", which has been widely used in sociology, particularly in the U.S.A., has been advocated by some writers as a substitute. This, again, is a term lacking in precision but has the advantage over "tribalism" in that it is more free from value-judgment and can be applied to a much wider variety of groupings.'[54] Drawing on Nathan Glazer and Daniel Patrick Moynihan's *Beyond the Melting Pot*, Cohen argued that ethnicity was a 'new social form' rather than 'an archaic survival arrangement carried over into the present by conservative people'.[55]

It is clear from the above that the ethnicity concept was imported into anthropology from American sociology: Wallerstein was working at the Department of Sociology at Columbia at the time, while both Lloyd and Cohen explicitly refer to the use of 'ethnicity' by sociologists. This reflects a broader rapprochement between the two disciplines in the mid twentieth century. 'Anthropology and sociology have converged', the American sociologist Robert Redfield proclaimed as early as 1940.[56] Redfield's claim may have been exaggerated, but there is no doubt that the traditional division of labour between the two disciplines – according to which anthropologists studied primitive tribes while sociologists focused on civilised nations – was becoming blurred. Indeed, the relational – processual approach developed by the Manchester School anthropologists bears a striking resemblance to the work of 'Chicago School' sociologists, including Redfield, during the 1930s and 1940s.[57] As industrialisation and urbanisation transformed the socioeconomic landscape in many parts of Africa, anthropologists were beginning to grapple with similar kinds of phenomena as urban sociologists a few decades earlier.

The Deconstruction of Primitive Society

When the concept of ethnicity first crept into Anglophone anthropological discourse in the 1960s, it was understood as a modern urban phenomenon distinct from primitive rural tribalism. Thus, even as the Manchester School anthropologists reconceptualised urban (ethnic)

---

[53] Cohen 1969, 3.   [54] Cohen 1969, 3–4.   [55] Cohen 1969, 190–192.
[56] Redfield 1940, 733.   [57] Kapferer 2006, 318–319; Mills 2006.

identities as dynamic phenomena, they did not problematise the concept of tribe: by and large, they continued to treat rural (tribal) identities in essentialist terms.[58] As Aristide Zolberg pointed out in 1967, the binary contrast between urban ethnic groups and rural tribes 'helps us understand the contemporary urban setting at the expense of our grasp of rural areas and of the past'.[59] To this extent, the work of the Manchester School anthropologists still fell within a unilinear modernisation narrative where tribal society represented the past of industrial society: the transformation of tribes into ethnic groups entailed, very concretely, the physical movement of tribespeople from a primitive rural context into a modern urban one. Ethnicity was the remainder of tribalism after modernisation, the residue of primitive society that the urban melting pot was unable to assimilate. Ethnicity was what remained of the past as it entered the present.

A more thorough critique of the tribe concept had to wait for the deconstruction of the civilised/primitive dichotomy from which it drew its meaning. In the words of Maurice Godelier, it was necessary for colonial anthropology to have 'lost its object' before the concept of tribe could wither away.[60] The first glimmerings of this process of deconstruction came with the publication of Elizabeth Colson's *The Makah Indians* in 1953. Instead of viewing tribes as relics of the primitive past, Colson suggested that tribes were products of colonial rule and thus 'of relatively recent origin'.[61] Two years later, the *Yearbook of Anthropology* published an article surveying the meaning and use of the terms 'native' and 'primitive'. 'Among anthropologists there is an increasing awareness that these terms are unsatisfactory and inadequate', the report noted. 'This is felt more keenly today because the societies which anthropologists have studied are themselves in ferment of change.'[62] The stream of critique turned into a flood in the 1960s, as the pages of *Current Anthropology* were inundated with critiques of the term 'primitive'.[63] According to one article, the term 'primitive' was 'not a legitimate concept' but an amorphous amalgam that encompassed 'all of the peoples of the world, past and present, except those which are part of Western Civilization and its

---

[58] Lentz 1995, 310. [59] Zolberg 1967, 452. [60] Godelier 1973, 25.
[61] Colson 1953, 75. See also Kroeber 1955. [62] Dozier 1955, 187.
[63] For example, Deuel and Lucas 1962; Gordon et al. 1961; Hsu 1964; Tax and Mednick 1960.

ancient progenitors'.[64] Another concluded that the dichotomy between civilised and primitive societies 'has neither empirical validity nor theoretical utility'.[65]

As colonial anthropology entered into a full-fledged identity crisis in the 1960s, the concept of tribe came under increasing scrutiny. Two of the concept's foremost critics were the American anthropologist Morton Fried and the aforementioned British anthropologist Aidan Southall, whose life's work has been characterised as a 'one-man crusade' against the concept of tribe.[66] In a paper published in 1966, Fried turned the traditional view of tribalism on its head, arguing that 'tribalism can be viewed as a reaction to the formation of complex political structure rather than a necessary preliminary stage in its evolution'.[67] Fried's article had an immediate impact and prompted the American Ethnological Society to arrange a symposium on the concept of tribe the following year.[68] No less significant was the publication of Southall's essay 'The Illusion of Tribe' in 1970. In a scathing attack on the state of the field, Southall argued that 'empirical divergences are so gross, widespread and frequent as to render the concept of tribe as it exists in the general literature untenable'.[69] Southall's essay has been said to mark 'the intersection between the essentialization of tribes, whether out of research pragmatism or *naïveté*, and their radical historicization since the late 1970s'.[70]

In the wake of Fried and Southall's seminal work, the 'invention' of tribalism through colonial practices has been highlighted by a range of influential scholars including John Iliffe, Terence Ranger, Jean-Loup Amselle, Leroy Vail, and more recently, Mahmood Mamdani.[71] From the vantage point of the postcolonial era, tribes no longer appear as primordial entities, but as products of a colonial governmentality that sought to establish and maintain order through the management of local differences. Ethnicity is thereby recast as a general process of constructing in-groups and out-groups regardless of the historical period, while tribalism becomes understood as a specifically colonial

---

[64] Tax and Mednick 1960, 441.   [65] Hsu 1964, 174.   [66] Ekeh 1990, 664.
[67] Fried 1966, 537. See also Fried 1975, 99–105.   [68] Helm 1968.
[69] Southall 1970, 32.   [70] Lentz 1995, 316.
[71] Amselle and M'Bokolo 1985; Iliffe 1979; Mamdani 2012; Ranger 1983; Vail 1989b. The historicisation of tribes was preceded by Marxist scholarship that analysed tribalism as a kind of 'false consciousness'. See, for example, Mafeje 1971.

form of ethnic differentiation. Put differently, ethnicity becomes the universal substrate out of which tribes are constructed: 'Tribalism is reified ethnicity. It is culture pinned to a homeland, culture in fixity, politicized, so that it does not move.'[72] In this way, through the deconstruction of primitive society, the Manchester School's understanding of the tribe/ethnicity relationship was turned on its head: tribes were no longer understood as primitive human communities that transform into nations or ethnic groups through modernisation, but as products of colonial practices that reify ethnicity in a particular manner. If the colonial view was that tribes would transform into ethnic groups, the postcolonial view is that ethnicity was moulded into tribes. A depoliticised and detemporalised concept of ethnicity is thus posited as the transcendental form of culture difference that makes possible the historicisation of tribes and tribalism.

The Antinomies of Anticolonial Nationalism

The deconstruction of primitive society and the critique of tribe concept in the 1960s went hand in hand with the rise of anticolonial nationalism and the independence of the colonial territories. This political transformation also gained substantial interest from IR scholars. In 1962, for instance, the *Journal of International Affairs* published a special issue on nation-building that featured an article by Leonard Doob charting the passage of Africa from 'tribalism' to 'nationalism'.[73] But if primitive tribes were transforming into modern nations, why was it the concept of ethnicity, rather than that of nation or nationality, that replaced the concept of tribe? To grasp the unique appeal of ethnicity, it is necessary to understand how anticolonial nationalism was conceptualised by Western scholars in the mid twentieth century. Recalling some of the themes of Chapter 1, it quickly becomes clear that the main issue was the tight link between nationhood and statehood. Due to the semantic baggage of 'tribe' and 'nation' – the former associated with primitive society, the latter with state sovereignty – neither of these concepts was able to suture the fault lines that anticolonial nationalism was creating in conceptual architecture of the imperial world order. Another concept was needed, and this concept was ethnicity.

[72] Mamdani 2012, 7. [73] Doob 1962.

Three distinct conceptualisations of anticolonial nationalism can be identified in mid twentieth-century Western scholarship. The first two emerge more or less concurrently in the 1950s, while the third does not appear until the deconstruction of primitive society in the 1960s.[74] Representative of the first approach are the former British imperial administrator William Malcolm Hailey, the German pioneer of African linguistics Diedrich Westermann, who had also been an active member of the research team behind Hailey's pathbreaking *An African Survey*,[75] and the American political scientist John Kautsky. In a nutshell, the position of all three men was that the term 'nationalism' was inappropriate for the colonies.[76] The main reason they gave for this was the artificiality of colonial borders, especially in Africa, and the consequent mismatch between ethnocultural and political units. The territorial entities in Africa had been formed 'by the accidents of history' and had 'missed the dynamic influence of the concept of territorial nationalism', Hailey explained in the revised 1957 edition of *An African Survey*. As a result, the peoples that constituted the territorial units of Africa had 'for the most part no tradition of a common origin nor common outlook on their political future'.[77] Given the inappropriateness of 'nationalism', Hailey proposed 'Africanism' as an alternative.[78] The lack of correspondence between political and ethnocultural units in Africa was likewise underlined by Diedrich Westermann in an article published posthumously in 1957: 'In Africa there are no nations, but only tribal groups, usually small, sometimes related to other groups in language, culture and tradition. There is no political power binding them together and forming a common will and outlook.'[79] John Kautsky's *Political Change in Underdeveloped Countries*, published in 1962, was less categorical on the terminological question and accepted that trying to prohibit the term 'nationalism' would be 'futile' given that it was already in widespread use. Still, he concurred with Hailey and Westermann that nationalism 'in the underdeveloped areas' was 'a phenomenon quite different from European nationalism' and concluded that 'it might

---

[74] For an excellent review of the literature on African nationalism in the 1950s, see Kilson 1958.
[75] Kallaway 2017, 872.
[76] Hailey 1957, 251–260; Kautsky 1962, 30–56; Westermann 1957, 1003.
[77] Hailey 1957, 251. [78] Hailey 1957, 252. [79] Westermann 1957, 1003.

therefore have been preferable to avoid the use of the term with reference to underdeveloped countries altogether'.[80]

A second group of scholars associated with modernisation theory was more willing to extend the concept of nationalism to the non-Western world. One of the earliest examples is James Smoot Coleman's pioneering work on Nigerian nationalism from the 1950s. Taking issue with Hailey's coinage of 'Africanism', Coleman pointed out that the contrast between Africanism and nationalism 'not only tends to perpetuate the erroneous notion that Africans are essentially different from the rest of mankind, but it also exaggerates the differences in the operation of the historical process of nation-building in Europe and in Africa'.[81] To this extent, Coleman was willing to place Europe and Africa on the same plane. When it came to the conceptualisation of the nation-building process, however, Coleman adopted the usual developmental hierarchy between primitive tribes and modern nations. His framework consisted of three tiers that he labelled 'tribe', 'nationality', and 'nation'. In developmental terms, the tribe came first and referred to 'the largest social group defined primarily in terms of kinship'.[82] Next came the nationality, which Coleman described as 'a convenient intermediary category introduced to refer to a people larger in population than a tribe, which is not yet and may never be a nation, but which offers the strongest cultural basis for nationhood at the highest level and on the largest scale of all traditional African groupings'.[83] Finally, there was the nation: 'A large group of people who feel that they form a single and exclusive community destined to be an independent state.'[84] A nation was thus conceived as a 'post-tribal' community that emerged through modernisation.[85] Although Coleman's analysis was concerned with 'the process of nation-building and national awakening in Nigeria', he emphasised that this process was not yet complete: 'Nigeria has never been and is not yet a nation.'[86] Where the likes of Hailey established a qualitative spatial dichotomy between Europe and Africa, Coleman's narrative was based on a quantitative difference: Africa was fundamentally similar to Europe, only temporally lagging behind.

Another influential exponent of the modernisation paradigm was Rupert Emerson, Professor of Government at Harvard University and

[80] Kautsky 1962, 33. [81] Coleman 1958, 478. [82] Coleman 1958, 424.
[83] Coleman 1958, 423. [84] Coleman 1958, 422. [85] Coleman 1954, 405.
[86] Coleman 1958, 423.

specialist on African and Asian nationalism. In 1960, he published his classic study of anticolonial nationalism, evocatively titled *From Empire to Nation: The Rise to Self-Assertion of Asian and African Peoples*. In Emerson's view, African and Asian claims for self-determination were evidence of the globalisation of European nationalism: '[T]he peoples of Asia and now, somewhat hesitatingly and often in embryonic fashion, the peoples of Africa are flowering out into luxuriant nationalisms of their own.'[87] This pivotal moment signalled 'the turning of the weapons – the ideas, the instruments, the institutions – of the West against itself'.[88] At the same time, Emerson emphasised that the progress of nationalism in the developing world might not be smooth sailing. 'It appears inevitable', Emerson warned, 'that Africa's further advance should be punctuated by a series of contests between tribal groups, each newly aware of its communal identity.'[89] In most of Asia and Africa, it was still the clan or the tribe, rather than the nation, that constituted 'the typical social and cultural units'.[90] The 'anti-character' of anticolonial nationalism created 'a deceptive sense of national unity'.[91]

The first two conceptualisations of nationalism – one reserving it for the European world, the other coupling it to the grand narrative of modernisation – reflect the two opposed yet complementary moments of European colonial ideology: the moment of difference, where the primitive 'other' is depicted as qualitatively different from the civilised 'self', and the moment of identity, where the primitive 'other' is depicted as fundamentally identical to, only temporally distanced from, the civilised 'self'.[92] From the mid-1960s, however, there emerged a third position that broke with this colonial logic. Instead of associating nations and nationalism with the modern state, this third group of scholars understood nationality as an ethnocultural identity, thus establishing a parallel between African tribes and European nationalities. Among the first to argue this point was the British anthropologist Ken Post in his 1964 study of new states in West Africa: '[I]f a nation is conceived as having a common culture,

---

[87] Emerson 1960a, 89.   [88] Emerson 1960a, 17.   [89] Emerson 1960a, 113.
[90] Emerson 1960b, 14.   [91] Emerson 1960b, 8.
[92] Antony Anghie (2005, 4) calls this oscillation between universalism and particularism the 'dynamic of difference'. On the aporetic logic of European colonial ideology, see also Bhabha 1994, 121–131; Young 1995, 1–26, 151–172; Young 2004, 158–198.

language, and historical experience, as the eighteenth- and nineteenth-century European writers held, then the closest approximation to national sentiment in West Africa must be the "tribalism" so often denounced by the nationalists.'[93] Five years later, W. J. Argyle extended Post's argument to the whole continent, asserting that 'African tribes and their tribalism can indeed be equated with European nations and their nationalism'.[94] One of the most influential representatives of this position was the American anthropologist Elizabeth Colson, who urged anthropologists to study European and African phenomena on equal terms: 'the so-called modern tribes have little in common with one another that they do not have with the so-called nationalities found in other parts of the world', she asserted at the symposium of the American Ethnological Society in 1967.[95] Colson further suggested that the word 'tribalism' be discarded altogether, given its erroneous and pejorative insinuation that political struggles in Africa were anachronistic survivals from an earlier age.[96] At the same symposium, Frank Bessac suggested that, if the evolutionary metanarrative was abandoned, a tribe was essentially 'a stateless nationality'.[97] The upshot of this conceptual reshuffling was to collapse the concept of tribe into the concept of nation and the concept of tribalism into the concept of nationalism.

By refusing to distinguish between tribes and nations, scholars such as Colson and Bessac closed the gap between the primitive and civilised worlds. However, this conceptual move was based on an ethnocultural definition of the nation that disregarded nationalism's political dimension. This shortcut left these scholars open to criticism, as seen in P. H. Gulliver's rearguard action in defence of the nationalism/tribalism distinction in 1969. To begin with, Gulliver pointed out that the meaning of the word 'nation' was not limited to sociocultural or ethnographical entities but was in fact more commonly associated with the *states* of Africa.[98] He then added that what was usually called 'tribalism' in Africa was not concerned with the establishment of a sovereign state, but with the acquisition of local or regional autonomy 'under the accepted superiority of the wider state'.[99] In other words, tribalism was not about political independence: '[U]nlike European nations, tribes are mainly in opposition to one another, rather than

---

[93] Post 1964, 66.   [94] Argyle 1969, 41.   [95] Colson 1968, 201.
[96] Colson 1968, 202.   [97] Bessac 1968, 60.   [98] Gulliver 1969, 27.
[99] Gulliver 1969, 28.

to the overarching authority of the encompassing state.'[100] For this reason, Gulliver suggested that instead of equating African tribalism with European nationalism, it was more fruitful to compare the phenomenon of tribalism 'with other kinds of particularism: regionalism, sectionalism, communalism, casteism, etc.'[101] It was through internal competition within existing state boundaries, rather than through outright secession, that tribalism challenged the unity of African states.[102]

What these scholars were struggling with was a case of a missing term: a conceptual lacuna had emerged between the primitive and the civilised worlds that neither the language of nationalism nor the language of tribalism was able to fill. On the one hand, the terms 'nation' and 'nationalism' had acquired connotations of sovereignty and political independence that were missing from most of the particularistic mobilisations taking place in the postcolonial states. On the other hand, the terms 'tribe' and 'tribalism' possessed a Eurocentric teleology and derogatory connotation of backwardness that most commentators were by now seeking to avoid. Ultimately, this gap was filled by the concept of ethnicity, which was able to avoid both of the above pitfalls: in contrast to nationalism, ethnicity had no association with statehood or secession; and in contrast to tribalism, ethnicity did not imply a civilisational hierarchy. The concept of ethnicity was thus able to provide a seemingly neutral and apolitical vocabulary through which particularistic identities could be discussed on equal terms in all places and times.

That said, the term 'ethnicity' also faced some resistance. For example, the use of the term 'ethnic group' as an alternative to 'tribe' was considered, but ultimately rejected, by Gulliver in 1969:

The sociological alternative is 'ethnic group', with its convenient 'ethnic' and 'ethnicity'. Unfortunately perhaps, this usage seems to be largely confined to intellectuals – mainly non-African ones too, and sometimes with an almost desperate air of self-righteousness in refusing to use the allegedly out-of-date

---

[100] Gulliver 1969, 28.   [101] Gulliver 1969, 30.
[102] Gulliver 1969, 30. The French anthropologist Paul Mercier (1961, 74–77) had made a similar distinction in an article published several years earlier: modernist or territorial nationalism was about secession, whereas traditionalist or tribal nationalism was about opposition to ethnic inequalities within the framework of the existing state. Mercier also identified 'para-nationalism' as an intermediate form.

and pejorative term, 'tribe'. Yet the advocates of this newer term mean, and refer to, precisely the same set of confused facts and elastically defined units of people as are encompassed by the older word. Moreover, this usage of a newer, seemingly scientific term wrongly suggests that the whole complex problem has somehow already been cleared up. But of course it has not been cleared up at all. Admittedly, there may be some value in avoiding some of the unfortunate associations of 'tribe', etc., by taking up the euphemism. Nevertheless I prefer to use the older term: partly because it is still the term used by East Africans themselves, but also because it may be valuable to eschew the somewhat spurious scientific certitude carried by the term 'ethnic'.[103]

In this passage, Gulliver raises an important point about the semantic politics that govern the choice between the register of tribalism and that of ethnicity. In the wake of decolonisation, 'tribe' and 'tribalism' became derogatory labels that are typically used to describe undesirable forms of behaviour, especially in Africa.[104] The choice between tribal and ethnic registers thus becomes, at least in part, a political one: 'If one disapproves of the phenomenon, "it" is "tribalism"; if one is less judgmental, "it" is "ethnicity".'[105] However, the fact that ethnicity lacks the derogatory connotations of tribalism should not be taken to imply that it is any less ideological, or any less problematic. It is rather the case that ethnicity is implicated in a different kind of ideological project and thus problematic in a different way: whereas the conceptual history of tribe is entangled with the history of colonialism, the conceptual history of ethnicity is entwined with the formation of the international order. Instead of positing a spatiotemporal hierarchy between civilised nations and primitive tribes, the concept of ethnicity presents itself as a morally neutral category applicable to all places and times. And, as Gulliver intimates, it is precisely in its apparent neutrality that the ideological power of ethnicity resides.

The Re-emergence of 'Ethnos' in Soviet Ethnography

In 1973, the French Marxist anthropologist Maurice Godelier suggested that the difficulties faced by Western anthropologists in defining the concept of tribe could, in part, be attributed to their failure to

---

[103] Gulliver 1969, 8.   [104] Ekeh 1990.   [105] Vail 1989a, 1.

Temporal Limits of the Tribe Concept 185

develop a coherent theory of social evolution.[106] In comparison, Soviet ethnography possessed a far more developed historical – materialist theory of social evolution derived from the work of Karl Marx and Friedrich Engels. Soviet ethnos-theory thus provides an even clearer illustration of how the new ethnos-based terms were taken up as transhistorical tools of diachronic analysis. As seen in Chapter 2, the term 'ethnos' had been introduced into Russian scholarly circles by Nikolai Mogilianskii, Sergei Rudenko, and Sergei Shirokogoroff already at the beginning of the twentieth century. After the Bolshevik Revolution, however, Mogilianskii and Shirokogoroff emigrated, while Rudenko – the only member of the trio to remain in Russia – was marginalised. What interests us in this section is the re-emergence of ethnos-theory in the Soviet Union in the second half of the twentieth century. To reconstruct this story, let us pick up the trail where we left off in Chapter 2: the Stalinist clamp-down on ethnology and ethnography at the end of the 1920s.

In April 1929, a conference was organised in Leningrad to legislate Soviet policy on the object and purpose of ethnology and ethnography. Valerian Aptekar spearheaded the attack against these fields, arguing that ethnology was premised on the separation of ethnic phenomena from their socioeconomic base and thus constituted a 'bourgeois' science.[107] The biosocial concept of ethnos came under heavy fire and the term 'biologisation' was coined specifically to denounce the linkage of the social and biological spheres in ethnos-theory.[108] In the end, the conference concluded that the scientific pretensions of ethnology were misguided, but that ethnographical work could be incorporated into the historical – materialist study of human societies.[109] Ethnography was thus relegated to the status of an auxiliary historical science comparable to palaeography or heraldry.[110] With the biosocial concept of ethnos discredited and Shirokogoroff's works banned, the object of ethnography came to be theorised through the Stalinist triad of tribes, nationalities, and nations. In this evolutionary framework, each concept of the triad was associated with a distinct phase in the historical – materialist development of society: the concept of tribe was associated with the primitive – communalist epoch, the concept of

---

[106] Godelier 1973.   [107] Slezkine 1991, 479.
[108] Alymov and Podrezova 2019, 183.   [109] Slezkine 1991, 479.
[110] Skalník 1986, 157.

nationality with the period of slavery and feudalism, and the concept of nation with the capitalist age.[111] The existence of multiple national groups within the Soviet Union was acknowledged, but it was assumed that over time these groups would fuse into a supraethnic 'Soviet people'.[112]

The outbreak of the Second World War and the prospect of international borders being redrawn gave ethnographical work a new lease of life. In 1942, the General Headquarters of the Red Army ordered Moscow-based geographers and ethnographers to prepare maps of the nationalities of the Soviet Union. It was in this context that Pavel Kushner – appointed as the head of the Department of Ethnic Statistics and Cartography at the Institute of Ethnography in Moscow in 1944 – reintroduced the term 'ethnos' into Soviet ethnography. In 1945, Kushner defended a doctoral thesis titled 'The Western Part of the Lithuanian Ethnographic Territory', parts of which were subsequently incorporated into an influential book titled *Ethnic Territories and Ethnic Borders*.[113] The publication of Kushner's book in 1951, coupled with Stalin's death two years later, created a new opening for the theorisation of ethnic identities in the Soviet Union.[114]

The two key figures behind the popularisation of ethnos-theory in the post-Stalinist era were Lev Gumilev and Yulian Bromley.[115] Gumilev first used the term 'ethnos' in a series of fourteen articles titled 'Landscape and Ethnos', published in both Russian and English between 1964 and 1973.[116] It seems likely that Gumilev borrowed the term 'ethnos' from Rudenko, who had been one of his most important mentors.[117] Gumilev's definition of ethnos was highly essentialised insofar as he considered each ethnos to be a self-contained and self-sustaining totality.[118] In line with the Marxist tradition, Gumilev drew a clear distinction between the social and natural spheres: the evolution of society from feudalism to socialism via capitalism took place in the social sphere, whereas an ethnos was a 'biophysical reality' that belonged to the natural sphere. 'Every human individual operated simultaneously in both modes of existence, as a member of society and a representative of an ethnos', Gumilev explained.[119] The 'naturalness'

---

[111] Skalník 1988, 162. [112] Skalník 1990, 184.
[113] Alymov, Anderson, and Arzyutov 2019, 42–43. [114] Skalník 1988, 162.
[115] Oushakine 2009, 86–95. [116] Bassin 2016, 135.
[117] Bassin 2016, 10, 160. [118] Bassin 2016, 23.
[119] Gumilev, quoted in Bassin 2016, 27.

of the ethnos had both an internal and an external source. Internally, it stemmed from the genetic properties of individual human beings, which were transmitted through the practice of endogamy within the ethnos. Externally, it was related to the geographical environment in which the ethnos was embedded.[120] Although each individual ethnos went through a life cycle that Gumilev called 'ethnogenesis', these ethnic processes were wholly divorced from social processes. Gumilev's conceptual segregation of the ethnos from the social realm transformed the ethnos into a transhistorical category that was applicable at every stage of human social evolution.[121]

Although Gumilev would become a hugely influential thinker in late Soviet and post-Soviet Eurasia, he remained a marginal and nonconformist figure in the Soviet academy.[122] By contrast, Yulian Bromley was at the epicentre of Soviet ethnography, serving as the director of the Institute of Ethnography of the Soviet Academy of Sciences from 1966 to 1989.[123] Owing to the bridge-building work of Western scholars such as Ernest Gellner, Bromley also became the best-known representative of Soviet ethnos-theory in the West.[124] The fact that Bromley published a substantial amount of work in English certainly helped to build his international reputation as well.[125] He first developed his theory of ethnos in the late 1960s, around the same time as Gumilev.[126] Although Bromley always referred to Gumilev's work critically and sought to distance his own theory from that of his rival, there are strong parallels between them. In fact, the parallels are so strong that Gumilev accused Bromley of plagiarising his ideas.[127]

At the core of Bromley's theory was a distinction between narrow and broad meanings of 'ethnos'. In the narrow sense, an ethnos was an 'ethnikos' or 'ethnic community proper', which Bromley defined as 'a historically formed aggregate of people who share common, relatively stable specific features of culture (including language) and psychology, realization of their unity and distinctiveness from other similar aggregates of people as well as the self-nomination'.[128] The ethnikos was

---

[120] Bassin 2016, 29–42. [121] Bassin 2016, 27.
[122] On Gumilev's influence, see Bassin 2016, 177–305; Sneath 2007, 176–177.
[123] Skalník 1990, 184. [124] For example, Gellner 1977, 1980.
[125] For example, Arutiunov and Bromley 1978; Bromley 1974a, 1977, 1978; Bromley and Kozlov 1989.
[126] Oushakine 2009, 87. [127] Bassin 2016, 172–173.
[128] Bromley 1978, 18. See also Bromley 1974b, 66–67.

also characterised by 'relative conservatism' and stability through time: 'For instance, Ukrainian ethnikos has existed during feudalism and capitalism, and it exists now, under socialism.'[129] By contrast, the broad meaning of 'ethnos' referred to an 'ethno-social organism' that combined the narrow definition of ethnikos with socioeconomic and political elements. Bromley singled out five distinct kinds of ethnosocial organisms, arranged in a developmental ladder: the tribe, the slave-owning nationality, the feudal nationality, the bourgeois nation, and the socialist nation.[130] The broad understanding of the ethnos thus allowed for the incorporation of Marxist socioeconomic stages into his theory.[131] It also ensured that the concept of ethnos could be applied to all peoples across all historical periods.[132] Under Bromley's leadership, the purpose of Soviet ethnography became the study of 'any and all ethnoses'.[133]

Akin to the emergence of ethnicity in Western anthropology, the return of ethnos-theory in the Soviet Union was an attempt to address the shortcomings of evolutionist theories. First, there was the manifest failure of particularistic ethnic identities to merge into a 'Soviet superethnicity' under socialism.[134] Against this backdrop, the concept of ethnos served as a 'morally neutral' category that made it possible for scholars to acknowledge the existence of ethnic diversity in the Soviet Union without raising the potentially dangerous issue of national self-determination or being accused of hindering the progress toward socialism.[135] Second, there was the theoretical problem presented by diachronic analysis. Traditionally, Marxist models of socioeconomic evolution had assumed that societies dissolved and re-formed as they passed through distinct historical stages. Within this stadial framework, it was impossible to explain ethnic continuities across the different stages of socioeconomic development. By positing a stable ethnic core that transcended different evolutionary stages, ethnos-theory offered a 'bridging mechanism' that made diachronic analysis possible without challenging the Marxist evolutionary paradigm.[136] In other words, the concept of ethnos served as a 'heuristic device' that reconciled the Marxist stages of socioeconomic development on the one hand with

---

[129] Bromley 1978, 19.
[130] Bromley 1978, 19. See also Bromley and Kozlov 1989, 431; Kozlov 1974, 84.
[131] Skalník 1990, 186–187.   [132] Bromley 1978, 15–16.
[133] Arutiunov and Bromley 1978, 12.   [134] Shanin 1989, 418.
[135] Banks 1996, 22.   [136] Banks 1996, 22–23.

the historical continuity of particular peoples on the other.[137] In this way, ethnos-theory was able to bring the object of ethnography in line with Soviet state ideology.[138] What the Soviet concept of ethnos shares with the concept of ethnicity in Western anthropology is a transhistorical quality that is not limited to a particular historical epoch.

Summary

This section has focused on the problematisation of evolutionary narratives in Western anthropology and Soviet ethnography in the second half of the twentieth century, demonstrating how ethnos-based terms were articulated to supplement existing frameworks. In the existing literature, scholars have tended to draw a sharp contrast between the Western concept of ethnicity and the Soviet concept of ethnos. According to Teodor Shanin, for example, the Western tradition views ethnicity as an epiphenomenon produced by underlying social, economic, or political processes, whereas the Soviet tradition understands ethnicity as an objective phenomenon that is 'socially real'.[139] One explanation for this divergence is the subordination of Soviet ethnos-theory to a historical – materialist ideology that established a very clear conceptual distinction between the natural and social spheres. Given that the concept of ethnos was restricted to the natural sphere, it is unsurprising that it acquired a more objective quality.

What is most striking, however, is not the differences but the similarities between Western and Soviet conceptions of ethnicity. In both cases, ethnos-based terms emerged out of the crisis of the evolutionary metanarratives that had previously ordered Western and Soviet science. In the West, the concept of ethnicity emerged specifically out of the crisis of the colonial order and the deconstruction of the civilised/primitive opposition. As urbanisation and industrialisation reshaped the African continent, Western anthropologists witnessed the transformation of primitive rural tribespeople into civilised urbanites before their very eyes. In parallel, the rise of anticolonial nationalism seemed to be fusing local tribal societies into political nations. The upshot of these transformations was the dismantling of the civilised/primitive opposition, the marginalisation of the concept of tribe, and the

---

[137] Dragadze 1990, 207.　[138] Skalník 1986, 1990.
[139] Shanin 1986, 118. See also Skalník 1988, 159.

articulation of ethnicity as a supplementary category that could be applied to peoples in all places and times. Meanwhile, in the Soviet Union, the persistence of particularistic identities under socialism put into question the prevailing metanarrative of socioeconomic evolution toward a supraethnic Soviet people. Through the articulation of a 'natural' concept of ethnos, it was possible for the likes of Gumilev and Bromley to reconcile the persistence of these particularistic identities with prevailing state ideology. In the same way that the Western concept of ethnicity served as a bridge between the primitive and civilised worlds, the Soviet concept of ethnos served as a bridge across different stages of socioeconomic development. What made these ethnos-based concepts so attractive in both contexts was that they lacked the temporal hierarchy of their neighbours: ethnicity and ethnos served as morally neutral tools of synchronisation that located difference in space rather than time. It is to the development of this spatial or geographical register of culture difference that the next section turns.

Spatial Limits of the Culture Concept

The synchronistic conception of culture, which locates differences in space rather than time, can be traced to the work of the German philosopher Johann Gottfried Herder in the late eighteenth century. In his concern for the individuality of every 'Volk' has been found the seed not only of the fascist ideologies of the twentieth century, but also of the relativist-pluralist concept of culture that dominates liberal discourses of multiculturalism.[140] Contrary to the hierarchical concept of culture or civilisation that would rise to dominate Anglophone and Francophone social theory in the nineteenth century, Herder understood culture 'more like a net or a web, with each person connected to others multilaterally'.[141] Herder's influence was manifest in the works of influential nineteenth-century German scholars, including the brothers Wilhelm and Alexander von Humboldt; the founders of 'Völkerpsychologie' Moritz Lazarus and Heymann Steinthal; the historical geographers Carl Ritter and Friedrich Ratzel; and the

---

[140] Broce 1986; Sikka 2011. [141] Carhart 2007, 26.

ethnologist Adolf Bastian.[142] In the second half of the century, Ratzel and Bastian in particular played an important role in systematising a geographical understanding of human cultures.[143]

In 1886, the Herderian legacy was carried to the United States by a young Jewish-German scholar named Franz Boas. Known today as the father of American anthropology, Boas had studied geography in Germany under Theobald Fischer, an ardent Ritterian historical geographer, and worked at the Royal Ethnological Museum in Berlin under Bastian, from whom he learned a profound appreciation for inductive empirical analysis.[144] During his first two years in the United States, Boas worked as the geographical editor for the journal *Science* and published an important article on 'The Study of Geography'.[145] When he accepted a docentship in anthropology at Clark University in 1889, he brought this geographical sensitivity to the study of culture.[146]

Boas's preference for inductive empirical analysis meant that he never showed much interest in formalising a theory of culture. Instead, the task of ordering the growing amount of ethnographical data on Native American tribal groups fell to his numerous students and colleagues. Despite individual differences, the new generation of Boasian anthropologists was broadly united in its condemnation of the civilisational understanding of culture. Whereas the civilisational approach had a unilinear notion of historical or temporal progress at its core, the geographical paradigm of the Boasians privileged spatial categories. Notably, the explicitly spatial concept of 'culture area' was launched into prominence by Clark Wissler, a leading American anthropologist who worked with Boas in the early twentieth century.[147] Although Wissler's racist inclinations and desire to develop a general theory of culture departed from Boas's egalitarian and idiographic preferences, both men were committed to a synchronistic understanding of culture that refused to classify people into civilisational hierarchies.[148] The culture area concept was subsequently taken

---

[142] Bunzl 1996. On Lazarus and Steinthal, see also Kalmar 1987. On Bastian, see also Köpping 1995.
[143] Santini 2018. [144] Bunzl 1996; Cole 1999, 38–62, 83–104; Renner 2004.
[145] Boas 1887a. [146] Speth 1978, 2.
[147] Wissler 1906, 1917, 1923, 1927, 1928. See also Kroeber 1931.
[148] Freed and Freed 1983; Barkan 1992, 108–111.

up by many of Boas's students, including Edward Sapir, Melville Herskovits, and Alfred Kroeber.[149]

Through the work of Boas and his numerous students, the temporalised understanding of culture as civilisational progress came under challenge from an alternative relativist-pluralist paradigm. The preceding section has already traced the crisis of the civilisational framework and demonstrated how it resulted in the displacement of the colonial concept of tribe by the seemingly timeless concept of ethnicity. This section provides the other half of the story, so to speak, by tracing the function of ethnicity within the new relativist-pluralist paradigm. In particular, I show how the relativisation and pluralisation of the culture concept threw into sharp relief what Ronald Cohen has called the 'unit problem' of anthropology: If cultures existed in the plural, how should cultures be identified and differentiated? What should be the basic unit of cultural analysis and cross-cultural comparison? Ultimately, it was the attempts to solve the unit problem that led to the popularisation of ethnicity as a new way of conceptualising human groups.[150]

Culture Areas and Museum Exhibits

In 1887, only a year after arriving on American soil, Franz Boas entered into a debate with Otis Tufton Mason, curator at the Smithsonian Institution, and John Wesley Powell, director of the Bureau of Ethnology.[151] On a theoretical level, the debate was about how to explain 'the occurrence of similar inventions in areas widely apart', to quote the title of Boas's article that started the debate.[152] On a practical level, it was about whether museum artefacts should be arranged according to a universal evolutionary series of inventions, as was the practice of the Smithsonian Institution at the time, or according to the particular tribal areas where they had been found, as Boas argued.[153] The debate offers valuable insight into turn-of-the-

---

[149] Herskovits 1924, 1930; Kroeber 1939; Sapir 1916, 44–51.
[150] Cohen 1978, 381–383.
[151] Boas 1887b, 1887c, 1887d; Mason 1887; Powell 1887. See also Buettner-Janusch 1957; Jacknis 1985; Stocking 1994a.
[152] Boas 1887b.
[153] Boas had previously been an assistant to Adolf Bastian at the Museum für Völkerkunde in Berlin, which displayed artefacts on an inductive basis rather than in an evolutionary series, and Boas's critique of the Smithsonian Institution's practice was no doubt inspired by his time with Bastian. It is worth

century world views insofar as the central function of a museum exhibit is to provide a rational ordering of artefacts, civilisations, and cultures: '[W]ithout representing a relation between things and conceptual structures, an institution is not a museum, but a storehouse.' In Foucauldian terms, a museum is an institution that puts the 'order of things' itself on display.[154]

Mason's premise for arranging exhibits in a universal evolutionary sequence was the assumption that 'like causes produce like effects' and that 'men will everywhere, under the same *stress* and with the same *resources*, make the same invention'.[155] To facilitate the study of their evolution over time, artefacts such as hunting implements should therefore be arranged into series ranging from the most primitive to the most advanced. In contrast, the central thrust of Boas's critique was that 'unlike causes produce like effects'.[156] A rattle, for example, could function as a ritual implement, a musical instrument, or a children's plaything – and it was impossible to tell which function it served without placing it in its particular tribal context.[157] Boas accordingly argued that artefacts should be arranged by tribal areas 'in order to teach the peculiar style of each group'.[158] The objective of museum exhibits, for Boas, was 'the dissemination of the fact that civilization is not something absolute, but that it is relative, and that our ideas and conceptions are true only so far as our civilization goes'.[159] In his reply, Mason suggested that a 'checkerboard' arrangement might be able to take into account both perspectives: moving in one direction the cases would represent 'races or tribes or locations', while moving in a perpendicular direction the cases would represent 'all the products of human activity in classes according to human wants'.[160] This compromise did not persuade Boas. 'In ethnology all is individuality', he insisted.[161]

Boas's proposal for a tribal classification of museum exhibits was next challenged by John Wesley Powell, director of the Bureau of Ethnology. Powell attacked what he saw as an implicit essentialism

---

noting here that Nikolai Mogilianskii, curator at the Russian Museum in St Petersburg and pioneer of Russian ethnos-theory, likewise followed Bastian's model of arranging exhibits by cultural or geographical areas. See Cvetkovski 2013.

[154] Lord 2006, 5. See also Hooper-Greenhill 1989. [155] Mason 1886, 248.
[156] Boas 1887b, 485. [157] Boas 1887c, 588. [158] Boas 1887b, 485.
[159] Boas 1887c, 589. [160] Mason 1887, 534. [161] Boas 1887c, 589.

in Boas's argument, pointing out that tribal groups were not stable entities: 'Most of the tribes best known to history have been absorbed, consolidated, and redivided again and again.'[162] To be representative, a museum collection arranged by tribal grouping would have to be collected 'by an army of collectors' in a single day.[163] Besides being 'monotonous and meaningless', such a collection was also 'an impossibility by reason of its magnitude'.[164] Powell was also sceptical about simplifying such a collection by classifying the different tribes on an 'ethnic' basis. After discussing the inadequacies of racial, linguistic, institutional, artistic, and geographical classifications, he concluded that 'there is and can be no ethnic classification of the tribes of America'.[165]

At first glance, Powell's argument may appear like a convincing refutation of Boas's position. Yet closer examination shows that the two men were in fact talking at cross-purposes. This becomes clearer from Boas's response to Powell:

The ideal plan of their arrangement is to exhibit a full set of a representative of an ethnical group, and to show slight peculiarities in small special sets. Experience shows that this can be done with collections from all parts of the world without over-burdening the collection with duplicates, and without making artificial classifications – only by grouping the tribes according to ethnic similarities. Such groups are not at all intended to be classifications, as Major Powell infers in his remarks on this subject. The principal difference between the plan advocated by Major Powell and adopted by Professor Mason, and that of other museums, is, that the latter exhibit the individual phenomenon, while the former make classifications that are not founded on the phenomenon, but in the mind of the student.[166]

Whereas Powell understood an 'ethnic' classification of American tribes as an intellectual exercise that entailed the organisation of abstract culture traits by scholars, Boas used the term 'ethnical group' with reference to concrete human communities that the anthropologist could visit and study in the field. For Boas, an 'ethnical group' was not an abstract category, but a concrete phenomenon that emerged out of social and cultural processes of group closure.

There was something of a convergence between Boas's and Mason's views in the 1890s, catalysed by the Chicago World's Fair of 1893. While preparing the Smithsonian Institution's display for the event,

[162] Powell 1887, 612.   [163] Powell 1887, 612.   [164] Powell 1887, 613.
[165] Powell 1887, 613.   [166] Boas 1887d, 614.

Mason came to the realisation that 'the character of the artifacts clustered not according to language or race, but according to local environmental zones'.[167] In the Smithsonian Institution's annual report of 1895, Mason identified eighteen 'American Indian environments or culture areas'.[168] Later, in an article on 'Environment' written for the *Handbook of American Indians North of Mexico* in 1907, he distinguished twelve 'ethnic environments'.[169] However, Mason's outline of these culture areas or ethnic environments was still premised on the scholarly classification of environmental zones and not on the actually existing group boundaries preferred by Boas. He also remained committed to a universal evolutionary scheme of cultural development, which Boas firmly rejected.[170] At the same time, Boas himself was becoming more aware of the difficulty of constructing a satisfactory tribal or ethnic context for collected artefacts.[171] In an article published in 1907, he acknowledged the limitations of the material collected by anthropologists, lamenting that the relations of different cultures 'can not be expressed by any arrangement based on so small a portion of the manifestation of ethnic life as is presented by specimens'.[172]

In 1902, William Henry Holmes, who succeeded Powell as director of the Bureau of Ethnology, ventured his opinion on the arrangement of museum exhibits. Recalling the debate between Boas and Mason, Holmes suggested that there were two principal ways of arranging exhibits: one based on 'culture-history' series and the other based on 'geo-ethnic' series.[173] The former entailed ordering social and political groups according to the evolutionary stages of savagery, barbarism, and civilisation. Holmes, like Boas, considered such an arrangement to be problematic, although more for pragmatic than methodological or normative reasons. On the one hand, he observed that most civilised polities, such as the British Empire, were 'too large and too complex to be used in classification'. On the other hand, 'inferior' political units tended to be so small that they would require 'thousands of exhibition units – too many entirely for practical purposes of grouping and installation'.[174] 'What is wanted', Holmes concluded, 'is a simple natural grouping of the very diversified ethnic phenomena.'[175] Such a

---

[167] Jacknis 1985, 80.   [168] Mason 1896, 646.   [169] Mason 1907, 427.
[170] Jacknis 1985, 82–83.   [171] Jacknis 1985, 108.   [172] Boas 1907, 928.
[173] Holmes 1902, 495–496. As an additional possibility, Holmes mentioned 'special' exhibits that could be designed to highlight particular cultural features.
[174] Holmes 1902, 488.   [175] Holmes 1902, 488–489.

'geographic-ethnic' or 'geo-ethnic' arrangement would include 'everything ethnical that the area produces, no matter what the race, the nation, the culture stage or the time represented'.[176] The term 'ethnical' here referred to 'the people and culture of the area represented. I say first *people* because, after all, it is the people we are studying, and a display of all the culture phenomena of a region without some definite illustration of the people concerned would be wholly unsatisfactory'.[177]

To sum up, there are two important themes that emerge out of the exchanges between Boas, Mason, and Powell, as well as the subsequent intervention by Holmes. The first is the stark contrast between temporal-historical and spatial-geographical frameworks for ordering the peoples of the world. Whenever the idea of ethnicity appears in these texts, it is associated with a spatial-geographical arrangement of exhibits and opposed to temporal-historical metanarratives about cultural or civilisational progress. The second theme, which emerges particularly strongly from Boas's and Holmes's contributions, is the understanding of ethnicity as a property of real and tangible human populations. Whereas culture traits and evolutionary schemas were free-floating abstractions, ethnic groups were concrete communities that anthropologists could encounter in their fieldwork. The remainder of this section traces how, over the course of the following decades, this incipient concept of ethnicity would become one of the most widely used concepts of Anglophone anthropology.

Society versus Culture

The twentieth century witnessed the successive elaboration of two conceptual distinctions pertaining to the concept of culture. The first was the conceptual distinction between heredity and environment, or nature and nurture, that began to coalesce in the second half of the nineteenth century and was well established by the second decade of the twentieth century (see Chapter 2). In 1917, Alfred Kroeber – a leading American anthropologist and former student of Franz Boas – expressed this distinction in terms of the 'organic' and 'superorganic' spheres. Whereas the organic sphere referred to biological qualities and processes, the superorganic sphere was the domain of social and

[176] Holmes 1902, 489.   [177] Holmes 1902, 489.

cultural activity. While similar contrasts such as body/soul and physical/mental stretched back centuries, Kroeber noted, 'the full import of the significance of the antithesis may be said to be only dawning upon the world'.[178]

The upshot of the conceptual separation of heredity and environment was the emergence of a 'condensed concept of culture-and-society' to designate what Kroeber had in 1917 labelled the 'superorganic' sphere. The terms 'culture' and 'society' were loosely employed, with little clarity on the specific relationship between them.[179] Very quickly, however, a second conceptual distinction between society and culture began to take shape. Already in 1917, the same year that Kroeber published his article differentiating the organic and superorganic spheres, Clark Wissler noted that 'no social group in the New World can be reckoned guilty of entire cultural independence'.[180] It was therefore necessary, Wissler argued, to distinguish between 'social, or tribal units' on the one hand and 'culture areas' on the other.[181]

The precise relationship between society and culture became a matter of sustained debate through the work of the American sociologist Talcott Parsons. Seeking to develop a more rational division of academic labour, Parsons established the interdisciplinary Department of Social Relations at Harvard in 1946 with the aim of bringing together psychologists, sociologists, and anthropologists under his leadership: psychologists would study the individual, sociologists would study the social system, and anthropologists would study the cultural system.[182] These rationalising initiatives engendered a flurry of attempts to clarify the proper relationship between society and culture, and by extension, the proper relationship between sociology and anthropology. 'The relation between what is biological and what is sociocultural has just been said to be a sort of central pivot of anthropology', Kroeber explained in 1948. 'It is now necessary to consider the more precise relation of society and culture within the "organic-plus".'[183]

The attempts at conceptual specification in the 1940s and the 1950s were characterised by the mobilisation of numerous dichotomies onto which the terms 'society' and 'culture' were mapped. Among the most

---

[178] Kroeber 1917, 163.   [179] Kroeber and Parsons 1958, 583.
[180] Wissler 1917, 204.   [181] Wissler 1917, 204, 206.   [182] Kuper 1999, 53.
[183] Kroeber 1948, 7.

influential were structure/function, quantity/quality, form/content, and animal/human. In each pairing, the first term was associated with the concept of society and treated as universal while the second term was associated with the concept of culture and treated as particular. The linkage of society with structure was especially commonplace and many anthropologists, including prominent figures such as A. R. Radcliffe-Brown and Meyer Fortes, referred to 'social structure' or 'structure' instead of 'society'.[184] In 1949, for example, Fortes mapped the distinction between structure and culture onto the quantity/quality dichotomy, arguing that structure referred to those features of social life 'which are actually or ideally susceptible of quantitative description and analysis' while culture referred to the 'qualitative aspect of social facts'.[185]

Two years later, a similar distinction between society and culture was outlined by S. F. Nadel in *The Foundations of Social Anthropology*. Nadel's premise was that social reality was composed of two dimensions:

> One rests on the criterion of the aim contents or the purposive character of action patterns; the other, on the criterion of the relationships between individuals and of their position towards or in regard to each other. The order of standardized purposive action patterns contains the social entities we know as *institutions*; the order of relationships, the social entities we know as *groups* or *groupings*.[186]

The set of purposive action patterns Nadel labelled 'culture' while the relationships between individuals that constituted social groupings he called 'society'.[187] Although both culture and society were abstractions, the latter was 'an abstraction of a higher order'.[188] Nadel therefore suggested that society could be understood as the 'structure' or 'form' of social reality whereas culture referred to its 'content' or 'function'. Crucially, however, Nadel cautioned against seeing this as a simple binary opposition: '[C]ulture, too, has a "pattern" or "form", as institutions or action patterns also exhibit "structural" features.'[189]

Nadel was not alone in highlighting the asymmetry that characterised the relationship between society and culture. The same point was made by Kroeber, who mapped the difference between society

---

[184] For example, Fortes 1949, 1953; Radcliffe-Brown 1940.
[185] Fortes 1949, 57. [186] Nadel 1951, 78. [187] Nadel 1951, 79–80.
[188] Nadel 1951, 82. [189] Nadel 1951, 83.

and culture onto the difference between animals and humans. For Kroeber, the concept of society referred broadly to 'group relations' whereas the concept of culture invoked 'the mass of learned and transmitted motor reactions, habits, techniques, ideas, and values – and the behavior they induce'. Hence, 'society precedes and underlies culture'. With regard to the distinction between animals and humans, Kroeber believed culture to be 'the special and exclusive product of men'. It was culture that differentiated human societies from the societies formed by social animals such as ants and bees: 'There is no culture on the subhuman level.'[190] Society and culture were therefore analytically distinguishable but in the case of human groups always occurred together: 'As something shared and supra-individual, culture can exist only when a society exists; and conversely every human society is accompanied by a culture.'[191] Yet the most important part of Kroeber's exploration of these concepts was relegated to a footnote of his *Anthropology*. In this critical footnote, which marked the self-deconstruction of the society/culture opposition, Kroeber observed that human societies, unlike anthills or beehives, 'are also culturally shaped and modeled'. While some level of social interaction was a necessary precondition of culture, 'specific human societies are more determined by culture than the reverse'. Echoing Nadel's aforementioned observation about cultural content possessing a 'pattern' or 'form' of its own, Kroeber was compelled to exclaim that 'social forms become part of culture!'[192]

The reason for the self-deconstruction of the society/culture opposition is the asymmetry between the two terms, which destabilises their relationship. The point becomes clearer when we consider the distinction between animals and humans, upon which Kroeber grounds his discussion of society and culture. What we have here is not a mutually exclusive binary, but a hierarchical distinction where one of the two terms occupies a privileged position relative to the other: the human is not only opposed to the animal, but is also a special kind of animal. The category of the human thus contains the category of the animal within itself, as the latter is sublated and elevated into the former. At the same time, the category of the animal contains the category of the human as a particular species. Each side of the dichotomy thus

---

[190] Kroeber 1948, 7–9.   [191] Kroeber 1949, 183.   [192] Kroeber 1948, 10n5.

overflows the slash to contaminate the other side. Similarly, as Kroeber was forced to conclude, there is a mutual contamination of culture and society. And, to anticipate the argument that follows later in this section, it was precisely to capture the self-deconstruction of the society/culture dichotomy – the becoming-cultural of the social and the becoming-social of the cultural – that the concept of ethnicity was adopted by anthropologists in the second half of the twentieth century. We must take Fredrik Barth very seriously and very literally when he characterises ethnicity as the 'social organization of culture difference'.[193]

The Quest for the Culture-Bearing Social Unit

The desire to clarify the relationship between 'society' and 'culture' was heightened by advances in statistical methods, which generated a newfound interest in cross-cultural comparisons. A fundamental challenge facing such comparative work was establishing a standardised unit of comparison that could be applied equally well in different cultural milieus. As one early twentieth-century study explained, 'Every rigid statistical inquiry supposes that the phenomena with which it deals can be stated in terms of some unit which is constant throughout its field. What is the unit social group?'[194] Traditionally, of course, the units that anthropologists studied in their fieldwork were 'tribes'. The problem was that the word 'tribe' lacked a standardised meaning and that its use varied immensely from author to author: '[A] population which is treated as a "tribe" by one writer might be regarded as a collection of many tribes by another.'[195] This was the most acute manifestation of what Ronald Cohen has called the 'unit problem' of anthropology.[196] And it was the quest to solve this problem that led to the emergence of ethnicity as an alternative way of conceptualising human groups.

Between 1926 and 1941, numerous regional classifications of cultural units were produced at the University of California under the oversight of Alfred Kroeber.[197] The largest of these studies was Stanislaw Klimek's *The Structure of California Indian Culture*, published in 1935. In the book, Klimek differentiated between two distinct

---

[193] Barth 1969a.   [194] Hobhouse, Wheeler, and Ginsberg 1915, 8.
[195] Hobhouse, Wheeler, and Ginsberg 1915, 8–9.   [196] Cohen 1978, 381–383.
[197] Driver et al. 1972, 311.

orders of facts: the territorial unit (the tribe or linguistic group) and the cultural elements. To determine the geographical distribution of the cultural elements, it was therefore necessary to satisfy three conditions: '(1) determined territorial entities, (2) knowledge of the presence, and (3) knowledge of the absence of the [cultural] element among the territorial entities'.[198] For our purposes, what is most significant in Klimek's study is his discussion of the term 'ethnic group' in a footnote:

> Both linguistic and cultural phenomena are products of social organizations. They owe their existence, their natures, and their distributions to definite human groups. Only in the fables of Andersen have cultural elements such as collars, pots, and baskets the ability to move by themselves and maintain independent existence. Of course we can connect some one ethnical group only with some particular cultural stratum, and not with the totality of the cultural inventory. That is why the structural analysis of culture is of such importance to ethnological research. Without this analysis, it is impossible to comprehend the observed phenomena.[199]

For Klimek, then, the ethnic group entailed the attachment of otherwise abstract cultural elements to a particular human population: '[E]ach cultural stratum has a connection with a definite ethnic group.'[200] The ethnic group was the critical link between the concepts of society and culture, connecting the territorial unit or tribe, on the one hand, with the cultural elements, on the other. For the time being, however, the concept of ethnicity remained a marginal one, relegated to an obscure footnote in Klimek's study. Its fuller elaboration in this context would take another three decades.

In 1935, the same year that Klimek's above study appeared, George Murdock set up the Cross-Cultural Survey at the Institute of Human Relations at Yale. The aim of the initiative was to produce a centralised database of material that would facilitate comparative studies and enable generalisations about human behaviour across different cultures.[201] At first intended as a purely intellectual endeavour, the onset of the Second World War also imbued the project with political and military significance, as the collation of cultural knowledge came to be seen as a valuable source of intelligence.[202] In 1946, Clellan Ford succeeded Murdock as the director of the Cross-Cultural Survey, and two years later the Carnegie Corporation arranged a conference at New

---

[198] Klimek 1935, 16.   [199] Klimek 1935, 49n9.   [200] Klimek 1935, 59.
[201] Murdock 1940.   [202] Ford 1970, 7–8.

Haven to discuss the future of the project. The conference was well attended, attracting participants from ten American universities as well as representatives from the Office of Naval Research, the Human Resources Development Board, the Carnegie Corporation, and the Rockefeller Foundation. At the end of the proceedings, the decision was made 'to establish an association cooperative in nature and national in scope, which will develop and distribute files of organized information related to human societies and cultures, the association to be known as the Human Relations Area Files'.[203] The Human Relations Area Files (HRAF) was officially created the following year, with funding from the Social Science Research Council and the Carnegie Corporation.[204]

Murdock and Ford identified three major figures as forerunners to the Cross-Cultural Survey and the HRAF: Herbert Spencer, William Graham Sumner, and Clark Wissler. All three scholars had dedicated their careers to collecting and classifying voluminous data about different peoples and cultures.[205] In particular, Murdock singled out Wissler's delineation of a 'universal culture pattern' as the main precursor of the HRAF.[206] According to Wissler, the universal culture pattern represented the essence of humanity: '[T]he pattern we have sketched here is the human pattern', he penned in 1923.[207] This universalistic approach to culture entailed a flattening of civilisational and racial hierarchies insofar as it was 'practically impossible to draw satisfactory distinctions between primitive and higher cultures, other than that they differ in complexity, or richness of content'.[208] Likewise, the aim of the Cross-Cultural Survey and the HRAF was to generate findings that would be 'applicable to any society from the most primitive to the most complex'.[209]

The key conceptual challenge faced by the HRAF was defining the basic social unit upon which cross-cultural comparison could be grounded. As Murdock explained, culture was always carried by and manifested through a particular social structure: '[T]he fate of a culture depends on the fate of the society which bears it.'[210] From smallest to

---

[203] Ford 1970, 10.
[204] On the history of the HRAF, see Ember 1997; Ford 1970, 1971; Murdock 1950.
[205] Ford 1970, 3–4; Ford 1971, 177–178; Murdock 1950, 718.
[206] Murdock 1950, 718. See also Murdock 1945; Wissler 1923, 73–98.
[207] Wissler 1923, 78.   [208] Wissler 1923, 78.   [209] Murdock 1950, 718.
[210] Murdock 1940, 365.

largest, the 'culture-bearing social units' discussed by Murdock were the community, the subtribe, the tribe, the nation, and the region. The corresponding cultural units were the local cultural variant, the subculture, the culture, the culture cluster, and the culture area.[211] Although the difference between these units was meant to be only a matter of size, civilisational hierarchies occasionally slipped in through the backdoor. For instance, Murdock reserved the category 'nation' for heterogeneous social units that were integrated politically and economically but not culturally – a situation that, he believed, was 'common enough in complex modern societies' but occurred 'infrequently on the primitive level'.[212]

The term 'ethnic group', which had been in sporadic use for several decades by now, acquired greater currency when the HRAF's Country Survey Series began to appear in 1956. The aim of the series was to facilitate cross-cultural comparisons by outlining the principal social, cultural, economic, and geographical features of selected Eurasian and African countries in a standardised format. All volumes in the series included a chapter on 'ethnic groups and languages'.[213] Although none of the HRAF's official publications unpacked the meaning of 'ethnic group', a valuable discussion of the concept can be found in a paper presented by Herbert Vreeland at a roundtable in 1958. The paper dealt with the difficulties that HRAF analysts, including Vreeland, faced when trying to identify ethnic groups. Using the ethnic categories that appeared in the existing literature proved problematic, as these were typically based on official censuses devised by British and French colonial administrators and tended to exaggerate religious factors. The HRAF team then attempted to base ethnic groups on objective criteria such as language, but this approach also ran into difficulties, as identity groups and language groups did not necessarily correspond. Ultimately, Vreeland concluded that it was necessary to consider subjective as well as objective criteria. Vreeland's conclusion also features the first written appearance of the word 'ethnicity' in this context:

In conclusion, the question raised here is: of what use is the concept ethnic groups to an integrated analysis of a whole society? The answer we have

---

[211] Murdock 1953, 478, table 1. [212] Murdock 1953, 479.
[213] For example, Blanchard 1958, 56–86; Fitzsimmons 1957, vol. I, 85–116; Harris 1956, 35–59; Harris 1957, 43–59; Steinberg 1957, 37–64; Vreeland 1957, 37–55.

come to is that a statement of the present ethnic groups should constitute the end, not the beginning of an analytic process. It should not be assumed that all the people in any given society are members of some ethnic group or community. Where concrete collectivities are discernible they may be ethnic groups, or ethnic communities, depending on the kind and degree of social cohesion, but provision should also be made for identifying and describing the function of more diffuse forms of cultural differentiation, or 'ethnicity,' within the total social system.[214]

Vreeland's insightful exploration of the difficulties of identifying ethnic groups touches upon a number of key themes that would be elaborated more fully over the ensuing decades. These include the disjuncture between observable linguistic or cultural traits and subjective group identities, as well as the importance of locating an ethnic group in relation to other groups in a broader social environment. When the concept of ethnicity was finally popularised in the 1960s, these themes would be front and centre.

The simmering debate around the 'unit problem' came to a boil with the publication of Raoul Naroll's article 'On Ethnic Unit Classification' in 1964. Naroll was an American anthropologist who had worked closely with the HRAF and was known for developing rigorous methodological tools for statistical analysis.[215] In his 1964 article, Naroll tackled 'the problem of defining the "tribe" or "society," conceived of as the basic culture-bearing unit'.[216] After discussing the shortcomings of existing definitions, Naroll introduced his own standardised unit for cross-cultural analysis. Curiously, despite the title of the article and the frequent references to 'ethnic units' in the text, Naroll decided to coin the term 'cultunit' to refer to the generic culture-bearing unit. He defined the cultunit as follows: '[p]eople who are domestic speakers of a common distinct language and who belong either to the same state or the same contact group'.[217] In other words, the cultunit was based on three criteria: language, territorial contiguity, and political organisation (although this third criterion only came into play when there existed 'a sufficiently authoritative political structure transcending the local community'). The combination of these criteria meant that the cultunit could

---

[214] Vreeland 1958, 88.   [215] For example, Naroll 1961.
[216] Naroll et al. 1964, 283.
[217] Naroll et al. 1964, 286. The term 'ethnic unit' appears in the title of Naroll's article and is interspersed throughout the text. Naroll also used the term 'ethnic unit' in an article published eight years earlier. See Naroll 1956.

be based on 'two different kinds of boundaries; a linguistic boundary and a communication-link (state or contract group) boundary. A cultunit boundary is formed by *either* of these boundaries'.[218] Based on the presence or absence of these two types of boundaries, Naroll distinguished four types of cultunits: the stateless linguistic group, the linguistically homogeneous state, the ruling group of a linguistically diverse state, and the subject group of a linguistically diverse state.

In specifying the analytical utility of the cultunit, Naroll entered into a discussion about the relationship between society and culture. He defined society as 'an actual system of social interaction' and culture as 'a pattern, a set of plans, a blueprint for living'. Like Alfred Kroeber and others, Naroll mapped the society/culture dichotomy onto the distinction between animals and humans: 'The distinction between culture and society becomes evident the moment we look at social insects. These have societies but lack cultures.' Naroll also seemed to acknowledge the asymmetry between these terms when he noted that the existence of culture presupposed some level of social interaction: 'Every culture includes as an element a social system, that is, a plan for social interaction.' However, Naroll was not interested in illuminating the interaction between social and cultural factors. What he wanted to do, instead, was to define a standardised analytical unit that would allow scholars to compare cultures from around the world. This ultimately required jettisoning the concept of society in favour of the ideal 'plans' that existed in the minds of individuals:

> The cultunit is offered as a unit of comparative statistical analysis of sets of *plans* – of social and cultural patterns as they exist in the minds of culture bearers. Study of actual social systems is of course relevant to the study of the plans which are supposed to govern them, but the unit of comparison is the plan, not the society.

Crucially, this meant that cultunits would not necessarily correspond to the societies that anthropologists encountered in the field: 'The cultunit sometimes may be a genuine social system but often will be only theoretical – an analytical abstraction.'[219]

Naroll's new concept sparked heated debate and featured prominently in the American Ethnological Society's symposium on the concept of tribe in 1967.[220] Most responses were unenthusiastic about the

---

[218] Naroll et al. 1964, 287.   [219] Naroll et al. 1964, 288.
[220] For the proceedings of the symposium, see Helm 1968.

new coinage. In an especially colourful commentary, Mervyn Jaspan raged that 'the "cultunit" is another linguistic monstrosity that does not clarify the notion of society or ethnic unit; it appears at first glance to have been emitted by a computer that had been fed a question having to do with certain socio-religious entities'.[221] George Murdock, the father of the Cross-Cultural Survey and a key force behind the HRAF, called the new term 'an ambiguous barbarism' and criticised Naroll for splitting the cultunit into four types. In Murdock's view, the culture-bearing unit had to be universal: '[A]ny culture must be comparable with any other, and this means that there can be only a single kind of "cultunit".'[222]

Significantly, a number of commentators wondered about the relationship between 'cultunits' and 'ethnic units'. 'Why should we continue to coin new terms', Paul Ducey asked, 'when established vocabulary would serve our purposes? Ethnic unit, it seems to me, would be equally appropriate and avoids possible religious associations.'[223] In the same vein, Frank Bessac observed that cultunits would 'approximate the actual ethnic units much of the time'. By 'ethnic unit' Bessac meant 'a group of people who often share a common, self-applied appellation, have a sense of common identity, and share a belief in a common heritage'.[224] Three years later at the American Ethnological Society's symposium, Bessac argued more forcefully that the ethnic unit would be a better category than the cultunit due to the restrictive association of the latter with communication: '[T]o the extent that we attempt to deal cross culturally with blue prints for culture and examine the relationship between the blue prints and actual behaviour, the identity group (i.e., ethnic units) is better suited for our needs than a communications group (i.e., cultunit) per se.'[225] This shift from the objective register of communication to the subjective register of identity is the key to the subsequent popularisation of ethnicity.

The critiques of Naroll's cultunit concept – and Bessac's observations in particular – reveal the structural rift between the concepts of society and culture from which the concept of ethnicity emerged. For Naroll, as we have seen, the value of the cultunit concept was its ability

---

[221] Naroll et al. 1964, 298.　[222] Naroll et al. 1964, 301.
[223] Naroll et al. 1964, 296.　[224] Naroll et al. 1964, 293.
[225] Bessac 1968, 69.

to provide an objective definition of the culture-bearing unit on the basis of mutual linguistic intelligibility and the presence of a communication link. The trouble with this definition, as critics pointed out and Naroll himself acknowledged, was that the resulting units often had little to no bearing on social reality. If the boundaries of cultunits corresponded to actual group boundaries, all the better, but this was by no means necessary for the application of the concept. Put differently, what Naroll's cultunit concept overlooked was the self-deconstruction of the society/culture dichotomy: by limiting his definition of the cultunit to ideal sets of plans, Naroll deliberately disregarded how social processes of group closure impact cultural activity and how social forms themselves become part of culture. A different approach, as Bessac suggested, was to focus on the actually existing human groups or 'ethnic units' that anthropologists encountered in their fieldwork. When the concept of ethnicity was added to the mix at the end of the 1960s, it was precisely with the aim of grounding the abstract concepts of society and culture in a more concrete setting. The result, as we shall see, was a dialectical reversal from an objective to a subjective understanding of human society and culture.

The Emergence of Ethnicity

Anthropologists had long been aware that the tribes they studied were somewhat arbitrary units. As Meyer Fortes observed in 1940, 'no "tribe" [...] can be circumscribed by a precise boundary – territorial, linguistic, cultural or political. Each merges with its neighbours in all these respects'.[226] Generally speaking, however, this problem was not addressed in any detail and A. R. Radcliffe-Brown's pragmatic solution was the norm: 'we take any convenient locality of a suitable size'.[227] The first serious considerations of the contradictions of the tribe concept came in 1942 with the publication of S. F. Nadel's *A Black Byzantium*. After considering and rejecting political, linguistic, and cultural definitions of the tribe, Nadel was left with only a 'tautological' definition: '[A] tribe or people is a group the members of which claim unity on the grounds of their conception of a specific common culture.'[228] It was Nadel's book, with its tentative shift from an

---

[226] Fortes 1940, 239–240. [227] Radcliffe-Brown 1940, 5.
[228] Nadel 1942, 17. See also Nadel 1951, 183–188.

objectivist to a subjectivist understanding of tribes, that initiated the deconstruction of the anthropological object and paved the way for the emergence of ethnicity.[229]

The next step came in 1954 with the publication of Edmund Leach's pathbreaking *Political Systems of Highland Burma*. Against the prevailing tendency to view social structures as the bearers of culture, Leach underscored the tension between these two orders: the same social structures could be represented by different cultural symbols and different social structures could be represented by the same cultural symbols.[230] In practice, therefore, the abstract concept of society was contaminated by the context-specific play of culture: '[W]hen social structures are expressed in cultural form, the representation is imprecise compared with that given by the exact categories which the sociologist, *qua* scientist, would like to employ.'[231] The abstract categories commonly used by the anthropologist 'exist only as logical constructions in his own mind'.[232] The 'real societies' where anthropologists conduct their ethnographic fieldwork could not be reduced to such categories because they were embedded within continually changing environments: 'Every real society is a process in time.'[233] The standard anthropological account of primitive society as a collection of autonomous culture-bearing societies or tribes had been predicated upon the systematic expulsion of time and process from the analysis.

Although the word 'ethnicity' never appears in *Political Systems of Highland Burma*, Leach's book was instrumental in setting the stage for its popularisation. Specifically, what the book did was open a debate on the relative significance of objective and subjective categories in determining analytical units: Should analytical units be determined by the criteria of the observer or by indigenous social distinctions?[234] The debate culminated in a series of exchanges between Raoul Naroll and Michael Moerman in the 1960s.[235] Representing the objectivist side, Naroll suggested that 'native concepts' could be helpful for describing particular cultures but were 'unsuited for cross-cultural comparisons'.[236] Representing the subjectivist camp, Moerman rejected the very premise that 'the world is composed of externally

---

[229] Amselle 1985, 20.   [230] Leach 1954, 17.   [231] Leach 1954, 4.
[232] Leach 1954, 5.   [233] Leach 1954, 5.   [234] Bentley 1987, 24.
[235] Moerman 1965, 1967, 1968; Naroll 1967, 1968; Naroll et al. 1964.
[236] Naroll 1967, 511.

discrete and internally homogeneous cultures'.[237] It was against this backdrop that Moerman launched the term 'ethnicity' into the fray.

Echoing Leach, Moerman made the case for a processual and relational approach to the study of human societies. Ethnic groups such as the Lue, he wrote, 'cannot be identified – cannot, in a sense, be said to exist – in isolation'. Without taking into account the broader sociocultural context within which the Lue were embedded, it was not possible to specify the 'Lue-ness' of the Lue.[238] Moerman further clarified his argument at the symposium organised by the American Ethnological Society in 1967:

> I am not asserting that the Lue are not in fact a tribe, and that they merely fooled me into thinking them one. Rather, I do assert that Lue ethnicity consists largely of the fact that persons in Chiengkham and neighboring districts often use ethnic labels when they talk about the people and the activities of Ban Ping and certain other villages. [...] Further, in order to call themselves by an ethnic label, villagers are semantically required to use or imply a contrastive ethnic label for others. To phrase the issue somewhat more generally and accurately, using one member of a set of identifications provides the context which makes other members of that set appropriate. Using the label 'Negro' provides the context which makes labels like 'White' or 'Mexican' appropriate.[239]

Put differently, Moerman was arguing for conceiving of ethnicity not as the inherent property of a group, but as an emergent effect of boundary-making processes in which other groups were also involved. This line of argument anticipated the publication of what is perhaps the most influential text on the concept of ethnicity to date: Fredrik Barth's introductory essay to the edited volume *Ethnic Groups and Boundaries*, published in 1969.

Barth had worked with Leach first at the London School of Economics and then at the University of Cambridge, and Leach's influence is manifest in his writings.[240] Thus, a recurring theme in Barth's work is the emphasis on the relational, processual, and contingent character of social reality: social forms are generated out of transactions between individuals and must therefore be understood as 'the outcome of social processes'.[241] In an article published in

---

[237] Moerman 1967, 513. [238] Moerman 1965, 1216.
[239] Moerman 1968, 161. [240] Eriksen and Nielsen 2013, 112–116.
[241] Barth 1966, 22.

1956, for instance, Barth introduced the idea of the 'ecologic niche' to describe 'the place of a group in the total environment, its relation to resources and competitors'. The environment of a group included not only the natural setting but also 'the presence and activities of the other ethnic groups on which it depends'.[242] In conceptual terms, the key corollary of Barth's argument was that the notion of discrete culture areas 'becomes inapplicable' in the face of a continuous social reality.[243] But aside from a few passing references to 'ethnic groups', Barth did not give the concept of ethnicity any sustained attention prior to convening a symposium on the subject in 1967. The proceedings of the symposium, held in Bergen, were published two years later as *Ethnic Groups and Boundaries*.

The significance of Barth's celebrated introductory essay to the 1969 volume is difficult to overstate, although this has not prevented scholars from trying – Leo Despres, for instance, has elevated Barth to the status of Christ by distinguishing between anthropology 'Before Barth' and 'After Barth'.[244] The key contribution of Barth's essay was to systematise and popularise the ongoing shift from an objectivist to a subjectivist conception of human groups. In his words, 'ethnic groups are categories of ascription and identification by the actors themselves'.[245] The concept of culture was thereby recast 'as an implication or result, rather than a primary and definitional characteristic of ethnic group organization'.[246] The defining characteristic of an ethnic group was not a particular set of culture traits, but the maintenance of a social boundary between themselves and others: 'The critical focus of investigation from this point of view becomes the ethnic *boundary* that defines the group, not the cultural stuff that it encloses. The boundaries to which we must give our attention are of course social boundaries, though they may have territorial counterparts.'[247] Moreover, these social boundaries are not static but 'entail social processes of exclusion and incorporation whereby discrete categories are maintained *despite* changing participation and membership in the course of individual life histories'.[248] With the reconceptualisation of culture as a result of social differentiation and the reconceptualisation of society as a

---

[242] Barth 1956, 1079. [243] Barth 1956, 1088. [244] Despres 1975, 189.
[245] Barth 1969b, 10. [246] Barth 1969b, 11. [247] Barth 1969b, 15.
[248] Barth 1969b, 10.

culturally mediated process of boundary construction, the structuralist-functionalist subordination of process to stasis was finally undone.

Summary

The first two sections of this chapter have traced how the concept of ethnicity emerged out of the interstices of existing categories. The first section focused on the dismantling of unilinear metanarratives of historical progress, with ethnicity emerging as a transhistorical category that cut across different evolutionary stages. This section has provided the other half of the story, so to speak, by demonstrating how the self-deconstruction of the structuralist-functionalist paradigm paved the way for a processual and relational understanding of ethnicity as an ongoing product of boundary-making processes. Taken together, these conceptual changes entailed a relocation of the temporal dimension of culture from the global realm to the domestic sphere: as the metanarrative of civilisational progress was subordinated to the territorial boundaries of the nation-state, the static societies studied by colonial anthropologists were recast as the dynamic products of social interactions unfolding through time. Even in the more objectivist and essentialist idiom of Soviet ethnos-theory, there was a clear emphasis on the growth and decline of ethnoses through time: they 'merge, change, evolve and "degrade"'.[249] The detemporalisation of the international plane thus coincided with the temporalisation of human cultural relations domestically. Crucially, this domestication of temporality was a necessary precondition for the transformation of the international plane into the 'timeless' space of 'contingency and repetition' so familiar to IR scholars today.[250] As the imperial world order was turned upside down and inside out, the discipline of IR accumulated the functions of colonial anthropology as the privileged scientific vehicle for the study of the modern state's 'other'.

From Primitive Anarchy to International Anarchy

There is a profound epistemological parallel between anthropology and IR. At their core, both disciplines are concerned with the 'other' of the modern state; their raison d'être is to distinguish what is foreign

---

[249] Anderson, Alymov, and Arzyutov 2019, 4.   [250] Walker 1990, 176.

or alien from what is domestic or native.[251] For anthropology, as we have seen, this 'other' was traditionally conceived in terms of those primitive tribal societies that lay both spatially and temporally beyond the West.[252] For IR, by contrast, the 'other' is the international system – an anarchical state of nature where sovereigns struggle for survival and vie with each other for hegemony. In the words of David Lake, 'we are drawn by our dominant theories to see the international system as an anarchy, a state of nature, a world of self-help'.[253] As a result, the object of both anthropology and IR has been defined in negative terms, as a set of residual phenomena that fall beyond the bounds of civilised life. In addition to these structural parallels, however, there also exist concrete historical threads connecting colonial anthropology to IR. As the rest of this section demonstrates, twentieth-century theories of international anarchy owe a profound debt to anthropological theories of primitive tribes.

John Mearsheimer has identified the British political scientist and philosopher G. Lowes Dickinson as the person who 'invented the concept of international anarchy'.[254] To be sure, the concept of anarchy features prominently in Dickinson's *The European Anarchy* and *The International Anarchy*, published in 1916 and 1926, respectively.[255] Written against the backdrop of the First World War, these works presented the condition of international anarchy as the logical corollary of 'the emergence of the sovereign State at the end of the fifteenth century'.[256] For Dickinson, sovereignty and anarchy were thus two sides of the same coin. Conflict between states represented 'the mutual aggression and defence of beings living in a "state of nature"'.[257] Similar conceptions of international anarchy can also be found in the early twentieth-century works of David Jayne Hill, Frederick Schuman, Nicholas Spykman, and others.[258] In an especially evocative passage, Schuman likened the 'anarchic jungle of sovereign political communities' to 'a pre-civil state of nature as Hobbes had described it, in which life was "solitary, poor, nasty, brutish, and

---

[251] Borneman 1995. [252] See Fabian 2014; Trouillot 2003.
[253] Lake 2009, 16. [254] Mearsheimer 2006, 234.
[255] Dickinson 1916, 1926. [256] Dickinson 1916, 13.
[257] Dickinson 1916, 16.
[258] Hill 1911, 15; Schuman 1933, 49–53; Spykman 1942, 15–19.

short" – in which might makes right – in which power is to the strongest, and the devil takes the hindmost'.[259]

The aforementioned scholars, like many IR scholars today, considered anarchy and sovereignty to be conjoined twins, each implying the other. However, as Jack Donnelly points out in a survey of early twentieth-century IR scholarship, other contemporary commentators saw 'sovereignty as *ending* anarchy, making "anarchic systems" and "systems of sovereign states" opposites'.[260] For this second group of scholars, anarchy was a feature of 'ancient'[261] or 'medieval'[262] international systems, which were contrasted with the modern international system of sovereign states. In this vein, authors such as T. J. Lawrence, Stephen Leacock, and Charles G. Fenwick believed that the Treaty of Westphalia had ended (rather than inaugurated or codified) a condition of international anarchy.[263] The sovereignty/anarchy binary was thus infused with a temporal dimension: anarchy symbolised the primitive past, and sovereignty the civilised present, of the states-system.

Pulling on this thread, we find interesting intersections between the concept of anarchy and the depiction of tribal societies in the European colonies. In 1898, for example, the well-known British sociologist Benjamin Kidd used the terms 'anarchy' and 'primitive savagery' as synonyms.[264] The vocabulary of many early twentieth-century structuralist-functionalist anthropologists also has a strikingly familiar ring to the ear of the IR scholar, with Meyer Fortes and E. E. Evans-Pritchard using terms such as 'ordered anarchy'[265] and 'self-help'[266] to describe African political systems. 'The ordered anarchy in which they live accords well with their character', Evans-Pritchard wrote in his influential study of the Nuer people of Sudan, 'for it is impossible to live among Nuer and conceive of rulers ruling over them'.[267]

Importantly, the parallel between primitive stateless societies and the international system has been repeatedly drawn by IR scholars themselves.[268] This analogy rests on an underlying conceptual distinction

---

[259] Schuman 1933, 53.   [260] Donnelly 2015, 406.
[261] For example, Walsh 1922, 57.
[262] For example, Potter 1922, 40; Russell 1936, 90.
[263] Fenwick 1924, 50; Lawrence 1895, 35; Leacock 1906, 95.
[264] Kidd 1898, 15. See also Schmidt 1998, 142–144.
[265] Evans-Pritchard 1940a, 6, 181; Evans-Pritchard 1940b, 296.
[266] Fortes and Evans-Pritchard 1940, 15–16.   [267] Evans-Pritchard 1940a, 181.
[268] Jahn 2000, 150–169.

between 'state societies' and 'stateless societies', with both primitive society and international society presented as exemplars of the latter.[269] In *Politics among Nations*, for instance, Hans Morgenthau compared international law to primitive law and likened international diplomatic practices to 'the chieftain of a primitive tribe maintaining political relations with a neighboring tribe'.[270] A more detailed exposition of these parallels can be found in an article that Roger Masters published in the journal *World Politics* in 1964. Drawing on influential anthropological studies – including the aforementioned work of Fortes and Evans-Pritchard – Masters theorised world politics as a primitive political system. 'Many primitive peoples have political systems which are very much like the international political system', read the provocative opening sentence of Masters's article.[271] Hedley Bull, the doyen of the English School of IR theory, later acknowledged this 'penetrating article' as a key inspiration for his own theorisation of the international system as an 'anarchical society'.[272] All in all, as Beate Jahn observes, the colonial notion of primitive society is 'very much present' in IR's conceptualisation of the international system as an anarchy of sovereign states.[273]

In his aforementioned survey, Donnelly finds a significant increase in the use of the term 'anarchy' by IR scholars following the publication of Kenneth Waltz's *Theory of International Politics* in 1979. Given that Donnelly credits Waltz with a 'decisive'[274] role in the popularisation of the concept, Waltz's theoretical writings deserve special attention. And as it turns out, Waltz's works are littered with references to structuralist-functionalist anthropologists and sociologists.[275] In a provocative article, Aaron Beers Sampson has argued that Waltz in fact 'derived all three components of his theory of international politics

---

[269] In anthropology, the distinction between state societies and stateless societies was systematised by Fortes and Evans-Pritchard (1940) in their introduction to *African Political Systems*. For discussions in IR, see Bull 1977, 59–65; Hinsley 1986, 15–22; Hoffman 1995, 1997.

[270] Morgenthau 1948, 211, 421. The parallel between primitive law and international law can be traced at least as far back as Henry Maine's (1861, 167) *Ancient Law*: 'Ancient jurisprudence, if perhaps a deceptive comparison may be employed, may be likened to International Law, filling nothing, as it were, except the interstices between the great groups which are the atoms of society.' See Maine 1861, 167.

[271] Masters 1964, 595.   [272] Bull 1977, 323. See also Terradas 2020.
[273] Jahn 2000, 153.   [274] Donnelly 2015, 394–407.
[275] Goddard and Nexon 2005, 22.

(ordering principles, functional differentiation, and the distribution of material capabilities) from a theory of primitive society published by Nadel in 1957'.[276] Waltz also repeatedly invoked the name of Émile Durkheim in support of his structuralist theory of international politics, arguing that the French sociologist's distinction between 'societies of mechanical and of organic solidarity' corresponded to his own distinction between 'the anarchic order of international politics and the hierarchic order of domestic politics'.[277] In this way, the civilised/primitive dichotomy that underlay Durkheim's work was mapped onto Waltz's distinction between state sovereignty and international anarchy.

Of course, even those IR scholars who drew an explicit parallel between primitive and international society recognised that the two were not identical. A recurring theme in this regard was the fact that international society is culturally much more diverse than a tightly knit tribal society. According to Masters, for instance, 'the international political system currently includes radically different political cultures'. By contrast, 'there is a marked tendency toward cultural homogeneity in primitive stateless societies'.[278] Bull concurred with this assessment, noting that 'whereas modern international society [...] is culturally heterogeneous, primitive stateless societies are marked by a high degree of cultural homogeneity'.[279] This is also the reason why Waltz's attempt to transpose Durkheim's structuralist-functionalist framework onto the international plane does not quite work. Faced with the cultural heterogeneity of the international order, Waltz had to reverse the causal logic and ultimately ended up turning Durkheim's argument on its head. Hence, as John Barkdull points out, Waltz's claim that the pressure of competition under anarchy moulds states into 'like units' directly contradicts Durkheim's original thesis 'that competition is the root cause of *differentiation*. Competition leads to an ever-greater division of labor and possibly to organic solidary society, not to the units' likeness or to mechanical society'.[280] For Durkheim, societies based on mechanical solidarity were not the result of anarchy, but to the contrary, of a central authority – a king, a chief, a priest – capable of creating respect for shared beliefs and traditions through moral

---

[276] Sampson 2002, 430.   [277] Waltz 1986, 323. See also Waltz 1979, 115n.
[278] Masters 1964, 614.   [279] Bull 1977, 64.   [280] Barkdull 1995, 674.

pressure.²⁸¹ To be clear, I am not simply claiming that Waltz's argument is wrong or that he misunderstood Durkheim. My point is, more specifically, that the transposition of the notion of anarchy from culturally homogeneous primitive societies to a culturally heterogeneous international society necessitated a dialectical reversal. This was not a straightforward translation of a concept from one domain to another, but a process of sublation that turned the colonial paradigm upside down and inside out all the while conserving its basic metaphysical presuppositions under a new form.

Given the parallels and continuities between colonial anthropology and IR, it is no surprise that the disciplines' attitudes toward their objects follow a similar logic. In the same way that Western colonial discourse oscillated between a register of difference and a register of identity, or a policy of assimilation and a policy of separate development, IR's theoretical canon oscillates between realism and liberalism. On the one hand, the realist tradition posits a qualitative binary contrast between a domestic society characterised by peace and progress and an international realm characterised by war and stasis: the old spatial divide between the civilised 'self' and the primitive 'other' is recast as an abstract and seemingly timeless opposition between the inside and the outside of the sovereign state. On the other hand, echoing the nineteenth-century civilising mission, IR's liberal or idealist wing is more optimistic about the possibility of international progress: the baneful effects of anarchy can be moderated, perhaps even fully overcome, through the spread of liberal – democratic institutions and norms. The constructivist approach popularised by Alexander Wendt also falls squarely within the liberal or idealist tradition insofar as it has faith in the improvement of the international system from a Hobbesian to a Lockean and finally to a Kantian state of nature.²⁸² In the words of R. B. J. Walker, 'the dominant urge has been to portray change in international life as either the perpetuation of difference and fragmentation or a move towards identity and integration'.²⁸³ The concept of international anarchy may have replaced the colonial concept of primitive society as the principal 'other' of the sovereign state, but the metaphysical framework through which the otherness of the 'other' is conceptualised has hardly changed.²⁸⁴

---

²⁸¹ Barkdull 1995, 674.   ²⁸² See Wendt 1992, 1999.   ²⁸³ Walker 1987, 83.
²⁸⁴ There is also an important gender dimension to these dichotomies. In the nineteenth century, the non-Western world was typically cast as a feminine space that could be penetrated by and subordinated to the will of the masculine

As the civilised/primitive dichotomy was negated, overturned, and reinscribed in the form of an abstract conceptual distinction between the inside and the outside of the state, the standard of civilisation between civilised and primitive societies was seemingly dismantled. Yet the legacies of this global hierarchy persist into the postcolonial era, as non-Western states continue to be stigmatised for failing to conform to the norms that have been set by the established states of the West.[285] Rather than being completely erased, old imperial distinctions have been rearticulated through 'pseudonyms'[286] or 'conceptual proxies'[287] such as 'development', 'dependency', and 'hegemony'. In his seminal study, Gerrit Gong identifies two successors to the nineteenth-century standard of civilisation: the standard of human rights and the standard of modernity.[288] What differentiates the standard of human rights from the standard of civilisation is its 'positive and universal' quality: human rights are based on a presumed similarity rather than a presumed difference among members, and demands are placed on established states as well as newcomers to conform to these universal values.[289] The same is true of the standard of modernity: developmental differences in the postcolonial era tend to be understood in purely quantitative terms, which allows both developed and developing countries to be portrayed as 'members of a single family'.[290] Following the sublation of the civilisational hierarchy, the outsiders remain outsiders, but they are now located inside the society of nations.

In many ways, the new universal standards of human rights and modernity are an improvement on the exclusionary and often explicitly racist standards that preceded them. When compared to the imperial world order of the nineteenth century, the standard of human rights and the standard of modernity provide a far more inclusive and egalitarian set of ground rules that are based on the fundamental sameness of people around the world. At the same time, however, these

---

West. As feminist IR scholars have underlined, the distinction between the inside and the outside of the state is similarly gendered: the success of the sovereign state is measured through masculine virtues such as power and autonomy, while the anarchical international system is characterised by feminine tropes of passivity and a cyclical temporality. See, for example, Tickner 1988.

[285] Zarakol 2011, 57–108.   [286] Long and Schmidt 2005b, 11.
[287] Guilhot 2014, 702.   [288] Gong 1984, 91–92.   [289] Donnelly 1998, 11.
[290] Rist 2008, 74.

seemingly universal standards are implicated in the obfuscation of those systemic violences through which the international order was forged. As Gilbert Rist points out in his classic study of development discourse, the assumption that the laws of development are the same for all serves to 'bracket out the effects of conquest, colonization, the slave trade, the dismantling of craft production in India, the breaking up of social structures, and so on'.[291] Similar critiques have been made of human rights, which tend to privilege a Eurocentric understanding of liberal democracy as the ideal form of political organisation.[292]

Because the nineteenth-century standard of civilisation was neither entirely erased nor retained unchanged, the postcolonial international order is characterised by a constitutive tension between the principle of formal sovereign equality, on the one hand, and new standards of civilisation that reinscribe sovereign inequalities, on the other. 'Our central problem', as Edward Keene writes, 'is that we still think in the same dualistic way as nineteenth-century international lawyers and diplomats about the purposes of order in world politics, but we have abandoned the discriminatory method that they used to resolve the resulting contradictions'.[293] As a result, the international order today is 'schizophrenically' committed to the realisation of two contradictory ideals at the same time: sovereignty and civilisation.[294] Whereas the ideal of sovereignty implies equality and autonomy among states, the ideal of civilisation implies inequality and justifies violations of sovereignty when certain conditions are met. The most common justifications for such violations are intervention in defence of human rights and the institutionalisation of global governance mechanisms to promote economic development, reflecting the standard of human rights and the standard of modernity, respectively. The spectre of imperialism rears its head whenever and wherever such violations of sovereignty occur.

Indigenous Rights

The legacies of colonialism are felt not only in IR theory, but also in international political and legal practice. In the latter domain, one of the main channels through which relations between the coloniser and

---

[291] Rist 2008, 74. See also McCarthy 2009.   [292] Mutua 2002.
[293] Keene 2002, 10.   [294] Keene 2002, 122. See also Aalberts 2014.

the colonised have been addressed is that of indigenous rights. The discourse of indigenous rights has two distinct lineages, both with colonial roots. The first leads back to Article 6 of the Final Act of the Berlin Conference in 1885, which formalised the so-called Scramble for Africa and committed the signatories to the 'protection of indigenous populations' on the African continent. In this context, the term 'indigenous' was intended to distinguish local inhabitants subjected to colonial rule from nationals of the colonial powers. There was also a racial element involved insofar as Article 6 was not considered applicable to the descendants of Dutch settlers subjected to British colonialism in South Africa.[295] This use of the term 'indigenous' continued after the First World War, with Article 22 of the Covenant of the League of Nations describing 'indigenous peoples' as 'peoples not yet able to stand by themselves under the strenuous conditions of the modern world' and contrasting them to 'advanced' societies.[296]

If the first lineage of indigenous rights takes us back to the governance of the European overseas empires, the second leads us to settler colonialism in the Americas. In this context, one of the earliest statements on indigenous rights is Resolution XI of the Pan-American Union (the predecessor of the Organization of American States) from 1938, which included the following passage: '[T]he indigenous populations, as descendants of the first inhabitants of the lands which today form America, and in order to offset the deficiency in their physical and intellectual development, have a preferential right to the protection of the public authorities.'[297] In this resolution and in its subsequent documentation, the Pan-American Union used 'indigenous' and 'Indian' interchangeably.[298] Whereas in European usage the term 'indigenous' referred to the non-European inhabitants of overseas colonies, in American usage it referred to pre-existing communities residing within state borders.[299] In both cases, however, the concept was inseparable from the history of European colonialism.

---

[295] UN Doc. E/CN.4/Sub.2/AC.4/1996/2, para. 11.
[296] Quoted in UN Doc. E/CN.4/Sub.2/AC.4/1996/2, para. 12.
[297] Quoted in UN Doc. E/CN.4/Sub.2/AC.4/1996/2, para. 15.
[298] UN Doc. E/CN.4/Sub.2/AC.4/1996/2, para. 15.
[299] UN Doc. E/CN.4/Sub.2/AC.4/1996/2, para. 16.

The Rise of Indigenous Rights

Of present-day international organisations, the International Labour Organization (ILO) – established in 1919 under the auspices of the League of Nations – has the longest pedigree in using the term 'indigenous'. This goes back to the ILO's attempts to draft international labour standards for the regulation of 'native labour' between 1919 and 1955. During this standard-setting activity, known collectively as the Colonial Code, the term 'indigenous' was applied to the inhabitants of colonial territories and 'served as a device for the regulation of the relations between the colonizer and the colonized'.[300] In 1957, the ILO adopted the first international agreement dedicated to indigenous rights: Convention No. 107 concerning the Protection and Integration of Indigenous and Other Tribal and Semi-Tribal Populations in Independent Countries. The convention was the first document to provide an internationally recognised definition of indigenous peoples, stating that populations could be 'regarded as indigenous on account of their descent from the populations which inhabited the country, or a geographical region to which the country belongs, at the time of conquest or colonisation'.[301] The convention's use of the term 'tribal' is also interesting: all indigenous populations were considered tribal populations, but not all tribal populations were considered indigenous populations. In other words, indigenous populations were a subset of tribal populations. A non-indigenous population was classed as a tribal population if its 'social and economic conditions are at a less advanced stage than the stage reached by the other sections of the national community, and whose status is regulated wholly or partially by their own customs or traditions or by special laws or regulations'.[302] The juxtaposition of 'tribal', 'semi-tribal', and 'national' communities underlines the convention's prioritisation of national integration over tribal autonomy: over time, tribal groups were expected to assimilate into the national community.[303] The intermediary category of 'semi-tribal' populations was accordingly defined as 'groups and persons who, although they are in the process of losing their tribal characteristics, are not yet integrated into the

---

[300] Rodríguez-Piñero 2005, 47. [301] ILO 1957, art. 1, para. 1.
[302] ILO 1957, art. 1, para. 1. [303] Rodríguez-Piñero 2005, 115–211.

national community'.[304] Governments had a responsibility not only to protect tribal communities, but also to ensure 'their progressive integration into the life of their respective countries'.[305]

In 1989, more than three decades after it had adopted Convention No. 107, the ILO adopted Convention No. 169 concerning Indigenous and Tribal Peoples in Independent Countries. The new convention included a number of important changes compared to its predecessor. First, the new convention referred to 'peoples' rather than 'populations'. This was an important shift insofar as the United Nations Charter grants 'peoples' but not 'populations' the right to self-determination, even if the ILO convention took care to specify that the use of the term 'shall not be construed as having any implications as regards the rights which may attach to the term under international law'.[306] Second, self-identification was introduced as 'a fundamental criterion' for determining the peoples to which the convention applied.[307] Third, integration was dropped as an objective. This was reflected in the fact that term 'semi-tribal' is nowhere to be found in the new convention and that 'tribal' peoples were no longer defined as being 'at a less advanced stage' than the rest of the national community. Finally, whereas the old convention had considered indigenous populations to be a subset of tribal populations, the 1989 convention split the two categories apart.[308] The new convention thus defined 'tribal' peoples as peoples 'whose social, cultural and economic conditions distinguish them from other sections of the national community, and whose status is regulated wholly or partially by their own customs or traditions or by special laws or regulations'. By contrast, 'indigenous' peoples were defined as peoples who could trace 'their descent from the populations which inhabited the country, or a geographical region to which the country belongs, at the time of conquest or colonisation or the establishment of present state boundaries and who, irrespective of their legal status, retain some or all of their own social, economic, cultural and political institutions'.[309] The key difference between the tribal and indigenous categories was thus the historical element of 'conquest or colonisation'. However, the inclusion of the phrase 'or the establishment of present state boundaries' minimised

---

[304] ILO 1957, art. 1, para. 2.   [305] ILO 1957, art. 2, para. 1.
[306] ILO 1989, art. 1, para. 3.   [307] ILO 1989, art. 1, para. 2.
[308] Macklem 2008, 195–197; Thornberry 2002, 44.
[309] ILO 1989, art. 1, para. 1.

this factor and effectively rendered indigenous and tribal peoples synonymous: both groups were defined primarily by their social, cultural, and economic distinctiveness in relation to the majority.[310] As of February 2020, Convention No. 107 is in force in seventeen states and Convention No. 169 in twenty-three.

The contrast between the two ILO conventions, as Patrick Thornberry observes, reflects a wider normative shift in the twentieth century from 'vertical and hierarchical narratives [...] towards a horizontal, equality-with-difference approach'.[311] This shift in attitude was largely the accomplishment of indigenous rights movements and activist anthropologists, who raised the question of indigenous rights to global prominence during the 1970s.[312] With regard to the conceptual history of ethnicity, it is important to underline that the rise of indigenous rights up the international agenda went hand in hand with the terminological shift from 'tribes' to 'ethnic groups'. So long as the anthropological object was represented through the colonial concept of tribe, the indigenous person's relationship to the anthropologist had been limited to that of a passive informant. Moreover, reflecting the subordination of tribes to nations in the civilisational hierarchy, any politicisation of indigenous identities was interpreted as an abandonment of traditional tribal values and hence as a sign of assimilation or acculturation. In the late 1960s, as we have seen, this conception of tribes as isolated and unchanging communities came under fire from a new processual and relational approach to ethnicity, epitomised by the work of Fredrik Barth. As Françoise Morin and Bernard Saladin d'Anglure explain, Barth's work 'created the theoretical preconditions enabling anthropology to consider the political development of indigenous peoples, as a subject for research and action'. The terminological shift from tribes to ethnic groups was nothing less than an 'epistemological rupture' that recast the role of indigenous groups from passive informants into active political players in their own right.[313] It was no coincidence that many of the participants of the Bergen symposium organised by Barth in

---

[310] UN Doc. E/CN.4/Sub.2/AC.4/1996/2, para. 28.
[311] Thornberry 2002, 44. See also Rodríguez-Piñero 2005, 215–331.
[312] Niezen 2003; Varese 1997.
[313] Morin and d'Anglure 1997, 161. Another important conceptual consequence of the indigenous rights movement was the popularisation of the term 'ethnocide' to describe the global destruction of indigenous cultures through development initiatives. See Heiskanen 2021b.

1967 were also founding members of the International Working Group on Indigenous Affairs, set up in Copenhagen in 1968.[314]

The epistemological shift heralded by the concept of ethnicity did not entail the wholesale disappearance of the older terminology. Words such as 'tribe' and 'tribal' continue to feature as alternatives to 'indigenous' in the work of many international organisations, including the United Nations. In 2004, the Permanent Forum on Indigenous Issues published a background paper which affirmed that 'the terms "indigenous" and "tribal" are used as synonyms in the UN system when the peoples concerned identify themselves under the indigenous agenda'.[315] A similar approach informs the language of the World Bank, which uses 'indigenous peoples' as a general category that encompasses more specific terms such as 'indigenous ethnic minorities', 'tribal groups', and 'scheduled tribes'.[316] In 1998, a World Bank discussion paper recommended a continuation of this flexible approach: '[T]he term indigenous peoples has come to subsume these different categories and usages, and its use is consistent with current United Nations and academic discussions of the topic.'[317] In some regional contexts, such as in India, the word 'tribe' remains the primary category.[318]

In many ways, the entanglements between the concept of tribe and the articulation of indigenous rights are comparable to the entanglements between the concept of nation and the articulation of minority rights. As seen in Chapter 1, the discourse of minority rights is primarily concerned with the non-sublated residues of the nation concept, even if the politically explosive word 'nation' and its cognates tend to be avoided. Similarly, the discourse of indigenous rights is primarily concerned with the non-sublated residues of the tribe concept, even if the derogatory word 'tribe' and its cognates are generally avoided. These terminological inheritances and continuities have generated a protracted debate about whether the category of indigenous peoples smuggles into anthropological scholarship and international law problematic colonial concepts such as 'tribe', 'native', and 'primitive'.[319]

---

[314] Morin and d'Anglure 1997, 161–162.
[315] UN Doc. PFII/2004/WS.1/3, para. 6.   [316] Kingsbury 1998, 420n20.
[317] World Bank, quoted in Sanders 1999, 8.
[318] Ekeh 1990, 664. See also Xaxa 1999.
[319] For example, Asch et al. 2004, 2006; Barnard 2006; Béteille 1998; Childs and Delgado-P 1999; Guenther et al. 2006; Kenrick and Lewis 2004; Kuper 2003; Kuper 2017, 169–181.

A crucial difference, however, is that the category of indigenous peoples – unlike its colonial precursors – has not simply been imposed by the coloniser. To the contrary, the key driver behind the elevation of indigenous rights into a global issue has been the activism of indigenous peoples themselves.

Indigenous Rights versus Minority Rights

Since the establishment of the United Nations Working Group on Indigenous Populations (WGIP) in 1982, international law- and policy-making on group rights has adopted a two-track approach differentiating between indigenous peoples and minorities.[320] Yet the two categories are not entirely symmetrical: following the promulgation of ILO Convention No. 169 in 1989 and the adoption of the United Nations Declaration on the Rights of Indigenous Peoples in 2007, indigenous status has become more advantageous than minority status. Most importantly, indigenous peoples have the right to self-determination, which minorities do not. These differences in legal rights have created rivalries among certain groups and underlined the need for clearer definitions. In particular, the appearance of groups of European descent at the WGIP – such as the Boers of South Africa in 1994 and the Rehoboth Basters of Namibia in 1993 and 1994 – has caused controversy. At the same time, however, the growing emphasis on self-identification as a key determinant of both indigenous and minority status has made it difficult to maintain an objective distinction between the two categories.[321]

The United Nations has produced a number of documents aiming to clarify the distinction between indigenous peoples and minorities. In 1996, a working paper prepared for the WGIP by Chairperson-Rapporteur Erica-Irene Daes claimed that it was possible to make a 'strict distinction' between indigenous and minority groups: 'Indigenous peoples are indeed peoples and not minorities or ethnic groups.'[322] Specifically, Daes pointed to two factors that had 'never been associated with the concept of "minorities"': priority in time and

---

[320] Kymlicka 2007, 36.
[321] Corntassel 2003, 76; Corntassel and Primeau 1995, 364–365; Thornberry 1995a, 64–65.
[322] UN Doc. E/CN.4/Sub.2/AC.4/1996/2, para. 47.

attachment to a particular territory'.³²³ Four years later, Daes prepared another working paper with Asbjørn Eide, the first chairperson of the WGIP. In the paper, Daes and Eide argued that 'the principal legal distinction between the rights of minorities and indigenous peoples in contemporary international law is with respect to internal self-determination: the right of a group to govern itself within a recognized geographical area, without State interference'.³²⁴ Minority rights sought to provide 'a space for pluralism in togetherness' whereas indigenous rights were about ensuring 'a high degree of autonomous development'.³²⁵ The paper concluded that minorities and indigenous peoples should be understood as ideal types, with the former focused on the group's experience of discrimination and the latter concerned with the group's aboriginality and territorial attachment.³²⁶

Another important point raised by Daes and Eide's working paper was the regional scope of applicability of minority rights and indigenous rights. According to the authors, minority rights were grounded on the European experience, whereas indigenous rights were centred on the American experience.³²⁷ Asia and Africa were thus left in an awkward position:

> Aboriginality (i.e. the characteristic of being autochthonous, or the original human inhabitants of a territory) appears to be obvious as a distinguishing characteristic of indigenous peoples. However, it fails to clarify many situations, especially in Asia and Africa, where dominant as well as non-dominant groups within the State can all claim aboriginality. In such situations, previous studies have proposed the use of subordination and cultural distinctiveness as further criteria, distinguishing vulnerable groups from the dominant sectors of society. But this approach fails to distinguish between indigenous peoples and minorities within African and Asian States, unless we are prepared to agree that the distinction is merely one of degree of aboriginality or cultural distinctiveness. In this case problems may arise from applying different approaches to different regions of the world: a qualitative

---

[323] UN Doc. E/CN.4/Sub.2/AC.4/1996/2, para. 60.
[324] UN Doc. E/CN.4/Sub.2/2000/10, para. 43.
[325] UN Doc. E/CN.4/Sub.2/2000/10, para. 8.
[326] UN Doc. E/CN.4/Sub.2/2000/10, paras. 47–50. From this perspective, the communitarian tradition of minority rights in Central and Eastern Europe, with its emphasis on self-determination and autonomy, could be seen as an intermediate category residing somewhere between the two ideal types defined by Daes and Eide. See Aukerman 2000.
[327] UN Doc. E/CN.4/Sub.2/2000/10, para. 25.

standard in the Americas (aboriginality), and a quantitative standard in Africa and Asia (degree of aboriginality or distinctiveness).[328]

This question of the geographical scope of indigenous rights has cropped up repeatedly in the United Nations. In 1985, for example, the British member of the Sub-Commission on the Prevention of Discrimination and Protection of Minorities wondered whether the distinction between indigenous peoples and minorities had any meaning in Europe. The Soviet ambassador likewise suggested that 'indigenous' situations could only arise in the Americas and in Australia, which contained 'imported' populations of Europeans.[329] As noted in Daes and Eide's aforementioned report, the distinction between minorities and indigenous peoples is especially problematic for Africa and Asia, where most groups can legitimately lay claim to indigenous status.[330] At the eleventh session of the WGIP in 1993, the Indian delegate argued that 'the application of the term "indigenous people" was not adequate for his country because its entire population had been living on its lands for several millennia. All these people were indigenous and any attempt to make a distinction between indigenous and non-indigenous would be artificial'.[331] In 1999, Special Rapporteur Miguel Alfonso Martínez suggested that the African and Asian situation should be analysed in the context of minority rights rather than indigenous rights.[332]

The distinction between indigenous peoples and minorities eludes attempts to construct objective definitions. As Miriam Aukerman observes, 'the actual implementation of rights must be flexible and case-specific'.[333] Yet this does not mean that the distinction is entirely arbitrary or ought to be abandoned. To the contrary, it is possible to identify an underlying logic to the construction of minorities and indigenous peoples as objects of international law. As demonstrated in Chapter 1, minority rights function as a safety valve to neutralise the threat that nationalism poses to the international order. Reflecting this orientation toward the future, both the Council of Europe and the OSCE justify minority protection primarily with reference to conflict

---

[328] UN Doc. E/CN.4/Sub.2/2000/10, para. 37.   [329] Barsh 1986, 375–376.
[330] Kingsbury 1998, 433–436; Niezen 2003, 72–76; Saugestad 2001a, 303–304; Saugestad 2001b, 52–54. On the African context, see also Werner 2023.
[331] UN Doc. E/CN.4/Sub.2/1993/29, para. 81.
[332] UN Doc. E/CN.4/Sub.2/1999/20, para. 90.
[333] Aukerman 2000, 1047. See also Kingsbury 1998.

prevention.[334] The preamble to the United Nations Declaration on the Rights of Persons Belonging to National or Ethnic, Religious and Linguistic Minorities likewise asserts that the protection of minority rights contributes to 'the political and social stability of States in which they live'.[335]

In contrast, indigenous rights are oriented toward the past of the international order. On a semantic level, this can be seen in the derivation of the term 'indigenous' from the Latin 'indigenae', which distinguished people who were born in a particular location from those who arrived there from elsewhere; the French 'autochtone' and the German 'Ursprung' likewise imply that a particular group was the first to live at a given location. As Daes pointed out in her 1996 working paper for the WGIP, all of these terms 'share a single conceptual element: priority in time'.[336] The category of indigenous peoples thus emerges out of a specifically postcolonial relationship between a people and a state – a relationship where a people that has historically occupied a particular territory is subjected to exploitation and domination within the political and economic structure of the state.[337] Whereas minority rights tend to be framed in terms of the prevention of future conflicts, indigenous rights seek to rectify the lasting legacies of past injustices. For example, the United Nations Declaration on the Rights of Indigenous Peoples is justified in the preamble on the basis that 'indigenous peoples have suffered from historic injustices as a result of, inter alia, their colonization and dispossession of their lands, territories and resources'.[338] Fundamentally, as Paul Keal argues, the articulation of indigenous rights is about the moral legitimacy of the international order.[339]

In sum, if the category of national minorities represents the internal 'other' of the international system – the excess of nations over states – then the category of indigenous peoples represents the system's external 'other'. Whereas minority rights are symptomatic of the aporetic logic of nationalism that threatens the stability of the international order from within, indigenous rights are a remainder and reminder of something that was once located outside the bounds of the states-system in both space and time. The categories through which group

[334] Aukerman 2000, 1044.   [335] UN Doc. A/RES/47/135, 3.
[336] UN Doc. E/CN.4/Sub.2/AC.4/1996/2, para. 10.
[337] Macklem 2008, 208; Saugestad 2001a, 304.
[338] UN Doc. A/RES/61/295, 2.   [339] Keal 2003.

rights have been articulated in international legal and political discourse thus serve particular purposes and arise logically out of the conceptual structures that constitute the international order: minority rights function as a safety valve that sutures the *future* of the international order against the threat of nationalist secession, while indigenous rights function as a corrective device that sutures the *past* of the international order against the injustices of colonialism. Taken together, minority rights and indigenous rights seek to address the foundational violences through which the *present* boundaries of states have been constituted – and, by doing so, to freeze the political map.

Conclusion

During the Second World War, the British-American anthropologist Ashley Montagu was among the first to propose replacing the word 'race' with the relatively unknown term 'ethnic group'. For Montagu, the value of this new term stemmed precisely from the fact that it was new and unfamiliar. As he put it, 'the concept of *ethnic group* implies a question mark, *not* a period'. This uncertainty over its meaning distinguished the concept of ethnic group from the established concept of race, which was often unthinkingly and problematically used precisely because everyone thought they knew what 'race' meant. Montagu believed that the strangeness of the new term 'ethnic group' would force people to stop and think whenever they encountered it, to reflect on its meaning, and thus guard it from ideological appropriation: 'Each time it is used it is likely to elicit the question, "What do you mean by *ethnic group*?"' The soundness of Montagu's strategy for 're-education' and 'self-enlightenment' is no doubt open to debate.[1] What is not open to debate is the fact that the concept of ethnic group has long since lost its novel and unfamiliar quality. Much like the early twentieth-century concept of race that Montagu was criticising, the concept of ethnic group today is often unthinkingly and problematically used, triggering all kinds of emotionally conditioned responses. Today, the concept of ethnic group implies a period, *not* a question mark.

The overarching aim of this book has been to turn the concept of ethnicity into a question mark once more: to dismantle its transhistorical veneer, to wrest away its natural appearance, and to lay bare its ideological functions. The first section of this conclusion ties together the narratives presented in the book's three substantive chapters to provide a panoramic overview of the conceptual history of ethnicity.

---

[1] Montagu 1951, 72.

It recounts how the concept of ethnicity transformed from a residual category inhabiting the margins of existing frameworks into one of the most widely used concepts in the English language. This universalisation of ethnicity entailed not only the problematisation of existing categories such as 'race' and 'tribe', but also the elevation of ethnicity itself into a seemingly 'neutral' descriptor of humanity's cultural diversity. The second section begins to chip away at ethnicity's non-ideological façade by examining the close relationship between ethnicity and culture, which has been a recurring theme throughout the book. Even as the twin concepts of ethnicity and culture contributed to the dismantling of European imperial ideology and the 'flattening' of the global sociopolitical imaginary, they also helped to reconfigure racial and civilisational hierarchies under a seemingly neutral form. It is precisely the neutral and timeless appearance of these concepts that lies behind their ideological power. Building on this argument, the third and final section of the conclusion draws inspiration from Carl Schmitt's *The Nomos of the Earth* to bring forward a speculative notion of 'ethnos'. If Schmitt's 'nomos' describes a constitutive ordering of land, then 'ethnos' describes a constitutive ordering of beings. Seen in the light of this more originary ethnos, the transhistorical appearance of ethnicity is exposed as a sham. The concept of ethnicity is no true transcendental, but a contingent historical effect of the concrete appropriations, divisions, and productions that constitute the international order.

From Supplement to Ground: The Universalisation of Ethnicity

The concept of ethnicity is a symptom of the epochal transition from a world of empires to a world of nation-states. When ethnos-based terms such as 'ethnicity' and 'ethnie' were first coined around the turn of the twentieth century, they served as extraneous additions to the established conceptual triad of nation, race, and tribe. Faced with scientific breakthroughs, socioeconomic dislocations, and political upheavals, scholars, lawyers, and policymakers turned to this new vocabulary in an effort to manage the shortcomings of existing categories. As the concepts of nation, race, and tribe began to creak and crack under the mounting weight of their contradictions, ethnos-based terms were plugged into the emerging gaps and fissures. The concept of ethnicity thus began its journey as a residual container of differences and discrepancies that could not be reconciled within existing classificatory schemas. Ethnicity, to borrow Judith Butler's memorable phrase, was born as the 'embarrassed "etc." at the end of the list'.[2]

The concept of ethnicity was born as a supplementary category designed to suture the contradictions of the Eurocentric imperial order. But as Jacques Derrida reminds us, supplements are dangerous things: precisely because a supplement is an extraneous addition to the system rather than a feature of the system proper, it does not merely complete the system, but also testifies to the system's incompleteness. A supplement is needed only because the system is lacking in some way.[3] This simple yet profound insight also applies to the conceptual history of ethnicity: as the supplementary concept of ethnicity was grafted onto the fracturing imperial system, the new concept inevitably foregrounded the limits and contradictions of that system, thereby furthering its disintegration. Seen in this light, it is hardly surprising that the meteoric popularisation of ethnicity in the second half of the century went hand in hand with the discrediting of scientific racism and the dismantling of the European colonial empires. As the world of empires gave way to a world of nation-states, the formerly residual and marginal concept of ethnicity was raised to the status of an all-encompassing master key. In Hegelian terms, the universalisation of ethnicity during the 1960s and 1970s was the world-historical moment where contradiction 'falls to the ground' and establishes itself as the foundation of an entire conceptual order.[4]

The universalisation of ethnicity entailed a dialectical reversal of the concept's relationship to its neighbours. At first, as noted above, ethnicity was conceived as an extraneous addition to the series of existing terms, a supplementary category that could be slotted alongside the established trinity of nation, race, and tribe. The situation changed decisively in the second half of the twentieth century. With the ethnos-based vocabulary spreading across the conceptual landscape like wildfire, nations, races, and tribes were themselves reconceptualised as particular forms of ethnicity: nations were recast as ethnic groups that had been politicised by the rise of nationalism, races were recast as ethnic groups that had been reified and naturalised through racialising practices, and tribes were recast as ethnic groups that had been fixed in time and place through colonial governance.

---

[2] Butler 1999, 182.   [3] Derrida 1976, 141–164.
[4] Hegel 1969, 440. See also Heiskanen 2021a.

By positing nations, races, and tribes as particular forms of itself – by remaking them in its own image – the concept of ethnicity played a pivotal role in the denaturalisation and historicisation of these older categories. Through the lens of ethnicity, nations, races, and tribes were revealed as contingent historical constructs rather than natural or primordial entities. In the very same movement, however, the concept of ethnicity also elevated *itself* into a seemingly transhistorical category. Even as it contributed to the historicisation and denaturalisation of its neighbours, the concept of ethnicity also insidiously naturalised itself, positing itself as the transcendental ground of their historicisation.

The transhistorical pretences of ethnicity are manifest in the language used to describe it. Time and again, as we have seen, ethnicity is depicted as a 'neutral', 'noncommittal', 'noncontaminating', 'apolitical', or 'natural' category that lacks the ideological baggage of its neighbours and precursors. A closely related semantic feature is the lack of a corresponding 'ism' or 'movement concept' to designate an ideological project centred on ethnicity.[5] Nations have been unveiled as products of nationalism, races as products of racism, and tribes as products of colonialism – but what ideological project is the concept of ethnicity a product of? Although the word 'ethnicism' does exist, it is almost entirely absent from public discourse and is rarely used even in specialised academic texts. Instead, any ethnic ideologies that arise tend to be given another (pejorative) label such as 'nationalism', 'racism', or 'tribalism'.[6] Sometimes a hybrid term such as 'ethnonationalism'[7] or 'ethnoracism'[8] might be used, but the implication is much the same: ethnicity itself is taken as a non-ideological phenomenon that is then mobilised by other (pathological) ideologies such as nationalism or racism. Whenever and wherever ethnicity acquires any political weight, it seems to metamorphose into something other than ethnicity.

There is, of course, the word 'ethnocentrism', coined by the American social scientist William Graham Sumner in 1906 to describe 'this view of things in which one's own group is the center of everything'.[9] Although

---

[5] See Koselleck 1997, 21; Koselleck 2004, 80; Koselleck 2011, 12.
[6] Jenkins 2008, 87.　　[7] For example, Connor 1994.
[8] For example, Aranda and Rebollo-Gil 2004.
[9] Sumner 1906, 13. Although Sumner was the first person to use the term 'ethnocentrism', the term 'ethnocentric' appears as early as 1861. It is likely that Sumner's use of 'ethnocentrism' was inspired by the work of the Polish sociologist

more widely used than ethnicism, ethnocentrism retains the transhistorical and non-ideological guise of ethnicity itself. Thus, ethnocentrism is typically understood as 'an age-old phenomenon' that is 'probably nearly as old as the human species'.[10] In this vein, the famed American sociologist Robert Park – among the earliest scholars to employ the term – referred to the 'incurable ethnocentrism of peoples'.[11] In contrast to nationalism, racism, or tribalism, but very much like ethnicity itself, ethnocentrism tends to be posited as an innate and therefore inescapable feature of human existence. All told, the seemingly transhistorical quality of ethnicity lends to this concept a mysterious resistance to ideologisation and politicisation.

Of course, as the vast literature on ethnic conflict testifies, it is widely recognised that ethnic identities can and do become politicised. But this kind of superficial politics is not what is at stake here. What is at stake is the persistent failure to theorise *the concept of ethnicity itself* as political. Even Rogers Brubaker's radically constructivist understanding of ethnic identities as 'perspectives *on* the world' rather than 'things *in* the world' falls into this trap insofar as it stops short of questioning the historical conditions of possibility of ethnicity as a category.[12] Contrary to appearances, what is actually being problematised in these kinds of constructivist approaches is not ethnicity as such, but associated concepts such as 'group' or 'identity'.[13] 'The problem', as Steve Fenton puts it in a widely cited study, 'is not the word "ethnic" but the word "group".'[14] No matter how radical the constructivist approach might be, the concept of ethnicity stubbornly retains a depoliticised and non-ideological guise. And this, precisely, is the source of its political and ideological power.

Ethnicity, Culture, Ideology

Ethnicity was not the only concept that first crept into European vocabulary at the turn of the twentieth century. Developing in parallel,

---

Ludwig Gumplowicz, who used the term 'Ethnocentrismus' in multiple publications in German and Polish between 1879 and 1905. See Bizumic 2014 and the entries for 'ethnocentrism' and 'ethnocentric' in the *Oxford English Dictionary*, available online at www.oed.com (last accessed 17 August 2020).
[10] McDonald 2007, 19; Smedley 1993, 31.   [11] Park 1950, 77.
[12] Brubaker 2004, 17.   [13] Brubaker 2004; Brubaker and Cooper 2000.
[14] Fenton 2010, 66. See also Brubaker 2004.

there was another newcomer that recurs in all three chapters of this book: the concept of culture. Thus, a central problematique in Chapter 1 was the tension between the political and cultural definitions of the nation; in Chapter 2, it was the splitting of the race concept between the biological and cultural spheres; and in Chapter 3, it was the relationship between tribal or social units on the one hand and culture areas or traits on the other. The form and function of the concept of ethnicity was thus structured around three key dichotomies, each involving the concept of culture: political/cultural (Chapter 1), biological/cultural (Chapter 2), and social/cultural (Chapter 3). As the imperial trinity of nation, race, and tribe split along these fault lines, the concept of ethnicity was adopted as a supplementary category to shore up the gaps. More specifically, this new concept was used to enclose each of its precursors within a distinct domain: the concept of nation was collapsed into the concept of the state and confined to the political domain; the concept of race was segregated from the concept of culture and limited to biological characteristics; and the concept of tribe was distinguished from modern urban patterns of culture difference and coupled to the notion of primitive social structure. This threefold conceptual restructuring, in turn, underwrote the emergence of 'culture' as a new domain of human activity distinct from the political, the biological, and the social. In short, the invention of ethnicity went hand in hand with the naturalisation of culture as 'the universal ground and horizon of difference'.[15]

Despite the conceptual linkages between ethnicity and culture, the former is not reducible to the latter – if it were, it would immediately render itself redundant. Rather than belonging purely or entirely to the sphere of culture, the concept of ethnicity belongs to those liminal border zones and marginal spaces that attach culture to the political, biological, and social domains. The concept of ethnicity marks a rupture, a fissure, a cut, in the totalising fabric of culture, a folding of culture along national, racial, and tribal lines. As the imperial trinity of nation, race, and tribe was negated by the work of sublation, the concept of ethnicity was articulated to fill in the empty spaces left behind. To quote Derrida, the concept of ethnicity is 'a mark of erasure, a *remainder* which is added to the subsequent text and which

---

[15] McGrane 1989, 113.

cannot be completely summed up within it'.[16] Ethnicity is the scarring left upon culture's supple surface by the violences of the imperial past.

Taken together, the twin concepts of ethnicity and culture have entailed a fundamental reconfiguration of the way in which the peoples of the world are ordered. In contrast to the vertical model of difference that prevailed in the nineteenth and early twentieth centuries, the postcolonial world order is defined by a lateral or horizontal model based on symmetrical and therefore reversible tropes. The civilisational metanarratives of the imperial era, which had arranged the peoples of the world along a gradated ladder from lowest to highest, have been displaced by a relativist-pluralist logic where a multiplicity of different cultures or ethnic groups can reside side by side 'on a single horizontal plane'.[17] This 'flattening' of the global sociopolitical imaginary, as Bernard McGrane writes, 'has rescued the non-European Other from the depths of the past and prehistory and reasserted him in the present; he is, once again, contemporary with us'.[18]

To the extent that the concept of ethnicity has contributed to the dismantling of racist doctrines and colonial ideologies, its popularisation can be seen as a benign – even positive – development. At the same time, however, the culturalisation and ethnicisation of the world also performs an important ideological function of its own. As David Scott notes, 'part of the appeal of the new culture-as-constructed-meaning concept is that it comports well with the new end-of-ideology conditions of liberal democratic discourse and practice'.[19] Framed through the depoliticising lens of culture, 'the otherness of the Other can be edifying without being threatening to the order of things'.[20] Whereas the imperial age was defined by the temporalisation and ideologisation of concepts in line with a Eurocentric metanarrative of historical progress, the postimperial age has witnessed the triumph of a 'monstrous' present that colonises both the past and the future.[21] By subordinating the peoples of the world to this detemporalised and deideologised imaginary, the twin concepts of ethnicity and culture help to freeze the present political map.

---

[16] Derrida 1981a, 9.   [17] Scott 2003, 104. See also Stolcke 1995, 7.
[18] McGrane 1989, 114.   [19] Scott 2003, 97.   [20] Scott 2003, 111.
[21] Hartog 2015, 203. See also Geulen 2010, 2012; Hoffmann and Kollmeier 2012; Lüdtke 2012; Sarasin 2012; Steinmetz 2012. On the temporalisation and ideologisation of concepts circa 1750–1850, see Koselleck 1997, 2011.

The erasure of colonial hierarchies and the naturalisation of a spatialised imaginary of formally equal and sovereign nation-states constitute two sides of the same movement of negation that dismantled the imperial order of the nineteenth century. However, the process of sublation also entails a simultaneous movement of preservation that eludes or exceeds this movement of negation. The contradictory doubleness of the dialectical process is reflected in the ideological functions of ethnicity: rather than merely confining nationalism, racism, and colonialism to a bygone era, the ethnic supplement also functions as the conceptual wedge that keeps the door to the imperial past ajar. Even as it appears to bring to an end the age of nationalism, racism, and colonialism, the concept of ethnicity also inaugurates the age of neo-nationalism, neoracism, and neocolonialism. In line with the inside/outside ontology of the international order, this reconfiguration and perpetuation of imperial hierarchies can be observed on three interrelated levels: inside nations, outside nations, and along the boundary lines between nations.[22]

Within the nation-state, the emergence of ethnicity has gone hand in hand with the institutionalisation of a domestic hierarchy between the hegemonic national culture, on the one hand, and national minorities and indigenous peoples, on the other. This is evident in the widely used 'minus one' model of ethnicity, according to which every state contains one group – the majority nation – that does not have an ethnic identity.[23] In many ways, this domestic hierarchy between nations and ethnic groups is a continuation of nineteenth-century distinctions between historical and non-historical peoples, or between civilised nations and primitive tribes. But whereas the old paradigm was premised on the eventual disappearance of these marginal groups, the advent of ethnicity entails a recognition that ethnic groups are here to stay and that their co-presence needs to be institutionally managed. Insofar as the new conceptual framework downplays the requirement of assimilation and drops the explicit reference to the standard of civilisation, it is no doubt an improvement on its nineteenth-century predecessors. Nevertheless, it continues to perpetuate an asymmetrical distinction between the majority nation and its various ethnic 'others'.

---

[22] On the inside/outside distinction, see especially Walker 1993.
[23] Banton 1983, 63–67.

A similar shift has taken place on the international plane, with long-standing civilisational and racial hierarchies recoded through ostensibly culture-neutral concepts such as 'capabilities', 'hegemony', and 'development'. Although the trend is, at least formally, toward greater inclusivity and pluralism, distinctions such as developed/underdeveloped still perpetuate an international hierarchy between the 'established' states of the West and the 'outsider' states of the non-West.[24] The emergence of ethnicity as a supplementary category was central to the recalibration of these long-standing hierarchies in more abstract and universalistic terms: by absorbing the residual cultural content of the nation-state and confining this to the domestic space, the concept of ethnicity allows states from all over the world to appear as interchangeable 'like units'. International hierarchies thus cease to be grounded on civilisational or racial differences and are instead expressed in more rational and merit-based terms. What is lost in this ostensibly benign reframing, however, is the long history of colonial extraction and expropriation through which these international differences were constituted in the first place. In facilitating a more culture-neutral understanding of international hierarchies, the concept of ethnicity also sweeps the legacies of imperialism under the carpet.

Last but not least, the universalisation of ethnicity has opened the door to new modes of discrimination between national groups, even as the formal equality of these groups is acknowledged. Two salient examples of this are the 'clash of civilisations' discourse and the new differentialist racism, both of which are grounded on notions of culture or ethnicity rather than race. These new discourses are often cloaked in superficially antiracist premises – such as protecting the cultural diversity of the world – yet they also feed into essentialist understandings of culture difference that legitimate discriminatory practices. Such post-racial and postcolonial patterns of prejudice are no doubt less objectionable than their imperial precursors, yet their ostensibly antiracist guise also renders them more resistant to critique.

The Ethnos of the Earth

Ethnicity, then, is far from the neutral or apolitical concept that it is typically presumed to be. In fact, it is precisely the non-ideological

[24] Zarakol 2011, 82–95.

guise of this concept that is the source of its ideological power: it is the ability of ethnicity to present itself as a seemingly transhistorical and value-free category that underlies both its rapid dissemination in the twentieth century and its ability to gloss over the contradictions of the international order. Yet this argument, in turn, throws up a new set of thorny theoretical questions: If ethnicity is not the transhistorical category it purports to be, then what are the conditions of possibility of demonstrating this? If the historicisation of nations, races, and tribes is predicated upon the naturalisation of ethnicity as the transhistorical ground for their historicisation, then what is the ground for historicising ethnicity itself?

To try and address these questions, this final section draws inspiration from Carl Schmitt's *The Nomos of the Earth* to conduct a speculative etymological analysis of the term from which ethnicity derives: the ancient Greek 'ethnos'. To be clear, the goal of this etymological exercise is neither to discover the 'original' meaning of ethnicity nor to juxtapose an ideological concept of ethnicity to a supposedly non-ideological concept of ethnos. Such efforts would merely repeat the ideological move exercised by the concept of ethnicity itself, that is, of positing a new concept as the transcendental ground for the historicisation of an existing concept, and ultimately pave the way for an endless regression of historicisations. Instead, the purpose of the etymological procedure is to unsettle the taken-for-grantedness of ethnicity by opening this concept to a broader range of historical and potential meanings. Hence, even as the notion of ethnos facilitates the denaturalisation and historicisation of the concept of ethnicity, it is not posited as the transcendental ground of this operation. Instead, the notion of ethnos is developed as an 'aconceptual concept'[25] that marks both the possibility and limit of the concept of ethnicity. This aconceptual concept functions as a pragmatic 'lever of intervention' that enables a 'regulated extension' of the meaning of ethnicity while keeping in touch with the existing system.[26] Through this strategic operation, the meaning of ethnicity is stretched to the point where its conceptual boundaries begin to break down, exposing the metaphysical

---

[25] Derrida 1988, 118.   [26] Derrida 1981c, 71.

presuppositions and sociohistorical processes that have gone into their formation.

Let us begin our etymological excursion with the uses of 'ethnos' in ancient Greece. Surveying the varied applications of this term, it quickly becomes clear that 'ethnos' had a diverse range of referents and served as a rather nebulous collective noun. In the works of Herodotus, for example, the word 'ethnos' could refer to almost any culturally, politically, or geographically defined grouping of people.[27] Although 'ethnos' always referred to 'a people, not a state',[28] it was also used by ancient Greeks to designate the population of a polis; the term 'ethnos' was thus deployed not only in a sociological or ethnographical sense, but also in a roughly legal or political sense to indicate citizenship of sorts (not unlike the words 'nation' and 'nationality' today). In Homer's *Iliad* and *Odyssey*, written several centuries earlier, the meanings of 'ethnos' are broader still, also including the ranks of the dead, groups of warriors, flocks of birds, herds of animals, and swarms of bees or flies – in short, any class of beings sharing a common identification.[29]

The etymological roots of the Greek 'ethnos' or 'ἔθνος' are shrouded in the mists of time. One hypothesis assumes that -νος is a suffix, which allows ἔθνος to be compared to ἔθος (signifying 'custom' or 'usage'). This parallel suggests that ἔθνος, like ἔθος, derives from the proto-Indo-European root *sued^h to which the suffix -νος (instead of -ος) has been added. At the core of *sued^h is the third person reflective anaphoric pronoun *s(u)e which is roughly equivalent to the English 'himself/herself/itself' but which was also used to designate the speaker's own social identity as in 'oneself' or 'ourselves'. The expansion *d^h may derive from *d^{h}eh$_1$-, meaning 'to put' or 'to situate'. Based on this speculative reconstruction, ἔθνος might have originally meant something like the placement of beings on the basis of their similarity to one another, the grouping of things with their own kind. This meaning certainly resonates with the wide-ranging use of the term by Homer.[30]

The wide range of referents enjoyed by the term 'ethnos' in ancient Greece has uncanny parallels in the present. Although the concept of ethnicity today is primarily used with reference to national, racial, and tribal communities, it has also been applied to a variety of other human

---

[27] Jones 1996. [28] Just 1989, 73.
[29] Hall 1997, 34; McInerney 2001, 54–57. [30] Beekes 2010, vol. I; Klein 1971.

groupings. Some of its more unconventional referents include social elites such as London bankers,[31] military organisations,[32] the community of deaf people,[33] the gay community,[34] and people who are HIV/AIDS positive.[35] The concept of ethnicity, as Carola Lentz notes, 'functions like the joker in a card-game: it can be introduced into various play sequences, taking on the characteristics [...] of the card it replaces'.[36] In structural terms, the apparent contentlessness of ethnicity recalls what the French anthropologist Claude Lévi-Strauss famously described as a 'floating' signifier: a sign of 'zero symbolic value' and 'therefore liable to take on any symbolic content whatever'.[37] The concept of ethnicity would thus be a signifier without a signified, hovering over an empty space in the signifying structure.

And yet, the concept of ethnicity is not entirely devoid of content. This can be seen in the tendency to qualify certain referents – such as the military or the gay community – as 'quasi-ethnicities' or 'quasi-ethnic communities' rather than treat them as ethnic groups proper.[38] Clearly, there are some uses of the concept that seem more natural or more appropriate, while others seem strange or unconventional. Despite its malleability, ethnicity still feels the gravitational pull of the concepts in relation to which it was articulated at the turn of the twentieth century – above all, the imperial triad of nation, race, and tribe. The empty space or structural void that the concept of ethnicity occupies is not a pure, abstract nothing, but the sublated product of the negation of certain concrete determinations: something was erased to create the structural void that ethnicity occupies, and the ghost of this something still haunts ethnicity from within. To make ethnicity 'float' away from these concrete historical moorings requires deliberate effort and belaboured justification. If ethnicity today seeks to constitute itself into the universal form of culture difference, there are nevertheless some differences that are different from this kind of difference. These deviant differences, which the concept of ethnicity struggles to hold within its grasp, are gathered up by the more expansive notion of ethnos. What the speculative notion of ethnos gestures at is a non-totalisable field of different kinds of differences that are structurally

---

[31] Cohen 1974. [32] Bah 2015; Zirker 2015.
[33] Eckert 2010; Erting 1978; Ladd and Lane 2013.
[34] Epstein 1992; Gamson 1995; Murray 1979. [35] Brock 2008.
[36] Lentz 1995, 304. [37] Lévi-Strauss 1987, 63–64.
[38] For example, Murray 1979; Zirker 2015.

barred from entering the domain of ethnicity, yet which continually threaten to breach its ramparts all the same.

In *The Nomos of the Earth*, Schmitt conducts a similar etymological exercise for the term 'nomos'. Tracing the uses of 'nomos' in ancient Greek sources, he identifies three primary meanings of this term: to take or appropriate, to divide or distribute, and to pasture or produce.[39] These three meanings of nomos are not equal, but follow from one another in a determinate sequence where appropriation precedes distribution and distribution precedes production: 'No man can give, divide, and distribute without taking.'[40] Schmitt thus identifies land-appropriation as the primeval sovereign act which 'constitutes the original spatial order, the source of all further concrete order and all further law'.[41] The act of land-appropriation orients the land-appropriating group both inward, toward the concrete socio-political order that it creates, and outward, toward other land-appropriating and land-owning groups.[42] It is worth quoting Schmitt's discussion at length:

> Not to lose the decisive connection between order and orientation, one should not translate *nomos* as law (in German, *Gesetz*), regulation, norm, or any similar expression. *Nomos* comes from *nemein* – a word that means both 'to divide' and 'to pasture.' Thus, *nomos* is the immediate form in which the political and social order of a people becomes spatially visible – the initial measure and division of pastureland, i.e. the land-appropriation as well as the concrete order contained in it and following from it. In Kant's words, it is the 'distributive law of mine and thine,' or, to use an English term that expresses it so well, it is the 'radical title.' *Nomos* is the *measure* by which the land in a particular order is divided and situated; it is also the form of political, social, and religious order determined by this process. Here, measure, order, and form constitute a spatially concrete unity.[43]

This originary meaning of nomos as a concrete spatial order was, however, 'destroyed by a series of distinctions and antitheses. Most important among them was the opposing of *nomos* and *physis*, whereby *nomos* became an imposed *ought* dissociated from and

---

[39] Schmitt 2003, 326–327.   [40] Schmitt 2003, 345.   [41] Schmitt 2003, 48.
[42] Schmitt 2003, 42–49. The term 'orientation' is apposite given how Western modernity was constructed in contradistinction to the Orient. Thus, it was Orientalism that provided the orientation for the imperial order. See also Said 2003.
[43] Schmitt 2003, 70.

opposed to *is*.[44] Through the elaboration of a conceptual opposition between nomos and physis, Schmitt argues, the meaning of nomos was transformed from a concrete spatial order into an abstract norm. A central aim of Schmitt's work was 'to restore to the word *nomos* its energy and majesty'.[45]

Schmitt's speculative genealogy of nomos is not without problems. As critics have pointed out, Schmitt's world view was deeply influenced by German conservative nationalist thought, and at times his theorisation of a primeval nomos strays close to a 'blut und boden' mentality that mythologises the earth as the privileged source of law and order.[46] Despite his mystification of the relationship between the law and the land, however, Schmitt's conception of nomos is by no means an essentialising or totalising one. For Schmitt, the sovereign act of appropriation is not only the constitutive force that founds the concrete order, but also, at the same time, the element of pure contingency that fractures that order from within and prevents it from ever constituting a self-enclosed totality. The act of appropriation is 'a founding rupture' that marks 'a void in the closure of order immanent to itself'.[47] The parallel between Schmitt's concrete order thinking and Derrida's insistence on the incompleteness of any conceptual system is evident here: every concrete order contains an immanent void, an outside on the inside, that opens the possibility of different appropriations and divisions of the earth.

'Prior to every legal, economic and social order, prior to every legal, economic or social theory,' Schmitt writes, 'there is this simple question: *Where and how was it appropriated? Where and how was it divided? Where and how was it produced?*'[48] It is in this spirit of concrete-order thinking that I wish to complement Schmitt's speculative notion of nomos with a speculative notion of ethnos. If Schmitt's nomos signifies a constitutive ordering of space, then ethnos signifies a constitutive ordering of beings. I refer deliberately to 'beings' rather than 'people' because the notion of ethnos should not be unthinkingly restricted to the sphere of living humans. The separation of the human from the animal, for instance, is an incredibly fraught distinction that in the modern era has been intertwined with discourses of racial

---

[44] Schmitt 2003, 69.   [45] Schmitt 2003, 67.
[46] For example, Benhabib 2012; Stergiopoulou 2014; Teschke 2011. See also Jurkevics 2017.
[47] Ojakangas 2007, 208.   [48] Schmitt 2003, 327–328.

hierarchy. A broader understanding of ethnos as the ordering of beings in general is also more in line with the flexible use of the term by Homer and the speculative proto-Indo-European etymology sketched out above.

This primeval meaning of ethnos, much like the primeval meaning of nomos, has been lost (or, perhaps, has never been found) due to the elaboration of a series of metaphysical antitheses stretching back to Aristotle's opposition between 'ethnos' and 'polis'. The meaning of 'ethnos' thus became associated with barbarian societies that lacked the political and legal institutions of the Greeks, while the polis came to be seen as a quintessentially Greek idea.[49] From this point on, the term 'ethnos' and its derivatives have been repeatedly (though not exclusively) associated with an 'other' separated and dissociated from the 'self', whether this be heathens and pagans in the medieval period or national minorities and non-Western peoples today.[50] To paraphrase Schmitt, it is time to restore to the word 'ethnos' its energy and majesty.

Seen in the light of a re-energised notion of ethnos, the transhistorical pretensions of ethnicity are exposed as a sham. Behind ethnicity's apolitical and non-ideological veneer lies an unacknowledged configuration of appropriations, divisions, and productions – an ethnos of the earth – that is the condition of possibility of ethnicity as such. The concept of ethnicity is no true transcendental, but a contingent symptom of those concrete historical processes that have produced the present global order of nation-states. Even as ethnicity's range of referents has expanded to embrace the darker side of the colour line and the lower rungs of the ladder of civilisation, it has also participated in the construction of new divisions and hierarchies. Above all, the concept of ethnicity has helped to erect a temporal boundary, a historical watershed, that segregates the states-system from its imperial past. It is this boundary work performed by the concept of ethnicity that allows the international order to take on a universalistic guise and to engulf the earth as a whole.

No ethnos is eternal. Like the imperial order that preceded it, the international order, too, must come to an end. On some level, it already has. In a Derridean twist, the emergence of ethnicity signals as much the end as the beginning of the international order: the

---

[49] Ehrenberg 1969, 22–25; Ward 2002, 17–19.
[50] Juteau-Lee 1983, 51; Neumann 2018; Shahabuddin 2016, 11–61.

concept of ethnicity is not only a 'filler' category that imbues the states-system with an aura of coherence and totality, but also, at the same time, a symptom of an inassimilable heterogeneity that discloses this system's contingency and incompleteness. As a phenomenon that resists absorption and assimilation, ethnicity signals the impossibility of the congruent nation-state, shattering the national space into a multiplicity of ethnic groups and exposing the limits of the international order. Over time, these indigestible differences will coalesce into oppositions, before maturing into contradictions that will impel the eventual breakdown of this order. The work of deconstruction has always-already begun.

References

Aalberts, Tanja E. 2014. Rethinking the Principle of (Sovereign) Equality as a Standard of Civilisation. *Millennium: Journal of International Studies* 42 (3): 767–789.
Abizadeh, Arash. 2005. Does Collective Identity Presuppose an Other? On the Alleged Incoherence of Global Solidarity. *The American Political Science Review* 99 (1): 45–60.
  2012. On the Demos and Its Kin: Nationalism, Democracy, and the Boundary Problem. *The American Political Science Review* 106 (4): 867–882.
Abramson, Harold J. 1973. *Ethnic Diversity in Catholic America*. New York: John Wiley & Sons.
Acharya, Amitav. 2022. Race and Racism in the Founding of the Modern World Order. *International Affairs* 98 (1): 23–43.
Acharya, Amitav, and Barry Buzan, eds. 2010. *Non-Western International Relations Theory: Perspectives from Asia*. London: Routledge.
  2019. *The Making of Global International Relations: Origins and Evolution of IR at Its Centenary*. Cambridge: Cambridge University Press.
Adas, Michael. 1989. *Machines as the Measure of Men: Science, Technology, and Ideologies of Western Dominance*. Ithaca: Cornell University Press.
Agier, Michel. 2017. Un pont sur la Manche: vers une anthropologie situationnelle. *Cahiers d'Études Africaines* 228: 921–932.
Alcoff, Linda Martín. 2000. Is Latina/o Identity a Racial Identity? In *Hispanics/Latinos in the United States: Ethnicity, Race, and Rights*, edited by Jorge J. E. Gracia and Pablo De Greiff, 23–44. New York: Routledge.
Alejandro, Audrey. 2019. *Western Dominance in International Relations? The Internationalisation of IR in Brazil and India*. London: Routledge.
Allen, Stephen Haley. 1920. *International Relations*. Princeton: Princeton University Press.
Allen, Tim, and John Eade. 1999. Introduction. In *Divided Europeans: Understanding Ethnicities in Conflict*, edited by Tim Allen and John Eade, 1–10. The Hague: Kluwer Law International.

Alymov, Sergei S. 2019. Ukrainian Roots of the Theory of Etnos. In *Life Histories of Etnos Theory in Russia and Beyond*, edited by David G. Anderson, Dmitry V. Arzyutov, and Sergei S. Alymov, 77–144. Cambridge: Open Book Publishers.

Alymov, Sergei S., and Svetlana V. Podrezova. 2019. Mapping Etnos: The Geographic Imagination of Fëdor Volkov and His Students. In *Life Histories of Etnos Theory in Russia and Beyond*, edited by David G. Anderson, Dmitry V. Arzyutov, and Sergei S. Alymov, 145–202. Cambridge: Open Book Publishers.

Amselle, Jean-Loup. 1985. Ethnies et espaces: pour une anthropologie topologique. In *Au cœur de l'ethnie: ethnies, tribalisme, et état en Afrique*, edited by Jean-Loup Amselle and Elikia M'Bokolo, 11–48. Paris: Éditions La Découverte.

2011. *L'ethnicisation de la France*. Paris: Lignes.

Amselle, Jean-Loup, and Elikia M'Bokolo, eds. 1985. *Au cœur de l'ethnie: ethnies, tribalisme, et état en Afrique*. Paris: Éditions La Découverte.

Anderson, Benedict. 2006. *Imagined Communities: Reflections on the Origin and Spread of Nationalism*. Revised edition. London: Verso.

Anderson, David G. 2019. Notes from His 'Snail's Shell': Shirokogoroff's Fieldwork and the Groundwork for Etnos Thinking. In *Life Histories of Etnos Theory in Russia and Beyond*, edited by David G. Anderson, Dmitry V. Arzyutov, and Sergei S. Alymov, 203–248. Cambridge: Open Book Publishers.

Anderson, David G., Dmitry V. Arzyutov, and Sergei S. Alymov, eds. 2019. *Life Histories of Etnos Theory in Russia and Beyond*. Cambridge: Open Book Publishers.

Anderson, David G., Dmitry V. Arzyutov, Sergei S. Alymov, Aurore Dumont, Andrei Golovnev, Chris Hann, Sergei Kan, Nathaniel Knight, Jeff Kochan, Marina Mogilner, Serguei A. Oushakine, Peter Schweitzer, Peter Skalník, and Hitoshi Yamada. 2019. The Etnos Archipelago: Sergei M. Shirokogoroff and the Life History of a Controversial Anthropological Concept [with Comments and Reply]. *Current Anthropology* 60 (6): 741–773.

Anderson, Mark. 2019b. *From Boas to Black Power: Racism, Liberalism, and American Anthropology*. Stanford: Stanford University Press.

Anghie, Antony. 2005. *Imperialism, Sovereignty and the Making of International Law*. Cambridge: Cambridge University Press.

Anievas, Alexander, Nivi Manchanda, and Robert Shilliam, eds. 2015. *Race and Racism in International Relations: Confronting the Global Colour Line*. London: Routledge.

Ansell, Amy Elizabeth. 1997. *New Right, New Racism: Race and Reaction in the United States and Britain*. Basingstoke: Macmillan.

Appiah, Kwame Anthony. 2014. *Lines of Descent: W. E. B. Du Bois and the Emergence of Identity*. Cambridge, MA: Harvard University Press.

Aranda, Elizabeth M., and Guillermo Rebollo-Gil. 2004. Ethnoracism and 'Sandwiched' Minorities. *American Behavioral Scientist* 47 (7): 910–927.

Archives d'Histoire de l'Ethnologie. 1993. *Georges Montandon et l'ethnie française*. Paris: Archives d'Historie de l'Ethnologie.

Arendt, Hannah. 1944. Race-Thinking Before Racism. *The Review of Politics* 6 (1): 36–73.

—— 1945. Imperialism, Nationalism, Chauvinism. *The Review of Politics* 7 (4): 441–463.

—— 1976. *The Origins of Totalitarianism*. New edition. New York: Harcourt, Brace & Company.

Argyle, W. J. 1969. European Nationalism and African Tribalism. In *Tradition and Transition in East Africa: Studies of the Tribal Element in the Modern Era*, edited by P. H. Gulliver, 41–58. Berkeley: University of California Press.

Armitage, David. 2013. *Foundations of Modern International Thought*. Cambridge: Cambridge University Press.

Arutiunov, Serghei A., and Yulian Bromley. 1978. Problems of Ethnicity in Soviet Ethnographic Studies. In *Perspectives on Ethnicity*, edited by Regina E. Holloman and Serghei A. Arutiunov, 11–13. The Hague: Mouton.

Arzyutov, Dmitry V. 2019. Order out of Chaos: Anthropology and Politics of Sergei M. Shirokogoroff. In *Life Histories of Etnos Theory in Russia and Beyond*, edited by David G. Anderson, Dmitry V. Arzyutov, and Sergei S. Alymov, 249–292. Cambridge: Open Book Publishers.

Arzyutov, Dmitry V., David G. Anderson, and Sergei S. Alymov. 2019a. Grounding Etnos Theory: An Introduction. In *Life Histories of Etnos Theory in Russia and Beyond*, edited by David G. Anderson, Dmitry V. Arzyutov, and Sergei S. Alymov, 1–20. Cambridge: Open Book Publishers.

—— 2019b. Etnos Thinking in the Long Twentieth Century. In *Life Histories of Etnos Theory in Russia and Beyond*, edited by David G. Anderson, Dmitry V. Arzyutov, and Sergei S. Alymov, 21–76. Cambridge: Open Book Publishers.

Asad, Talal, ed. 1973. *Anthropology and the Colonial Encounter*. London: Ithaca Press.

—— 1991. Afterword: From the History of Colonial Anthropology to the Anthropology of Western Hegemony. In *Colonial Situations: Essays on the Contextualization of Ethnographic Knowledge*, edited by George W. Stocking, 314–324. Madison: University of Wisconsin Press.

Asch, Michael, Colin Samson, Dieter Heinen, Justin Kenrick, Jerome Lewis, Sidsel Saugestad, Terry Turner, and Adam Kuper. 2004. On the Return of the Native. *Current Anthropology* 45 (2): 261–267.

Asch, Michael, Colin Samson, Ulf Dahre, and Adam Kuper. 2006. More on the Return of the Native. *Current Anthropology* 47 (1): 145–149.

Ashley, Richard K. 1988. Untying the Sovereign State: A Double Reading of the Anarchy Problematique. *Millennium: Journal of International Studies* 17 (2): 227–262.

Aukerman, Miriam J. 2000. Definitions and Justifications: Minority and Indigenous Rights in a Central/East European Context. *Human Rights Quarterly* 22 (4): 1011–1050.

Avrutin, Eugene M. 2007. Racial Categories and the Politics of (Jewish) Difference in Late Imperial Russia. *Kritika: Explorations in Russian and Eurasian. History* 8 (1): 13–40.

Aydin, Cemil. 2007a. A Global Anti-Western Moment? The Russo-Japanese War, Decolonization, and Asian Modernity. In *Competing Visions of World Order: Global Moments and Movements, 1880s–1930s*, edited by Sebastian Conrad and Dominic Sachsenmeier, 213–236. Basingstoke: Palgrave Macmillan.

2007b. *The Politics of Anti-Westernism in Asia: Visions of World Order in Pan-Islamic and Pan-Asian Thought*. New York: Columbia University Press.

2013. Pan-Nationalism of Pan-Islamic, Pan-Asian, and Pan-African Thought. In *The Oxford Handbook of the History of Nationalism*, edited by John Breuilly, 672–693. Oxford: Oxford University Press.

Bah, Mamadou Diouma. 2015. The Military and Politics in Guinea: An Instrumental Explanation of Political Stability. *Armed Forces & Society* 41 (1): 69–95.

Baji, Tomohito. 2016. Zionist Internationalism? Alfred Zimmern's Post-Racial Commonwealth. *Modern Intellectual History* 13 (3): 623–651.

2021. *The International Thought of Alfred Zimmern: Classicism, Zionism and the Shadow of Commonwealth*. Basingstoke: Palgrave Macmillan.

Baker, Ray Stannard. 1923. *Woodrow Wilson and World Settlement: Written from His Unpublished and Personal Material*. London: William Heinemann.

Balandier, Georges. 1951. La situation coloniale: approche théorique. *Cahiers Internationaux de Sociologie* 11: 44–79.

1953. Messianismes et nationalismes en Afrique noire. *Cahiers Internationaux de Sociologie* 114: 41–65.

1955. *Sociologie actuelle de l'Afrique noire: changements sociaux au Gabon et au Congo*. Paris: Presses Universitaires de France.

1960. Structures sociales traditionnelles et changements économiques. *Cahiers d'Études Africaines* 1 (1): 1–14.

Balibar, Étienne. 1991a. Is There a 'Neo-Racism'? In *Race, Nation, Class: Ambiguous Identities*, by Étienne Balibar and Immanuel Wallerstein, translated by Chris Turner, 17–28. London: Verso.

1991b. Racism and Nationalism. In *Race, Nation, Class: Ambiguous Identities*, by Étienne Balibar and Immanuel Wallerstein, translated by Chris Turner, 37–67. London: Verso.

1994. Racism as Universalism. In *Masses, Classes, Ideas: Studies on Politics and Philosophy Before and After Marx*, by Étienne Balibar, translated by James Swenson, 191–204. New York: Routledge.

2008. Racism Revisited: Sources, Relevance, and Aporias of a Modern Concept. *PMLA: Publications of the Modern Language Association of America* 123 (5): 1630–1639.

Ballard, Roger. 1996. Negotiating Race and Ethnicity: Exploring the Implications of the 1991 Census. *Patterns of Prejudice* 30 (3): 3–33.

Banks, Marcus. 1996. *Ethnicity: Anthropological Constructions*. London: Routledge.

Banton, Michael. 1983. *Racial and Ethnic Competition*. Cambridge: Cambridge University Press.

2007. Max Weber on 'Ethnic Communities': A Critique. *Nations and Nationalism* 13 (1): 19–35.

Barder, Alexander D. 2021. *Global Race War: International Politics and Racial Hierarchy*. Oxford: Oxford University Press.

Barkan, Elazar. 1992. *The Retreat of Scientific Racism: Changing Concepts of Race in Britain and the United States between the World Wars*. Cambridge: Cambridge University Press.

Barkawi, Tarak, Christopher Murray, and Ayşe Zarakol. 2023. The United Nations of IR: Power, Knowledge, and Empire in Global IR Debates. *International Theory* 15 (3): 445–461.

Barkdull, John. 1995. Waltz, Durkheim, and International Relations: The International System as an Abnormal Form. *The American Political Science Review* 89 (3): 669–680.

Barker, Martin. 1981. *The New Racism: Conservatives and the Ideology of the Tribe*. Frederick, MD: University Publications of America.

Barnard, Alan. 2006. Kalahari Revisionism, Vienna and the 'Indigenous Peoples' Debate. *Social Anthropology* 14 (1): 1–16.

Barnes, Harry Elmer. 1919. Nationalism, the Historical Development of. In *The Encyclopedia Americana*, Vol. XIX, 743–765. New York: The Encyclopedia Americana Corporation.

1920. National Self-Determination and the Problems of the Small Nations. In *The League of Nations: The Principle and the Practice*, edited by Stephen Pierce Duggan, 161–183. London: Allen & Unwin.

Barnett, Michael. 2020. The Jewish Problem in International Society. In *Culture and Order in World Politics*, edited by Andrew Phillips and Christian Reus-Smit, 232–249. Cambridge: Cambridge University Press.

Barrington, Lowell W. 1997. 'Nation' and 'Nationalism': The Misuse of Key Concepts in Political Science. *PS: Political Science and Politics* 30 (4): 712–716.

Barsh, Russel Lawrence. 1986. Indigenous Peoples: An Emerging Object of International Law. *The American Journal of International Law* 80 (2): 369–385.

Bartelson, Jens. 1995. *A Genealogy of Sovereignty*. Cambridge: Cambridge University Press.

Barth, Fredrik. 1956. Ecologic Relationships of Ethnic Groups in Swat, North Pakistan. *American Anthropologist* 58 (6): 1079–1089.

 1966. *Models of Social Organization*. London: Royal Anthropological Institute of Great Britain and Ireland.

 ed. 1969a. *Ethnic Groups and Boundaries: The Social Organization of Culture Difference*. Boston: Little, Brown and Company.

 1969b. Introduction. In *Ethnic Groups and Boundaries: The Social Organization of Culture Difference*, edited by Fredrik Barth, 9–38. Boston: Little, Brown and Company.

Barzun, Jacques. 1938. *Race: A Study in Modern Superstition*. London: Methuen.

Bassin, Mark. 2016. *The Gumilev Mystique: Biopolitics, Eurasianism, and the Construction of Community in Modern Russia*. Ithaca: Cornell University Press.

Bastid-Bruguière, Marianne. 2004. The Japanese-Induced German Connection of Modern Chinese Ideas of the State: Liang Qichao and the Guojia lun of J. K. Bluntschli. In *The Role of Japan in Liang Qichao's Introduction of Modern Western Civilization to China*, edited by Joshua A. Fogel, 105–124. Berkeley: Institute of Asian Studies.

Bauman, Zygmunt. 1989. *Modernity and the Holocaust*. Cambridge: Polity.

 1991. *Modernity and Ambivalence*. Cambridge: Polity.

Becquet, Charles. 1963. *L'ethnie française d'Europe*. Paris: Nouvelles Éditions Latines.

Beekes, Robert. 2010. *Etymological Dictionary of Greek*. Leiden: Brill.

Beer, George Louis. 1917. *The English-Speaking Peoples: Their Future Relations and Joint International Obligations*. New York: Macmillan.

Béjin, André. 1982. Le sang, le sense et le travail: Georges Vacher de Lapouge darwinista social fondateur de l'anthroposociologie. *Cahiers Internationaux de Sociologie* 73: 323–343.

Bell, Duncan. 2007. *The Idea of Greater Britain: Empire and the Future of World Order, 1860–1900*. Princeton: Princeton University Press.

2011. Empire and Imperialism. In *The Cambridge History of Nineteenth-Century Political Thought*, edited by Gareth Stedman Jones and Gregory Claeys, 864–892. Cambridge: Cambridge University Press.

2012. The Project for a New Anglo Century: Race, Space, and Global Order. In *Anglo-America and Its Discontents: Civilizational Identities beyond West and East*, edited by Peter J. Katzenstein, 33–55. London: Routledge.

2013. Race and International Relations: Introduction. *Cambridge Review of International Affairs* 26 (1): 1–4.

2014. What Is Liberalism? *Political Theory* 42 (6): 682–715.

2018. Founding the World State: H. G. Wells on Empire and the English-Speaking Peoples. *International Studies Quarterly* 62 (4): 867–879.

2020. *Dreamworlds of Race: Empire and the Utopian Destiny of Anglo-America*. Princeton: Princeton University Press.

Benedict, Ruth. 1934. *Patterns of Culture*. Boston: Houghton Mifflin.

1940. *Race: Science and Politics*. New York: Modern Age.

1942. *Race and Racism*. London: Routledge.

Benhabib, Seyla. 2012. Carl Schmitt's Critique of Kant: Sovereignty and International Law. *Political Theory* 40 (6): 688–713.

Bentley, G. Carter. 1987. Ethnicity and Practice. *Comparative Studies in Society and History* 29 (1): 24–55.

Benveniste, Émile. 1971. *Problems in General Linguistics*. Translated by Mary Elizabeth Meek. Coral Gables: University of Miami Press.

Berenskoetter, Felix. 2017. Approaches to Concept Analysis. *Millennium: Journal of International Studies* 45 (2): 151–173.

Berkson, Isaac B. 1920a. A Community Theory of American Life. *Menorah Journal* 6 (6): 311–321.

1920b. *Theories of Americanization: A Critical Study with Special Reference to the Jewish Group*. New York: Teachers College Press.

1921. The Jewish Right to Live: A Defense of Ethnic Loyalty. *Menorah Journal* 7 (1): 41–51.

Berman, Nathaniel. 1998. The International Law of Nationalism: Group Identity and Legal History. In *International Law and Ethnic Conflict*, edited by David Wippman, 25–57. Ithaca: Cornell University Press.

Bernasconi, Robert. 2007. Ethnic Race. In *Race or Ethnicity? On Black and Latino Identity*, edited by Jorge J. E. Gracia, 123–136. Ithaca: Cornell University Press.

2011. The Great White Error and the Great Black Mirage: Frantz Fanon's Critical Philosophy of Race. In *Living Fanon: Global Perspectives*, edited by Nigel C. Gibson, 85–92. Basingstoke: Palgrave Macmillan.

Bernier, Bernard, Mikhael Elbaz, and Gilles Lavigne. 1978. Ethnicité et lutte de classes. *Anthropologie et Sociétés* 2 (1): 15–60.

Bessac, Frank D. 1968. Cultunit and Ethnic Unit – Processes and Symbolism. In *Essays on the Problem of Tribe: Proceedings of the 1967 Annual Spring Meeting of the American Ethnological Society*, edited by June Helm, 58–71. Seattle: University of Washington Press.

Béteille, André. 1998. The Idea of Indigenous People. *Current Anthropology* 39 (2): 187–192.

Bettiza, Gregorio. 2014. Civilizational Analysis in International Relations: Mapping the Field and Advancing a 'Civilizational Politics' Line of Research. *International Studies Review* 16 (1): 1–28.

Bhabha, Homi K. 1994. *The Location of Culture*. London: Routledge.

Bhambra, Gurminder K. 2010. Historical Sociology, International Relations and Connected Histories. *Cambridge Review of International Affairs* 23 (1): 127–143.

Bilgin, Pinar. 2008. Thinking Past 'Western' IR? *Third World Quarterly* 29 (1): 5–23.

2016. 'Contrapuntal Reading' as a Method, an Ethos, and a Metaphor for Global IR. *International Studies Review* 18 (1): 134–146.

Billig, Michael. 1995. *Banal Nationalism*. London: Sage.

Birkenmaier, Anke. 2016. *The Specter of Races: Latin American Anthropology and Literature between the Wars*. Charlottesville: University of Virginia Press.

Bizumic, Boris. 2014. Who Coined the Concept of Ethnocentrism? A Brief Report. *Journal of Social and Political Psychology* 2 (1): 3–10.

Blakeslee, George H. 1910. Introduction. *The Journal of Race Development* 1 (1): 1–4.

Blanchard, Wendell. 1958. *Thailand: Its People, Its Society, Its Culture*. New Haven: Human Relations Area Files.

Blatt, Jessica. 2004. 'To Bring Out the Best That Is in Their Blood': Race, Reform, and Civilization in the Journal of Race Development (1910–1919). *Ethnic and Racial Studies* 27 (5): 691–709.

2014. John W. Burgess, the Racial State and the Making of the American Science of Politics. *Ethnic and Racial Studies* 37 (6): 1062–1079.

2018. *Race and the Making of American Political Science*. Philadelphia: University of Pennsylvania Press.

Blauner, Robert. 1972. *Racial Oppression in America*. New York: Harper & Row.

Bloom, Leonard. 1948. Concerning Ethnic Research. *American Sociological Review* 13 (2): 171–182.

Bluntschli, Johann Kaspar. 1877. *Théorie générale de l'état*. Translated by Armand de Riedmatten. Paris: Librairie Guillaumin.

1885. *The Theory of the State*. Translated by David George Ritchie, Percy Ewing Matheson, and Richard Lodge. Oxford: Clarendon.

1886. *Lehre vom modernen Staat.* 6th edition. Stuttgart: Verlag der J. G. Cotta'sche Buchhandlung.
Boas, Franz. 1887a. The Study of Geography. *Science* 9 (210): 137–141.
1887b. The Occurrence of Similar Inventions in Areas Widely Apart. *Science* 9 (224): 485–486.
1887c. Museums of Ethnology and Their Classification. *Science* 9 (228): 587–589.
1887d. Museums of Ethnology and Their Classification. *Science* 9 (229): 614.
1907. Some Principles of Museum Administration. *Science* 25 (650): 921–933.
1940. *Race, Language and Culture.* New York: Free Press.
Boehm, Max Hildebert, and Carlton J. H. Hayes. 1933. Nationalism. In *Encyclopaedia of the Social Sciences*, Vol. XI, 231–249. London: Macmillan.
Bonilla-Silva, Eduardo. 2022. *Racism without Racists: Color-Blind Racism and the Persistence of Racial Inequality in America.* 6th edition. Lanham: Rowman & Littlefield.
Bonnett, Alastair. 2004. From White to Western: 'Racial Decline' and the Rise of the Idea of the West in Britain, 1890–1930. In *The Idea of the West: Culture, Politics and History*, 14–39. Basingstoke: Palgrave Macmillan.
Borde, Jean. 1950. Le problème ethnique dans l'Union Sud-Africaine. *Cahiers d'outre-mer* 3 (12): 319–342.
Borneman, John. 1995. American Anthropology as Foreign Policy. *American Anthropologist* 97 (4): 663–672.
Boulenger, Jacques. 1943. *Le sang français.* Paris: Éditions Denoël.
Bowden, Brett. 2009. *The Empire of Civilization: The Evolution of an Imperial Idea.* Chicago: University of Chicago Press.
Boyon, Jacques. 1963. Pouvoir et autorité en Afrique noire: état des travaux. *Revue Française de Science Politique* 13 (4): 993–1018.
Brace, C. L., Carleton S. Coon, Earl W. Count, Stanley M. Garn, Julian Huxley, and Ashley Montagu. 1964. On the Race Concept [with Comments and Reply]. *Current Anthropology* 5 (4): 313–320.
Braithwaite, Lloyd. 1953. Social Stratification in Trinidad: A Preliminary Analysis. *Social and Economic Studies* 2 (2–3): 5–175.
Brattain, Michelle. 2007. Race, Racism, and Antiracism: UNESCO and the Politics of Presenting Science to the Postwar Public. *American Historical Review* 112 (5): 1386–1413.
Breton, Roland. 1992. *Les ethnies.* 2nd edition. Paris: Presses Universitaires de France.
Breuilly, John. 1993. *Nationalism and the State.* 2nd edition. Manchester: Manchester University Press.

2011. On the Principle of Nationality. In *The Cambridge History of Nineteenth-Century Political Thought*, edited by Gareth Stedman Jones and Gregory Claeys, 77–109. Cambridge: Cambridge University Press.

Brincat, Shannon, and L. H. M. Ling. 2014. Dialectics for IR: Hegel and the Dao. *Globalizations* 11 (5): 661–687.

Brinton, Daniel G. 1890. *Races and Peoples: Lectures on the Science of Ethnography*. New York: N. D. C. Hodges.

Broce, Gerald. 1986. Herder and Ethnography. *Journal of the History of the Behavioral Sciences* 22 (2): 150–170.

Brock, Richard. 2008. An 'Onerous Citizenship': Globalization, Cultural Flows and the HIV/AIDS Pandemic in Hari Kunzru's Transmission. *Journal of Postcolonial Writing* 44 (4): 379–390.

Bromley, Yulian, ed. 1974a. *Soviet Ethnology and Anthropology Today*. The Hague: Mouton.

1974b. The Term Ethnos and Its Definition. In *Soviet Ethnography and Anthropology Today*, edited by Yulian Bromley, 55–72. The Hague: Mouton.

1977. The Object and the Subject-Matter of Ethnography. In *Ethnography and Related Sciences*, edited by E. Veselkin, 7–23. Moscow: USSR Academy of Sciences.

1978. On the Typology of Ethnic Communities. In *Perspectives on Ethnicity*, edited by Regina E. Holloman and Serghei A. Arutiunov, 15–21. The Hague: Mouton.

Bromley, Yulian, and Viktor Kozlov. 1989. The Theory of Ethnos and Ethnic Processes in Soviet Social Sciences. *Comparative Studies in Society and History* 31 (3): 425–438.

Broom, Leonard. 1954. The Social Differentiation of Jamaica. *American Sociological Review* 19 (2): 115–125.

Brouard, Carl, Lorimer Denis, Clément Magloire fils, and François Duvalier. 1938. Declaration. *Les Griots: La Revue Scientifique et Littéraire d'Haïti* 1 (1): 1.

Brown, Michael E., ed. 1993. *Ethnic Conflict and International Security*. Princeton: Princeton University Press.

Brown, Philip Marshall. 1923. *International Society: Its Nature and Interests*. New York: Macmillan.

Brubaker, Rogers. 2004. *Ethnicity without Groups*. Cambridge, MA: Harvard University Press.

2017. Between Nationalism and Civilizationism: The European Populist Moment in Comparative Perspective. *Ethnic and Racial Studies* 40 (8): 1191–1226.

Brubaker, Rogers, and Frederick Cooper. 2000. Beyond 'Identity'. *Theory and Society* 29 (1): 1–47.

Brunhes, Jean, and Camille Vallaux. 1921. *La géographie de l'histoire: géographie de la paix et de la guerre sur terre et sur mer*. Paris: Félix Alcan.
Bruyneel, Kevin. 2007. *The Third Space of Sovereignty: The Postcolonial Politics of U.S.-Indigenous Relations*. Minneapolis: University of Minnesota Press.
Bryce, James. 1912. *South America: Observations and Impressions*. London: Macmillan.
  1922. *International Relations: Eight Lectures Delivered in the United States in August, 1921*. London: Macmillan.
Buck, Carl Darling. 1916. Language and the Sentiment of Nationality. *The American Political Science Review* 10 (1): 44–69.
Buell, Raymond Leslie. 1926. *International Relations*. London: Sir Isaac Pitman & Sons.
Buettner-Janusch, John. 1957. Boas and Mason: Particularism versus Generalization. *American Anthropologist* 59 (2): 318–324.
Bukovansky, Mlada. 1999. The Altered State and the State of Nature: The French Revolution and International Politics. *Review of International Studies* 25 (2): 197–216.
Bull, Hedley. 1977. *The Anarchical Society: A Study of Order in World Politics*. London: Macmillan.
  1984. The Emergence of a Universal International Society. In *The Expansion of International Society*, edited by Hedley Bull and Adam Watson, 117–126. Oxford: Clarendon.
Bull, Hedley, and Adam Watson, eds. 1984. *The Expansion of International Society*. Oxford: Clarendon.
Bunzl, Matti. 1996. Franz Boas and the Humboldtian Tradition: From Volksgeist and Nationalcharakter to an Anthropological Concept of Culture. In *Volksgeist as Method and Ethic: Essays on Boasian Ethnography and the German Anthropological Tradition*, edited by George W. Stocking, 17–78. Madison: University of Wisconsin Press.
Burgess, John W. 1890. *Political Science and Comparative Constitutional Law*. Boston: Ginn.
Burke, Roland. 2010. *Decolonization and the Evolution of International Human Rights*. Philadelphia: University of Pennsylvania Press.
Burles, Regan. 2023. Globalizing the International: Bull's Metaphysics of Order. *International Theory* 15 (2): 184–207.
Burtscher, Michael. 2012. A Nation and a People? Notes Toward a Conceptual History of the Terms Minzoku and Kokumin in Early Meiji Japan. *Journal of Political Science & Sociology* 16: 47–106.
Butler, Judith. 1999. *Gender Trouble: Feminism and the Subversion of Identity*. London: Routledge.

Cadiot, Juliette. 2007. *Le laboratoire impérial: Russie-URSS, 1870–1940*. Paris: CNRS Éditions.
Caffrey, Margaret M. 1989. *Ruth Benedict: Stranger in This Land*. Austin: University of Texas Press.
Cahen, Michel. 1994. *Ethnicité politique: pour une lecture réaliste de l'identité*. Paris: L'Harmattan.
Caputo, John D., ed. 1997. *Deconstruction in a Nutshell: A Conversation with Jacques Derrida*. New York: Fordham University Press.
Carhart, Michael C. 2007. *The Science of Culture in Enlightenment Germany*. Cambridge, MA: Harvard University Press.
Carmichael, Stokely, and Charles V. Hamilton. 1968. *Black Power: The Politics of Liberation in America*. London: Jonathan Cape.
Carr, E. H. 1945. *Nationalism and After*. London: Macmillan.
Carter, Jacoby Adeshei. 2016. *African American Contributions to the Americas' Cultures*. New York: Palgrave Macmillan.
Césaire, Aimé. 1955. *Discourse on Colonialism*. Translated by Joan Pinkham. New York: Monthly Review Press.
Chakrabarty, Dipesh. 2000. *Provincializing Europe: Postcolonial Thought and Historical Difference*. Princeton: Princeton University Press.
Chapman, Malcolm. 1993. Social and Biological Aspects of Ethnicity. In *Social and Biological Aspects of Ethnicity*, edited by Malcolm Chapman, 1–46. Oxford: Oxford University Press.
Childs, John Brown, and Guillermo Delgado-P. 1999. On the Idea of the Indigenous. *Current Anthropology* 40 (2): 211–212.
Chowdhry, Geeta. 2007. Edward Said and Contrapuntal Reading: Implications for Critical Interventions in International Relations. *Millennium: Journal of International Studies* 36 (1): 101–116.
Ciccariello-Maher, George. 2017. *Decolonizing Dialectics*. Durham: Duke University Press.
Coakley, John. 2012. *Nationalism, Ethnicity and the State: Making and Breaking Nations*. London: Sage.
Cohen, Abner. 1969. *Custom and Politics in Urban Africa: A Study of Hausa Migrants in Yoruba Towns*. London: Routledge & Kegan Paul.
——— 1974. Introduction: The Lesson of Ethnicity. In *Urban Ethnicity*, edited by Abner Cohen, ix–xxiv. London: Tavistock.
Cohen, Ronald. 1978. Ethnicity: Problem and Focus in Anthropology. *Annual Review of Anthropology* 7: 379–403.
Cole, Douglas. 1999. *Franz Boas: The Early Years, 1858–1906*. Vancouver: Douglas & McIntyre.
Coleman, James S. 1954. Nationalism in Tropical Africa. *The American Political Science Review* 48 (2): 404–426.

    1958. *Nigeria: Background to Nationalism*. Berkeley: University of California Press.
Colson, Elizabeth. 1953. *The Makah Indians: A Study of an Indian Tribe in Modern American Society*. Manchester: Manchester University Press.
    1968. Contemporary Tribes and the Development of Nationalism. In *Essays on the Problem of Tribe: Proceedings of the 1967 Annual Spring Meeting of the American Ethnological Society*, edited by June Helm, 201–206. Seattle: University of Washington Press.
Commission Mixte d'Émigration Gréco-Bulgare. 1921. *Procès-verbaux des séances*. Geneva: League of Nations Library.
Conklin, Alice L. 2013. *In the Museum of Man: Race, Anthropology, and Empire in France, 1850–1950*. Ithaca: Cornell University Press.
Connor, Walker. 1972. Nation-Building or Nation-Destroying? *World Politics* 24 (3): 319–355.
    1978. A Nation Is a Nation, Is a State, Is an Ethnic Group, Is a .... *Ethnic and Racial Studies* 1 (4): 377–400.
    1981. Nationalism and Political Illegitimacy. *Canadian Review of Studies in Nationalism* 8 (2): 201–228.
    1991. From Tribe to Nation? *History of European Ideas* 13 (1–2): 5–18.
    1994. *Ethnonationalism: The Quest for Understanding*. Princeton: Princeton University Press.
Cooper, Frederick. 2014. *Citizenship between Empire and Nation: Remaking France and French Africa, 1945–1960*. Princeton: Princeton University Press.
Copans, Jean. 2001. La 'situation coloniale' de Georges Balandier: notion conjoncturelle ou modèle sociologique et historique? *Cahiers Internationaux de Sociologie* 1 (110): 31–52.
Corntassel, Jeff. 2003. Who Is Indigenous? 'Peoplehood' and Ethnonationalist Approaches to Rearticulating Indigenous Identity. *Nationalism and Ethnic Politics* 9 (1): 75–100.
Corntassel, Jeff, and Tomas Hopkins Primeau. 1995. Indigenous 'Sovereignty' and International Law: Revised Strategies for Pursuing 'Self-Determination'. *Human Rights Quarterly* 17 (2): 343–365.
Cox, Oliver C. 1944. The Racial Theories of Robert E. Park and Ruth Benedict. *The Journal of Negro Education* 13 (4): 452–463.
    1948. *Caste, Class, and Race: A Study in Social Dynamics*. New York: Doubleday & Company.
Crampton, Jeremy W. 2006. The Cartographic Calculation of Space: Race Mapping and the Balkans at the Paris Peace Conference of 1919. *Social & Cultural Geography* 7 (5): 731–752.

Cruse, Harold. 1967. *The Crisis of the Negro Intellectual*. New York: William Morrow & Company.

1968. *Rebellion or Revolution*. New York: William Morrow & Company.

Cvetkovski, Roland. 2013. Empire Complex: Arrangements in the Russian Ethnographic Museum, 1910. In *An Empire of Others: Making Ethnographic Knowledge in Imperial Russia and the USSR*, edited by Roland Cvetkovski and Alexis Hofmeister, 211–252. Budapest: Central European University Press.

de Azcárate, Pablo. 1945. *League of Nations and National Minorities: An Experiment*. Washington, DC: Carnegie Endowment for International Peace.

de Heusch, Luc. 1997. L'ethnie: les vicissitudes d'un concept. *Archives Européennes de Sociologie* 38 (2): 185–206.

Deloria, Vine Jr. 1969. *Custer Died for Your Sins: An Indian Manifesto*. Norman: University of Oklahoma Press.

Delos, Joseph Thomas. 1928. L'internationalisme: synthèse de la culture et de la civilisation. *Revue des Sciences Philosophiques et Théologiques* 17 (4): 659–679.

1944. *Le problème de civilisation: la nation*. Montreal: Éditions de l'Arbre.

Deniker, Joseph. 1900a. *Les races et les peuples de la terre: éléments d'anthropologie et d'ethnographie*. Paris: Schleicher.

1900b. *The Races of Man: An Outline of Anthropology and Ethnography*. London: Walter Scott.

1904. Les six races composant la population actuelle de l'Europe. *The Journal of the Anthropological Institute of Great Britain and Ireland* 34: 181–206.

Denis, Lorimer, and François Duvalier. 1936. La civilisation haïtienne: notre mentalité est-elle africaine ou gallo-latine. *Revue de la Société d'Histoire et de Géographie d'Haïti* 7 (23): 1–31.

1938a. Le noir d'Afrique et la civilisation européenne. *Les Griots: La Revue Scientifique et Littéraire d'Haïti* 1 (1): 3–13.

1938b. L'essentiel de la doctrine des griots. *Les Griots: La Revue Scientifique et Littéraire d'Haïti* 2 (2): 151–153.

1939. Question d'anthropo-sociologie: le déterminism racial. *Les Griots: La Revue Scientifique et Littéraire d'Haïti* 1 (3): 303–309.

Derrida, Jacques. 1976. *Of Grammatology*. Baltimore: The Johns Hopkins University Press.

1978. From Restricted to General Economy: A Hegelianism without Reserve. In *Writing and Difference*, by Jacques Derrida, translated by Alan Bass, 251–277. London: Routledge & Kegan Paul.

1981a. *Dissemination*. Translated by Barbara Johnson. London: Athlone Press.

1981b. Economimesis. Translated by R. Klein. *Diacritics* 11 (2): 2–25.
1981c. *Positions*. Translated by Alan Bass. London: Athlone Press.
1986. *Glas*. Translated by John P. Leavey and Richard Rand. Lincoln: University of Nebraska Press.
1988. *Limited Inc*. Evanston: Northwestern University Press.
1991. Letter to a Japanese Friend. In *A Derrida Reader: Between the Blinds*, edited by Peggy Kamuf, translated by David Wood and Andrew Benjamin, 269–276. New York: Harvester Wheatsheaf.
1999. Hospitality, Justice and Responsibility: A Dialogue with Jacques Derrida. In *Questioning Ethics: Contemporary Debates in Philosophy*, edited by Richard Kearney and Mark Dooley, 65–83. London: Routledge.

de Saussure, Ferdinand. [1916] 1995. *Cours de linguistique générale*. Paris: Payot.
1959. *Course in General Linguistics*. Translated by Wade Baskin. New York: Philosophical Library.

de Sauvigny, G. d. B. 1970. Liberalism, Nationalism and Socialism: The Birth of Three Words. *The Review of Politics* 32 (2): 147–166.

Desoille, H. 1938. Félix Regnault: notice nécrologique. *Bulletins et Mémoires de la Société d'Anthropologie de Paris* 9 (4–6): 120.

Despres, Leo A. 1975. Towards a Theory of Ethnic Phenomena. In *Ethnicity and Resource Competition in Plural Societies*, edited by Leo A. Despres, 187–208. The Hague: Mouton.

Deuel, Thorne, and Jack A. Lucas. 1962. Terminology: Relative to Primitive. *Current Anthropology* 3 (2): 206.

De Swaan, Abram. 2001. *Words of the World: The Global Language System*. Cambridge: Polity.

Dickinson, G. Lowes. 1916. *The European Anarchy*. New York: Macmillan.
1926. *The International Anarchy, 1904–1914*. London: Allen & Unwin.

Dike, Edwin Berck. 1935. Obsolete English Words: Some Recent Views. *The Journal of English and Germanic Philology* 34 (3): 351–365.

Doak, Kevin M. 2007. *A History of Nationalism in Modern Japan: Placing the People*. Leiden: Brill.

Donnelly, Jack. 1998. Human Rights: A New Standard of Civilization? *International Affairs* 74 (1): 1–23.
2015. The Discourse of Anarchy in IR. *International Theory* 7 (3): 393–425.

Doob, Leonard W. 1962. From Tribalism to Nationalism in Africa. *Journal of International Affairs* 16 (2): 144–155.

Dose, Ralf. 2014. *Magnus Hirschfeld: The Origins of the Gay Liberation Movement*. Translated by Edward H. Willis. New York: Monthly Review Press.

Doty, Roxanne Lynn. 1993. The Bounds of 'Race' in International Relations. *Millennium: Journal of International Studies* 22 (3): 443–461.
Douglass, William A., and Stanford M. Lyman. 1976. L'ethnie: structure, processus et saillance. Translated by Alain Kihm. *Cahiers Internationaux de Sociologie* 61: 197–220.
Dover, Cedric. 1935. The Racial Myth. *Nature* 136 (3445): 736–737.
Dozier, Edward P. 1955. The Concepts of 'Primitive' and 'Native' in Anthropology. *Yearbook of Anthropology* 187–202.
Dragadze, Tamara. 1980. The Place of 'Ethnos' Theory in Soviet Anthropology. In *Soviet and Western Anthropology*, edited by Ernest Gellner, 161–170. New York: Columbia University Press.
  1990. Some Changes in Perspectives on Ethnicity Theory in the 1980's: A Brief Sketch. *Cahiers du Monde Russe et Soviétique* 31 (2–3): 205–212.
Driver, Harold E., James A. Kenny, Herschel C. Hudson, and Ora May Engle. 1972. Statistical Classification of North American Indian Ethnic Units. *Ethnology* 11 (3): 311–339.
Dryhurst, N. F., ed. 1910. *Nationalities and Subject Races: Report of Conference Held in Caxton Hall, Westminster June 28–30, 1910*. London: P. S. King & Sons.
Duara, Prasenjit. 2001. The Discourse of Civilization and Pan-Asianism. *Journal of World History* 12 (1): 99–130.
Du Bois, W. E. B. 1897. *The Conservation of Races*. The American Negro Academy Occasional Papers, No. 2. Washington, DC: The American Negro Academy.
  1903. *The Souls of Black Folk: Essays and Sketches*. Chicago: A. C. McClurg.
  [1936] 1985. The Negro and Social Reconstruction. In *Against Racism: Unpublished Essays, Papers, Addresses, 1887–1961*, edited by Herbert Aptheker, 103–158. Amherst: University of Massachusetts Press.
Durkheim, Émile. 1893. *De la division du travail social: étude sur l'organisation des sociétés supérieures*. Paris: Félix Alcan.
Eckert, Richard Clark. 2010. Toward a Theory of Deaf Ethnos. *Journal of Deaf Studies and Deaf Education* 15 (4): 317–333.
Ehrenberg, Victor. 1969. *The Greek State*. 2nd edition. London: Methuen.
Ejdus, Filip, Alexandra Gheciu, Jozef Bátora, and Einar Wigen. 2014. The Expansion of International Society after 30 Years: Views from the European Periphery. *International Relations* 28 (4): 445–478.
Ekeh, Peter P. 1990. Social Anthropology and Two Contrasting Uses of Tribalism in Africa. *Comparative Studies in Society and History* 32 (4): 660–700.

Ember, Melvin. 1997. Evolution of the Human Relations Area Files. *Cross-Cultural Research* 31 (1): 3–15.
Emerson, Rupert. 1960a. *From Empire to Nation: The Rise to Self-Assertion of Asian and African Peoples*. Cambridge, MA: Harvard University Press.
 1960b. Nationalism and Political Development. *The Journal of Politics* 22 (1): 3–28.
Epstein, A. L. 1958. *Politics in an Urban African Community*. Manchester: Manchester University Press.
Epstein, Steven. 1992. Gay Politics, Ethnic Identity: The Limits of Social Constructionism. In *Forms of Desire: Sexual Orientation and the Social Constructionist Controversy*, edited by Edward Stein, 239. London: Routledge.
Eriksen, Thomas Hylland. 2010. *Ethnicity and Nationalism: Anthropological Perspectives*. 3rd edition. London: Pluto Press.
Eriksen, Thomas Hylland, and Finn Sivert Nielsen. 2013. *A History of Anthropology*. 2nd edition. London: Pluto Press.
Erting, Carol. 1978. Language Policy and Deaf Ethnicity in the United States. *Sign Language Studies* 19: 139–152.
Evans, Ivan. 1997. *Bureaucracy and Race: Native Administration in South Africa*. Berkeley: University of California Press.
Evans-Pritchard, E. E. 1940a. *The Nuer: A Description of the Modes of Livelihood and Political Institutions of a Nilotic People*. Oxford: Clarendon.
 1940b. The Nuer of the Southern Sudan. In *African Political Systems*, edited by Meyer Fortes and E. E. Evans-Pritchard, 272–296. London: Oxford University Press.
Evens, T. M. S., and Don Handelman. 2006. Introduction: The Ethnographic Praxis of the Theory of Practice. In *The Manchester School: Practice and Ethnographic Praxis in Anthropology*, edited by T. M. S. Evens and Don Handelman, 1–12. New York: Berghahn.
Fabian, Johannes. 2014. *Time and the Other: How Anthropology Makes Its Object*. New York: Columbia University Press.
Fall, Juliet J. 2010. Artificial States? On the Enduring Geographical Myth of Natural Borders. *Political Geography* 29 (3): 140–147.
Fanon, Frantz. 1956. Racisme et culture. *Présence Africaine* VIII–IX–X (3): 122–131.
 2002. *Les damnés de la terre*. Paris: La Découverte.
Febvre, Lucien. 1973. Civilisation: Evolution of a Word and a Group of Ideas. In *A New Kind of History and Other Essays: Lucien Febvre*, edited by Peter Burke, translated by K. Folca, 219–257. New York: Harper & Row.

Fenton, Steve. 2010. *Ethnicity*. 2nd edition. Cambridge: Polity.
Fenwick, Charles G. 1924. *International Law*. London: Allen & Unwin.
Fink, Carole. 2004. *Defending the Rights of Others: The Great Powers, the Jews, and International Minority Protection, 1878–1938*. Cambridge: Cambridge University Press.
Fischer, Hans. 1970. 'Völkerkunde', 'Ethnographie', 'Ethnologie': Kritische Kontrolle der frühesten Belege. *Zeitschrift für Ethnologie* 95 (2): 169–182.
Fishberg, Maurice. 1911. *The Jews: A Study of Race and Environment*. New York: Walter Scott.
Fitzsimmons, Thomas, ed. 1957. *RSFSR: Russian Soviet Federated Socialist Republic*. New Haven: Human Relations Area Files.
Flournoy, Richard W. 1933. Nationality. In *Encyclopaedia of the Social Sciences*, Vol. XI, 249–252. London: Macmillan.
Ford, Clellan S. 1970. Human Relations Area Files: 1949–1969. A Twenty-Year Report. *Behavior Science Notes* 5 (1): 1–61.
  1971. The Development of the Outline of Cultural Materials. *Behavior Science Notes* 6 (3): 173–185.
Fortes, Meyer. 1940. The Political System of the Tallensi of the Northern Territories of the Gold Coast. In *African Political Systems*, edited by Meyer Fortes and E. E. Evans-Pritchard, 239–271. London: Oxford University Press.
  1949. Time and Social Structure: An Ashanti Case Study. In *Social Structure: Studies Presented to A. R. Radcliffe-Brown*, edited by Meyer Fortes, 54–84. Oxford: Clarendon.
  1953. The Structure of Unilineal Descent Groups. *American Anthropologist* 55 (1): 17–41.
Fortes, Meyer, and E. E. Evans-Pritchard. 1940. Introduction. In *African Political Systems*, edited by Meyer Fortes and E. E. Evans-Pritchard, 1–24. London: Oxford University Press.
Foucault, Michel. 1972. *The Archaeology of Knowledge*. Translated by A. M. Sheridan Smith. London: Routledge.
  1984. Nietzsche, Genealogy, History. In *The Foucault Reader*, edited by Paul Rabinow, 76–100. New York: Pantheon Books.
  2003. *'Society Must Be Defended': Lectures at the Collège de France, 1975–76*. Edited by Mauro Bertani and Alessandro Fontana. Translated by David Macey. New York: Picador.
Fouillée, Alfred. 1898. *Psychologie du peuple français*. Paris: Félix Alcan.
Francis, E. K. 1947. The Nature of the Ethnic Group. *American Journal of Sociology* 52 (5): 393–400.
Fredrickson, George M. 2002. *Racism: A Short History*. Princeton: Princeton University Press.

Freed, Stanley A., and Ruth S. Freed. 1983. Clark Wissler and the Development of Anthropology in the United States. *American Anthropologist* 85 (4): 800–825.

Freeden, Michael. 1996. *Ideologies and Political Theory: A Conceptual Approach*. Oxford: Clarendon.

Fried, Morton H. 1966. On the Concepts of 'Tribe' and 'Tribal Society'. *Transactions of the New York Academy of Sciences* 28 (4): 527–540.

   1975. *The Notion of Tribe*. Menlo Park: Cummings Publishing Company.

Füredi, Frank. 1998. *The Silent War: Imperialism and the Changing Perception of Race*. London: Pluto Press.

Gamson, Joshua. 1995. Must Identity Movements Self-Destruct? A Queer Dilemma. *Social Problems* 42 (3): 390–407.

Gannett, Lisa. 2001. Racism and Human Genome Diversity Research: The Ethical Limits of 'Population Thinking'. *Philosophy of Science* 68 (3): S479–S492.

Garner, James Wilford. 1919. Nationality. In *The Encyclopedia Americana*, Vol. XIX, 765–766. New York: The Encyclopedia Americana Corporation.

   1928. *Political Science and Government*. New York: American Book Company.

Gelfand, Lawrence E. 1963. *The Inquiry: American Preparations for Peace, 1917–1919*. New Haven: Yale University Press.

Gellner, Ernest. 1977. Ethnicity and Anthropology in the Soviet Union. *European Journal of Sociology* 18 (2): 201–220.

   ed. 1980. *Soviet and Western Anthropology*. New York: Columbia University Press.

   1983. *Nations and Nationalism*. Oxford: Blackwell.

Georges-Jacob, Kléber. 1941. *L'ethnie haïtienne*. Port-au-Prince: Imprimerie de l'État.

   1946. *Contribution à l'étude de l'homme haïtien, au service de l'histoire ethno-sociale de l'ethnie haïtienne*. Port-au-Prince: Imprimerie de l'État.

Getachew, Adom. 2019. *Worldmaking after Empire: The Rise and Fall of Self-Determination*. Princeton: Princeton University Press.

Geulen, Christian. 2007. The Common Grounds of Conflict: Racial Visions of World Order 1880–1940. In *Competing Visions of World Order: Global Moments and Movements, 1880s–1930s*, edited by Sebastian Conrad and Dominic Sachsenmeier, 69–96. Basingstoke: Palgrave Macmillan.

   2010. Plädoyer für eine Geschichte der Grundbegriffe des 20. Jahrhunderts. *Zeithistorische Forschungen/Studies in Contemporary History* 7: 79–97.

   2012. Reply. *Contributions to the History of Concepts* 7 (2): 118–128.

2017. Ideology's Logic: The Evolution of Racial Thought in Germany from the Völkisch Movement to the Third Reich. In *Beyond the Racial State: Rethinking Nazi Germany*, edited by Devin O. Pendas, Mark Roseman, and Richard F. Wetzell, 197–212. Cambridge: Cambridge University Press.

Ghosh, Amitav, and Dipesh Chakrabarty. 2002. A Correspondence on Provincializing Europe. *Radical History Review* 2002 (83): 146–172.

Giddens, Anthony. 1985. *The Nation-State and Violence: Volume Two of a Contemporary Critique of Historical Materialism*. Cambridge: Polity.

Gilroy, Paul. 1987. *'There Ain't No Black in the Union Jack': The Cultural Politics of Race and Nation*. London: Hutchinson.

Gingrich, Andre. 2005. The German-Speaking Countries. In *One Discipline, Four Ways: British, German, French, and American Anthropology*, by Fredrik Barth, Robert Parkin, Andre Gingrich, and Sydel Silverman, 61–153. Chicago: University of Chicago Press.

Glazer, Nathan, and Daniel P. Moynihan. 1963. *Beyond the Melting Pot: The Negroes, Puerto Ricans, Jews, Italians, and Irish of New York City*. Cambridge, MA: The MIT Press.

1975. Introduction. In *Ethnicity: Theory and Experience*, edited by Nathan Glazer and Daniel P. Moynihan, 1–28. Cambridge, MA: Harvard University Press.

Gleason, Philip. 1983. Identifying Identity: A Semantic History. *The Journal of American History* 69 (4): 910–931.

Gluckman, Max. 1960. Tribalism in Modern British Central Africa. *Cahiers d'Études Africaines* 1 (1): 55–70.

1965. *Politics, Law and Ritual in Tribal Society*. Oxford: Basil Blackwell.

Goddard, Stacie E., and Daniel H. Nexon. 2005. Paradigm Lost? Reassessing Theory of International Politics. *European Journal of International Relations* 11 (1): 9–61.

Godelier, Maurice. 1973. The Concept of Tribe: Crisis of a Concept or Crisis of the Empirical Foundations of Anthropology? *Diogenes* 21 (81): 1–25.

GoGwilt, Chris. 1995. True West: The Changing Idea of the West from the 1880s to the 1920s. In *Enduring Western Civilization: The Construction of the Concept of Western Civilization and Its 'Others'*, edited by Silvia Federici, 37–62. Westport: Praeger.

Goldberg, David Theo. 1993. *Racist Culture: Philosophy and the Politics of Meaning*. Oxford: Blackwell.

1997. *Racial Subjects: Writing on Race in America*. New York: Routledge.

2002. *The Racial State*. London: Blackwell.

Goldenweiser, Alexander A. 1921. *Early Civilization: An Introduction to Anthropology*. London: G. G. Harrap & Company.

Goldstein, Eric L. 2006. *The Price of Whiteness: Jews, Race, and American Identity*. Princeton: Oxford University Press.
Goldstein, Erik. 1991. *Winning the Peace: British Diplomatic Strategy, Peace Planning, and the Paris Peace Conference, 1916–1920*. Oxford: Clarendon.
Gong, Gerrit W. 1984. *The Standard of 'Civilization' in International Society*. Oxford: Clarendon.
Gordon, D. H., Catherine H. Berndt, Robert H. Edwards, Douglas G. Haring, Albert C. Spaulding, Rosalie H. Wax, Murray Wax, William W. Stein, and Sol Tax. 1961. Terminology: Primitive. *Current Anthropology* 2 (4): 396–397.
Gordon, Milton M. 1964. *Assimilation in American Life: The Role of Race, Religion, and National Origins*. New York: Oxford University Press.
Gorski, Philip S. 2000. The Mosaic Moment: An Early Modernist Critique of Modernist Theories of Nationalism. *American Journal of Sociology* 105 (5): 1428–1468.
Gosselin, Gabriel. 1985. Ethnicité au-delà, régionalisme en-deçà. *L'Homme et la Société* 77–78: 111–120.
Gosselin, Gabriel, and Jean-Pierre Lavaud, eds. 2001. *Ethnicité et mobilisations sociales*. Paris: L'Harmattan.
Greene, Daniel. 2011. *The Jewish Origins of Cultural Pluralism: The Menorah Association and American Diversity*. Bloomington: Indiana University Press.
Greenfeld, Liah. 1992. *Nationalism: Five Roads to Modernity*. Cambridge, MA: Harvard University Press.
Gruffydd Jones, Branwen. 2008. Race in the Ontology of International Order. *Political Studies* 56 (4): 907–927.
Guenther, Mathias, Justin Kenrick, Adam Kuper, Evie Plaice, Trond Thuen, Patrick Wolfe, Werner Zips, and Alan Barnard. 2006. The Concept of Indigeneity. *Social Anthropology* 14 (1): 17–32.
Guilhot, Nicolas, ed. 2011a. *The Invention of International Relations Theory: Realism, the Rockefeller Foundation, and the 1954 Conference on Theory*. New York: Columbia University Press.
  2011b. The Realist Gambit: Postwar American Political Science and the Birth of IR Theory. In *The Invention of International Relations Theory: Realism, the Rockefeller Foundation, and the 1954 Conference on Theory*, edited by Nicolas Guilhot, 128–161. New York: Columbia University Press.
  2014. Imperial Realism: Post-War IR Theory and Decolonisation. *The International History Review* 36 (4): 698–720.
  2017. *After the Enlightenment*. Cambridge: Cambridge University Press.
Guldin, Gregory Eliyu. 1994. *The Saga of Anthropology in China: From Malinowksi to Moscow to Mao*. Armonk: M. E. Sharpe.

Gulliver, P. H. 1969. Introduction. In *Tradition and Transition in East Africa: Studies of the Tribal Element in the Modern Era*, edited by P. H. Gulliver, 5–40. Berkeley: University of California Press.

Gutiérrez, Ramón A. 2004. Internal Colonialism: An American Theory of Race. *Du Bois Review* 1 (2): 281–295.

Haddon, Alfred C. 1909. *The Races of Man and Their Distribution*. London: Milner and Company.

Hager, Don J., A. de Froe, Cedric Dover, and J. C. Trevor. 1951. Race. *Man* 51: 53–56.

Hailey, William Malcolm. 1957. *An African Survey, Revised 1956: A Study of Problems Arising in Africa South of the Sahara*. Oxford: Oxford University Press.

Hall, Jonathan M. 1997. *Ethnic Identity in Greek Antiquity*. Cambridge: Cambridge University Press.

Hall, Martin, and Patrick Thaddeus Jackson, eds. 2007. *Civilizational Identity: The Production and Reproduction of "Civilizations" in International Relations*. Basingstoke: Palgrave Macmillan.

Hall, Stuart. 1996. New Ethnicities. In *Stuart Hall: Critical Dialogues in Cultural Studies*, edited by David Morley and Kuan-Hsing Chen, 441–449. London: Routledge.

Halter, Marilyn. 2006. Ethnic and Racial Identity. In *A Companion to American Immigration*, edited by Reed Ueda, 161–176. Oxford: Blackwell.

Hankins, Frank H. 1926. *The Racial Basis of Civilization: A Critique of the Nordic Doctrine*. New York: Alfred A. Knopf.

Haraway, Donna. 1991. *Simians, Cyborgs, and Women: The Reinvention of Nature*. New York: Routledge.

Harff, Barbara, and Ted Robert Gurr. 2004. *Ethnic Conflict in World Politics*. 2nd edition. Boulder: Westview.

Harris, George L., ed. 1956. *North Borneo, Brunei, Sarawak (British Borneo)*. New Haven: Human Relations Area Files.

——— ed. 1957. *Egypt*. New Haven: Human Relations Area Files.

Harrison, Austin. 1920. The Africanisation of Europe. *The English Review* 30: 363–371.

Hart, Bradley W. 2015. *George Pitt-Rivers and the Nazis*. London: Bloomsbury.

Hartog, François. 2015. *Regimes of Historicity: Presentism and Experiences of Time*. Translated by Saskia Brown. New York: Columbia University Press.

Hattam, Victoria. 2007. *In the Shadow of Race: Jews, Latinos, and Immigrant Politics in the United States*. Chicago: University of Chicago Press.

Havertz, Ralf. 2023. Ethnopluralism and Its Ambiguities: Racism with and without Race. *Journal of Political Ideologies* (online first): 1–16.

Hayes, Carlton J. H. 1928. Two Varieties of Nationalism: Original and Derived. *Proceedings of the Association of History Teachers of the Middle States and Maryland* 26: 70–83.

   1931. *The Historical Evolution of Modern Nationalism*. New York: Macmillan.

   1933. *Essays on Nationalism*. New York: Macmillan.

Headlam-Morley, James. 1972. *A Memoir of the Paris Peace Conference 1919*. Edited by Agnes Headlam-Morley, Russell Bryant, and Anna Cienciala. London: Methuen.

Hecht, Jennifer Michael. 2000. Vacher de Lapouge and the Rise of Nazi Science. *Journal of the History of Ideas* 61 (2): 285–304.

Hegel, Georg Wilhelm Friedrich. 1969. *Science of Logic*. Translated by A. V. Miller. London: Routledge.

   1991a. *Elements of the Philosophy of Right*. Edited by Allen W. Wood. Translated by H. B. Nisbet. Cambridge: Cambridge University Press.

   1991b. *The Encyclopaedia Logic (with the Zusätze)*. Translated by T. F. Geraets, W. A. Suchting, and H. S. Harris. Indianapolis: Hackett Publishing Company.

   2001. *The Philosophy of History*. Translated by J. Sibree. Kitchener: Batoche Books.

Heiskanen, Jaakko. 2019. Spectra of Sovereignty: Nationalism and International Relations. *International Political Sociology* 13 (3): 315–332.

   2021a. Found in Translation: The Global Constitution of the Modern International Order. *International Theory* 13 (2): 231–259.

   2021b. In the Shadow of Genocide: Ethnocide, Ethnic Cleansing, and International Order. *Global Studies Quarterly* 1 (4): ksab030.

   2021c. Nations and Nationalism in International Relations. In *The Routledge Handbook of Historical International Relations*, edited by Julia Costa López, Halvard Leira, and Benjamin de Carvalho, 244–252. London: Routledge.

   2021d. The Nationalism-Populism Matrix. *Journal of Political Ideologies* 26 (3): 335–355.

   2023. Mind the Gap: The Nation Form and the Kohn Dichotomy. *Nations and Nationalism* 29 (4): 1179–1195.

Helm, June, ed. 1968. *Essays on the Problem of Tribe: Proceedings of the 1967 Annual Spring Meeting of the American Ethnological Society*. Seattle: University of Washington Press.

Henderson, Errol A. 2013. Hidden in Plain Sight: Racism in International Relations Theory. *Cambridge Review of International Affairs* 26 (1): 71–92.

2019. *The Revolution Will Not Be Theorized: Cultural Revolution in the Black Power Era.* Albany: State University of New York Press.

Henrard, Kristin. 2000. *Devising an Adequate System of Minority Protection: Individual Human Rights, Minority Rights and the Right to Self-Determination.* The Hague: Martinus Nijhoff.

Heraud, Guy. 1963. *L'Europe des ethnies.* Paris: Presses d'Europe.

Herberg, Will. 1960. *Protestant-Catholic-Jew: An Essay in American Religious Sociology.* Revised edition. New York: Anchor Books.

Herbert, Sydney. 1920. *Nationality and Its Problems.* London: Methuen.

Herod, Charles C. 1976. *The Nation in the History of Marxist Thought: The Concept of Nations with History and Nations without History.* The Hague: Martinus Nijhoff.

Herskovits, Melville J. 1924. A Preliminary Consideration of the Culture Areas of Africa. *American Anthropologist* 26 (1): 50–63.

1930. The Culture Areas of Africa. *Africa: Journal of the International African Institute* 3 (1): 59–77.

Hesse, Barnor. 2004. Im/Plausible Deniability: Racism's Conceptual Double Bind. *Social Identities* 10 (1): 9–29.

Hicks, Frederick Charles. 1920. *The New World Order: International Organization, International Law, International Coöperation.* Garden City: Doubleday, Page, & Company.

Higham, John. 1984. *Send These to Me: Immigrants in Urban America.* Revised edition. Baltimore: The Johns Hopkins University Press.

Hill, David Jayne. 1911. *World Organization as Affected by the Nature of the Modern State.* New York: Columbia University Press.

Hinsley, F. H. 1986. *Sovereignty.* 2nd edition. Cambridge: Cambridge University Press.

Hirsch, Francine. 2005. *Empire of Nations: Ethnographic Knowledge and the Making of the Soviet Union.* Ithaca: Cornell University Press.

Hirschfeld, Magnus. 1938. *Racism.* Translated by Eden Paul and Cedar Paul. London: Victor Gollancz.

Hirschi, Caspar. 2012. *The Origins of Nationalism: An Alternative History from Ancient Rome to Early Modern Germany.* Cambridge: Cambridge University Press.

Hobhouse, L. T., G. C. Wheeler, and M. Ginsberg. 1915. *The Material Culture and Social Institutions of the Simpler Peoples: An Essay in Correlation.* London: Routledge & Kegan Paul.

Hobsbawm, Eric J. 1992. *Nations and Nationalism since 1780: Programme, Myth, Reality.* Cambridge: Cambridge University Press.

Hobsbawm, Eric J., and Terence Ranger, eds. 1983. *The Invention of Tradition.* Cambridge: Cambridge University Press.

Hobson, John A. 1902. *Imperialism: A Study*. London: James Nisbet & Company.

Hobson, John M. 2013. The Other Side of the Westphalian Frontier. In *Postcolonial Theory and International Relations: A Critical Introduction*, edited by Sanjay Seth, 32–48. London: Routledge.

2014. The Twin Self-Delusions of IR: Why 'Hierarchy' and Not 'Anarchy' Is the Core Concept of IR. *Millennium: Journal of International Studies* 42 (3): 557–575.

2022. Unmasking the Racism of Orthodox International Relations/International Political Economy Theory. *Security Dialogue* 53 (1): 3–20.

Hobson, John M., and Alina Sajed. 2017. Navigating Beyond the Eurofetishist Frontier of Critical IR Theory: Exploring the Complex Landscapes of Non-Western Agency. *International Studies Review* 19 (4): 547–572.

Hoffman, John. 1995. *Beyond the State: An Introductory Critique*. Cambridge: Polity.

1997. Is It Time to Detach Sovereignty from the State? In *Reclaiming Sovereignty*, edited by Laura Brace and John Hoffman, 9–25. London: Pinter.

Hoffmann, Stefan-Ludwig, and Kathrin Kollmeier. 2012. Introduction: Geschichtliche Grundbegriffe Reloaded? Writing the Conceptual History of the Twentieth Century. *Contributions to the History of Concepts* 7 (2): 79–86.

Holcombe, Arthur N. 1923. *The Foundations of the Modern Commonwealth*. New York: Harper & Brothers.

Holland Rose, John. 1916. *Nationality as a Factor in Modern History*. London: Rivingtons.

Holmes, William Henry. 1902. Classification and Arrangement of the Exhibits of an Anthropological Museum. *Science* 16 (404): 487–504.

Hooper-Greenhill, Eilean. 1989. The Museum in the Disciplinary Society. In *Museum Studies in Material Culture*, edited by Susan M. Pearce, 61–72. London: Leicester University Press.

Horigan, Stephen. 1988. *Nature and Culture in Western Discourses*. London: Routledge.

Horowitz, Donald L. 1985. *Ethnic Groups in Conflict*. Berkeley: University of California Press.

Hsu, Francis L. K. 1964. Rethinking the Concept 'Primitive'. *Current Anthropology* 5 (3): 169–178.

Hudson, Nicholas. 1996. From 'Nation' to 'Race': The Origin of Racial Classification in Eighteenth-Century Thought. *Eighteenth-Century Studies* 29 (3): 247–264.

Hughan, Jessie Wallace. 1924. *A Study of International Government*. London: G. G. Harrap & Company.
Hughes, Everett Cherrington, and Helen MacGill Hughes. 1952. *Where Peoples Meet: Racial and Ethnic Frontiers*. Glencoe: Free Press.
Huntington, Samuel P. 1993. The Clash of Civilizations? *Foreign Affairs* 72 (3): 22–49.
Hutchings, Kimberly. 2011. Dialogue between Whom? The Role of the West/Non-West Distinction in Promoting Global Dialogue in IR. *Millennium: Journal of International Studies* 39 (3): 639–647.
Hutton, Christopher M. 2005. *Race and the Third Reich: Linguistics, Racial Anthropology and Genetics in the Dialectic of Volk*. Cambridge: Polity.
Huxley, Julian S. 1941. The Concept of Race. In *The Uniqueness of Man*, 106–126. London: Chatto & Windus.
Huxley, Julian S., and Alfred C. Haddon. 1935. *We Europeans: A Survey of 'Racial' Problems*. London: Jonathan Cape.
Ignatieff, Michael. 1994. *Blood and Belonging: Journeys into the New Nationalism*. London: Vintage.
Ikenberry, G. John. 2020. Liberal Internationalism and Cultural Diversity. In *Culture and Order in World Politics*, edited by Andrew Phillips and Christian Reus-Smit, 137–158. Cambridge: Cambridge University Press.
Iliffe, John. 1979. *A Modern History of Tanganyika*. Cambridge: Cambridge University Press.
Inayatullah, Naeem, and David L. Blaney. 2004. *International Relations and the Problem of Difference*. London: Routledge.
Intercollegiate Menorah Association. 1914. *The Menorah Movement for the Study and Advancement of Jewish Culture and Ideals: History, Purposes, Activities*. Ann Arbor: Intercollegiate Menorah Association.
Jacknis, Ira. 1985. Franz Boas and Exhibits: On the Limitations of the Museum Method of Anthropology. In *Objects and Others: Essays on Museum and Material Culture*, edited by George W. Stocking, 75–111. Madison: University of Wisconsin Press.
Jackson Preece, Jennifer. 1998. *National Minorities and the European Nation-States System*. Oxford: Oxford University Press.
Jacobson, Matthew Frye. 1998. *Whiteness of a Different Color: European Immigrants and the Alchemy of Race*. Cambridge, MA: Harvard University Press.
Jacques, T. Carlos. 1997. From Savages and Barbarians to Primitives: Africa, Social Typologies, and History in Eighteenth-Century French Philosophy. *History and Theory* 36 (2): 190–215.
Jahn, Beate. 2000. *The Cultural Construction of International Relations: The Invention of the State of Nature*. Basingstoke: Palgrave.

James, C. L. R. 1980. *Notes on Dialectics: Hegel, Marx, Lenin*. Westport: Lawrence Hill & Co.
Janowsky, Oscar L. 1933. *The Jews and Minority Rights (1898–1919)*. New York: Columbia University Press.
Jenkins, Richard. 2008. *Rethinking Ethnicity: Arguments and Explorations*. 2nd edition. London: Sage.
Johannet, René. 1918. *Le Principe des Nationalités*. Paris: Nouvelle Librairie Nationale.
Jones, C. P. 1996. ἔθνος and γένος in Herodotus. *The Classical Quarterly* 46 (2): 315–320.
Jordheim, Helge, and Iver B. Neumann. 2011. Empire, Imperialism and Conceptual History. *Journal of International Relations and Development* 14 (2): 153–185.
Joseph, Bernard. 1929. *Nationality: Its Nature and Problems*. London: Allen & Unwin.
Jurkevics, Anna. 2017. Hannah Arendt Reads Carl Schmitt's *The Nomos of the Earth*: A Dialogue on Law and Geopolitics from the Margins. *European Journal of Political Theory* 16 (3): 345–366.
Just, Roger. 1989. Triumph of the Ethnos. In *Ethnicity and History*, edited by Elizabeth Tonkin, Maryon McDonald, and Malcolm Chapman, 71–88. London: Routledge.
Juteau-Lee, Danielle. 1983. La production de l'ethnicité ou la part réelle de l'idéal. *Sociologie et Sociétés* 15 (2): 39–54.
Jutila, Matti. 2009. Taming Eastern Nationalism: Tracing the Ideational Background of Double Standards of Post-Cold War Minority Protection. *European Journal of International Relations* 15 (4): 627–651.
Kallaway, Peter. 2017. Diedrich Westermann and the Ambiguities of Colonial Science in the Inter-war Era. *The Journal of Imperial and Commonwealth History* 45 (6): 871–893.
Kallen, Horace M. 1906. The Ethics of Zionism. *The Maccabaean* 11 (2): 61–71.
  [1910] 1932. Judaism, Hebraism and Zionism. In *Judaism at Bay: Essays toward the Adjustment of Judaism to Modernity*, 28–41. New York: Bloch.
  1915a. Democracy versus the Melting-Pot: A Study of American Nationality: Part I. *The Nation* 100 (2590): 190–194.
  1915b. Democracy versus the Melting-Pot: A Study of American Nationality: Part II. *The Nation* 100 (2591): 217–220.
  1915c. Nationality and the Hyphenated American. *Menorah Journal* 1 (2): 79–86.
  [1924] 1998. *Culture and Democracy in the United States*. Brunswick: Transaction Publishers.

1957. Alain Locke and Cultural Pluralism. *The Journal of Philosophy* 54 (5): 119–127.
Kalmar, Ivan. 1987. The Völkerpsychologie of Lazarus and Steinthal and the Modern Concept of Culture. *Journal of the History of Ideas* 48 (4): 671–690.
Kapferer, Bruce. 2006. Coda: Recollections and Refutations. In *The Manchester School: Practice and Ethnographic Praxis in Anthropology*, edited by T. M. S. Evens and Don Handelman, 311–321. New York: Berghahn.
Katzenstein, Peter J., ed. 2010. *Civilizations in World Politics: Plural and Pluralist Perspectives*. London: Routledge.
  ed. 2012a. *Anglo-America and Its Discontents: Civilizational Identities beyond West and East*. London: Routledge.
  ed. 2012b. *Sinicization and the Rise of China: Civilizational Processes beyond East and West*. Abingdon: Routledge.
Kautsky, John H. 1962. *Political Change in Underdeveloped Countries: Nationalism and Communism*. New York: John Wiley & Sons.
Keal, Paul. 2003. *European Conquest and the Rights of Indigenous Peoples: The Moral Backwardness of International Society*. Cambridge: Cambridge University Press.
Keene, Edward. 2002. *Beyond the Anarchical Society: Grotius, Colonialism and Order in World Politics*. Cambridge: Cambridge University Press.
  2014. The Standard of 'Civilisation', the Expansion Thesis and the 19th-Century International Social Space. *Millennium: Journal of International Studies* 42 (3): 651–673.
Keith, Arthur. 1919. *Nationality and Race from an Anthropologist's Point of View*. London: Oxford University Press.
  1931a. *Ethnos: Or the Problem of Race Considered from a New Point of View*. London: Kegan Paul.
  1931b. *The Place of Prejudice in Modern Civilization*. London: Williams & Norgate.
Kemiläinen, Aira. 1964. *Nationalism: Problems Concerning the Word, the Concept and Classification*. Jyväskylä: Jyväskylän Kasvatusopillinen Korkeakoulu.
Kennedy, Ruby Jo Reeves. 1944. Single or Triple Melting-Pot? Intermarriage Trends in New Haven, 1870–1940. *American Journal of Sociology* 49 (4): 331–339.
Kenrick, Justin, and Jerome Lewis. 2004. Indigenous Peoples' Rights and the Politics of the Term 'Indigenous'. *Anthropology Today* 20 (2): 4–9.
Kettunen, Pauli. 2018. The Concept of Nationalism in Discussions on a European Society. *Journal of Political Ideologies* 23 (3): 342–369.
Kidd, Benjamin. 1898. *The Control of the Tropics*. New York: Macmillan.

Kilson, Martin L. 1958. The Analysis of African Nationalism. *World Politics* 10 (3): 484–497.
Kingsbury, Benedict. 1998. 'Indigenous Peoples' in International Law: A Constructivist Approach to the Asian Controversy. *The American Journal of International Law* 92 (3): 414–457.
Kitsikis, Dimitri. 1972. *Le rôle des experts à la Conférence de la Paix de 1919: gestation d'une technocratie en politique internationale.* Ottawa: Éditions de L'Université d'Ottawa.
Klein, Ernest. 1971. *Klein's Comprehensive Etymological Dictionary of the English Language.* Amsterdam: Elsevier.
Klimek, Stanislaw. 1935. *The Structure of California Indian Culture.* Berkeley: University of California Press.
Knight, Nathaniel. 2000. Ethnicity, Nationality and the Masses: Narodnost and Modernity in Imperial Russia. In *Russian Modernity: Politics, Knowledge, Practices*, edited by David L. Hoffmann and Yanni Kotsonis, 41–64. Basingstoke: Macmillan.
Knobel, Marc. 1988. L'ethnolgue à la dérive: George Montandon et l'ethnoracisme. *Ethnologie française* 18 (2): 107–113.
Kohn, Hans. 1934. Race Conflict. In *Encyclopaedia of the Social Sciences*, Vol. XIII, 36–41. London: Macmillan.
    [1944] 2005. *The Idea of Nationalism: A Study of Its Origins and Background.* New Brunswick: Transaction Publishers.
Köpping, Klaus-Peter. 1995. Enlightenment and Romanticism in the Work of Adolf Bastian: The Historical Roots of Anthropology in the Nineteenth Century. In *Fieldwork and Footnotes: Studies in the History of European Anthropology*, edited by Han F. Vermeulen and Arturo Alvarez Roldán, 75–91. London: Routledge.
Korelitz, Seth. 1997. The Menorah Idea: From Religion to Culture, from Race to Ethnicity. *American Jewish History* 85 (1): 75–100.
Koselleck, Reinhart. 1996. A Response to Comments on the Geschichtliche Grundbegriffe. In *The Meaning of Historical Terms and Concepts: New Studies on Begriffsgeschichte*, edited by Hartmut Lehmann and Melvin Richter, translated by Melvin Richter and Sally E. Robertson, 59–70. Washington, DC: German Historical Institute.
    1997. The Temporalisation of Concepts. Translated by Klaus Sondermann. *Redescriptions: Political Thought, Conceptual History and Feminist Theory* 1 (1): 16–24.
    2004. *Futures Past: On the Semantics of Historical Time.* Translated by Keith Tribe. New York: Columbia University Press.
    2011. Introduction and Prefaces to the Geschichtliche Grundbegriffe. Translated by Michaela Richter. *Contributions to the History of Concepts* 6 (1): 1–5, 7–25, 27–37.

Kozlov, Viktor. 1974. On the Concept of Ethnic Community. In *Soviet Ethnography and Anthropology Today*, edited by Yulian Bromley, 73–87. The Hague: Mouton.

Krehbiel, Edward. 1916. *Nationalism, War and Society: A Study of Nationalism and Its Concomitant, War, in Their Relation to Civilization; and of the Fundamentals and the Progress of the Opposition to War*. New York: Macmillan.

Krieg-Planque, Alice. 2005. Le mot ethnie: nommer autrui. Origine et fonctionnement du terme ethnie dans l'univers discursif français. *Cahiers de Lexicologie* 2 (87): 141–161.

Krishna, Sankaran. 2001. Race, Amnesia, and the Education of International Relations. *Alternatives: Global, Local, Political* 26 (4): 401–424.

Kroeber, Alfred L. 1917. The Superorganic. *American Anthropologist* 19 (2): 163–213.

  1931. Culture Area. In *Encyclopaedia of the Social Sciences*, Vol. IV, 646–647. London: Macmillan.

  1939. *Culture and Natural Areas of Native North America*. Berkeley: University of California Press.

  1948. *Anthropology: Race, Language, Culture, Psychology, Prehistory*. London: G. G. Harrap & Company.

  1949. The Concept of Culture in Science. *The Journal of General Education* 3 (3): 182–196.

  1955. Nature of the Land-Holding Group. *Ethnohistory* 2 (4): 303–314.

Kroeber, Alfred L., and Talcott Parsons. 1958. The Concepts of Culture and of Social System. *American Sociological Review* 23 (5): 582–583.

Kronfeldner, Maria E. 2009. 'If There Is Nothing beyond the Organic…': Heredity and Culture at the Boundaries of Anthropology in the Work of Alfred L. Kroeber. *NTM: Zeitschrift für Geschichte der Wissenschaften, Technik und Medizin* 17 (2): 107–133.

Kumar, Krishan. 2014. The Return of Civilization – And of Arnold Toynbee? *Comparative Studies in Society and History* 56 (4): 815–843.

Kunz, Josef L. 1954. The Present Status of the International Law for the Protection of Minorities. *The American Journal of International Law* 48 (2): 282–287.

Kuper, Adam. 1999. *Culture: The Anthropologists' Account*. Cambridge, MA: Harvard University Press.

  2003. The Return of the Native. *Current Anthropology* 44 (3): 389–402.

  2017. *The Reinvention of Primitive Society: Transformations of a Myth*. 2nd edition. London: Routledge.

Kymlicka, Will. 2001. Reply and Conclusion. In *Can Liberal Pluralism Be Exported? Western Political Theory and Ethnic Relations in*

Eastern Europe, edited by Will Kymlicka and Magda Opalski, 347–414. Oxford: Oxford University Press.
2007. *Multicultural Odysseys: Navigating the New International Politics of Diversity*. Oxford: Oxford University Press.
2015. Multiculturalism and Minority Rights: West and East. *Journal on Ethnopolitics and Minority Issues in Europe* 14 (4): 4–25.
Labouret, Henri. 1931. *Les tribus du rameau Lobi*. Paris: Institut d'Ethnologie.
Ladas, Stephen P. 1932. *The Exchange of Minorities: Bulgaria, Greece and Turkey*. New York: Macmillan.
Ladd, Paddy, and Harlan Lane. 2013. Deaf Ethnicity, Deafhood, and Their Relationship. *Sign Language Studies* 13 (4): 565–579.
Lake, David A. 2009. *Hierarchy in International Relations*. Ithaca: Cornell University Press.
Lake, Marilyn, and Henry Reynolds. 2008. *Drawing the Global Colour Line: White Men's Countries and the International Challenge of Racial Equality*. Cambridge: Cambridge University Press.
Larbiou, Benoît. 2005. René Martial, 1873–1955. De l'hygiénisme à la raciologie, une trajectoire possible. *Genèses* 3 (60): 98–120.
Lawrence, T. J. 1895. *The Principles of International Law*. London: Macmillan.
Leach, Edmund R. 1954. *Political Systems of Highland Burma: A Study of Kachin Social Structure*. London: G. Bell and Sons.
Leacock, Stephen. 1906. *Elements of Political Science*. London: Archibald Constable.
League of Nations. 1927. *The League of Nations and the Protection of Minorities of Race, Language and Religion*. Revised edition. Geneva: League of Nations Information Section.
Leff, Lisa Moses. 2005. Self-Definition and Self-Defense: Jewish Racial Identity in Nineteenth-Century France. *Jewish History* 19 (1): 7–28.
Le Fur, Louis. 1921. Race et nationalité. *Revue Catholique des Institutions et du Droit* 59: 199–243.
1922. *Races, nationalités, états*. Paris: Alcan.
Leibold, James. 2007. *Reconfiguring Chinese Nationalism: How the Qing Frontier and Its Indigenes Became Chinese*. Basingstoke: Palgrave Macmillan.
Leigh, Joseph. 2021. Geoculture and Unevenness: Occidentalism in the History of Uneven and Combined Development. *Cambridge Review of International Affairs* 34 (2): 186–206.
Leira, Halvard. 2019. The Emergence of Foreign Policy. *International Studies Quarterly* 63 (1): 187–198.

Lentin, Alana. 2005. Replacing 'Race', Historicizing 'Culture' in Multiculturalism. *Patterns of Prejudice* 39 (4): 379–396.
Lentz, Carola. 1995. 'Tribalism' and Ethnicity in Africa: A Review of Four Decades of Anglophone Research. *Cahiers des Sciences Humaines* 31 (2): 303–328.
Lerner, Adam B. 2022. Pathological Nationalism? The Legacy of Crowd Psychology in International Theory. *International Affairs* 98 (3): 995–1012.
Lévi-Strauss, Claude. 1987. *Introduction to the Work of Marcel Mauss*. Translated by Felicity Baker. London: Routledge & Kegan Paul.
Lichtenberger, Henri. 1923. *Relations between France and Germany*. Washington, DC: Carnegie Endowment for International Peace.
Lloyd, P. C. 1967. *Africa in Social Change*. Harmondsworth: Penguin.
Locke, Alain. [1916] 1992. *Race Contacts and Interracial Relations: Lectures on the Theory and Practice of Race*. Edited by Jeffrey C. Stewart. Washington, DC: Howard University Press.
   [1924] 1989. The Concept of Race as Applied to Social Culture. In *The Philosophy of Alain Locke: Harlem Renaissance and Beyond*, edited by Leonard Harris, 188–199. Philadelphia: Temple University Press.
   [1943] 2009. *Le rôle du nègre dans la culture des Amériques*. Paris: L'Harmattan.
Long, David, and Brian C. Schmidt, eds. 2005a. *Imperialism and Internationalism in the Discipline of International Relations*. New York: State University of New York Press.
Long, David, and Brian C. Schmidt. 2005b. Introduction. In *Imperialism and Internationalism in the Discipline of International Relations*, edited by David Long and Brian C. Schmidt, 1–21. New York: State University of New York Press.
Lord, Beth. 2006. Foucault's Museum: Difference, Representation, and Genealogy. *Museum and Society* 4 (1): 1–14.
Lorimer, Douglas. 2005. From Victorian Values to White Virtues: Assimilation and Exclusion in British Racial Discourse, c.1870–1914. In *Rediscovering the British World*, edited by Phillip Buckner and R. Douglas Francis, 109–134. Calgary: University of Calgary Press.
   2009. From Natural Science to Social Science: Race and the Language of Race Relations in Late Victorian and Edwardian Discourse. In *Lineages of Empire: The Historical Roots of British Imperial Thought*, edited by Duncan Kelly, 181–212. Oxford: Oxford University Press.
Lüdtke, Alf. 2012. History of Concepts, New Edition: Suitable for a Better Understanding of Modern Times? *Contributions to the History of Concepts* 7 (2): 111–117.

Lurie, Nancy Oestreich. 1965. An American Indian Renascence? *Midcontinent American Studies Journal* 6 (2): 25–50.
Macartney, C. A. 1934. *National States and National Minorities*. London: Oxford University Press.
Macklem, Patrick. 2008. Indigenous Recognition in International Law: Theoretical Observations. *Michigan Journal of International Law* 30 (1): 177–210.
Mafeje, Archie. 1971. The Ideology of 'Tribalism'. *The Journal of Modern African Studies* 9 (2): 253–261.
Maine, Henry Sumner. 1861. *Ancient Law: Its Connection with the Early History of Society, and Its Relation to Modern Ideas*. London: John Murray.
Maitre, Henri. 1912. *Les jungles moï*. Paris: Emile Larose.
Malabou, Catherine. 2005. *The Future of Hegel: Plasticity, Temporality and Dialectic*. Translated by Lisabeth During. London: Routledge.
Malešević, Siniša. 2010. Ethnicity in Time and Space: A Conceptual Analysis. *Critical Sociology* 37 (1): 67–82.
Mamdani, Mahmood. 2012. *Define and Rule: Native as Political Identity*. Cambridge, MA: Harvard University Press.
Manchanda, Nivi. 2018. The Imperial Sociology of the 'Tribe' in Afghanistan. *Millennium: Journal of International Studies* 46 (2): 165–189.
Mancini, Elena. 2010. *Magnus Hirschfeld and the Quest for Sexual Freedom: A History of the First International Sexual Freedom Movement*. Basingstoke: Palgrave Macmillan.
Mandelbaum, Moran M. 2013. One State-One Nation: The Naturalisation of Nation-State Congruency in IR Theory. *Journal of International Relations and Development* 16 (4): 514–538.
  2020. *The Nation/State Fantasy: A Psychoanalytical Genealogy of Nationalism*. Basingstoke: Palgrave Macmillan.
Mandler, Peter. 2000. 'Race' and 'Nation' in Mid-Victorian Thought. In *History, Religion, and Culture: British Intellectual History 1750–1950*, edited by Stefan Collini, 224–244. Cambridge: Cambridge University Press.
Manela, Erez. 2007. *The Wilsonian Moment: Self-Determination and the International Origins of Anticolonial Nationalism*. Oxford: Oxford University Press.
Mann, Michael. 2005. *The Dark Side of Democracy: Explaining Ethnic Cleansing*. Cambridge: Cambridge University Press.
Mantena, Karuna. 2010. *Alibis of Empire: Henry Maine and the Ends of Liberal Imperialism*. Princeton: Princeton University Press.
Mantoux, Paul. 1955. *Les délibérations du Conseil des Quatre (24 mars – 28 juin 1919)*. Paris: Centre National de la Recherche Scientifique.

Markell, Patchen. 2003. *Bound by Recognition*. Princeton: Princeton University Press.
Markwell, D. J. 1986. Sir Alfred Zimmern Revisited: Fifty Years On. *Review of International Studies* 12 (4): 279–292.
Martial, René. 1934. *La race française*. Paris: Mercure de France.
   1938. *Race, hérédité, folie: étude d'anthropo-sociologie appliquée à l'immigration*. Paris: Mercure de France.
   1939. *Vie et constance des races*. Paris: Mercure de France.
   1942a. *Français, qui es-tu?* Paris: Mercure de France.
   1942b. *Les métis: nouvelle étude sur les migrations, le mélange des races, le métissage, la retrempe de la race française et la révision du code de la famille*. Paris: Flammarion.
   1943. *Notre race et ses aïeux*. Paris: Perceval.
Martin, Gary W. 1963. Concerning Ashley Montagu and the Term 'Race'. *American Anthropologist* 65 (2): 402–403.
Martiniello, Marco. 2013. *Penser l'ethnicité: identité, culture et relations sociales*. Liège: Presses Universitaires de Liège.
Marx, Karl. 1976. *Capital: A Critique of Political Economy: Volume One*. Translated by Ben Fowkes. London: Penguin.
Mason, David. 1999. The Continuing Significance of Race? Teaching Ethnic and Racial Studies in Sociology. In *Ethnic and Racial Studies Today*, edited by Martin Bulmer and John Solomos, 13–28. London: Routledge.
Mason, Otis T. 1886. Resemblances in Arts Widely Separated. *The American Naturalist* 20 (3): 246–251.
   1887. The Occurrence of Similar Inventions in Areas Widely Apart. *Science* 9 (226): 534–535.
   1896. Influence of Environment upon Human Industries or Arts. In *Annual Report of the Board of Regents of the Smithsonian Institution, Showing the Operations, Expenditures, and Condition of the Institution to July, 1895*, 639–665. Washington, DC: Government Printing Office.
   1907. Environment. In *Handbook of American Indians North of Mexico*, Vol. I, 427–430. Washington, DC: Government Printing Office.
Masters, Roger D. 1964. World Politics as a Primitive Political System. *World Politics* 16 (4): 595–619.
Matin, Kamran. 2011. Redeeming the Universal: Postcolonialism and the Inner Life of Eurocentrism. *European Journal of International Relations* 19 (2): 353–377.
   2020. Deciphering the Modern Janus: Societal Multiplicity and Nation-Formation. *Globalizations* 17 (3): 436–451.
Mazower, Mark. 1997. Minorities and the League of Nations in Interwar Europe. *Daedalus* 126 (2): 47–63.

2006. An International Civilization? Empire, Internationalism and the Crisis of the Mid-twentieth Century. *International Affairs* 82 (3): 553–566.
Mazrui, Ali A. 1968. From Social Darwinism to Current Theories of Modernization: A Tradition of Analysis. *World Politics* 21 (1): 69–83.
McCarthy, Thomas. 2009. *Race, Empire, and the Idea of Human Development*. Cambridge: Cambridge University Press.
McDonald, Jason. 2007. *American Ethnic History: Themes and Perspectives*. Edinburgh: Edinburgh University Press.
McGrane, Bernard. 1989. *Beyond Anthropology: Society and the Other*. New York: Columbia University Press.
McInerney, Jeremy. 2001. Ethnos and Ethnicity in Early Greece. In *Ancient Perceptions of Greek Ethnicity*, edited by Irad Malkin, 51–74. Cambridge, MA: Harvard University Press.
Mead, Margaret, ed. 1937. *Cooperation and Competition among Primitive Peoples*. New York: McGraw-Hill.
Mearsheimer, John J. 2006. Conversations in International Relations: Interview with John J. Mearsheimer (Part II). *International Relations* 20 (2): 231–243.
Mehta, Pratap Bhanu. 2012. Liberalism, Nation, and Empire: The Case of J. S. Mill. In *Empire and Modern Political Thought*, edited by Sankar Muthu, 232–260. Cambridge: Cambridge University Press.
Meloni, Maurizio. 2016. From Boundary-Work to Boundary Object: How Biology Left and Re-entered the Social Sciences. *The Sociological Review* 64 (1): 61–78.
Mercier, Paul. 1951. *Les tâches de la sociologie*. Dakar: Institut Français d'Afrique Noire.
  1954. Aspects des problèmes de stratification sociale dans l'ouest Africain. *Cahiers Internationaux de Sociologie* 17: 47–65.
  1961. Remarques sur la signification du 'tribalisme' actuel en Afrique noire. *Cahiers Internationaux de Sociologie* 31: 61–80.
Michael, Michális S., and Fabio Petito, eds. 2009. *Civilizational Dialogue and World Order: The Other Politics of Cultures, Religions, and Civilizations in International Relations*. Basingstoke: Palgrave Macmillan.
Miles, Robert, and Malcolm Brown. 2003. *Racism*. 2nd edition. London: Routledge.
Mill, John Stuart. 1859. A Few Words on Non-intervention. *Fraser's Magazine* 60 (360): 766–776.
  1861. Of Nationality, as Connected with Representative Government. In *Considerations on Representative Government*, 287–297. London: Parker, Son, and Bourn.

Miller, Alexey. 2008. Natsiia, Narod, Narodnost' in Russia in the 19th Century: Some Introductory Remarks to the History of Concepts. *Jahrbücher für Geschichte Osteuropas* 56 (3): 379–390.

Miller, Benjamin. 2007. *States, Nations, and the Great Powers: The Sources of Regional War and Peace.* Cambridge: Cambridge University Press.

Miller, David Hunter. 1924. *My Diary at the Conference of Paris.* New York: Printed for the author by the Appeal Printing Company.

  1928. *The Drafting of the Covenant.* New York: G. P. Putnam's Sons.

Mills, Charles W. 1997. *The Racial Contract.* Ithaca: Cornell University Press.

Mills, David. 2006. Made in Manchester? Methods and Myths in Disciplinary History. In *The Manchester School: Practice and Ethnographic Praxis in Anthropology*, edited by T. M. S. Evens and Don Handelman, 165–179. New York: Berghahn.

Mitchell, J. Clyde. 1956. *The Kalela Dance: Aspects of Social Relationships among Urban Africans in Northern Rhodesia.* Manchester: Manchester University Press.

Mittelman, James H. 2009. The Salience of Race. *International Studies Perspectives* 10 (1): 99–107.

Moerman, Michael. 1965. Ethnic Identification in a Complex Civilization: Who Are the Lue? *American Anthropologist* 67 (5): 1215–1230.

  1967. Reply to Naroll. *American Anthropologist* 69 (5): 512–513.

  1968. Being Lue: Uses and Abuses of Ethnic Identification. In *Essays on the Problem of Tribe: Proceedings of the 1967 Annual Spring Meeting of the American Ethnological Society*, edited by June Helm, 153–169. Seattle: University of Washington Press.

Mogilner, Marina. 2013. *Homo Imperii: A History of Physical Anthropology in Russia.* Lincoln: University of Nebraska Press.

Montag, Warren. 1997. The Universalization of Whiteness: Racism and Enlightenment. In *Whiteness: A Critical Reader*, edited by Mike Hill, 281–293. New York: New York University Press.

Montagu, Ashley. 1941a. Race, Caste and Scientific Method. *Psychiatry* 4 (3): 337–338.

  1941b. The Concept of Race in the Human Species in the Light of Genetics. *Journal of Heredity* 32 (8): 243–248.

  1942. *Man's Most Dangerous Myth: The Fallacy of Race.* New York: Columbia University Press.

  1945. *Man's Most Dangerous Myth: The Fallacy of Race.* 2nd edition. New York: Columbia University Press.

  1950. A Consideration of the Concept of Race [with Discussion]. *Cold Spring Harbor Symposia on Quantitative Biology* 15: 315–336.

1951. *Statement on Race: An Extended Discussion in Plain Language of the UNESCO Statement by Experts on Race Problems*. New York: Henry Schuman.

1962. The Concept of Race. *American Anthropologist* 64 (5): 919–928.

1972. *Statement on Race: An Annotated Elaboration and Exposition of the Four Statements on Race Issued by the United Nations Educational, Scientific, and Cultural Organization*. 3rd edition. New York: Oxford University Press.

Montandon, George. 1928. *L'ologenèse humaine (ologénisme)*. Paris: Félix Alcan.

1931. Remarques sur la classification des sciences anthropologiques du Dr Félix Regnault. *Revue d'Anthropologie* 41: 127–130.

1933. *La race, les races: mise au point d'ethnologie somatique*. Paris: Payot.

1935a. La race française [review]. *Revue Anthropologique* 45: 192.

1935b. *L'ethnie française*. Paris: Payot.

1940. *Comment reconnaître le juif?* Paris: Nouvelles Éditions Françaises.

1941. Ce que signifie l'ethnie française. *L'Ethnie Française* 1: 2–4.

1943. Racisme et juifs. *L'Ethnie Française* 7: 2–6.

1944. Synthèse de la notion d'ethnicité. *Je Vous Hais!*

Moon, Parker Thomas. 1925. *Syllabus on International Relations*. New York: Macmillan.

Moret, Alexandre, and Georges Davy. 1923. *Des clans aux empires: l'organisation sociale chez les primitifs et dans l'orient ancien*. Paris: La Renaissance du Livre.

Morgenthau, Hans J. 1948. *Politics among Nations: The Struggle for Power and Peace*. New York: Alfred A. Knopf.

1957. The Paradoxes of Nationalism. *Yale Review* 46 (4): 481–496.

Morin, Françoise. 1981. Minorités, revendications d'identité ethnique, mouvements nationalistes. *Bulletin de l'Association Française des Anthropologues* 5: 16–21.

Morin, Françoise, and Bernard Saladin d'Anglure. 1997. Ethnicity as a Political Tool for Indigenous Peoples. In *The Politics of Ethnic Consciousness*, edited by Cora Govers and Hans Vermeulen, 157–193. Basingstoke: Macmillan.

Mufti, Aamir R. 2016. *Forget English! Orientalisms and World Literature*. Cambridge, MA: Harvard University Press.

Mühlmann, Wilhelm. 1938. *Methodik der Völkerkunde*. Stuttgart: Ferdinand Enke Verlag.

1964. *Rassen, Ethnien, Kulturen*. Neuwied: Luchterhand.

Muir, Ramsay. 1919. *Nationalism and Internationalism: The Culmination of Modern History*. 2nd edition. London: Constable.

Murdock, George P. 1940. The Cross-Cultural Survey. *American Sociological Review* 5 (3): 361–370.

   1945. The Common Denominator of Cultures. In *The Science of Man in the World Crisis*, edited by Ralph Linton, 123–142. New York: Columbia University Press.

   1950. Feasibility and Implementation of Comparative Community Research: With Special Reference to the Human Relations Area Files. *American Sociological Review* 15 (6): 713–720.

   1953. The Processing of Anthropological Materials. In *Anthropology Today: An Encyclopedic Inventory*, edited by Alfred L. Kroeber. Chicago: University of Chicago Press.

Murray, Christopher. 2020. Imperial Dialectics and Epistemic Mapping: From Decolonisation to Anti-Eurocentric IR. *European Journal of International Relations* 26 (2): 419–442.

Murray, Gilbert. 1910. Empire and Subject Races. In *Nationalities and Subject Races: Report of Conference Held in Caxton Hall, Westminster June 28–30, 1910*, edited by N. Dryhurst, 3–10. London: P. S. King & Sons.

Murray, James A. H., ed. 1897. *A New English Dictionary on Historical Principles Founded Mainly on the Materials Collected by the Philological Society*. Oxford: Clarendon.

Murray, Stephen O. 1979. The Institutional Elaboration of a Quasi-Ethnic Community. *International Review of Modern Sociology* 9 (2): 165–177.

Mutua, Makau. 2002. *Human Rights: A Political and Cultural Critique*. Philadelphia: University of Pennsylvania Press.

Myrdal, Gunnar. 1944. *An American Dilemma: The Negro Problem and Modern Democracy*. New York: Harper & Brothers.

Nadel, S. F. 1942. *A Black Byzantium: The Kingdom of Nupe in Nigeria*. London: Oxford University Press.

   1951. *The Foundations of Social Anthropology*. London: Cohen & West.

Nagel, Joane. 1996. *American Indian Ethnic Renewal: Red Power and the Resurgence of Identity and Culture*. Oxford: Oxford University Press.

Naroll, Raoul. 1956. A Preliminary Index of Social Development. *American Anthropologist* 58 (4): 687–715.

   1961. Two Solutions to Galton's Problem. *Philosophy of Science* 28 (1): 15–39.

   1967. Native Concepts and Cross-Cultural Surveys. *American Anthropologist* 69 (5): 511–512.

   1968. Who the Lue Are. In *Essays on the Problem of Tribe: Proceedings of the 1967 Annual Spring Meeting of the American Ethnological Society*, edited by June Helm, 72–79. Seattle: University of Washington Press.

Naroll, Raoul, Ronald M. Berndt, Frank D. Bessac, Eliot D. Chapple, Gertrude E. Dole, Harold E. Driver, Paul Ducey, Melvin Ember,

Helmuth Fuchs, Hans Hoffmann, Mervyn Jaspan, David Landy, Edmund Leach, Otto Von Mering, Simon D. Messing, Frank W. Moore, Ramkrishna Mukherjee, George P. Murdock, Artur Hehl Neiva, Gideon, Andree F. Sjoberg, Andrée F. Sjoberg, Leigh M. Triandis, C. F. Voegelin, Linvill Watson, and John W. M. Whiting. 1964. On Ethnic Unit Classification [with Comments and Reply]. *Current Anthropology* 5 (4): 283–312.

Nestor, Stelios. 1962. Greek Macedonia and the Convention of Neuilly (1919). *Balkan Studies* 3 (1): 169–185.

Neumann, Iver B. 1999. *Uses of the Other: 'The East' in European Identity Formation*. Manchester: Manchester University Press.

2011. Entry into International Society Reconceptualised: The Case of Russia. *Review of International Studies* 37 (2): 463–484.

2018. Security, Ethnicity, Nationalism. *Nations and Nationalism* 24 (2): 348–368.

Nicholls, David. 1996. *From Dessalines to Duvalier: Race, Colour and National Independence in Haiti*. 3rd edition. New Brunswick: Rutgers University Press.

Nicolas, François J. 1952. La question de l'ethnique 'Gourounsi' en Haute-Volta (A.O.F.). *Africa: Journal of the International African Institute* 22 (2): 170–172.

Nicolas, Guy. 1973. Fait 'ethnique' et usages du concept d' 'ethnie'. *Cahiers Internationaux de Sociologie* 54: 95–126.

Nielsen, Kai. 1999. Cultural Nationalism, neither Ethnic nor Civic. In *Theorizing Nationalism*, edited by Ronald Beiner, 119–130. Albany: State University of New York Press.

Niezen, Ronald. 2003. *The Origins of Indigenism: Human Rights and the Politics of Identity*. Berkeley: University of California Press.

Nimni, Ephraim. 1989. Marx, Engels and the National Question. *Science & Society* 53 (3): 297–326.

Nisancioglu, Kerem. 2020. Racial Sovereignty. *European Journal of International Relations* 26 (S1): 39–63.

Noiriel, Gérard. 1995. Socio-histoire d'un concept: les usages du mot 'nationalité' au XIXe siècle. *Genèses* 20: 4–23.

2007. *Immigration, antisémitisme et racisme en France (XIXe-XXe siècle): discours publics, humiliations privées*. Paris: Fayard.

Novak, Michael. 1972. *The Rise of the Unmeltable Ethnics: Politics and Culture in the Seventies*. New York: Macmillan.

O'Hagan, Jacinta. 2002. *Conceptualizing the West in International Relations: From Spengler to Said*. Basingstoke: Palgrave Macmillan.

Ojakangas, Mika. 2007. A Terrifying World without an Exterior: Carl Schmitt and the Metaphysics of International (Dis)Order. In *The*

International Political Thought of Carl Schmitt: Terror, Liberal War and the Crisis of Global Order, edited by Louiza Odysseos and Fabio Petito, 205–221. London: Routledge.

Olson, William C., and A. J. R. Groom. 1991. *International Relations Then and Now: Origins and Trends in Interpretation*. London: Harper Collins Academic.

Omi, Michael, and Howard Winant. 1994. *Racial Formation in the United States*. 2nd edition. New York: Routledge.

Osterhammel, Jürgen. 2013. Nationalism and Globalization. In *The Oxford Handbook of the History of Nationalism*, edited by John Breuilly, 694–707. Oxford: Oxford University Press.

Oushakine, Serguei A. 2009. *The Patriotism of Despair: Nation, War, and Loss in Russia*. Ithaca: Cornell University Press.

Özkirimli, Umut. 2005. *Contemporary Debates on Nationalism: A Critical Engagement*. Basingstoke: Palgrave Macmillan.

Palsky, Gilles. 2002. Emmanuel de Martonne and the Ethnographical Cartography of Central Europe (1917–1920). *Imago Mundi* 54: 111–119.

Papillault, Georges. 1908. L'anthropologie est-elle une science unique? *Revue de l'École d'Anthropologie* 18: 117–132.

Park, Robert Ezra. 1950. *Race and Culture*. New York: Free Press.

Pasha, Mustapha Kamal. 2011. Untimely Reflections. In *International Relations and Non-Western Thought: Imperialism, Colonialism and Investigations of Global Modernity*, edited by Robbie Shilliam, 12–26. London: Routledge.

PCIJ. 1930. *Greco-Bulgarian 'Communities'*. PCIJ Advisory Opinion, Series B, No. 17. Leyden: A. W. Sijthoff's Publishing Company.

Pennybacker, Susan D. 2005. The Universal Races Congress, London Political Culture, and Imperial Dissent, 1900–1939. *Radical History Review* 92: 103–117.

Pernau, Margrit. 2012. Whither Conceptual History? From National to Entangled Histories. *Contributions to the History of Concepts* 7 (1): 1–11.

Persaud, Randolph, and Alina Sajed, eds. 2018. *Race, Gender, and Culture in International Relations: Postcolonial Perspectives*. London: Routledge.

Persaud, Randolph, and R. B. J. Walker. 2001. Apertura: Race in International Relations. *Alternatives: Global, Local, Political* 26 (4): 373–376.

Petersen, William. 1980. Concepts of Ethnicity. In *Harvard Encyclopedia of American Ethnic Groups*, edited by Stephan Thernstrom, 234–242. Cambridge, MA: Harvard University Press.

Piana, Francesca. 2016. The Dangers of 'Going Native': George Montandon in Siberia and the International Committee of the Red Cross. *Contemporary European History* 25 (2): 253–274.
Pianko, Noam. 2008. 'The True Liberalism of Zionism': Horace Kallen, Jewish Nationalism, and the Limits of American Pluralism. *American Jewish History* 94 (4): 299–329.
  2009. Cosmopolitan Wanderer or Zionist Activist? Sir Alfred Zimmern's Ambivalent Jewishness and the Legacy of British Internationalism. *Ab Imperio* 4: 211–247.
Pinson, Koppel S. 1935. *A Bibliographical Introduction to Nationalism*. New York: Columbia University Press.
Pitt-Rivers, George Henry Lane Fox. 1927a. *The Clash of Culture and the Contact of Races: An Anthropological and Psychological Study of the Laws of Racial Adaptability, with Special Reference to the Depopulation of the Pacific and the Government of Subject Races*. London: George Routledge & Sons.
  1927b. The Effect on Native Races of Contact with European Civilisation. *Man* 27: 2–10.
Pitts, Jennifer. 2005. *A Turn to Empire: The Rise of Imperial Liberalism in Britain and France*. Princeton: Princeton University Press.
Plamenatz, John. 1960. *On Alien Rule and Self-Government*. London: Longmans.
  1973. Two Types of Nationalism. In *Nationalism: The Nature and Evolution of an Idea*, edited by Eugene Kamenka, 22–37. Canberra: Australian National University Press.
Pocock, J. G. A. 1996. Concepts and Discourses: A Difference in Culture? Comment on a Paper by Melvin Richter. In *The Meaning of Historical Terms and Concepts: New Studies on Begriffsgeschichte*, edited by Hartmut Lehmann and Melvin Richter, 47–58. Washington, DC: German Historical Institute.
Polgar, Steven. 1964. An Operational Approach to 'Race'. *American Anthropologist* 66 (2): 423–426.
Post, Ken. 1964. *The New States of West Africa*. Harmondsworth: Penguin.
Potter, Pitman B. 1922. *An Introduction to the Study of International Organization*. New York: Century.
Poutignat, Philippe, and Jocelyne Streiff-Fenart. 1995. *Théories de l'ethnicité*. Paris: Presses Universitaires de France.
Powell, John Wesley. 1887. Museums of Ethnology and Their Classification. *Science* 9 (229): 612–614.
Preston, Paul. 2000. The Great Civil War: European Politics, 1914–1945. In *The Oxford History of Modern Europe*, edited by T. C. W. Blanning, 153–185. Oxford: Oxford University Press.

Prott, Volker. 2014. Tying up the Loose Ends of National Self-Determination: British, French, and American Experts in Peace Planning, 1917–1919. *The Historical Journal* 57 (3): 727–750.
Quane, Helen. 1998. The United Nations and the Evolving Right to Self-Determination. *The International and Comparative Law Quarterly* 47 (3): 537–572.
Quinlan, Sean. 1998. The Racial Imagery of Degeneration and Depopulation: Georges Vacher de Lapouge and 'Anthroposociology' in Fin-de-Siècle France. *History of European Ideas* 24 (6): 393–413.
Radcliffe-Brown, Alfred Reginald. 1940. On Social Structure. *The Journal of the Royal Anthropological Institute of Great Britain and Ireland* 70 (1): 1–12.
Rae, Heather. 2002. *State Identities and the Homogenisation of Peoples.* Cambridge: Cambridge University Press.
Ramaga, Philip Vuciri. 1992. The Bases of Minority Identity. *Human Rights Quarterly* 14 (3): 409–428.
Ranger, Terence. 1983. The Invention of Tradition in Colonial Africa. In *The Invention of Tradition*, edited by Eric J. Hobsbawm and Terence Ranger, 211–262. Cambridge: Cambridge University Press.
Rasmussen, Kim Su. 2011. Foucault's Genealogy of Racism. *Theory, Culture & Society* 28 (5): 34–51.
Raum, Johannes W. 1995. Reflections on Max Weber's Thoughts concerning Ethnic Groups. *Zeitschrift für Ethnologie* 120 (1): 73–87.
Raveau, François. 1976. Ethnicité et mécanismes de défense. In *L'autre et l'ailleurs: hommages à Roger Bastide*, edited by Jean Poirier and François Raveau, 475–479. Paris: Berger-Levrault.
Ravndal, Ellen. 2020. Colonies, Semi-severeigns, and Great Powers: IGO Membership Debates and the Transition of the International System. *Review of International Studies* 46 (2): 278–298.
Redfield, Robert. 1940. The Folk Society and Culture. *American Journal of Sociology* 45 (5): 731–742.
Rees, Richard W. 2007. *Shades of Difference: A History of Ethnicity in America.* Lanham: Rowman & Littlefield.
Regnault, Félix. 1919. Il convient de différencier l'ethnie linguistique de la race anatomique. *Bulletins et Mémoires de la Société d'Anthropologie de Paris* 10 (6): 55–56.
   1920. Quelques considérations sur l'étude des races en anthropologie et en zootechnie. *Revue de Pathologie Comparée* 165: 26–29.
   1921. Distinguons la race anatomique et l'ethnie psychique. *Revue de Pathologie Comparée* 178: 87–89.

1928. La question des races devant l'anatomie et la linguistique. In *III session Amsterdam, 20–29 Septembre 1927*, 193–197. Paris: Librairie E. Nourray.

1931. Classification des sciences anthropologiques. *Revue d'Anthropologie* 41: 121–127.

Reinsch, Paul S. 1900. *World Politics at the End of the Nineteenth Century as Influenced by the Oriental Situation*. New York: Macmillan.

1902. *Colonial Government: An Introduction to the Study of Colonial Institutions*. New York: Macmillan.

Renner, Egon. 2004. Franz Boas, l'anthropologie allemande et son transfert aux États-Unis. In *Quand Berlin pensait les peuples: anthropologie, ethnologie et psychologie (1850–1890)*, edited by Céline Trautmann-Waller, 211–224. Paris: CNRS Éditions.

Reus-Smit, Christian, and Timothy Dunne. 2017a. Introduction. In *The Globalization of International Society*, edited by Timothy Dunne and Christian Reus-Smit, 3–17. Cambridge: Cambridge University Press.

2017b. The Globalization of International Society. In *The Globalization of International Society*, edited by Timothy Dunne and Christian Reus-Smit, 18–40. Cambridge: Cambridge University Press.

Reynaud-Paligot, Carole. 2010. L'émergence de l'antisémitisme scientifique chez les anthropologues français. *Archives Juives* 43: 66–76.

Rich, Paul. 1984. 'The Baptism of a New Era': The 1911 Universal Races Congress and the Liberal Ideology of Race. *Ethnic and Racial Studies* 7 (4): 534–550.

Richard, Nathalie. 2012. Volkov in France: Cultural Transfers in Anthropology and Prehistoric Archaeology at the End of the 19th Century. In *History of Archaeology Conference Proceedings: Arkheolohiia i davnia istoriia Ukraïny*, 9: 220–227.

Richard-Molard, Jacques. 1952. Groupements ethniques et civilisations nègres d'Afrique noire. *Cahiers d'Outre-Mer* 5 (17): 5–25.

Riesman, David. 1953. Some Observations on Intellectual Freedom. *The American Scholar* 23 (1): 9–25.

Rist, Gilbert. 2008. *The History of Development: From Western Origins to Global Faith*. Translated by Patrick Camiller, 3rd edition. London: Zed Books.

Robinson, Cedric. 2020. *Black Marxism: The Making of the Black Radical Tradition*. 3rd edition. Chapel Hill: University of North Carolina Press.

Rodríguez-Piñero, Luis. 2005. *Indigenous Peoples, Postcolonialism, and International Law: The ILO Regime (1919–1989)*. Oxford: Oxford University Press.

Rohan-Csermak, Geza de. 1967. La première apparition du terme 'ethnologie'. *Ethnologia Europaea* 1 (1): 170–184.

Rony, Fatimah Tobbing. 1996. *The Third Eye: Race, Cinema, and Ethnographic Spectacle*. Durham: Duke University Press.
Rösch, Felix, ed. 2014. *Émigré Scholars and the Genesis of International Relations: A European Discipline in America?* Basingstoke: Palgrave Macmillan.
Rosdolsky, Roman. 1986. *Engels and the 'Nonhistoric' Peoples: The National Question in the Revolution of 1848*. Translated by John-Paul Himka. Glasgow: Critique.
Rosenau, James N. 1970. *Race in International Politics: A Dialogue in Five Parts*. Denver: University of Denver Press.
Rosenthal, Lawrence, and Vesna Rodic, eds. 2015. *The New Nationalism and the First World War*. Basingstoke: Palgrave Macmillan.
Roshchin, Evgeny. 2017. *Friendship among Nations: History of a Concept*. Manchester: Manchester University Press.
Rouch, Jean. 1956. Migrations au Ghana. *Journal de la Société des Africanistes* 26 (1): 33–196.
Rousseau, Jérôme. 1978. Classe et ethnicité. *Anthropologie et Sociétés* 2 (1): 61–69.
Royal Institute of International Affairs. 1939. *Nationalism: A Report by a Study Group of Members of the Royal Institute of International Affairs*. London: Oxford University Press.
Russell, Frank M. 1936. *Theories of International Relations*. New York: Appleton-Century-Crofts.
Ruyssen, Théodore. 1916. The World War and the Principle of Nationality. *International Conciliation* 3: 307–328.
  1917. What Is a Nationality? The Principle of Nationality, Part II. *International Conciliation* 4: 71–94.
  1919. La controverse nationalitaire. *Revue de Métaphysique et de Morale* 26 (6): 771–803.
Sabaratnam, Meera. 2020. Is IR Theory White? Racialised Subject-Positioning in Three Canonical Texts. *Millennium: Journal of International Studies* 49 (1): 3–31.
Said, Edward W. 1985. *Beginnings: Intention and Method*. New York: Columbia University Press.
  2003. *Orientalism*. London: Penguin.
Sampson, Aaron Beers. 2002. Tropical Anarchy: Waltz, Wendt, and the Way We Imagine International Politics. *Alternatives: Global, Local, Political* 27 (4): 429–457.
Sanders, Douglas E. 1999. Indigenous Peoples: Issues of Definition. *International Journal of Cultural Property* 8 (1): 4–13.
Santini, Carlotta. 2018. Can Humanity Be Mapped? Adolf Bastian, Friedrich Ratzel and the Cartography of Culture. *History of Anthropology*

Newsletter 42. https://histanthro.org/notes/can-humanity-be-mapped/ (last accessed 25 June 2024).
Sapir, Edward. 1916. *Time Perspective in Aboriginal American Culture, A Study in Method*. Ottawa: Government Printing Bureau.
Saramago, André. 2022. Post-Eurocentric Grand Narratives in Critical International Theory. *European Journal of International Relations* 28 (1): 6–29.
Sarasin, Philipp. 2012. Is a 'History of Basic Concepts of the Twentieth Century' Possible? A Polemic. *Contributions to the History of Concepts* 7 (2): 101–110.
Sartre, Jean-Paul. 1951. Black Orpheus. Translated by S. W. Allen. *Présence Africaine* 10–11: 219–247.
Saugestad, Sidsel. 2001a. Contested Images: 'First Peoples' or 'Marginalized Minorities' in Africa. In *Africa's Indigenous Peoples: 'First Peoples' or 'Marginalized Minorities'*, edited by Alan Barnard and Justin Kenrick, 299–322. Edinburgh: Centre of African Studies, University of Edinburgh.
    2001b. *The Inconvenient Indigenous: Remote Area Development in Botswana, Donor Assistance, and the First People of the Kalahari*. Uppsala: Nordic Africa Institute.
Schippers, Thomas K. 2009. Le fait ethnique, histoires d'une notion controversée. In *Le nom des langues en Afrique sub-saharienne: pratiques, dénominations, catégorisations*, edited by Carole de Férale, 19–37. Louvain-La-Neuve: Peeters.
Schmidt, Brian C. 1998. *The Political Discourse of Anarchy: A Disciplinary History of International Relations*. Albany: State University of New York Press.
Schmitt, Carl. 2003. *The Nomos of the Earth in the International Law of the Jus Publicum Europaeum*. Translated by G. L. Ulmen. New York: Telos Press.
Schneider, William H. 1990. *Quality and Quantity: The Quest for Biological Regeneration in Twentieth-Century France*. Cambridge: Cambridge University Press.
Schuman, Frederick L. 1933. *International Politics: An Introduction to the Western State System*. New York: McGraw-Hill.
Scott, David. 2003. Culture in Political Theory. *Political Theory* 31 (1): 92–115.
Selcer, Perrin. 2012. Beyond the Cephalic Index: Negotiating Politics to Produce UNESCO's Scientific Statements on Race. *Current Anthropology* 53 (S5): S173–S184.
Seton-Watson, Hugh. 1977. *Nations and States: An Enquiry into the Origins of Nations and the Politics of Nationalism*. London: Methuen.

Seton-Watson, Robert William. 1908. *Racial Problems in Hungary*. London: Archibald Constable.
Sewell, William H. 2004. The French Revolution and the Emergence of the Nation Form. In *Revolutionary Currents: Nation Building in the Transatlantic World*, edited by Michael A. Morrison and Melinda Zook, 91–126. Lanham: Rowman & Littlefield.
Shahabuddin, Mohammad. 2016. *Ethnicity and International Law: Histories, Politics and Practices*. Cambridge: Cambridge University Press.
Shanin, Teodor. 1986. Soviet Theories of Ethnicity: The Case of a Missing Term. *New Left Review* 158: 113–122.
  1989. Ethnicity in the Soviet Union: Analytical Perceptions and Political Strategies. *Comparative Studies in Society and History* 31 (3): 409–424.
Sharma, Nandita. 2020. *Home Rule: National Sovereignty and the Separation of Natives and Migrants*. Durham: Duke University Press.
Sharp, John. 1980. Two Separate Developments: Anthropology in South Africa. *RAIN* 36: 4–6.
  1981. The Roots and Development of Volkekunde in South Africa. *Journal of Southern African Studies* 8 (1): 16–36.
Shaw, Malcolm N. 1992. The Definition of Minorities in International Law. In *The Protection of Minorities and Human Rights*, edited by Yoram Dinstein and Mala Tabory, 1–32. Dordrecht: Martinus Nijhoff.
Shepherd, George W., and Tilden J. LeMelle, eds. 1970. *Race among Nations: A Conceptual Approach*. Lexington: Lexington Books.
Shilliam, Robbie. 2011. The Perilous but Unavoidable Terrain of the Non-West. In *International Relations and Non-Western Thought: Imperialism, Colonialism and Investigations of Global Modernity*, edited by Robbie Shilliam, 12–26. London: Routledge.
Shirokogoroff, S. M. 1924. *Ethnical Unit and Milieu: A Summary of the Ethnos*. Shanghai: Edward Evans and Sons.
  1931. *Ethnological and Linguistical Aspects of the Ural–Altaic Hypothesis*. Peking: The Commercial Press.
  1933. *Social Organization of the Northern Tungus: With Introductory Chapters Concerning Geographical Distribution and History of These Groups*. Shanghai: The Commercial Press.
  1935. *Psychomental Complex of the Tungus*. London: Kegan Paul, Trench, Trubner & Company.
  1936. La théorie de l'ethnos et sa place dans le système des sciences anthropologiques. *L'Ethnographie* 32: 85–115.
Sidgwick, Henry. 1891. *The Elements of Politics*. London: Macmillan.
Sikka, Sonia. 2011. *Herder on Humanity and Cultural Difference: Enlightened Relativism*. Cambridge: Cambridge University Press.

Singer, L. 1962. Ethnogenesis and Negro-Americans Today. *Social Research* 29 (4): 419–432.
Sirina, Anna Anatol'evna, Vladimir Nikolaevich Davydov, Olga Alekseevna Povoroznyuk, and Veronika Vital'evna Simonova. 2016. S. M. Shirokogoroff's Book Social Organization of the Northern Tungus and Its Russian Translation: History, Structure, and Interpretations. *Asian Ethnicity* 17 (1): 31–47.
Sirina, Anna Anatol'evna, and Aleksey Aleksandrovich Zakurdaev. 2016. Shirokogoroff: A Portrait of the Anthropologist (From His Letters to the Sinologist Alekseev). *Asian Ethnicity* 17 (1): 15–30.
Skalník, Peter. 1986. Towards an Understanding of Soviet Etnos Theory. *South African Journal of Ethnology* 9 (4): 157–166.
  1988. Union soviétique – Afrique du Sud: les 'théories' de l'etnos. *Cahiers d'Études Africaines* 28 (110): 157–176.
  1990. Soviet Etnografiia and the National(ities) Question. *Cahiers du Monde Russe et Soviétique* 31 (2–3): 183–193.
Skinner, Quentin. 1979. The Idea of a Cultural Lexicon. *Essays in Criticism* 24 (3): 205–224.
  1988. A Reply to My Critics. In *Meaning and Context: Quentin Skinner and His Critics*, edited by James Tully, 231–288. Cambridge: Polity.
Slezkine, Yuri. 1991. The Fall of Soviet Ethnography, 1928-38. *Current Anthropology* 32 (4): 476–484.
Sluga, Glenda. 2002. Narrating Difference and Defining the Nation in Late Nineteenth and Early Twentieth Century 'Western' Europe. *European Review of History: Revue Européenne d'Histoire* 9 (2): 183–197.
Smedley, Audrey. 1993. *Race in North America: Origin and Evolution of a Worldview*. Boulder: Westview.
Smith, Anthony D. 1981. *The Ethnic Revival*. Cambridge: Cambridge University Press.
  1986. *The Ethnic Origins of Nations*. Oxford: Basil Blackwell.
Smith, Edmund Munroe. 1899. Nationality, Law of. In *Cyclopædia of Political Science, Political Economy, and the Political History of the United States*, Vol. II, 941–956. New York: Maynard, Merrill, and Company.
Smith, M. G. 1955. *A Framework for Caribbean Studies*. Mona: University College of the West Indies.
  1957. Ethnic and Cultural Pluralism in the British Caribbean. In *Ethnic and Cultural Pluralism in Intertropical Communities: Report of the XXXth Meeting Held in Lisbon on the 15th, 16th, 17th and 18th April 1957*, 439–447. Brussels: International Institute of Differing Civilizations.
  1982. Ethnicity and Ethnic Groups in America: The View from Harvard. *Ethnic and Racial Studies* 5 (1): 1–22.

Smith, Matthew J. 2009. *Red and Black in Haiti: Radicalism, Conflict, and Political Change, 1934–1957*. Chapel Hill: University of North Carolina Press.

Smith, Neil. 2003. *American Empire: Roosevelt's Geographer and the Prelude to Globalization*. Berkeley: University of California Press.

Smith, Rogers M. 2004. The Puzzling Place of Race in American Political Science. *PS: Political Science and Politics* 37 (1): 41–45.

Sneath, David. 2007. *The Headless State: Aristocratic Orders, Kinship Society, and Misrepresentations of Nomadic Inner Asia*. New York: Columbia University Press.

Snyder, Louis L. 1954. *The Meaning of Nationalism*. New Jersey: Rutgers University Press.

  1968. *The New Nationalism*. Ithaca: Cornell University Press.

Sollors, Werner. 1986. *Beyond Ethnicity: Consent and Descent in American Culture*. New York: Oxford University Press.

Southall, Aidan. 1961. Introductory Summary. In *Social Change in Modern Africa: Studies Presented and Discussed at the First International African Seminar, Makerere College, Kampala, January 1959*, edited by Aidan Southall, 1–66. London: Oxford University Press.

  1970. The Illusion of Tribe. In *The Passing of Tribal Man in Africa*, edited by Peter C. W. Gutkind, 28–50. Leiden: Brill.

Spanu, Maja. 2020. The Hierarchical Society: The Politics of Self-Determination and the Constitution of New States After 1919. *European Journal of International Relations* 26 (2): 372–396.

Speth, William W. 1978. The Anthropogeographic Theory of Franz Boas. *Anthropos* 73 (1–2): 1–31.

Spiller, G., ed. 1911. *Papers on Inter-racial Problems Communicated to the First Universal Races Congress Held at the University of London, July 26–29, 1911*. London: P. S. King & Sons.

Spykman, Nicholas John. 1942. *America's Strategy in World Politics: The United States and the Balance of Power*. New York: Harcourt, Brace & Company.

Stagl, Justin. 1995. August Ludwig Schlözer and the Study of Mankind According to Peoples. In *A History of Curiosity: The Theory of Travel 1550–1800*. London: Routledge.

  1998. Rationalism and Irrationalism in Early German Ethnology: The Controversy between Schlözer and Herder, 1772/73. *Anthropos* 93 (4–6): 521–536.

Staum, Martin S. 2011. *Nature and Nurture in French Social Sciences, 1859–1914 and Beyond*. Montreal: McGill-Queen's University Press.

Stead, W. T., ed. 1902. *The Last Will and Testament of Cecil John Rhodes with Elucidatory Notes to Which Are Added Some Chapters Describing the Political and Religious Ideas of the Testator.* London: Review of Reviews Office.

Steger, Brigitte. 2019. The Stranger and Others: The Life and Legacy of the Japanese Ethnologist Oka Masao. *Vienna Journal of East Asian Studies* 11 (1): 60–91.

Steinberg, David J. 1957. *Cambodia: Its People, Its Society, Its Culture.* New Haven: Human Relations Area Files.

Steinberg, Stephen. 1989. *The Ethnic Myth: Race, Ethnicity, and Class in America.* Updated and expanded edition. Boston: Beacon Press.

Steinmetz, Willibald. 2012. Some Thoughts on a History of Twentieth-Century German Basic Concepts. *Contributions to the History of Concepts* 7 (2): 87–100.

Stergiopoulou, Katerina. 2014. Taking 'Nomos': Carl Schmitt's Philology Unbound. *October* 149: 95–122.

Stewart, Jeffrey C. 1992. Introduction. In *Race Contacts and Interracial Relations: Lectures on the Theory and Practice of Race*, edited by Jeffrey C. Stewart, ix–lix. Washington, DC: Howard University Press.

    2018. *The New Negro: The Life of Alain Locke.* Oxford: Oxford University Press.

Stocking, George W. 1982. *Race, Culture, and Evolution: Essays in the History of Anthropology.* Chicago: University of Chicago Press.

    1987. *Victorian Anthropology.* New York: Free Press.

Stocking, George W., ed. 1991. *Colonial Situations: Essays on the Contextualization of Ethnographic Knowledge.* Madison: University of Wisconsin Press.

    1994a. Dogmatism, Pragmatism, Essentialism, Relativism: The Boas/Mason Museum Debate Revisited. *History of Anthropology Newsletter* 21 (1): 3–12.

    1994b. The Turn-of-the-Century Concept of Race. *Modernism/Modernity* 1 (1): 4–16.

Stoddard, Lothrop. 1920. *The Rising Tide of Color against White World-Supremacy.* New York: Charles Scribner's Sons.

Stolcke, Verena. 1995. Talking Culture: New Boundaries, New Rhetorics of Exclusion in Europe. *Current Anthropology* 36 (1): 1–24.

Stoler, Ann Laura. 1995. *Race and the Education of Desire: Foucault's History of Sexuality and the Colonial Order of Things.* Durham: Duke University Press.

Stourzh, Gerald. 1994. Ethnic Attribution in Late Imperial Austria: Good Intentions, Evil Consequences. In *The Habsburg Legacy: National Identity in Historical Perspective*, edited by Ritchie Robertson and Edward Timms, 67–83. Edinburgh: Edinburgh University Press.

Stuurman, Siep. 2000. François Bernier and the Invention of Racial Classification. *History Workshop Journal* 50 (1): 1–21.

Subotic, Jelena, and Ayşe Zarakol. 2013. Cultural Intimacy and International Relations. *European Journal of International Relations* 19 (4): 915–938.

Subrahmanyam, Sanjay. 1997. Connected Histories: Notes towards a Reconfiguration of Early Modern Eurasia. *Modern Asian Studies* 31 (3): 735–762.

Sumner, William Graham. 1906. *Folkways: A Study of the Sociological Importance of Usages, Manners, Customs, Mores, and Morals*. Boston: Ginn.

Suzuki, Shogo. 2005. Japan's Socialization into Janus-Faced European International Society. *European Journal of International Relations* 11 (1): 137–164.

  2009. *Civilization and Empire: China and Japan's Encounter with European International Society*. London: Routledge.

Taguieff, Pierre-André. 1994. Immigrés, métis, juifs: les raisons de l'inassimilabilité. In *Nationalismes, féminismes, exclusions: mélanges en l'honneur de Rita Thalmann*, edited by Liliane Crips, Michel Cullin, Nicole Gabriel, and Fritz Taubert, 177–221. Frankfurt am Main: Peter Lang.

  2000. Sélectionnisme et socialisme dans une perspective aryaniste: théories, visions et prévisions de Georges Vacher de Lapouge. *Mil Neuf Cent: Revue d'Histoire Intellectuelle* 18: 7–51.

  2001. *The Force of Prejudice: On Racism and Its Doubles*. Translated and edited by Hassan Melehy. Minneapolis: University of Minnesota Press.

Taras, Raymond, and Rajat Ganguly. 2010. *Understanding Ethnic Conflict: The International Dimension*. 4th edition. Boston: Longman.

Tardieu, André. 1921. *The Truth about the Treaty*. London: Hodder & Stoughton.

Tax, Sol, and Lois Mednick. 1960. Terminology: 'Primitive' Peoples. *Current Anthropology* 1 (5–6): 441–445.

Temperley, H. W. V. 1921. *A History of the Peace Conference of Paris*. London: Henry Frowde and Hodder & Stoughton.

Terradas, Nicolás. 2020. The Quest for Order in Anarchical Societies: Anthropological Investigations. *International Studies Review* 22 (1): 98–121.

Teschke, Benno. 2011. Fatal Attraction: A Critique of Carl Schmitt's International Political and Legal Theory. *International Theory* 3 (2): 179–227.

Thakur, Vineet, and Peter Vale. 2020. *South Africa, Race and the Making of International Relations*. London: Rowman & Littlefield.

Thakur, Vineet, Alexander E. Davis, and Peter Vale. 2017. Imperial Mission, 'Scientific' Method: An Alternative Account of the Origins of IR. *Millennium: Journal of International Studies* 46 (1): 3–23.

Thernstrom, Stephan, ed. 1980. *Harvard Encyclopedia of American Ethnic Groups*. Cambridge, MA: Harvard University Press.
Thernstrom, Stephan, Ann Orlov, and Oscar Handlin. 1980. Introduction. In *Harvard Encyclopedia of American Ethnic Groups*, edited by Stephan Thernstrom, v–ix. Cambridge, MA: Harvard University Press.
Thomas, James M. 2020. Du Bois, Double Consciousness, and the 'Jewish Question'. *Ethnic and Racial Studies* 43 (8): 1333–1356.
Thomas, Nicholas. 1994. *Colonialism's Culture: Anthropology, Travel and Government*. Cambridge: Polity.
Thomas, Robert K. 1968. Pan-Indianism. In *The American Indian Today*, edited by Stuart Levine and Nancy Oestreich Lurie, 128–140. Baltimore: Penguin.
Thompson, Debra. 2013. Through, against and beyond the Racial State: The Transnational Stratum of Race. *Cambridge Review of International Affairs* 26 (1): 133–151.
Thornberry, Patrick. 1991. *International Law and the Rights of Minorities*. Oxford: Clarendon.
  1995a. On Some Implications of the UN Declaration on Minorities for Indigenous Peoples. In *Indigenous and Tribal Peoples' Rights: 1993 and After*, edited by Eyassu Gayim and Kristian Myntti, 46–91. Rovaniemi: University of Lapland.
  1995b. The UN Declaration on the Rights of Persons Belonging to National or Ethnic, Religious and Linguistic Minorities: Background, Analysis, Observations, and an Update. In *Universal Minority Rights*, edited by Alan Phillips and Allan Rosas, 13–76. Turku/Åbo: Åbo Akademi Universal Institute for Human Rights.
  2002. *Indigenous Peoples and Human Rights*. Manchester: Manchester University Press.
Tickner, Arlene B., and Ole Wæver, eds. 2009. *International Relations Scholarship around the World*. London: Routledge.
Tickner, J. Ann. 1988. Hans Morgenthau's Principles of Political Realism: A Feminist Reformulation. *Millennium: Journal of International Studies* 17 (3): 429–440.
Tilley, Helen. 2011. *Africa as a Living Laboratory: Empire, Development, and the Problem of Scientific Knowledge, 1870–1950*. Chicago: University of Chicago Press.
  2014. Racial Science, Geopolitics, and Empires: Paradoxes of Power. *Isis* 105 (4): 773–781.
Tinker, Hugh. 1977. *Race, Conflict and the International Order: From Empire to United Nations*. London: Macmillan.
Todorov, Tzvetan. 1993. *On Human Diversity: Nationalism, Racism, and Exoticism in French Thought*. Translated by Catherine Porter. Cambridge, MA: Harvard University Press.

Tönnies, Ferdinand. 1887. *Gemeinschaft und Gesellschaft: Abhandlung des Communismus und des Socialismus als empirischer Culturformen*. Leipzig: Fues.
Tonooka, Chika. 2021. World History's Eurocentric Moment? British Internationalism in the Age of Asian Nationalism, c.1905–1931. *Modern Intellectual History* 18 (1): 95–120.
Topinard, Paul. 1879. De la notion de race en anthropologie. *Revue d'Anthropologie* 2 (2): 589–660.
  1885. *Éléments d'anthropologie générale*. Paris: Adrien Delahaye et Émile Lecrosnier.
Toynbee, Arnold J. 1915. *The New Europe: Some Essays in Reconstruction*. Toronto: J. M. Dent & Sons.
  1918. Race. In *Encyclopædia of Religion and Ethics*, edited by James Hastings, 550–558. Edinburgh: T. & T. Clark.
  1934. *A Study of History: Volume One*. London: Oxford University Press.
Trouillot, Michel-Rolph. 2003. *Global Transformations: Anthropology and the Modern World*. Basingstoke: Palgrave Macmillan.
UNESCO. 1969. *Four Statements on the Race Question*. Paris: United Nations Educational, Scientific and Cultural Organization.
  1971. Dimensions de la situation raciale. *Revue Internationale des Sciences Sociales* 23 (4): 501–651.
United Nations. 1954. *Documents of the United Nations Conference on International Organization, San Francisco, 1945*. New York: United Nations.
United States Department of State. 1919. *Papers Relating to the Foreign Relations of the United States, 1919: The Paris Peace Conference*. Washington, DC: US Government Printing Office.
Urquhart, F. F. 1916. The Causes of Modern Wars. In *An Introduction to the Study of International Relations*, by A. J. Grant, Arthur Greenwood, J. D. L. Hughes, Philip Henry Kerr, and F. F. Urquhart, 37–65. London: Macmillan.
Vacher de Lapouge, Georges. 1896. *Les sélections sociales: cours libre de science politique professé à l'université de Montpellier (1888–1889)*. Paris: Albert Fontemoing.
  1897. Préface du traducteur. In *Le monisme, lien entre la religion et la science: profession de foi d'un naturaliste*, by Ernst Haeckel, translated by Georges Vacher de Lapouge, 1–8. Paris: Schleicher.
Vail, Leroy. 1989a. Introduction: Ethnicity in Southern African History. In *The Creation of Tribalism in Southern Africa*, edited by Leroy Vail, 1–18. Berkeley: University of California Press.
  1989b. *The Creation of Tribalism in Southern Africa*. Berkeley: University of California Press.

Vallois, Henri V. 1943. *Anthropologie de la population française.* Paris: Didier.
Vallois, Henri V., H. J. Fleure, W. C. Osman Hill, and K. L. Little. 1951. U.N.E.S.C.O. on Race. *Man* 51: 15–18.
Van den Berghe, Pierre L. 1965. Introduction. In *Africa: Social Problems of Change and Conflict,* edited by Pierre L. Van den Berghe, 1–12. San Francisco: Chandler Publishing Company.
  1970. *Race and Ethnicity: Essays in Comparative Sociology.* New York: Basic Books.
  1978. *Race and Racism: A Comparative Perspective.* 2nd edition. New York: John Wiley & Sons.
  1983. Class, Race and Ethnicity in Africa. *Ethnic and Racial Studies* 6 (2): 221–236.
van der Kerken, Georges. 1944. *L'ethnie Mongo: histoire, groupements, sous-groupements, origines; visions, représentations et explications du monde; sociologie, économie, ergologie, langues et arts des peuples Mongo, politique indigène, contacts avec peuples voisins.* Brussels: Librairie Falk.
van Evera, Stephen. 1994. Hypotheses on Nationalism and War. *International Security* 18 (4): 5–39.
Varese, Stefano. 1997. Memories of Solidarity: Anthropology and the Indigenous Movement in Latin America. *Cultural Survival Quarterly* 21 (3): 23–26.
Varouxakis, Georgios. 2020. When Did Britain Join the Occident? On the Origins of the Idea of 'the West' in English. *History of European Ideas* 46 (5): 563–581.
Vasilaki, Rosa. 2012. Provincialising IR? Deadlocks and Prospects in Post-Western IR Theory. *Millennium: Journal of International Studies* 41 (1): 3–22.
Vermeulen, Han F. 1992. The Emergence of 'Ethnography' ca. 1770 in Göttingen. *History of Anthropology Newsletter* 19 (2): 6–9.
  1995. Origins and Institutionalization of Ethnography and Ethnology in Europe and the USA, 1771–1845. In *Fieldwork and Footnotes: Studies in the History of European Anthropology,* edited by Han F. Vermeulen and Arturo Alvarez Roldán, 39–59. London: Routledge.
  2006. The German Invention of Völkerkunde: Ethnological Discourse in Europe and Asia, 1740–1798. In *The German Invention of Race,* edited by Sara Eigen and Mark Larrimore, 123–145. Albany: State University of New York Press.
  2015. *Before Boas: The Genesis of Ethnography and Ethnology in the German Enlightenment.* Lincoln: University of Nebraska Press.
Verna, Chantalle F. 2017. *Haiti and the Uses of America: Post-U.S. Occupation Promises.* New Brunswick: Rutgers University Press.

Vincent, R. J. 1982. Race in International Relations. *International Affairs* 58 (4): 658–670.
Vitalis, Robert. 2000. The Graceful and Generous Liberal Gesture: Making Racism Invisible in American International Relations. *Millennium: Journal of International Studies* 29 (2): 331–356.
  2010. The Noble American Science of Imperial Relations and Its Laws of Race Development. *Comparative Studies in Society and History* 52 (4): 909–938.
  2015. *White World Order, Black Power Politics: The Birth of American International Relations*. Ithaca: Cornell University Press.
von Treitschke, Heinrich. 1916. *Politics*. Translated by Blanche Dugdale and Torben de Bille. New York: Macmillan.
Vreeland, Herbert H. 1957. *Iran*. New Haven: Human Relations Area Files.
  1958. The Concept of Ethnic Groups as Related to Whole Societies. In *Report on the Ninth Annual Round Table Meeting on Linguistics and Language Studies: Anthropology and African Studies*, edited by William M. Austin, 81–88. Washington, DC: Georgetown University Press.
Vucetic, Srdjan. 2011. *The Anglosphere: A Genealogy of a Racialized Identity in International Relations*. Stanford: Stanford University Press.
Wade, Peter. 2002. *Race, Nature and Culture*. London: Pluto Press.
Walby, Sylvia. 2003. The Myth of the Nation-State: Theorizing Society and Polities in a Global Era. *Sociology* 37 (3): 529–546.
Walker, R. B. J. 1987. Realism, Change, and International Political Theory. *International Studies Quarterly* 31 (1): 65–86.
  1990. Sovereignty, Identity, Community: Reflections on the Horizons of Contemporary Political Practice. In *Contending Sovereignties: Redefining Political Community*, edited by R. B. J. Walker and Saul H. Mendlovitz, 159–186. Boulder: Lynne Rienner.
  1993. *Inside/Outside: International Relations as Political Theory*. Cambridge: Cambridge University Press.
Wallerstein, Immanuel. 1960. Ethnicity and National Integration in West Africa. *Cahiers d'Études Africaines* 1 (3): 129–139.
Wallerstein, Immanuel. 1972. La conscience ethnique en Asie soviétique. Translated by Jean-Claude Robert. *Sociologie et Sociétés* 4 (2): 225–232.
Walsh, Edmund A. 1922. *The History and Nature of International Relations*. New York: Macmillan.
Waltz, Kenneth. 1959. *Man, the State and War: A Theoretical Analysis*. New York: Columbia University Press.
  1979. *Theory of International Politics*. Boston: McGraw-Hill.
  1986. Reflections on Theory of International Politics: A Response to My Critics. In *Neorealism and Its Critics*, edited by Robert O. Keohane, 322–345. New York: Columbia University Press.

Ward, Julie K. 2002. Ethnos in the Politics: Aristotle and Race. In *Philosophers on Race: Critical Essays*, edited by Julie K. Ward and Tommy L. Lott, 14–37. Oxford: Blackwell.
Ware, Caroline F. 1931. *Ethnic Communities. Encyclopaedia of the Social Sciences*. London: Macmillan.
　1935. *Greenwich Village, 1920–1930: A Comment on American Civilization in the Post-war Years*. Boston: Houghton Mifflin.
Warner, W. Lloyd, and Paul S. Lunt. 1941. *The Social Life of a Modern Community*. New Haven: Yale University Press.
　1942. *The Status System of a Modern Community*. New Haven: Yale University Press.
Warner, W. Lloyd, and Leo Srole. 1945. *The Social Systems of American Ethnic Groups*. New Haven: Yale University Press.
Weber, Cynthia. 2016. *Queer International Relations: Sovereignty, Sexuality and the Will to Knowledge*. New York: Oxford University Press.
Weber, Max. 1922. *Wirtschaft und Gesellschaft: Grundriss der Sozialökonomik*. Tübingen: Mohr.
　1978. *Economy and Society: An Outline of Interpretive Sociology*. Edited by Guenther Roch and Claus Wittich. Berkeley: University of California Press.
Weitz, Eric D. 2008. From the Vienna to the Paris System: International Politics and the Entangled Histories of Human Rights, Forced Deportations, and Civilizing Missions. *The American Historical Review* 113 (5): 1313–1343.
Wendt, Alexander. 1992. Anarchy Is What States Make of It: The Social Construction of Power Politics. *International Organization* 46 (2): 391–425.
　1999. *Social Theory of International Politics*. Cambridge: Cambridge University Press.
Werner, Karolina. 2023. Who Is Indigenous in Africa? The Concept of Indigeneity, Its Impacts, and Progression. *Millennium: Journal of International Studies* 51 (2): 379–404.
Werner, Michael, and Benedicte Zimmermann. 2006. Beyond Comparison: Histoire Croisée and the Challenge of Reflexivity. *History and Theory* 45 (1): 30–50.
Wessel, Bessie Bloom. 1931. *An Ethnic Survey of Woonsocket, Rhode Island*. Chicago: University of Chicago Press.
Westermann, Diedrich. 1957. The Cultural History of Negro Africa. *Cahiers d'Histoire Mondiale* 3 (4): 985–1004.
Wheatley, Natasha. 2017. Spectral Legal Personality in Interwar International Law: On New Ways of Not Being a State. *Law and History Review* 35 (3): 753–787.

Wheatley, Steven. 2005. *Democracy, Minorities and International Law*. Cambridge: Cambridge University Press.

Wheeler, Roxan. 2000. *The Complexion of Race: Categories of Difference in Eighteenth-Century British Culture*. Philadelphia: University of Pennsylvania Press.

Whitman, James Q. 2017. *Hitler's American Model: The United States and the Making of Nazi Race Laws*. Princeton: Princeton University Press.

Williams, Brackette F. 1989. A Class Act: Anthropology and the Race to Nation across Ethnic Terrain. *Annual Review of Anthropology* 18: 401–444.

Williams, Michael C. 2013. In the Beginning: The International Relations Enlightenment and the Ends of International Relations Theory. *European Journal of International Relations* 19 (3): 647–665.

Wilson, Godfrey. 1941. *An Essay on the Economics of Detribalization in Northern Rhodesia: Part I*. Livingstone: The Rhodes-Livingstone Institute.

1942. *An Essay on the Economics of Detribalization in Northern Rhodesia: Part II*. Livingstone: The Rhodes-Livingstone Institute.

Wilson, Godfrey, and Monica Wilson. 1968. *The Analysis of Social Change Based on Observations in Central Africa*. Cambridge: Cambridge University Press.

Wissler, Clark. 1906. Ethnic Types and Isolation. *Science* 23 (578): 147–149.

1917. *The American Indian: An Introduction to the Anthropology of the New World*. New York: Douglas C. McMurtrie.

1923. *Man and Culture*. London: G. G. Harrap & Company.

1927. The Culture-Area Concept in Social Anthropology. *American Journal of Sociology* 32 (6): 881–891.

1928. The Culture Area Concept as a Research Lead. *American Journal of Sociology* 33 (6): 894–900.

Wolff, Stefan. 2006. *Ethnic Conflict: A Global Perspective*. Oxford: Oxford University Press.

Woodwell, Douglas. 2007. *Nationalism in International Relations: Norms, Foreign Policy, and Enmity*. Basingstoke: Palgrave Macmillan.

Woofter, T. J. 1933. *Races and Ethnic Groups in American Life*. New York: McGraw-Hill.

Xaxa, Virginius. 1999. Tribes as Indigenous People of India. *Economic and Political Weekly* 34 (51): 3589–3595.

Yack, Bernard. 2001. Popular Sovereignty and Nationalism. *Political Theory* 29 (4): 517–536.

Yapp, Malcolm. 1983. Tribes and States in the Khyber, 1838–1842. In *The Conflict of Tribe and State in Iran and Afghanistan*, edited by Richard Tapper, 150–191. London: Croom Helm.

Young, Robert J. C. 1995. *Colonial Desire: Hybridity in Theory, Culture and Race*. London: Routledge.
  2002. Race and Language in the Two Saussures. In *Philosophies of Race and Ethnicity*, edited by Peter Osborne and Stella Sandford, 63–78. London: Continuum.
  2004. *White Mythologies: Writing History and the West*. 2nd edition. London: Routledge.
Younis, Musab. 2017. 'United by Blood': Race and Transnationalism during the Belle Époque. *Nations and Nationalism* 23 (3): 484–504.
Zarakol, Ayşe. 2011. *After Defeat: How the East Learned to Live with the West*. Cambridge: Cambridge University Press.
  2014. What Made the Modern World Hang Together: Socialisation or Stigmatisation? *International Theory* 6 (2): 311–332.
  ed. 2017. *Hierarchies in World Politics*. Cambridge: Cambridge University Press.
  2018. Sovereign Equality as Misrecognition. *Review of International Studies* 44 (5): 848–862.
  2022. *Before the West: The Rise and Fall of Eastern World Orders*. Cambridge: Cambridge University Press.
Zernatto, Guido. 1944. Nation: The History of a Word. *The Review of Politics* 6 (3): 351–366.
Zimmerer, Jürgen. 2005. The Birth of Ostland out of the Spirit of Colonialism: A Postcolonial Perspective on the Nazi Policy of Conquest and Extermination. *Patterns of Prejudice* 39 (2): 197–219.
Zimmern, Alfred E. 1918a. *Nationality and Government with Other War-Time Essays*. London: Chatto & Windus.
  1918b. True and False Nationalism. In *Nationality and Government with Other War-Time Essays*, by Alfred E. Zimmern, 61–86. London: Chatto & Windus.
  1923. Nationalism and Internationalism. *Foreign Affairs* 1 (4): 115–126.
Zirker, Daniel G. 2015. *Forging Military Identity in Culturally Pluralistic Societies: Quasi-Ethnicity*. Lanham: Lexington Books.
Žižek, Slavoj. 2011. Hegel and Shitting: The Idea's Constipation. In *Hegel and the Infinite: Religion, Politics, and Dialectic*, edited by Slavoj Žižek, Clayton Crockett, and Creston Davis, 221–232. New York: Columbia University Press.
Zolberg, Aristide R. 1967. Patterns of National Integration. *Journal of Modern African Studies* 5 (4): 449–467.

Index

Abramson, Harold, 114–115
Africanism, 179
Allen, Stephen Haley, 46
American Jewish Congress, 60
Amselle, Jean-Loup, 177
anarchy
   international relations and, 2–3, 21, 42–43, 166, 211–217
   nationalism and, 38
   primitive, 14, 73, 213–214
Anderson, David, 133, 139
Anglo-America, 161
anthropology
   colonialism and, 168
   convergence with sociology, 175
   international relations and, 21, 166, 213–216
   Manchester School of, 171–176, 178
   unit problem of, 192, 200–207
antisemitism, 107, 119, 121, 125–127, 141–142, 145
Anuchin, Dmitrii, 134
apartheid, 142, 150
Arendt, Hannah, 57
Aristotle, 243
Armitage, David, 1
Arzyutov, Dmitry, 133, 139
assimilation, 41, 107, 109–110, 114, 158, 216, 222, 236
Aufhebung, See sublation
Aukerman, Miriam, 226
Austria-Hungary, 11, 35, 46, 49, 58, See also Habsburg empire
Azcárate, Pablo de, 47, 60

Balandier, Georges, 171
Balbi, Adrien, 133
Balfour, Arthur, 61
Balibar, Étienne, 84, 154, 161

Balkanization, 39
Balkans, 37, 39
Barkdull, John, 215
Barnes, Harry Elmer, 48
Barruel, Augustin, 36
Barth, Fredrik, 200, 209–211, 222
Barzun, Jacques, 149–150
Bastian, Adolf, 133
Bauman, Zygmunt, 85
Bell, Duncan, 79
Benedict, Ruth, 89, 95, 148–149, 151
Berkson, Isaac, 101, 103–105, 107, 145
Berlin Conference, 219
Berthelot, Philippe, 59, 63
Black Power, 111, 113–114, 145
Blauner, Robert, 112
Bluntschli, Johann Kaspar, 51–52, 72
Boas, Franz, 89–90, 94–95, 106, 140, 149, 160, 191–196
Bolshevik Revolution, 136, 185
Bonilla-Silva, Eduardo, 152
Bonnett, Alastair, 164
Boulenger, Jacques, 125–126, 140
Brinton, Daniel, 133
British Union of Fascists, 141
Bromley, Yulian, 186, 190
Brubaker, Rogers, 233
Brunhes, Jean, 56
Bryce, James, 47, 53
Bulgaria, 57–58, 64–66, 75
Bull, Hedley, 9, 12, 166, 214
Burgess, John William, 48, 54
Burles, Regan, 12
Butler, Judith, 231

capitalism, 151–152, 186, 188
Capotorti, Francesco, 69
Carr, E. H., 37, 39, 59
Cecil, Robert, 59

Index

Césaire, Aimé, 151, 153
China, 11, 137–139, *See also* minzu
citizenship, 5, 46–47, 53, 103, 135, 239
civilisation
  culture and, 89–90, 164, 190
  as detribalisation, 173
  race and, 89–90, 157–158, 162
  relativisation and pluralisation of, 82, 89–90, 163–164
  standard of, 4, 21, 73, 157–159, 217–218, 236
clash of civilisations, 156–157, 164, 237
Clemenceau, Georges, 60–61
Cohen, Abner, 174–175
Cohen, Ronald, 192, 200
Cold War, 8, 76, 79, 156
Coleman, James Smoot, 180
colonialism, 11, 27, 128, 145, 165, 184, 189, 219, 228, 232, 236, *See also* domestic colonialism
colour line, 26, 105, 107, 115, 156–157, 159, 165
Colson, Elizabeth, 176, 182
Comité d'Études, 56
Committee on New States and the Protection of Minorities, 57, 59–61, 64
concepts
  aconceptual, 238
  contestability of, 6–7
  discourse and, 6
  history of, 5–9, 13–14
  temporalisation of, 235
  words and, 6
Conference on Nationalities and Subject Races, 160
Conference on Security and Co-operation in Europe (CSCE), 69, 76
Congress of Vienna, 55
connected histories, 8
Connor, Walker, 40
Council of Europe, 69, 226
Cox, Oliver, 151
Cross-Cultural Survey, 201–202, 206, *See also* Human Relations Area Files (HRAF)
Cruse, Harold, 111–112
culture
  civilisation and, 89–90, 164, 190
  ethnicity and, 143–144, 233–235
  race and, 87–90, 102–105, 143–144
  relativisation and pluralisation of, 89–90, 192, 235
culture area, 191, 195, 197, 203, 210

d'Anglure, Bernard Saladin, 222
Daes, Erica-Irene, 224–225
Darwin, Charles, 88
Declaration of the Rights of Man and of the Citizen, 33
decolonisation, 2, 15, 27, 166, 168, 184
deconstruction
  of civilised/primitive dichotomy, 168, 172, 175–179, 189
  of international order, 244
  of society/culture dichotomy, 199–200, 207
  of structuralist-functionalist paradigm, 173, 211
  sublation and, 19–21
Deloria, Vine Jr, 113
Delos, Joseph Thomas, 54
Deniker, Joseph, 55, 91–93, 118, 120, 125, 133
Denis, Lorimer, 129–130, 132, 140
Derrida, Jacques, 19–20, 22–23, 231, 234, 242
Deschênes, Jules, 69
development
  as conceptual proxy, 4, 21, 217–218, 237
  nationalism and, 34, 51, 74–75, 77, 180–181
  policy of separate, 143, 216
  race and, 86, 157
  stages of, 75, 166–167, 184–190, 195, 211, 220
  tribalism and, 172, 174–178
dialectical reversal, 21–22, 25, 32, 35, 90, 216, 231, *See also* sublation
Dickinson, G. Lowes, 212
domestic colonialism, 112–113
Donnelly, Jack, 213–214
Du Bois, W. E. B., 26, 105–107, 111, 151, 153, 156, 159–160
Dunne, Timothy, 11–12
Durkheim, Émile, 165, 215–216
Duvalier, François, 129–131, 140

Eide, Asbjørn, 225
Emerson, Rupert, 180–181
Engels, Friedrich, 72, 185
Epstein, A. L., 173–174
Estimé, Dumarsais, 131
ethnic cleansing, 1, 8, 31
ethnic race, 106, 115, 131
ethnicism, 101, 121, 232
ethnicity
  as apolitical, 7, 25, 32, 43, 53, 64, 66, 178, 183–184, 232–233, 237, 243
  black, 106, 111–113, 145
  constructivist approaches to, 233
  culture and, 143–144, 233–235
  groupness and, 129, 233
  as heathen or pagan superstition, 4, 91, 100–101
  identity and, 114, 206, 233
  Indian, 113
  indigenous rights and, 222–223
  minus one model of, 108, 236
  nation and, 31–32, 43
  nationality and, 25, 53–55, 102–104, 113, 138, 182
  race and, 81, 108–109, 143–144
  as supplement, 22–24, 26, 55, 143–144, 189–190, 230–231, 234, 236–237, 244
  tribe and, 27, 167, 174–178, 183–184
ethnie
  in France, 116–128, 169–172
  in Haiti, 129–132
  translation into English of, 128–129
  tribu and, 128, 169–172
ethnisme, 5, 117–118, 121–122, 126, 131, 138
ethnocentrism, 5, 105, 232
ethnography
  concept of, 4, 133
  in imperial Russia, 134–136
  in Soviet Union, 184–189
ethnology
  concept of, 4, 133
  in Germany, 142
  in Japan, 139
  in Soviet Union, 185
ethnorace, 115
ethnoracisme, 121, 126, 131, 147
ethnos
  in ancient Greece, 4, 239, 243
  in China, 138–139
  etymology of, 239
  in France, 120, 125, 133–134
  in Germany, 142
  in imperial Russia, 5, 7, 133–136
  in Japan, 139–140
  in South Africa, 142–143
  in Soviet Union, 7, 184–190, 211
  in United Kingdom, 140–142
  in United States, 101
eugenics, 116, 141–142
Eurocentrism
  civilisation and, 27, 157–159, 167, 183
  human rights and, 218
  international relations and, 13, 16–19, 80
  racism and, 81, 150–152
Evans-Pritchard, E. E., 172–173, 213–214

Fabian, Johannes, 28
Fanon, Frantz, 14, 151, 153
fantasy, 40, 43, 77, 84, 161
Fei Xiaotong, 139
Fenton, Steve, 233
Fenwick, Charles G., 213
Fishberg, Maurice, 102
floating signifier, 240
Fortes, Meyer, 198, 207, 213–214
Foucault, Michel, 6
Fouillée, Alfred, 116
France, 7, 9, 59–60, 76, 91, 119, 121, 126–127, 129, 137, 140, 148
French Revolution, 33
Fried, Morton, 177
Füredi, Frank, 150

Galton, Francis, 88
Gandhi, Mohandas, 160
Garner, James Wilford, 38, 46–47, 50
Gaultier, Jules de, 122
Gellner, Ernest, 30, 40, 187
Georges-Jacob, Kléber, 130–131
Germany, 34, 37, 41, 74, 117, 142, 144, 147, 170, 191
Ginsberg, Asher, 103
Glazer, Nathan, 109–111, 114, 175
Gleason, Philip, 114
Gluckman, Max, 171, 173–174

Gobineau, Arthur de, 119, 158
Godelier, Maurice, 166, 176, 184
Goldberg, David Theo, 115
Goldenweiser, Alexander, 90, 164
Gong, Gerrit, 217
González Casanova, Pablo, 112
Gordon, Milton, 110
Grant, Madison, 117
Greece, 57–58, 64–66, 75, 239
Guilhot, Nicholas, 44
Gulliver, P. H., 182–184
Gumilev, Lev, 186–187, 190
Gumplowicz, Ludwig, 233
Günther, Hans, 117, 127, 144

Habsburg empire, 56, 73, 87, *See also* Austria-Hungary
Haddon, Alfred Cort, 93–94, 148
Hailey, William Malcolm, 179–180
Haiti, 9, 91, 129–132, 140, 145
Hall, Stuart, 115
Hankins, Frank, 148
Haraway, Donna, 24
Hayes, Carlton, 47, 53, 73
Headlam-Morley, James, 59, 61
Hegel, Georg Wilhelm Friedrich, 13–14, 16, 21, 30, 72
Henderson, Errol, 80
Herder, Johann Gottfried, 190
Herodotus, 94, 239
Herskovits, Melville, 191
Herz, John, 41
Hesse, Barnor, 151
Hill, David Jayne, 212
Hirschfeld, Magnus, 148
Hitler, Adolf, 121, 141
Hobsbawm, Eric, 30, 34
Holcombe, Arthur, 48
Holland Rose, John, 50
Holmes, William Henry, 195–196
Holocaust, 81, 150
Homer, 239, 243
Hughes, Everett Cherrington, 108
Hughes, Helen MacGill, 108
Human Relations Area Files (HRAF), 202–204
human rights, 15, 153, 217–218
Huntington, Samuel, 156, 164
Hutchings, Kimberly, 17
Huxley, Julian, 93–94, 96–97, 148

Ikenberry, John, 3
Inquiry, 56–57, 63
Intercollegiate Menorah Association, 101
internal colonialism, *See* domestic colonialism
International Covenant on Civil and Political Rights (ICCPR), 68–69
International Labour Organization (ILO), 220–222
international relations
  anthropology and, 21, 166, 213–216
  Eurocentrism in, 13, 16–19, 80
  expansion thesis, 9–13
  problem of difference, 40–43, 71
International Working Group on Indigenous Affairs, 223
irredentism, 25, 31, 58, 66, 71
Isla, José Francisco de, 100
Italy, 34, 37, 59–60

Jahn, Beate, 214
James, C. L. R., 13
Japan, 11, 18, 59, 137, 139–140, 158–159, *See also* minzoku
Johannet, René, 55

Kallen, Horace, 101–104, 107
Kautsky, John, 179
Keal, Paul, 167, 227
Keene, Edward, 10–12, 162, 218
Keith, Arthur, 120, 140–141
Kidd, Benjamin, 213
kinship, 75, 92, 168, 180
Klimek, Stanislaw, 200–201
Kohn, Hans, 74–75, 162
Koselleck, Reinhart, 5–6
Kroeber, Alfred, 89, 192, 196–200, 205

Lake, David, 212
Lamarckism, 87–89, 102–103
Lawrence, T. J., 213
Le Fur, Louis, 50, 54, 63
Leach, Edmund, 208–209
Leacock, Stephen, 213
League of Nations, 46–47, 56–58, 60, 66, 75, 141, 219
Légitime, François, 160
Leibold, James, 139
Lévi-Strauss, Claude, 154, 240

liberal internationalism, 103, 163
liberalism
  nationalism and, 33–34, 74
  racism and, 79–81, 144, 146, 151, 153
Lloyd George, David, 60–61
Lloyd, P. C., 174–175
Locke, Alain, 106–107, 115, 131

Macartney, C. A., 57
Mack, Julian, 60
Magloire, Paul, 132
Maine, Henry, 165, 214
Malabou, Catharine, 23
Malcolm X, 111
Mamdani, Mahmood, 165, 177
Mantoux, Paul, 61
Marshall, Louis, 60
Martial, René, 122–124, 126, 130
Martonne, Emmanuel de, 56
Marx, Karl, 42–43, 72, 185
Mason, Otis T., 192–193
Masters, Roger, 214–215
Maurras, Charles, 36
McGrane, Bernard, 235
Mead, Margaret, 89
Mearsheimer, John, 212
Mendel, Gregor, 88–89
Mercier, Paul, 171
Mill, John Stuart, 34, 72
Miller, David Hunter, 57, 59
minzoku, 9, 139
minzu, 9, 139
Mitchell, J. Clyde, 173
modernisation, 4, 21, 172, 174, 176, 178, 180–181, *See also* development
Mogilianskii, Nikolai, 133, 135–136, 185
Montagu, Ashley, 95–100, 144–145, 229
Montandon, George, 119–125, 127–128, 130–131, 137, 140, 144, 147, 170
Moon, Parker Thomas, 44
Morgenthau, Hans, 31, 38–42, 214
Morin, Françoise, 128, 222
Moynihan, Daniel Patrick, 109–111, 114, 175
Mühlmann, Wilhelm, 139, 142–144
multiculturalism, 77, 190
Murdock, George, 201–203, 206
Murray, Christopher, 17
Myrdal, Gunnar, 110

Nadel, S. F., 198–199, 207–208
narod, 135
narodnost, 135
Naroll, Raoul, 204–208
nation
  ethnicity and, 31–32, 43
  race and, 83–87, 140–141
  state and, 25, 29–31, 40–42, 45–46
  tribe and, 180–184
nationalism
  anticolonial, 15, 178–184, 189
  black, 111–113, 129
  civic and ethnic, 33, 71–78
  contradictions of, 29–32, 43, 83–84
  liberalism and, 33–34, 74
  official, 35
  racism and, 83–85
  transformation of, 25, 40
  tribalism and, 178, 181–184
nationality
  as citizenship, 53
  as developmental stage, 180, 186, 188
  ethnicity and, 25, 54–55, 102–104, 113, 138, 182
  principle of, 33, 36
Neuilly, Convention of, 64, 75
Neuilly, Treaty of, 64
Novak, Michael, 114
Nugent, Thomas, 100

Oka Masao, 139
Organization for Security and Co-operation in Europe (OSCE), 69, 226
Orientalism, 80, 241
Ottoman empire, 56, 73, *See also* Turkey
Özkirimli, Umut, 83

Paderewski, Ignacy Jan, 61
Pan-African Conference, 159
pan-Africanism, 15, 159
Pan-American Union, 219
pan-Asianism, 15, 159
pan-Germanism, 36, 147, 161
pan-Indianism, 113
pan-Islamism, 159
pan-Slavism, 36, 161
Papillault, Georges, 133–134
Park, Robert, 233

Parsons, Talcott, 197
Pasha, Mustapha Kamal, 18
Permanent Court of International Justice, 75–76
Pinson, Koppel S., 44
Pitt-Rivers, George, 140–142, 145
Political Intelligence Department, 56
Powell, John Wesley, 192–196
Price-Mars, Jean, 129–130

race
  caste and, 95, 110
  civilisation and, 157–158, 162
  culture and, 87–90, 102–105, 143–144
  domestication of, 26, 81–82, 156
  ethnicity and, 81, 108–109, 143–144
  nation and, 83–87, 140–141
racialism, 147–150
racism
  differentialist, 4, 131, 146, 154–155, 237
  Eurocentric concept of, 81, 150–152
  liberalism and, 79–81, 144, 146, 151, 153
  nationalism and, 83–85
  systemic concept of, 151–154
Radcliffe-Brown, A. R., 172–173, 198, 207
Red Power, 113–114
Redfield, Robert, 175
Rees, Richard, 112
Regnault, Félix, 118–119, 122–123, 133, 138, 169
Reinsch, Paul S., 35, 160
Republic of New Africa, 111
Reus-Smit, Christian, 11–12
Rhodes, Cecil, 35
Riesman, David, 109
Rist, Gilbert, 218
Romanov empire, 56, 73, *See also* Russia
Rouch, Jean, 171
Rudenko, Sergei, 133, 136, 185
Russia, 5, 7, 11, 35, 91, 133–134, 136, 159, 185, *See also* Romanov empire, Soviet Union
Ruyssen, Théodore, 50, 74

Sapir, Edward, 192
Sartre, Jean-Paul, 154

Saussure, Ferdinand de, 117–118, 138
Schippers, Thomas, 134
Schmitt, Carl, 230, 238, 241–242
Schuman, Frederick, 212
Scott, David, 235
secession, 25, 31, 38, 66, 70–71, 168, 183, 226, 228
segregation, 107, 150
self-determination, 15, 25, 31, 34, 37, 56–58, 67, 69, 73, 111, 181, 188, 221, 224–225
Seton-Watson, Robert, 87
Shanin, Teodor, 189
Sharma, Nandita, 155
Shirokogoroff, Sergei, 125, 130, 133, 137–143, 185
Sidgwick, Henry, 47
Singer, Lester, 111
Skinner, Quentin, 5–6
slavery, 109, 112, 151, 186
social race, *See* ethnic race
South Africa, 91, 142–143, 147, 150, 219, 224
Southall, Aidan, 174, 177
Soviet Union, 68, 137, 161, 184–190, *See also* Russia
Spykman, Nicholas, 212
state
  artificial, 77
  contradictions of, 30, 83
  legitimacy of, 25, 29–30, 32, 35, 37
  nation and, 25, 29–31, 40–42, 45–46
Stoddard, Lothrop, 161
Stoler, Ann Laura, 80
sublation, 14–16, 19–25, 32, 71, 81, 89, 146, 234, 236, *See also* dialectical reversal
Sumner, William Graham, 202, 232
Switzerland, 117, 119

Taguieff, Pierre-André, 84, 86, 126
Tönnies, Ferdinand, 67, 165
Topinard, Paul, 88
Toynbee, Arnold, 38, 56, 163–164
translation, 9, 51, 62–64, 76, 92, 100, 117, 121, 128–129, 134–135, 138, 147
Treitschke, Heinrich von, 74
tribe
  ethnicity and, 167, 174–178, 183–184
  indigenous rights and, 220–224

tribe (cont.)
  nation and, 180–184
  urbanisation and, 27, 168, 171–175, 189
Turkey, 11, 58, 74, See also Ottoman empire

United Kingdom, 59–60, 140
United Nations
  Charter of, 67–70, 221
  Declaration on the Rights of Indigenous Peoples, 224, 227
  Declaration on the Rights of Persons Belonging to National or Ethnic, Religious and Linguistic Minorities, 69–70, 227
  Educational, Scientific and Cultural Organization (UNESCO), 69, 96–98, 147, 150, 153, 155
  ethnic group and, 5, 90, 96, 144
  Human Rights Commission, 69
  imperial legacies and, 22
  Permanent Forum on Indigenous Issues, 223
  Sub-Commission on the Prevention of Discrimination and Protection of Minorities, 96, 226
  Working Group on Indigenous Populations (WGIP), 224–227
United States, 7, 41, 59–60, 100–115, 117, 120, 131, 140, 145, 150, 191
Universal Races Congress, 160

Vacher de Lapouge, Georges, 116–118, 120, 122, 127, 144
Vallois, Henri, 127
van den Berghe, Pierre, 115, 171
van der Kerken, Georges, 169–170
van Gennep, Arnold, 121, 138
Venizelos, Eleftherios, 63–64
Vitalis, Robert, 79
Volk, 127, 142–144, 162, 190
Volkov, Fiodor, 133, 135–136

Walker, R. B. J., 216
Wallerstein, Immanuel, 174–175
Waltz, Kenneth, 29, 166, 214–216
Warner, W. Lloyd, 107
Watson, Adam, 9
Weber, Max, 92–93
Weismann, August, 88
Wells, H. G., 160, 163
Westermann, Diedrich, 179
Wheeler, Roxann, 83
white supremacism, 161
whiteness, 86, 102, 161–162, 164
Wight, Martin, 163
Wilson, Woodrow, 56–61
Wissler, Clark, 191, 197, 202
World Bank, 223
World War, the First, 14, 25, 33, 36, 38–39, 45, 56–57, 66–67, 73–74, 87, 91, 119, 147, 159, 161, 212, 219
World War, the Second, 2, 14, 41, 67, 79, 81, 90, 147–148, 151, 162, 170, 186, 201, 229

xenophobia, 147

Zangwill, Israel, 160
Zarakol, Ayşe, 13, 37
Zimmern, Alfred, 45–46, 56, 73, 103, 159
Zionism, 101–103
Žižek, Slavoj, 23

www.ingramcontent.com/pod-product-compliance
Lightning Source LLC
Chambersburg PA
CBHW050804070225
21590CB00023B/67